DEATH ANXIETY
HANDBOOK

SERIES IN DEATH EDUCATION, AGING, AND HEALTH CARE

HANNELORE WASS, CONSULTING EDITOR

ADVISORY BOARD

Herman Feifel, Ph.D.
Jeanne Quint Benoliel, R.N., Ph.D.
Balfour Mount, M.D.

DEATH ANXIETY HANDBOOK

Research, Instrumentation, and Application

Edited by

Robert A. Neimeyer

Taylor & Francis
Publishers since 1798

USA	Publishing Office:	Taylor & Francis
		1101 Vermont Avenue, N.W., Suite 200
		Washington, DC 20005-3521
		Tel: (202) 289-2174
		Fax: (202) 289-3665
	Distribution Center:	Taylor & Francis
		1900 Frost Road, Suite 101
		Bristol, PA 19007-1598
		Tel: (215) 785-5800
		Fax: (215) 785-5515
UK		Taylor & Francis Ltd.
		4 John St.
		London WC1N 2ET
		Tel: 071 405 2237
		Fax: 071 831 2035

DEATH ANXIETY HANDBOOK: Research, Instrumentation, and Application

2 3 4 5 6 7 8 9 0   B R B R   9 8 7 6 5

This book was set in Times Roman by Harlowe Typography, Inc. The editors were Deborah Klenotic and Joyce Duncan; the production supervisor was Peggy M. Rote. Cover design by Michelle M. Fleitz. Printing and binding by Braun-Brumfield, Inc.

A CIP catalog record for this book is available from the British Library. ⊗ The paper in this publication meets the requirements of the ANSI Standard Z39.48-1984 (Permanence of Paper)

Library of Congress Cataloging-in-Publication Data
Death anxiety handbook: research, instrumentation, and application /
  Robert A. Neimeyer, editor.
    p.   cm.

    1. Death—Psychological aspects. 2. Anxiety. 3. Death—Psychological aspects—Testing. 4. Anxiety—Testing.
I. Neimeyer, Robert A., 1954–
BF789.D4D347   1933
155.9'37—dc20

ISBN 1-56032-282-9   93-28596
ISSN 0275-3510   CIP

Contents

CHAPTER 7   **Death Competency: Bugen's Coping with Death
                              Scale and Death Self-Efficacy**
                              Rosemary A. Robbins   149

PART 3: APPLICATIONS

CHAPTER 8   **Reduced Death Threat in Near-Death
                              Experiencers**
                              Bruce Greyson   169

CHAPTER 9   **Death Threat, Parental Loss, and Interpersonal
                              Style: A Personal Construct Investigation**
                              Christopher M. Meshot and Larry M. Leitner   181

PART 4: CONCLUSION

Contributors

Gordon G. Cappelletty, Ph.D.
California School of Professional
  Psychology
Fresno, CA 93740

Stephen J. DePaola, Ph.D.
Department of Psychology
Memphis State University
Memphis, TN 38152

Joseph A. Durlak, Ph.D.
Department of Psychology
Lake Shore Campus
Loyola University
6525 N. Sheridan Road
Chicago, IL 60626-5385

Jayne Fiedler, M.A.
Department of Psychology
Memphis State University
Memphis, TN 38152

Robert W. Firestone, Ph.D.
The Glendon Association
2049 Century Park East, Suite 3000
Los Angeles, CA 90067

Winston Frederick, M.D.
Howard University
2400 6th Street N.W.
Washington, DC 20059

Gina Gesser, M.A. [deceased]
Department of Behavioral Science
University of Toronto
Toronto, Ontario, Canada

Bruce Greyson, M.D.
School of Medicine
University of Connecticut Health Center
Farmington, CT 06030

Julie Hintze, Ph.D.
California School of Professional
  Psychology
Fresno, CA 93740

Larry M. Leitner, Ph.D.
Department of Psychology
Miami University
Oxford, OH 45056

David Lester, Ph.D.
Stockton State College
Jim Leeds Road
Pomona, NJ 08240

Michael B. Lupfer, Ph.D.
Department of Psychology
Memphis State University
Memphis, TN 38152

Christopher M. Meshot, Ph.D.
School of Medicine
Indiana University
Indianapolis, IN 46206

Marlin K. Moore, Ph.D.
1034 Washington Blvd.
Abilene, TX 79601-3815

Robert A. Neimeyer, Ph.D.
Department of Psychology
Memphis State University
Memphis, TN 38152

F. C. Powell, Ph.D.
Department of Gerontology
College of Public Affairs and Community
  Service
Omaha, NE 68182-0202

Gary T. Reker, Ph.D.
Department of Psychology
Trent University
Peterborough, Ontario
Canada K9J 7B8

Rosemary A. Robbins, Ph.D.
Pain Management Service
Department of Anesthesia
P.O. Box 850
Hershey, PA 17033

Donald I. Templer, Ph.D.
California School of Professional
  Psychology
Fresno, CA 93740

James A. Thorson, Ed.D.
Department of Gerontology
College of Public Affairs and Community
  Service
University of Nebraska
Omaha, NE 68182-0202

Adrian Tomer, Ph.D.
Department of Psychology, 52001
Shippensburg University
Shippensburg, PA 17257

Paul T. P. Wong, Ph.D.
Department of Psychology
Trent University
Peterborough, Ontario
Canada K9J 7B8

Preface

In a sense, this book represents a long answer to a short question. Over the past 10 years, I have been approached by scores of researchers, students, and practitioners in a range of helping professions, who with minor variations have said, "I'm interested in studying the relation between death anxiety and ____ (religiosity, physical illness, living in dangerous urban environments, etc.). What measure of death anxiety should I use?" My response, "That depends on ____ (your goals, your implicit theory of death anxiety, your population, etc.)," often opened the door to substantial consultation before an intelligent answer could be given. Moreover, this consultation was often complicated by the rarity with which the strengths and limitations of existing scales were discussed in the published literature. As a result, the earnest questioners who have approached me have often had no convenient resources on which to draw in focusing their hypotheses, selecting appropriate measures, and constructing a design for a study likely to yield informative answers.

Two more recent experiences have also contributed to my decision to edit the current volume. The first was my collaboration in 1988 with Hannelore Wass and Felix Berardo in editing *Dying: Facing the facts* (2nd edition), a high-level survey text in thanatology. One of my responsibilities for the project was to review the voluminous published literature on death anxiety, which even at that time numbered well over 500 articles. Unfortunately, it was hard to evade the conclusion that the impressive quantity of this literature was not matched by its quality. My impression upon completing that review is equally relevant today, in spite of some acknowledged improvements in the empirical and theoretical sophistication of studies over the past 5 years. Summarizing what was known about the demographic, personal, and situational correlates of death attitudes, I noted that

> despite this admittedly substantial literature, many of even the best researched areas contain unanswered questions. To a large degree, this reflects certain persistent conceptual and methodological inadequacies in the study of death anxiety. For example, although methodological advances have indeed occurred, they typically had only a local impact, with the majority of investigators continuing to rely on simply administered but psychometrically ambiguous instruments devised in the early days of this literature. On the other hand, even those investigators who have devised new and more revealing assessment techniques typically have been too impatient in their use, rushing into application of their scales before undertaking the arduous work of establishing their reliability and validity. As a consequence of these two trends, the death anxiety literature too often resembles a gray mosaic of randomly assembled studies, embellished by an occasionally brilliant, but fragile and isolated investigation. . . . [F]ar too much of the research on death orientation is atheoretical and opportunistic, addressing easily investigated issues rather than more scientifically incisive questions. When this is compounded by a heavy reliance on correlational, rather than genuinely experimental designs, the result is a body of knowledge that is vaguely suggestive, rather than clearly authoritative (Neimeyer, 1988).

My work as editor of the peer-reviewed journal *Death Studies* since 1991 has reinforced these concerns. Too often, the authors of papers submitted for review seemed to choose a particular method of measuring death attitudes simply because it had an appropriate sounding name, or because it had ''face validity'' in asking something about the respondent's views of death. Perhaps equally regrettable were the growing number of studies defending their selection of a given measure on the basis of a single number—often an internal consistency estimate—that was a poor surrogate for temporal reliability or that more elusive psychometric desideratum, construct validity. This tendency to ''seek safety in numbers,'' at the expense of serious conceptual development of the measure or the study of which it was a part, undoubtedly contributed substantially to the equivocal results often obtained in such investigations.

The *Death anxiety handbook* represents a response to this state of affairs. The core of the volume consists of six chapters that provide in-depth reviews of the best available measures of death attitudes, from extensions and refinements of widely used instruments for measuring death anxiety, threat, and fear, to more recent scales assessing a range of death concerns and competencies. Not only do these chapters discuss the available data on the psychometric properties of each instrument and summarize research using them, but they also provide a copy of the instruments (with scoring keys) to facilitate their use by interested researchers and professionals. In the past, these instruments either have been unpublished, available only by contacting the author, or have been dispersed through widely scattered journals, making them onerous to locate. I hope that the present format, including each instrument as an appendix to the related chapter, promotes their accessibility and intelligent use in the future.

Although these concerns with improving the caliber of research on death attitudes was a major motivation for the present text, it was not the only one. Even the best conducted empirical research loses meaning unless it is embedded in a more abstract theory, on the one hand, and more concrete practical impli-cations, on the other. For this reason, I invited a chapter on major philosophical and psychological theories of the causes and consequences of death anxiety in adult life, providing a broad framework for interpreting the various research programs that follow later in the volume. This opening chapter also is richly suggestive of important hypotheses for subsequent research, as well as possibil-ities for integrating existing conceptualizations of death attitudes to yield a more comprehensive theory of the role of death in human life.

Just as research on death attitudes should make some contribution to a broader theory, it should also make contact with a range of human applications. For this reason, I have included several chapters of varying lengths illustrating the potential relevance of death anxiety in applied contexts such as nursing homes, psychotherapy, and death education, and in understanding the experience of bereaved young adults, persons with AIDS, and near-death experiencers. Because applications to many of these areas are germinal, some chapters repre-sent initial empirical forays into the study of death attitudes in these applied areas, while others consolidate and discuss what is known from the perspective of more substantial research literature or the author's own clinical experience.

Despite the broad scope of this handbook, no single volume can accomplish everything, particularly in a field that is as large and diverse as the study of death attitudes. Thus, I had to consider what would be omitted from, as well as included in the present compendium. As a result, I decided to forgo a lengthy review of empirical studies and measurement issues, instead deferring coverage of this material to the separate chapters of the book. Tomer's integrative theo-retical review, for example, discusses empirical support for various models of death anxiety—from classical analytic and existential positions to more recent constructivist and "positive illusion" theories. Similarly, each of the chapters reviewing the development of instruments for assessing death attitudes includes discussion of research using the scale, although with only a few exceptions, these chapters are "agnostic" with respect to conceptual model. Rather than risk redundancy with this extensive coverage of the literature throughout the book, I have chosen only to highlight certain issues and problems in my concluding chapter, and to refer the reader to other sources (e.g., Neimeyer, 1988) for a more systematic review and evaluation of existing research in a single chapter.

In compiling this text, I have been fortunate to recruit some of the most significant contributors to the study of death attitudes. The authors whose work appears here include both long-time leaders in the field, who are responsible for much of the popularity that the study of death anxiety has enjoyed in the past, as well as newer contributors, whose fresh vision will help assure the continued vitality of the field in the future. Finally, I have benefitted from the enthusiasm and patience of Ron Wilder, my friend and colleague at Taylor & Francis, whose occasional prompts kept the project moving forward in the face of other commitments. I hope the resulting handbook will be useful to both individual readers and to the field of death studies as a whole, as we pursue in a psychological context perennial questions concerning the human encounter with death.

REFERENCE

Neimeyer, R. A. (1988). Death anxiety. In Wass, H., Berardo, F. M., and Neimeyer, R. A. (Eds.). *Dying: Facing the Facts* (2nd ed.). New York: Hemisphere.

Robert A. Neimeyer

Part I

Theoretical Overview

Chapter 1

Death Anxiety in Adult Life— Theoretical Perspectives

Adrian Tomer

The purpose of this review is to present several theoretical approaches that are relevant to the study of death anxiety. Neimeyer's (1988) examination of the empirical papers dealing with death anxiety reveals, in general, a richness of findings together with a relative weakness in the theoretical justification of the research strategy in this area (Neimeyer & Moore, 1989). This observation, together with the realization that there are rich theoretical systems that can be used in a more efficient way in the study of death anxiety, was the main motivation for writing this review.

The review is by necessity selective with several restrictions to help define its scope. First, the age span reviewed is adult and old age. Childhood and adolescence are very important ages in the study of death anxiety but they are beyond the scope of this review. Second, a limitation was imposed on the subject matter: Death anxiety as defined here is that experienced in ''daily life,'' not the anxiety experienced in coping with immediate threats to one's life. Moreover, the main interest here is anxiety caused by the anticipation of the state in which one is dead, excluding related aspects such as fear of dying or death of significant others. Third, when several related theories were similar from the point of view of their implications for death anxiety, only one of them was presented.

Many terms have been used in the literature to relate to the issue of (negative) attitudes toward death. The most common terms, besides death anxiety, are fear of death, death threat, death concern, and death acceptance. Although these terms sometimes can be (and have been) used interchangeably, in other cases they reflect important conceptual distinctions, often accompanied by attempts to develop scales focused on one concept or another (see Warren, 1989, ch. 4). For example, the term *anxiety* has a connotation of "nonspecific" distress (Kastenbaum & Ainsberg, 1972) and "confusion" (Kelly, 1955), which distinguishes it from other terms such as *fear* or *threat*. In fact, a theory such as personal construct theory (Kelly, 1955) makes a systematic distinction between *threat* and *anxiety*. In this review the usage was adapted to match the usage made by the proponents of the various theories. For general discussions I have used *death anxiety* as a generic term that subsumes more specific terms.

For reasons of space, no general exposition of the theories discussed is attempted. Rather, these theories are presented in the context of death anxiety and selected empirical results are used to indicate to the reader the existence of relevant evidence.

The review divides the theoretical approaches into several categories, beginning with philosophical perspectives. Several psychological theories are then reviewed including: self-realization theories, search-for-meaning theories, personal construct theory, theories of denial, self-concept discrepancy theory, and developmental approaches such as Erikson's psychosocial theory or theories of intellectual development. Recurrent themes in these approaches are the annihilation of the self, death as radical transformation, death as threat to life's meaningfulness, and death as threat to realization of basic life projects. These aspects are discussed in the concluding section. The discussion also formulates several "challenges" faced by the researcher in the field of death anxiety.

SELECTED PHILOSOPHICAL APPROACHES

Philosophical approaches usually cannot serve as psychological theories, and philosophical approaches toward death are no exception. There are, however, at least three reasons to include a brief review of philosophical perspectives in a psychologically oriented review. First, existential and phenomenological approaches in psychology are based upon firm philosophical foundations. Second, there have been interesting occasional attempts to use insightful philosophical descriptions of death as psychological models. Thus, Neimeyer and Chapman (1980) applied Sartre's existentialism to make predictions regarding death anxiety. Third, both philosophical and psychological perspectives emphasize the need to "integrate" or make sense of death. For these reasons I will begin by considering several philosophical approaches to death.

Heidegger's View

Martin Heidegger (1927/1962) is well known for his statement in *Being and Time* that *being* (Dasein) is freedom toward death. Characteristic of our being-in-the-world is our being as not-yet, as no-thing. The realization of the inability to become a full being brings about (actually, is) the state of mind called anxiety. Death shows that there is no hope in being what we are. On the other hand, as pointed out by Carse (1980), death holds also a positive promise: The promise to *being* that it always will be in the manner of being-toward-an-end. One can choose oneself authentically only by choosing oneself as a being-toward-the-end-of-oneself. Only then is freedom, including freedom from fear of death, realized.

Heidegger's position implies that death is on one hand a threat—the threat of nonexistence. On the other hand, according to Heidegger a realization of our future nonexistence is a precondition of a fuller understanding of our life and, eventually, a precondition for freeing ourselves from anxiety. A psychological model based on this approach may be expected to explain and perhaps to predict when one or another construction of death (as threat to existence or as condition of meaning) will prevail. While the philosophical analysis supplies the main variables that need to be explained, it remains the task of the psychological theory to specify mechanisms, circumstances, etc., in order to achieve a model that represents a scientific explanation of human behavior.

Sartre's View

While for Heidegger death is the foundation of one's freedom, for Sartre (1943/1966) death prevents an individual from realizing his or her possibilities. Death is in the future but *my death* is not in my future. Death is the "in-itself" that cannot be experienced because there is no "for-itself" to experience it. Ultimately, death reduces one's existence to what this existence really is: a "useless passion," nothing. Reflection on death is, from this point of view, reflection on the meaninglessness of existence. It seems, therefore, that we should predict higher death anxiety to the extent one spends more time thinking about death.

A more positive interpretation of Sartre's thought was provided, however, by Neimeyer and Chapman (1980) in their use of the existential theory to connect death anxiety to self-actualization. The researchers elaborated upon Sartre's statement in *Being and Nothingness* that death reduces one to one's essence, which is his past, to what one *has been*. Given this, a person who has realized his or her central life projects to a great extent is less likely to be anxious about death than one whose projects remain incomplete. It seems, however, that on this point Sartre agrees basically with Heidegger's position that presents refuge in the past as unauthentic. There cannot be any refuge in the past for a being whose mode of being is *not* to be one's own essence. A different way of explaining the relationship between death anxiety and self-actualization would be through self-actualization theories and/or "search of meaning" theories in which a person "detects" oneself rather than "invents" oneself (Frankl, 1963). Both sets of theories will be reviewed below.

A Logician's Point of View—Hofstadter's Metaphors

Hofstadter (1979) contrasts two levels at which personal nonexistence might be considered. At one level one looks upon oneself as "just another human being." It is clear then that personal nonexistence is, in the long run, unavoidable. At another level one tries to consider nonexistence as an attribute of the self. However, a "nonexistent self" is inconceivable. For Hofstadter personal nonexistence is perhaps "the best metaphorical analogue of Gödel's Theorem" (p. 698).

It is instructive to pursue this analogy a bit further. It was shown by Gödel (1931/1962) that a system or calculus including arithmetic and also some propositional logic may be constructed in such a way that, in a precise sense, it may mirror statements about properties of expressions of the calculus in the calculus itself. This system is shown to include a formula that mirrors a statement known (in the metalanguage) to be true but that is not provable in the language of the calculus itself. The analogy may be realized by interpreting the self as a structure including beliefs that correspond to the theorems of a formal calculus. Axioms may be interpreted as fundamental beliefs. A belief of complete nonexistence is incompatible with these axioms and therefore cannot be added to them.

Hofstadter's philosophical formulation reminds us of Kelly's (1955) psychological formulation (see the section on the Personal Constructs Theory), with the difference that in Hofstadter's view no "death integration" (more correctly no "nonexistence integration") is possible. Of course, the idea that death is unimaginable is hardly original. Freud, for example, contended that "in the unconscious every one of us is convinced of his own immortality" (Freud, 1915/1959, p. 313). What is peculiar to Hofstadter's argument is the presentation of this impossibility as an almost logical necessity.

Summary

Philosophical approaches, perhaps not surprisingly, differ in their conclusions as to the possibility that reflection on death might confer meaning to life. Heidegger's approach, as well as other phenomenological approaches that have not been reviewed here (e.g., Koestenbaum, 1971), make the meditation on personal death a precondition for achieving meaning and freedom of fear in everyday life. In contradistinction, for Hofstadter the ultimate understanding and assimilation of death is an impossibility. The question to what extent, under what circumstances, etc., a person may achieve integration, is an empirical question. It is the task of psychological theories to drive the research that, eventually, will provide satisfactory answers to these questions.

PSYCHOLOGICAL THEORIES

Self-Realization Theories

Several personological theorists, in particular Maslow (1968, 1970) and Rogers (1959), posited that individuals are motivated to realize their innate potentials.

Maslow's self-actualizing person has among other theoretical characteristics a greater acceptance of him- or herself, a lower anxiety, and a lower death fear. For Rogers, self-actualization is an important aspect of the "actualizing tendency." Actualization is an inherent tendency to maintain and enhance the organism. Roger's theory of personality presents the self and the corresponding urge for self-actualization as an upshot of the process of differentiation (which is a manifestation of the fundamental actualizing tendency). The same process of differentiation generates, besides the self (a symbolic representation of what one is), the ideal self, which constitutes a representation of what one wishes to be.

The notions of threat, anxiety, and defense are based in the Rogerian system on the concepts of positive regard, congruence, and conditions of worth. The individual has a need for warmth and support from other human beings—a need for positive regard. The need for self-regard develops when the individual learns to experience positive regards in relation to his or her self-experiences and independently of transactions with significant others. In this process the individual starts avoiding or seeking self-experiences because these experiences are discriminated as being more or less worthy of self-regard. At this point the individual is said to have acquired "conditions of worth," a kind of "introjected values" that reflect the evaluation of self-experiences in terms of their contribution to self-regard. The individual protects himself or herself against experiences that are perceived (or rather "subceived," since the perception is at a subliminal level) as not fitting these conditions of worth. The process of defense against this threat consists of selective perception or distortion of the experience and/or complete denial of the experience or part of it. A break of these defenses, with the subsequent realization in awareness of the aforementioned incongruence, produces anxiety.

The "theory of the fully functioning person" (pp. 234–235) assumes that in an ideal individual there is a perfect harmony between self-experiences, the general actualizing and self-actualizing tendency, and the needs for positive regard and self-regard. The fully functioning person has no "conditions of worth," no need to use defenses, and is completely open to experiences.

Death anxiety should be examined in the light of Rogers' concepts of defense and in light of his theory about the fully functioning person. Being alive may be considered a fundamental condition of worth for people who fall short of the theoretical ideal. Correspondingly, awareness of approaching death threatens these individuals, who protect themselves against it through distortions and denial. However, Rogers' notion of complete openness to experience in ideal individuals changes the status of death as a fundamental threat. Indeed, for a fully functioning person, death may be an interesting experience (Rogers, 1980).

Rogers' theory presents several notions that may be fruitful in an analysis of death attitudes. An individual may loosen this condition of worth by constructing himself as a worthy person in spite of unavoidable death. The critical notion here is an ability to maintain self-esteem in conditions that are interpreted as movement toward death. Another useful concept defined by Rogers is that of the ''ideal self''—the representation of one's wishes. Death may threaten to finalize a discrepancy between the self and the ideal self. This latter point is elaborated in the section on self-concept discrepancy theory below.

Self-actualization theories have been criticized for several methodological and theoretical reasons. Writers representing the point of view of ''mainstream psychology'' have criticized the vagueness of some of the constructs, or the emphasis on private experience with little attention being paid to overt action (e.g., Singer, 1984). Other critics, from a humanistic perspective, have argued that there are contradictions in self-realization theories, which also have a pre-scriptive (rather than descriptive), moralistic character (e.g., Daniels, 1988; Geller, 1982). A self-actualization motivation appears to be accepted, however, in recent self-concept models as a basic type of motivation (Markus & Wurf, 1987). Moreover, an important and rather consistent finding is that of an inverse relationship between the level of death anxiety and measures of self-actualization (Neimeyer, 1988). We therefore can expect a theoretical approach to the study of death anxiety to be based, at least in part, on this kind of motivation.

Search-for-Meaning Theories

Theories emphasizing the search for meaning (Antonowski, 1979; Frankl, 1963; Maddi, 1970; Taylor, 1983; Thompson & Janigian, 1988) often describe pro-cesses of reformulation of perceptions, life schemes, and attitudes happening in circumstances of intense adversity, which help one to regain a sense of purpose in life.

An important question regarding the search for meaning relates to one's relationship to one's past. With respect to this, ''search-for-meaning theories'' may be seen as complementary to self-actualization theories. One of the clearest statements to this effect is that of Frankl, who in *Man's Search for Meaning* says, ''in the past, nothing is irrecoverably lost but everything irrevocably stored'' (Frankl, 1963, p. 122), and ''having been is the surest kind of being'' (p. 123). Such a position may be contrasted with Sartre's position, according to which the past as the essence or the ''being-in-itself'' is the lack of any possi-bilities, the lack of freedom and meaning.

A systematic description of the ''search-for-meaning'' was provided by Thompson and Janigian (1988) using the concept of *life scheme* as a main theoretical and methodological concept. In their formulation, meaning consists of both order (of the world and one's place in it) and purpose (of one's life). Negative events can be dealt with by changing one's life scheme so that it accommodates negative events, for example cancer (Weisman & Worden, 1975), or by changing one's perception of the event.

In the present context we can interpret the first alternative to mean an attempt to validate life in spite of death. A change in attitude towards one's past, which may be considered as the ''surest kind of being'' (Frankl, 1963) rather than as "something which is not here anymore," seems to be of this type. A larger definition of the self to include significant others (thus creating an "extended self") is also illustrative of this possibility. An extended self was indeed found to be accompanied by less fear of death (Westman & Canter, 1985). On the other hand, the perception of death itself may be changed from an absolute evil to a significant event that eventually gives life meaning (see the section on Heidegger). In fact it seems likely that both these strategies are needed for a successful resolution of death anxiety.

A number of studies on death anxiety, drawing on Frankl's perspective, have investigated the existence of a positive correlation between purpose in life and death anxiety. The results, in general, have upheld this expectation (Aronow, Rauchway, Peller, & DeVitto, 1980; Bolt, 1978; Durlak, 1972).

A conceptual framework such as that presented by Thompson and Janigian suggests the existence of two components of death integration: one focuses on the self, its achievements, past, etc., and another focuses on death itself, which may be reconstructed to fit the need for meaningfulness.

Personal Construct Theory

According to Kelly's theory of personal constructs (Kelly, 1955), a person construes events in order to be able to anticipate thematically similar events in the future. In formulating constructs, an individual abstracts some important ways in which "elements" (things, persons, events, etc.) are similar and different, gradually developing a belief system that is hierarchically organized. Some constructs are at a relatively low level (peripheral) and can be easily revised without needing to revise the whole system. Others—core constructs—are much higher in the hierarchy and their revision implies radical changes in the person's outlook. Kelly allows, through his "fragmentation corollary," contradictions between subsystems but limitations on these are imposed by other corollaries in his theory.

Kelly uses death several times in his book as the paradigmatic example for "threat," which is defined as "the awareness of imminent change in one's core structures" (p. 489). Death is considered here as an alternative core structure, one which is incompatible with the present structure. As a function of one's beliefs one may anticipate a more or less radical change and therefore may feel a more or less serious threat. Some findings concerning the relationship between religious belief and fear of death seem to be consistent with this prediction (Florian & Kravetz, 1983).

Although Kelly uses death only in the context of "threat" and in order to illustrate this concept, his theory also provides a definition of "anxiety" that allows for a definition of death anxiety separate from death threat. Anxiety is defined to be "the recognition that the events with which one is confronted lie outside the range of convenience of one's construct system" (p. 490). Death may be considered as an element (event) that is difficult to make sense of. Assuming that this element cannot be subsumed under the existent structure, anxiety should ensue. A difficulty in conceiving one's own death should be accompanied by higher anxiety. Findings of empirical research are consistent with this hypothesis, as discussed below.

Kelly's original theory and methodology (e.g., the repertory grid technique, see Kelly, 1955) have been fruitfully extended to the study of death attitudes, generating the creation of an instrument—the Threat Index (TI) (Krieger & Epting, 1974)—and several lines of research (Neimeyer & Moore, 1989). The TI is based on the idea that death is threatening to the extent to which a person is reluctant to subsume his or her self-concept and the concept of death under the same poles of a sample of personal constructs. This threat has been found to be less for people believing in afterlife (Krieger & Epting, 1974), since for these people death implies a smaller change in their core beliefs than for other people. In addition, scores on the TI should be greater for people who are less able to conceive their own deaths. Again, evidence in support of these hypotheses has been provided by personal construct researchers (see Neimeyer & Moore, 1989, and Chapter 4, this volume, for a review of this literature and data regarding the construct validity and other psychometric properties of two versions of the TI).

Additional work dealing with systems of death-related beliefs, from a structural or content point of view, has been conducted by Neimeyer and his colleagues (Neimeyer, Bagley, & Moore, 1986; Neimeyer & Moore, 1989). In particular, a Death Attitude Repertory Test (DART) based on Kelly's grid technique measures the way respondents rate death-related situations on 15 scales elicited from the respondents themselves. Structural measures are obtained, for example, by correlating the ratings of different situations and computing a measure of coherence (high relationships) vs. complexity (low relationships). These measures may be valuable in studying changes in death attitudes across the life span (Neimeyer & Moore, 1989).

More work regarding "the theory of death threat" remains to be done (Chambers, 1986; Neimeyer, 1986). For example, in its present form, the TI fails to discriminate between threat engendered by the process of dying versus the state of being dead (Neimeyer, 1986). It might be fruitful to distinguish different aspects of death threat and the self in measuring threat. In addition, as an aggregate measure, the traditional TI may obscure the specific ways in which self and death are viewed as compatible or incompatible by the subject. Confirmatory factor analysis by Neimeyer, Moore, and Bagley (1988) indeed disconfirmed the hypothesis of one general factor for the 30-item self-report Threat Index, indicating that it may be measuring not one, but several dimensions of death threat. A subsequent analysis of a large data set, also using confirmatory procedures, suggests that the TI can be scored to yield useful measures of Fatalism, Threat to Well-being, and Uncertainty, in addition to the Global Threat measure used by previous investigators (Moore & Neimeyer, 1991).

Building on the work of Neimeyer and Chapman (1980), Robinson and Wood (1983, 1984) used the TI methodology to investigate the aspect of death threat, or conversely, "integration," together with self-actualization. Their additive model was tested in several studies by these and other researchers (Neimeyer, 1985). The model hypothesizes that death concern is an additive function of two factors: actualization and integration. An actualization score reflects the extent to which self and ideal self are rated similarly on a sample of construct dimensions. An integration score is similarly computed, but is based on the ratings of self and death. The evidence for the model is mixed (Neimeyer, 1985) and one can only agree with Neimeyer that additional explanatory variables are needed for a fuller explanation of death anxiety. The additive model, which is consistent with both a theory of personal constructs and with a self-actualization approach, seems to be a promising step toward a comprehensive model of death anxiety.

A personal construct conceptualization provides a rich system for measuring and studying death attitudes in theoretically consistent ways. Kelly's theory also describes different ways by which incompatibility between subsystems can be reduced (e.g., dilation vs. constriction), which are of interest in the context of death threat. An application of the theory to development (Morrison & Cometa, 1982) might constitute a powerful tool in the study of death anxiety and its intra-individual change over time.

Theories of Denial and Positive Illusions

An important concept in the Freudian and Neo-Freudian approaches is that of defense mechanisms used by the ego to guard against anxiety provoked by internal or external stimuli (Freud, 1946). A natural next step would be to invoke these defenses as protection against unacceptable personal death. This step was not taken by Freud himself but was taken by psychoanalytic thinkers, such as Rank and Brown, as described by Becker (1973). From this point of view, high levels of (conscious) death anxiety may be interpreted as a breakdown of protective mechanisms and mainly of the mechanism of denial. Conversely, an ability to deny death without being much bothered by ones's own "lies" may be considered "the essence of normality" (Becker, p. 178).

Recently, Snyder (1988) described the development of the classic self-defense mechanism into the present "self-protection" processes involving processes such as "self-serving attributional bias" (Weary, 1979) or "ego-defensive attribution" (Miller, 1976). This approach is consistent with a new influential view (e.g., Taylor, 1983; Taylor & Brown, 1988), according to which mental health is achieved through adaptive positive illusions.

The notion of illusion is perhaps consistent with some views of symbolic immortality, according to which a person finds an antidote to his terror of death in identification with the cultural system (Becker, 1975). This section reviews several theoretical models or approaches that assume that persons need to protect themselves against the specter of death using repressions or illusions and/or that symbolic systems are effective means in creating and maintaining an illusion of immortality.

The Two-Factor Model of Death Anxiety   According to this model (Gilliland & Templer, 1985–86; Lonetto & Templer, 1986; Templer, 1976), death anxiety is determined by two factors. One factor reflects overall psychological health as evidenced by measures of general anxiety and depression. The second factor reflects specific life experiences concerning the topic of death. Gilliland and Templer (1985–86) proposed that the first factor represents death anxiety (presumably in a relatively narrow sense) while the second factor represents "straightforward" fear of death. The nature of this second factor remains somewhat unclear since, in spite of being an experiential factor, the authors suggest that "it is almost inevitably present in humans and depends minimally upon learning" (p. 163).

A breakdown of defense mechanisms may bring about death anxiety, together with other psychopathological conditions such as depression, types of neurosis, and psychosis. The relevant literature includes empirical findings regarding the relationship between death anxiety and maladjustment symptoms and between death anxiety and life experiences. Reviewing this literature, Lonetto and Templer (1986) arrived at the conclusion that the evidence, in general, "meshes well" with a two-factor interpretation.

Terror Management Theory   Terror management theory (e.g., Rosenblatt, Greenberg, Solomon, Pyszczynski, & Lyon, 1989), which is based on Becker's writings (Becker, 1962, 1973, 1975), assumes that cultural systems serve the function of buffers against human awareness of vulnerability and eventual mortality. Cultural systems encourage conceptions of the world as a just place and promise "symbolic" immortality through identification with the system and "real" immortality through religion. However, to enjoy these benefits one has to abide by the system's rules and to live up the common cultural standards. In this way one achieves the feeling of being a worthy participant in the cultural system (self-esteem). Thus, people are motivated to believe in their cultural systems and in their belonging to them. The theory predicts that making death more salient for subjects should motivate them to respond especially positively toward people who uphold cultural values and especially negatively toward those who violate them. The model also predicts that increasing self-esteem in subjects should enable them to experience less anxiety in response to threatening stimuli, such as video-taped scenes of death. There is empirical evidence consistent with these predictions (Greenberg, Pyszczynski, & Solomon, 1986; Rosenblatt, Greenberg, Solomon, Pyszczynski, & Lyon, 1989). In addition, results indicative of a negative correlation between self-esteem and death anxiety (e.g., Davis, Martin, Wilee, & Voorhees, 1978) are also consistent with the terror management theory.

Illusions of Self Control   According to the general view presented by Taylor and other researchers (Taylor & Brown, 1988; Taylor, Collins, Skokan, & Aspinwall, 1989), most people develop and maintain positive illusions regarding themselves, the world, their ability to control the environment and the future. Moreover, these positive illusions may be distinguished from defense mechanisms (Taylor & Brown, 1988; Taylor, Collins, Skokan, & Aspinwall, 1989) and they foster positive psychological adjustment (Taylor, 1983; Taylor & Brown, 1988). Being "higher-order beliefs" (Epstein, 1980), positive illusions may be not tested very often (Janoff-Bulman, 1989). When they are tested, however, and disconfirmed, they are changed in accordance with reality (Janoff-Bulman, 1989; Taylor, Collins, Skokan, & Aspinwall, 1989).

What are the illusions related to death? This topic was discussed extensively (mostly in terms of denial) in the context of a person facing life threatening diseases and in the context of the dying person (e.g., Kübler-Ross, 1969; Taylor & Brown, 1988; Weisman, 1972). Our interest here, however, is in death anxiety as a phenomenon accompanying "normal life." People may acknowledge the inevitability of their own death and still consider this as an event belonging to the remote future, without any relevance to their present. Such a belief is important (a "core belief") and has adaptive value, and consequently the inclination to disconfirm it is very low (Epstein, 1980). Ironically, an individual may strengthen his belief that death is always (at safe distance) in the future by a type of learning that makes denying only more effective. This view was expressed by Breznitz (1983) in his book on the phenomenon of false alarms. As he states, "denial itself can be particularly effective in view of the fact that death is a single-trial experience, and as long as we are alive we have been through false alarms only. The many threats that did not materialize encourage the illusion of invulnerability so necessary to one's psychological security and well-being" (p. 233).

Positive illusions regarding one's death seem to imply a structure of personal time as well as beliefs of high control. Regarding the first point there are two possibilities: One may construe himself or herself as having a long subjective life expectancy or, alternatively, one may define his or her life projects to cover the immediate but not the remote future. This second possibility involves less denial and has more the character of an illusion than of a defense (Taylor, Collins, Skokan, & Aspinwall, 1989). Indeed, the empirical evidence suggests that individuals high in death anxiety use the first strategy of postponing death (Neimeyer, Bagley, & Moore, 1986), while those low in death anxiety have a more pronounced present orientation than others (Vargo & Batsel, 1981). A theory of positive illusions will predict that death anxiety will correlate negatively with internal locus of control and positively with external locus of control. Substantial evidence is consistent with this assumption (e.g., Hayslip & Stewart-

Bussey, 1986–87; Kuperman & Golden, 1978; Peterson, 1985; Sadowski, Davis, & Loftus-Vergari, 1979; Stewart, 1975; Vargo & Black, 1984). There are, however, many exceptions to this pattern (e.g., Hunt, Lester, & Ashton, 1983; O'Dowd, 1984–85; Nehrke, Belluci, & Gabriel, 1977–78), suggesting that additional variables may be involved.

An application of a theory of adaptive positive illusions to everyday death anxiety seems promising. Particularly intriguing is the distinction between positive illusions and defenses. Theoretically, a person using defensive mechanisms to combat death anxiety would have a high level of unconscious death anxiety. A theory of positive illusions, on the other hand, does not assume the existence of unconscious death anxiety. Moreover, since illusions are beliefs, a deeper understanding of inter- and intra-individual differences in death anxiety may be achieved via an investigation of the systems of beliefs of the individuals involved and of changes in these systems. This is a conclusion consistent with many of the approaches reviewed here, especially personal construct theory.

Finally, a positive illusions view on death seems consistent with the notion of "middle knowledge" of death as a partial awareness, partial denial. This last notion was applied first to dying patients (Weisman & Hackett, 1961) and then generalized by Lifton to the "rest of us" (Lifton, 1979).

Multiple Selves and the Self-Concept Discrepancy Theory

Most of the approaches reviewed here are based on the notion of self. For example, self-actualization theories describe a self striving to achieve its potential, to become actualized. Roger's formulation included the possibility of a discrepancy between the actual self and the ideal self with implications for self-regard. Erikson's psychosocial theory (see next section) describes a self that constructs and transforms itself in the process of growth. This notion of a "dynamic" self (e.g., Markus & Wurf, 1987) is prevalent indeed in recent theories. Closely linked to this are the notions of multiple selves and possible or potential selves (Markus & Nurius, 1986). According to this last notion, motivations become translated or embodied in structures, which contain cognitive representations of goals and threats related to future events. These representations, in Markus and Nurius' formulation, beyond their functioning as incentives "provide an evaluative and interpretive context for the now self" (p. 962). The relevance to our topic is clear. We may say that attitudes toward death are determined by the way one sees himself or herself in the future as a "dying self" (Marshall, 1980) or even as a "dead self" (of course, a self-contradictory notion).

One theory that makes use of the notion of multiple selves and its relevance to the study of death anxiety is the self-concept discrepancy theory (Higgins, 1987). The theory postulates three domains of the self: the *actual* self, the *ideal* self, and the *ought* self. The actual self includes representations of attributes that someone (self or significant other) believes that the person actually possesses. The ideal self refers to representations of characteristics someone (or a significant other) would like himself or herself to possess. The ought self includes representation of characteristics that the person (or significant others) believes he or she should possess. Perceived discrepancies between the actual self and the ideal self are assumed to generate feelings of disappointment and failure, whereas discrepancies between the real self and the ought self are assumed to generate fear, threat, and anxiety.

This model was applied to distinguish between different aspects of depression and anxiety (Higgins, Klein, & Strauman, 1985). The actual-ideal discrepancy was associated to dejection-related emotions, whereas the actual-ought discrepancy was associated to agitation-related emotions. A possible application to death anxiety might involve an attempt to distinguish (and predict) feelings of failure associated with death from feelings of anxiety and fear, also associated with personal death. The first, according to the self-discrepancy theory, are connected to unfulfilled wishes, whereas the second are connected to unfulfilled duties and responsibilities.

An application of the theory to the area of death anxiety might also have to consider the fact that death is a future event. Death anxiety may be a result of the self imagining a future self facing death. This imagined self facing death might have many characteristics of the imagining (present) self. In particular, it has a structure of ought self, real self, and ideal self that might be very similar to the present structure. If this interpretation is true, it means that it is not fulfillment of wishes and responsibilities that is a determinant of (lower) death anxiety, but the amount of *anticipated* fulfillment. Obviously, with increased age, the present fulfillment and the anticipated one become closer and therefore the whole topic of self-realization (in terms of wishes and responsibilities) becomes more critical (cf. Erikson, 1963). We should expect therefore an interaction of age (or, maybe, subjective life expectancy) and self-realization in their impact on death anxiety.

Admittedly, this is speculative and advanced as an illustration of possible use (and integration) of newly developed theories from the field of social and developmental psychology in the research on death anxiety.

Erikson's Psychosocial Theory

Erikson's psychosocial theory of development (Erikson, 1963, 1982; Erikson, Erikson, & Kivnick, 1986) provides a broad view of human development with important implications regarding the role of death anxiety in adult life, as well as regarding the eventual fate of the struggle with the death threat. The part of the theory commonly referred to in this context is the last stage of *integrity versus despair*. A person who sees his life in this stage as a meaningful whole would positively resolve the crises of this stage. In Lifton's (1979) formulation this person realizes symbolic immortality. A negative solution would be that of a person looking at his or her entire life as wrongly lived or wasted. Such a person will show a high fear of death. Erikson may be interpreted as maintaining that positive resolution of one stage depends on positive resolutions of prior stages (Meacham, 1989). Correspondingly, the development of ego integrity has antecedents, the most important of which is the resolution of the *generativity vs. stagnation* stage. Two aspects of this stage are of special interest in the present context.

First, it is the awareness of mortality and closeness of death that precipitates the crisis of this stage (Gould, 1978; Jacques, 1965; Neugarten, 1977). The development of generativity in the form of care to children, to grandchildren, to society, etc., is a response to this challenge. Second, this form of "transcending death" is of an interpersonal nature; it involves construing or extending the self to include significant others and possibly the whole social and cultural system (Meacham, 1989). Some evidence (Westman & Canter, 1985) about a negative relationship between fear of death and an extended self is consistent with Erikson's theory.

The conjunction between the seventh and the eighth stages suggests an interesting dynamic: Death anxiety has a causal effect in producing the crisis of one stage whose positive resolution enables one to move to the next stage. A positive resolution in this last stage presumably will be accompanied by a low fear of death. However, as Meacham (1989) rightly mentions, it is not clear whether or not Erikson believes that a positive resolution in the last stage represents a stable state or whether one has to struggle continuously to maintain one's integrity and one's low fear.

Erikson's psychosocial theory constitutes a rich conceptual system for the study of death anxiety. As a theory centered on the self, it is consistent with recent developments in the concept of self and its basic motivations. Thus, the "dynamic self" (Markus & Wurf, 1987) is often assumed to include a self esteem need and a self-consistency need (Breytspraak, 1984). The last stage of *integrity vs. despair* emphasizes this second need. Attempts to formulate developmental models based on the concept of self (e.g., Dickstein, 1977; Lewis, 1979) are at least partially compatible with Erikson's approach. Thus, Dickstein (1977) proposed a model based on different types of self-esteem realized at different stages. The last stages are the "self as integrated whole" and the "selfless self." In the latter stage the self tends to lose its boundaries (which are now conceived to be arbitrary), a phenomenon described by Erikson (1959) as "identity diffusion." Both integration and the realization of a selfless self may be conceived as different approaches to "solve" the problem of personal death. An interesting empirical question indeed regards the differential effectiveness of these two approaches as protective shields against death anxiety.

The concept of life review (Butler, 1961; Romaniuk, 1981) and the similar concept of biography construction (Marshall, 1980) fit also neatly in Erikson's model. On one hand they represent efforts at achieving cohesiveness and integrity, and in this way they are preparation for death (Marshall, 1980). On the other hand, these processes include biases, which are much studied in recent approaches to self structures. These are biases, reflected in selective recall explained using, for example, implicit theories of self-consistency (e.g., Ross, 1989), as well as biases in the interpretation of the past, which were found to be consistent with the existence of a need for self-enhancement (Greenwald, 1980). While Erikson emphasizes the achievement of integrity via the construction of one's personal history as a valid activity, these empirically demonstrated biases reflect the importance of the task at hand: to prepare a self very much aware of its approaching death (Marshall, 1980). The self-serving processes are also consistent with recent theories of adjustment through positive illusions (see the section "Theories of Denial and Positive Illusions").

Application of the theory in empirical research is difficult. For example, the operationalization of notions like positive resolution of crises is problematic (Meacham, 1989). It should be clear that, to the extent that testable hypotheses are derived, they should be tested using the kind of design (e.g., longitudinal) that is appropriate to the structure of Erikson's theory. This comment applies also to other stage theories similar to Erikson's (e.g., Gould, 1978; Levinson, Darrow, Klein, Levinson, & McKee, 1978). While several studies on death anxiety have used Erikson's theory to derive hypotheses or to interpret findings (Flint, Grayton, & Ozmon, 1983; Nehrke, Belluci, & Gabriel, 1977–78; Reker, Peacock, & Wong, 1987), they have used cross-sectional designs and, sometimes, rather simplified interpretations.

In conclusion, the psychosocial theory in conjunction with other concepts and theoretical models, as indicated above, may become a rich source of ideas and, eventually, of testable hypotheses in the area of death anxiety.

Theories of Intellectual Development in Adult Age— Postformal Models and Models of Wisdom

Discontentment with Piagetian theory, in particular in respect to its ability to describe adequately development in late adolescence and adulthood, has recently generated several models of postformal thinking (Broughton, 1984). The concepts of dialectic and of dialectical operations (Basseches, 1984; Riegel, 1973) are of special importance in the formulation of these models. Our interest in these developments resides in their implications for the possibility for growing individuals to integrate their own death into their self structures by using dialectic thinking. Indeed, a classic definition considers dialectic thinking to be the capacity to integrate contradictory facets (Carse, 1980).

A good example of a postformal theory is the model proposed by Labouvie-Vief (1982). In her model, the first postformal stage, the *intersystemic*, replaces a logical and universal concept of truth with a relativistic one, which accepts as equally valid several points of view. During the next stage, *autonomy*, "truth" becomes relative to personal and social goals. It is at this stage that the individual can fully accept responsibility for his development. The notion of truth as anchored in personal and interpersonal interests, rather than in an "objective" world, is important in the present context. This concept of truth seems to imply, for example, that "symbolic immortality" (Lifton, 1979) is not a dubious surrogate for the "real thing" (real immortality) but *is* the real thing. The model also implies that the capacity to realize this kind of symbolic immortality develops throughout adulthood.

There is still a need for empirical evidence for the existence of postformal thinking in Labouvie-Vief's model or, for that matter, in other models of post formal thinking. The possibility of fundamental changes in ways and structures of thinking or in styles of thinking (Rybash, Hoyer, & Roodin, 1986) is intriguing. In particular, it may allow us to explain changes in the concept of death and in death attitudes with increased age and to relate them to changes in many other domains on the basis of changes in intellectual functioning.

Other theories of intellectual development suggest an increase in the ability of individuals to pass judgments regarding uncertain matters of life and/or their increased expertise in the pragmatics of life (Baltes, 1987; Dittman-Kohli & Baltes, 1990; Dixon & Baltes, 1986). Dittman-Kohli and Baltes (1990) made a distinction between practical wisdom relating to one's personal life and philosophical wisdom. Practical wisdom includes knowledge about personally relevant real-life situations. Philosophical wisdom includes cognitive activities related to solutions for general, social, and cultural problems. A development in practical wisdom should facilitate optimal transitions at all stages of development. In old age practical wisdom would allow a construction of self and the world "that permits, for instance, the anchoring of one's increasing losses and one's finitude into the context of intergenerational transmission and cultural movement" (p. 75). One implication of the approach of Dittman-Kohli and Baltes seems to be that an increased ability to accept death is a result of an increase in practical wisdom. On the other hand, a development in philosophical wisdom, which exists at a higher level of abstraction and generalization, may also, perhaps, enable one to "transcend" and to accept personal death.

There is some empirical evidence that seems to confirm the notion that there is a development in wisdom (see Dittman-Kohli and Baltes, 1990). Should the wisdom models prove to be successful, their integration with psychosocial theories of development, such as Erikson's theory (Dittman-Kohli & Baltes, 1990), might provide a promising developmental model for the study of changes in death anxiety in adulthood.

DISCUSSION

The focus in the present review was on death of self. Four aspects may be subsumed under this general category. They are the annihilation of the self (nonexistence), death as radical transformation and separation, death as threat to the meaningfulness of life, and death as threat to realization of life's basic goals and propensities. This conceptualization is quite similar to that used by Lifton (1979). Lifton's inner disintegration and separation correspond to the first two categories. Stasis, which for Lifton means the opposite of movement and growth, is replaced here by two related threats: to the meaningfulness of life and to self-realization. These categories may be considered as types of death-related "threats" that are recurrent themes in different theoretical approaches to death anxiety. Self-annihilation may be considered to be a main theme for theories of denial. Death as radical transformation is addressed by Kelly's theory of personal constructs. Search-for-meaning theories deal with threats to meaningfulness of existence of which death is the paradigmatic example. Self-realization and self theories are especially relevant to the realization of basic goals and inherent inclinations. Finally, developmental theories may offer an insight about developmental changes that may help the individual to cope with all four types of death-related threats. In addition, these theories consider the impact death threats have on development.

There is a substantial amount of overlap among theories. As a result, some hypotheses may be derived from more than one theory. For example, the hypothesis that an expanded self will be accompanied by less fear of death can be derived from the theory of personal constructs: from the standpoint of an expanded self, death may imply a less radical transformation of the self structure. But an expanded self also lessens the threat of meaninglessness, is consistent with the concept of generativity, or, when constructed to include whole cultural systems, is consistent with the terror management theory.

The richness in theoretical models relevant to the study of death is accompanied by several important challenges. They may be conveniently placed under the following headings: operationalization, creative application, integration, and selection of appropriate methods.

Operationalization

There is a need to operationalize vague concepts, such as the successful resolution of a life crisis in Erikson's theory. This problem of definition is inextricably linked to the problem of derivation of unambiguous, testable hypotheses. The problem is likely to be especially difficult when the attempt is made to derive empirical hypotheses on the basis of philosophical analyses.

An important part of the operationalization process has to do with the definition of aspects of death anxiety or to related terms. There are a multitude of measurement tools (see Neimeyer, 1988, for a review), but only a few of them were constructed on the basis of a well defined theoretical approach. As a result, the researcher in this area might need to select carefully (and sometimes to construct) his or her tools. For example, some theoretical approaches will suggest important distinctions between awareness of (or preoccupation with) death and death anxiety. Thus, Heidegger's approach makes the awareness of imminent death a condition for the eventual liberation from the fear of death and for the finding of meaningfulness in life. The empirical investigation of this hypothesis will necessitate using an instrument such as the Death Concern Scale (Dickstein, 1972) that allows the calculation of a separate score for the two dimensions of awareness and negative evaluation of death (cf. Klug & Boss, 1976; Warren, 1989).

Another example of the importance of adequate operationalization concerns the extent to which death anxiety is stable and trait-like in character, and the extent to which it is variable and state-like. Most of the theories reviewed here seem to encourage a view of death anxiety as a relatively stable characteristic, possibly changing over extended periods of time. Some empirical evidence was interpreted to mean that death anxiety is indeed mainly a trait (e.g., Pettigrew & Dawson, 1979). It has been increasingly recognized, however, that many variables have both a trait-like and a state-like character and that the measurement of states may well necessitate special instruments (Nesselroade, 1991).

Creative Application

The present review included several theories that were considered to be relevant to the understanding of death anxiety, although for some of them, no specific application has yet been suggested in the investigation of death anxiety. An example is the self-concept discrepancy theory. In still other cases (e.g., search-for-meaning theories), applications of potentially promising approaches are scarce. On these occasions I added speculative comments to make the relevance of the theory to the study of death anxiety clear and to suggest directions of possible application. The derivation of testable hypotheses from these theories and their investigation may serve the dual purpose of promoting the understanding of death anxiety and of testing the particular theory.

Of special interest is the possible application of philosophical theories. Philosophical analyses may provide insightful descriptions of the possible meaning (or lack of meaning) of death and may even suggest empirical relationships (e.g., Neimeyer & Chapman, 1980). They may also provide us with "exemplars" against which informal or "implicit" theories about personal death may be examined. The simultaneous consideration of two or more approaches may be fruitful. For example, a logical analysis such as that of Hofstadter suggests the impossibility of a complete integration, whereas Heidegger's analysis may suggest the reverse. The question whether intense meditation on the subject of death is conducive to integration, or is doomed to failure, is of course an empirical question. We can, in fact, anticipate that a specification of accompanying circumstances, experiences, etc. will be needed before an answer to this question may be provided. It is, therefore, the task of the psychologist not only to operationalize vague philosophical concepts but also to build (perhaps using psychological models) upon the selected philosophical foundation in order to derive a testable model. This brings us to the next challenge.

Integration

A need for integration is suggested by the multitude of approaches and by their similarities as well as differences. An examination of the empirical literature (for a review, see Neimeyer, 1988) reveals considerable complexity and, frequently, discrepancies and inconsistencies among various studies. This situation suggests the necessity for a complex model, possibly based on an integration of theories, to account for such a complex phenomenon as death anxiety.

Thus, many may feel that a denial approach based on defense mechanisms captures an important truth. At the same time, the consideration of additional factors may be necessary for a more complete explanation. For example, a second factor representing specific experiences related to death was incorporated in Templer's two-factor model. A two-factor model is, however, still incomplete since this model does not deal with the possibility of integration of death with other self-structures. One has to have recourse to other approaches, for example to personal construct theory or to Erikson's psychosocial developmental theory, in order to find interesting treatments of this topic. Indeed, Lonetto and Templer (1986) recognize that it might be necessary to add a third, "existential" factor to the other two factors in their approach.

The last example suggests the possibility that different explanatory concepts may be needed to explain death anxiety at different levels within a range spreading from "pathological," through "common," to almost complete lack of fear of death (White & Handal, 1990–91). An explanation based on breakdown of defenses seems pertinent to the first level, while an explanation based on integration of death may be useful at the third level. From a developmental point of view, such an approach would be consistent with recent calls to distinguish between "successful aging," "usual aging," and pathological changes (Rowe & Kahn, 1987).

Finally, a different type of integration is suggested by general theories such as Erikson's psychosocial approach. Many other models (e.g., a life review approach, theories of selective recall, or a theory of development of practical wisdom) may be used *within* the global psychosocial approach, as they specify mechanisms of coping with developmental challenges. The researcher in thanatology may play an important role in suggesting these types of integration and in applying them in his or her own research.

Selection of Appropriate Methods

It is likely that one result of an integration of several theoretical approaches would be a model of death anxiety that recognizes the multidimensionality of death anxiety, its existence at different levels of consciousness (Epting, Rainey, & Weiss, 1979; Kunzendorf, 1985), and its causation by multiple factors. In addition, aspects of death anxiety might serve in a developed model both as independent variables (e.g., precipitating important life decisions and changes in time perspective in midlife) and as dependent variables multiply determined. Complex, elaborated models necessitate appropriate methods for their investigation.

A persistent problem in most of the death anxiety studies is their almost exclusive reliance on cross-sectional designs and on unsophisticated exploratory methods of analysis. Particularly in the case of developmental theories, cross-sectional designs prevent appropriate tests of the model under study, and they should be replaced by longitudinal designs. Also, in addition to long-term longitudinal designs, short-term longitudinal designs may provide information regarding intra-individual variability in death anxiety over short periods of time and possible antecedents of this variability.

Structural equation models using multiple indicators for the latent variables and specifying an elaborated pattern of relationships (''paths'') between the latent variables (e.g., Hertzog, 1987) may significantly improve the ability to test complex models. Confirmatory factor analyses of the type performed by Neimeyer and his colleagues (Moore & Neimeyer, 1991; Neimeyer, Moore, & Bagley, 1988) are an important step in this direction. In particular, it is possible to construct identifiable structural equation models to model longitudinal relationships and reciprocal relationships (e.g., Gollob & Reichardt, 1987; Jöreskog & Sörbom, 1988).

Experimental designs may also be used. Some of the theoretical approaches surveyed lend themselves more easily than others to investigation based on experimental designs. This is the case, for example, with terror management theory that has already generated substantial experimental work. For example, self-esteem is a variable that may be manipulated experimentally, and its effects on death anxiety may be studied.

In conclusion, I hope that the careful use of theoretical models for derivation of hypotheses about death anxiety and the use of sophisticated experimental and correlational techniques will deepen our understanding of death attitudes and of human nature in general.

ACKNOWLEDGMENTS

Acknowledged is support of the MacArthur Foundation Network on Successful Aging. The author thanks Bob Intrieri, James Reid, and Scott Hershberger from the Department of Human Development and Family Studies, Pennsylvania State University, for their insightful comments on various drafts of this paper. In addition, multiple thanks are due to the editor of *Death Studies* and to two anonymous reviewers for their invaluable comments on the form and substance of a previous version of this paper.

REFERENCES

Antonowski, A. (1979). *Health, stress and coping*. San Francisco: Jossey-Bass.

Aronow, E., Rauchway, A., Peller, M., & DeVitto, A. (1980). The value of the self in relation to fear of death. *Omega, 11*, 37–44.

Baltes, P. B. (1987). Theoretical, propositions of life span developmental psychology: On the dynamics between growth and decline. *Developmental Psychology, 23*, 611–626.

Basseches, M. A. (1984). Dialectical thinking as a metasystematic form of cognitive organization. In M. L. Commons, F. A. Richards, & C. Armon (Eds.), *Beyond formal operations: Latent adolescent and adult cognitive development* (pp. 216–238). New York: Praeger.

Becker, E. (1962). *The birth and death of meaning*. New York: Free Press.

Becker, E. (1973). *The denial of death*. New York: Free Press.

Becker, E. (1975). *Escape from evil*. New York: Free Press.

Bolt, M. (1978). Purpose in life and death concerns. *Journal of Geriatric Psychology, 132*, 159–160.

Breytspraak, L. (1984). *The development of the self in later life*. Boston: Little, Brown.

Breznitz, S. (1983). *Cry wolf*. Hillsdale, NJ: Lawrence Erlbaum.

Broughton, J. M. (1984). Not beyond formal operations but beyond Piaget. In M. L. Commons, F. A. Richards, & C. Armon (Eds.), *Beyond formal operations* (pp. 395–411). New York: Praeger.

Butler, R. N. (1961). The life review: An interpretation of reminiscence in the aged. In B. L. Neugarten (Ed.), *Middle age and aging* (pp. 486–496). Chicago: University of Chicago Press.

Carse, J. P. (1980). *Death and existence*. New York: John Wiley & Sons, Inc.

Chambers, W. V. (1986). Inconsistencies in the theory of death threat. *Death Studies, 10*, 165–175.

Daniels, M. (1988). The myth of self-actualization. *Journal of Humanistic Psychology, 28*, 7–38.

Davis, S. F., Martin, D. A., Wilee, C. T., & Voorhees, J. W. (1978). Relationship of fear of death and level of self-esteem in college students. *Psychological Reports, 42*, 419–422.

Dickstein, E. (1977). Self and self esteem: Theoretical foundations and their implications for research. *Human Development, 20*, 129–140.

Dickstein, L. S. (1972). Death concern: Measurement and correlates. *Psychological Reports, 30,* 563–571.

Dickstein, L. S. (1977–78). Attitudes toward death, anxiety, and social desirability. *Omega, 8,* 369–378.

Dittman-Kohli, F., & Baltes, P. B. (1990). Toward a neofunctionalist conception of adult intellectual development: Wisdom as a prototypical case of intellectual growth. In C. Alexander & E. Langer (Eds.), *Beyond formal operations: Alternative endpoints to human development* (pp. 54–78). New York: Oxford University Press.

Dixon, R. A, & Baltes, P. B. (1986). Toward life-span research on the functions and pragmatics of intelligence. In R. J. Sternberg & R. K. Wagner (Eds.), *Practical intelligence: Nature and origins of competence in the everyday world* (pp. 203–235). New York: Cambridge University Press.

Durlak, J. (1972). Relationship between individual attitudes toward life and death. *Journal of Consulting and Clinical Psychology, 38,* 463.

Epstein, S. (1980). The self-concept: A review and the proposal of an integrated theory of personality. In E. Staub (Ed.), *Personality: Basic issues and current research* (pp. 81–132). Englewood Cliffs, NJ: Prentice-Hall.

Epting, F. R., Rainey, L. C., & Weiss, M. J. (1979). Constructions of death and levels of death fear. *Death Education, 3,* 21–30.

Erikson, E. H. (1959). Identity and the life-cycle. *Psychological Issues Monograph, 1,* (1, Whole No. 1), 50–100.

Erikson, E. H. (1963). *Childhood and society* (rev. ed.) New York: Norton.

Erikson, E. H. (1982). *The life cycle completed.* New York: Norton.

Erikson, E. H., Erikson J. M., & Kivnick, H. Q. (1986). *Vital involvement in old age.* New York: Norton.

Flint, G. A., Grayton, W. F., & Ozmon, K. L. (1983). Relationships between life satisfaction and acceptance of death by elderly persons. *Psychological Reports, 53,* 290.

Florian, V., & Kravetz, S. (1983). Fear of personal death; Attribution, structure, and relation to religious belief. *Journal of Personality and Social Psychology, 44,* 600–607.

Frankl, V. E. (1963). *Man's search for meaning.* Boston: Beacon Press. (Original work published 1959)

Freud, A. (1946). *The ego and the mechanism of defence.* NY: International Univ. Press.

Freud, S. (1959). Thoughts for the time on war and death. In *Collected papers of Sigmund Freud* (Vol. 4, pp. 288–317). Boston: Beacon Press. (Original work published 1915)

Geller, L. (1982). The failure of self-actualization theory: A critique of Carl Rogers and Abraham Maslow. *Journal of Humanistic Psychology, 22,* 56–73.

Gilliland, J. C., & Templer, D. I. (1985–86). Relationship of death anxiety scale factors to subjective states. *Omega, 16,* 155–167.

Gödel, K. (1962). *On formally undecidable propositions.* New York: Basic Books. (translation of the original 1931 paper).

Gollob, H. F., & Reichardt, C. S. (1987). Taking account of time lags in causal models. *Child Development, 58,* 80–92.

Gould, R. (1978). *Transformations: Growth and change in adult life.* New York: Simon and Shuster.

Greenberg, J., Pyszczynski, T., & Solomon, S. (1986). The causes and consequences of a need for self-esteem: A terror management theory. In R. F. Baumeister (Ed.), *Public self and private self* (pp. 189–212). New York: Springer-Verlag.

Greenwald, A. G. (1980). The totalitarian ego: Fabrication and revision of personal history. *American Psychologist, 35,* 603–618.

Hayslip, B., & Stewart-Bussey, D. (1986–87). Locus of control—levels of death anxiety relationships. *Omega, 17,* 41–50.

Heidegger, M. (1962). *Being and time* (J. Macquarrie and E. Robinson, Trans.). London: SCM Press LTD. (Original work published 1927)

Hertzog, C. (1987). Applications of structural equation models in gerontological research. In K. W. Schaie (Ed.) *Annual review of gerontology and geriatrics* (Vol. 7, pp. 265–293). New York: Springer-Verlag.

Higgins, E. T. (1987). Self-discrepancy: A theory relating self and affect. *Psychological Review, 94,* 319–340.

Higgins, E. T., Klein, R., & Strauman, T. (1985). Self-concept discrepancy theory: A psychological model for distinguishing among different aspects of depression and anxiety. *Social Cognition, 3,* 51–76.

Hofstadter, D. R. (1979). *Gödel, Escher, Bach: An eternal golden braid.* New York: Vintage Books.

Hunt, D. M., Lester, D., & Ashton, N. (1983). Fear of death, locus of control and occupation. *Psychological Reports, 53,* 1022.

Jacques, E. (1965). Death and the midlife crisis. *International Journal of Psychoanalysis, 46,* 502–514.

Janoff-Bulman, R. (1989). The benefits of illusions, the threat of disillusionment, and the limitations of inaccuracy. *Journal of Social and Clinical Psychology 8*(2), 158–175.

Jöreskog, K. G., & Sörbom, D. (1988). *LISREL 7: A guide to the program and its application.* Chicago: SPSS Inc.

Kastenbaum, R. H., & Ainsberg, R. (1972). *The psychology of death.* New York: Springer.

Kelly, G. A. (1955). *The psychology of personal constructs.* New York: Norton.

Klug, L., & Boss, M. (1976). Factorial structure of the death concern scale. *Psychological Reports, 38,* 107–112.

Koestenbaum, P. (1971). Death and finitude. *The Journal of Existentialism, 20,* 437–439.

Krieger, S. R., & Epting, F. R. (1974). Personal constructs, threat and attitudes toward death. *Omega, 5,* 299–310.

Kübler-Ross, E. (1969). *On death and dying.* New York: Macmillan.

Kunzendorf, R. G. (1985). Repressed fear of inexistence and its hypnotic recovery in religious students. *Omega, 16,* 23–33.

Kuperman, S. K., & Golden, C. J. (1978). Personality correlates of attitude toward death. *Journal of Clinical Psychology, 34,* 661–663.

Labouvie-Vief, G. (1982). Dynamic development and mature autonomy: A theoretical prologue. *Human Development, 25,* 161–191.

Levinson, D. J., Darrow, C. N., Klein, B. B., Levinson, M. H., & McKee, B. (1978). *The seasons of a man's life.* New York: Knopf.

Lewis, M. (1979). The self as a developmental concept. *Human Development, 22,* 416–419.

Lifton, R. J. (1979). *The broken connection.* New York: Simon & Schuster.

Lonetto, R., & Templer, D. I. (1986). *Death anxiety.* Washington, DC: Hemisphere Publishing Corp.

Maddi, S. (1970). The search for meaning. In W. J. Arnold & M. M. Page (Eds.), *Nebraska Symposium of Motivation* (pp. 137–186). Lincoln: University of Nebraska Press.

Markus, H., & Nurius, P. (1986). Possible selves. *American Psychologist, 41,* 954–969.

Markus, H., & Wurf, E. (1987). The dynamic self-concept: a social psychological perspective. *Annual Review of Psychology, 38,* 299–337.

Marshall, V. W. (1980). *Last chapters: A sociology of aging and dying.* Monterey, CA: Brooks/Cole.

Maslow, A. H. (1968). *Toward a psychology of being* (2nd ed.). New York: Van Nostrand Reinhold.

Maslow, A. H. (1970). *Motivation and personality* (2nd ed.). New York: Harper & Row.

Meacham, J. A. (1989). Autonomy, despair, and generativity in Erikson's theory. In P. S. Fry (Ed.), *Psychological perspectives of helplessness and control in the elderly* (pp. 63–98). Amsterdam, The Netherlands (New York): Elsevier Science Publishers B.V.

Miller, D. T. (1976). Ego involvement and attribution for success and failure. *Journal of Personality and Social Psychology, 34,* 901–906.

Moore, M. K., & Neimeyer, R. A. (1991). A confirmatory factor analysis of the Threat Index. *Journal of Personality and Social Psychology, 60,* 122–129.

Morrison, J. K., & Cometa, M. C. (1982). Variations in developing construct systems: The experience corollary. In J. C. Mancuso & J. R. Adams-Webber (Eds.), *The construing person* (pp. 152–169). New York: Praeger.

Nehrke, M. F., Belluci, G., & Gabriel, S. (1977–78). Death anxiety, locus of control and life satisfaction in the elderly: Toward a definition of ego-integrity. *Omega, 8*(4), 359–368.

Neimeyer, R. A. (1985). Actualization, integration and fear of death: A test of the additive model. *Death Studies, 9,* 235–250.

Neimeyer, R. A. (1986). The threat hypothesis: a conceptual and empirical defense. *Death Studies, 10,* 177–190.

Neimeyer, R. A. (1988). Death anxiety. In H. Wass, F. M. Berardo, & R. A. Neimeyer (Eds.), *Dying: Facing the facts* (2nd ed., pp. 97–136). Washington, DC: Hemisphere Publishing Corporation.

Neimeyer, R. A., Bagley, K. J., & Moore, M. K. (1986). Cognitive structure and death anxiety. *Death Studies, 10,* 273–288.

Neimeyer, R. A., & Chapman, K. M. (1980). Self/ideal discrepancy and fear of death: testing an existential hypothesis. *Omega, 11,* 233–240.

Neimeyer, R. A., & Moore, M. K. (1989). Assessing personal meanings of death: Empirical refinements in the Threat Index. *Death Studies, 13,* 227–245.

Neimeyer, R. A., Moore, M. K, & Bagley, K. J. (1988). A preliminary factor structure for the Threat Index. *Death Studies, 12,* 217–225.

Nesselroade, J. R. (1991). The warp and the woof of the developmental fabric. In R. Downs, L. Liben, & D. S. Palermo (Eds.), *Visions of development, the environment, and aesthetics: The legacy of Joachim F. Wohlwill*. Hillsdale, NJ: Lawrence Erlbaum Associates.

Neugarten, B. (1977). Personality and aging. In J. E. Birren & K. W. Schaie (Eds.), *Handbook of the psychology of aging* (pp. 625–649). New York: Van Nostrand Reinhold.

O'Dowd, W. (1984–85). Locus of control and level of conflict as correlates of immortality orientation. *Omega, 15,* 25–35.

Peterson, S. A. (1985). Death anxiety and politics. *Omega, 16,* 169–174.

Pettigrew, C. G., & Dawson, J. G. (1979). Death anxiety: "State" or "trait"? *Journal of Clinical Psychology, 35,* 154–158.

Reker, G. T., Peacock, E. J., & Wong, P. T. (1987). Meaning and purpose in life and well-being: A life-span perspective. *Journal of Gerontology, 42,* 44–49.

Riegel, K. F. (1973). Dialectic operations: The final period of cognitive development. *Human Development, 16,* 346–370.

Robinson, P. J., & Wood, K. (1983). The Threat Index: An additive approach. *Omega, 14,* 139–144.

Robinson, P. J., & Wood, K. (1984). Fear of death and physical illness: A personal construct approach. In F. Epting & R. A. Neimeyer (Eds.), *Personal meanings of death* (pp. 127–142). Washington, DC: Hemisphere.

Rogers, C. R. (1959). A theory of therapy, personality, and interpersonal relationships, as developed in the client-centered framework. In S. Koch (Ed.), *Psychology: A study of a science* (Vol. 3, pp. 184–256). New York: McGraw-Hill.

Rogers, C. R. (1980). *A way of being*. Boston: Houghton-Mifflin.

Romaniuk, M. (1981). Reminiscence and the second half of life. *Experimental Aging Research, 7,* 315–336.

Rosenblatt, A., Greenberg, J., Solomon, S., Pyszczynski, T., & Lyon, D. (1989). Evidence for terror management theory: I. The effects of mortality salience on reactions to those who violate or uphold cultural values. *Journal of Personality and Social Psychology, 57,* 681–690.

Ross, M. (1989). Relation of implicit theories to the construction of personal histories (1989). *Psychological Review, 96,* 341–357.

Rowe, W. J., & Kahn, R. L. (1987). Human aging: Usual and successful. *Science, 237,* 143–149.

Rybash, J. M., Hoyer, W. J., & Roodin, P. A. (1986). *Adult cognition and aging: developmental changes in processing, knowing and thinking*. New York: Pergamon Press.

Sadowski, C. J., Davis, S. F., & Loftus-Vergari, M. (1979). Locus of control and death anxiety: A reexamination. *Omega, 10,* 203–210.

Sartre, J. P. (1966). *Being and nothingness: An essay on phenomenological ontology* (H. Barnes, Trans.). New York: Citadel Press. (Original work published 1943)

Singer, J. L. (1984). *The human personality*. New York: Harcourt Brace Jovanovich.

Snyder, C. R. (1988). From defenses to self-protection: An evolutionary perspective. *Journal of Social and Clinical Psychology, 6,* 155–158.

Stewart, D. W. (1975). Religious correlates and the fear of death. *Journal of Thanatology, 3,* 161–164.

Taylor, S. E. (1983). Adjustment to threatening events: A theory of cognitive adaptation. *American Psychologist, 38,* 1161–1173.

Taylor, S. E., & Brown, J. D. (1988). Illusions and well-being: A social psychological perspective on mental health. *Psychological Bulletin, 103,* 193–210.

Taylor, S. E., Collins, R. L., Skokan, L. A., & Aspinwall, L. G. (1989). Maintaining positive illusions in the face of negative information: Getting the facts without letting them to get you. *Journal of Social and Clinical Psychology, 8,* 114–129.

Templer, D. I. (1971). Death anxiety as related to depression and health of retired persons. *Journal of Gerontology, 26,* 521–523.

Templer, D. I. (1976). Two factor theory of death anxiety: A note. *Essence, 1,* 91–93.

Thompson, S. C., & Janigian, A. S. (1988). Life schemes: A framework for understanding the search for meaning. *Journal of Social and Clinical Psychology, 7,* 260–280.

Vargo, M. E., & Batsel, W. M. (1981). Relationship between death anxiety and components of the self-actualization process. *Psychological Reports, 48,* 89–90.

Vargo, M. E., & Black, F. W. (1984). Attribution of control and the fear of death among first year medical students. *Journal of Clinical Psychology, 40,* 1525–1528.

Warren, W. G. (1989). *Death education and research: Critical perspectives.* New York: The Haworth Press.

Weary, G. (1979). Self-serving attributional biases: Perceptual or response distortions? *Journal of Personality and Social Psychology, 37,* 1418–1420.

Weisman, A. D. (1972). *On dying and denying: A psychiatric study of terminality.* New York: Behavioral Publications.

Weisman, A. D., & Hackett, T. (1961). Predilection to death: Death and dying as a psychiatric problem. *Psychosomatic Medicine, 23,* 232–255.

Weisman, A. D., & Worden, J. W. (1975). Psychological analysis of cancer deaths. *Omega, 6,* 61–75.

Westman, A. S., & Canter, F. M. (1985). Fear of death and the concept of extended self. *Psychological Reports, 56,* 419–425.

White, W., & Handal, P. J. (1990–91). The relationship between death anxiety and mental health/distress. *Omega, 22,* 13–24.

Part II

Research Instruments

Chapter 2

A Revised Death Anxiety Scale

James A. Thorson
F. C. Powell

Recognition that the fear of death is universal goes back at least as far as the work of Hall in 1896; it is a concept elaborated upon by Becker (1973), among many others; it is normal, according to Butler (1963), and Momeyer (1986) says that it should not be considered to be unusual. Several approaches, many of which are detailed in this volume, have been taken in recent years in an effort to develop instruments useful for measuring the different dimensions of death anxiety.

A number of studies have approached death anxiety as a unidimensional construct. For example, studies by Bengtson, Cuellar, and Ragan (1977), and by Kalish (1986) simply used a single Likert item asking for a self-rating of fear of death. Most, however, have taken the approach that a number of different factors or elements make up the personal fear of death. Detailing the great number of different approaches to measuring these various elements of death anxiety goes beyond the scope of this paper; however, Marshall (1982) has published a review chapter on measurement of death anxiety, and several different researchers more recently have reviewed a number of approaches to the measurement of death anxiety (Conte, Weiner, & Plutchik, 1982; Epting & Neimeyer, 1984; Lonetto & Templer, 1986; Neimeyer, 1988; Thorson & Powell, 1988). The purpose of this article is, of course, to elaborate and expand upon this work.

Scales for the assessment of death anxiety have the virtue, usually, of ease of administration, making them convenient for use with large groups for comparison purposes. Marshall (1982) has observed, however, that many demonstrate little in the way of age differentiation, perhaps because the bulk of the work done with them has consisted of their administration to sophomore psychology students. Also, because of the singular lack of validation studies in this realm (and the student of death anxiety must appreciate just how difficult it would be to validate such a scale), we have pointed out the difficulty of determining what these various scales really measure (Thorson & Powell, 1988).

An exception to this general pattern of equivocal information on validity is the recent work of Neimeyer and his colleagues (Epting & Neimeyer, 1984; Neimeyer & Moore, 1989; Moore & Neimeyer, 1991), in which it is demonstrated that the Threat Index differentiates between known groups that ought to differ with reference to their level of fear of death, such as death education students versus controls, adults who have planned for disposition of their bodies compared to those who have not, and medical students who are more and less willing to inform terminally ill patients of their diagnosis. One is forced to take the leap of faith with most other instruments, however, that face validity is manifest, and that construct validity can be demonstrated by correlating these various scales one with another.

Theoretical and methodological difficulties notwithstanding, most psychological scales for the assessment of death anxiety generally are convenient to score and administer, and comparisons of relative differences in scores can be made. By far the most frequently used of these instruments has been the Death Anxiety Scale developed by Donald Templer in 1970; elaboration on various studies using this scale can be found in Lonetto and Templer (1986).

Templer's Death Anxiety Scale (DAS) was, however, thought at one time to measure only a single general death anxiety construct (Nehrke, 1973), although the scale has subsequently been shown to have a diverse factor structure (Lonetto & Templer, 1986). Nehrke (1973) thought to combine the Templer DAS with a Fear of Death scale developed in a dissertation study by Boyar (1964). Nehrke also added one item of his own construction and used the combined scale in several subsequent studies (Nehrke, 1974; Nehrke, Bellucci, & Gabriel, 1978; Nehrke, Morganti, Willrich, & Hulicka, 1979). Thus, modification of the DAS had begun. We have since factor-analyzed Nehrke's modified scale and revised it over the course of five major studies.

METHOD AND RESULTS

Our first use of the Nehrke modification of Templer's and Boyar's scales was in 1977 (Thorson, 1977). It was presented at that time as a 34-item true-false inventory, scored with one point being given for each response that indicated anxiety (negatively phrased items being reversed in the scoring process), so that higher scores indicated higher death anxiety. This instrument was administered to 208 University of Georgia graduate and undergraduate students (97 males, 111 females; age range from 18 to 53 years, median = 23 years). They also completed a standard personality inventory, the Edwards Personal Preference Schedule (EPPS), a 225-item questionnaire that reports scores on 15 different personality traits (Edwards, 1959).

We reported in that study that death anxiety correlated with gender (r = .22, p < .01), females in the sample indicating higher death anxiety scores, a relationship confirmed by analysis of variance (F = 10.31, p < .002). Despite the fairly broad age spread of the sample, however, the correlation between age and death anxiety score was not significant. It appeared that the scale might not be sensitive to age differences within the sample. There were several low-level, significant relationships between what we were then calling the NTB (for Nehrke–Templer–Boyar) scale and several traits identified by the EPPS: with Succorance (r = .22, p < .01), Exhibition (r = .23, p < .001), Endurance (r = −.14, p < .05), and Aggression (r = −.18, p < .01).

We gathered additional data with the NTB 34-item scale and reported upon a second sample that same year (Thorson & Perkins, 1977). With 659 respondents (172 males, 487 females, and a better age distribution: 115 under age 22, 302 aged 22–35, 203 aged 36–55, and 39 aged 55+), we found small but significant relationships with both age and death anxiety score (r = −.15, p < .001) and sex and death anxiety score (r = .11, p < .01). These were also confirmed by ANOVA: NTB score and age F = 6.18 (p < .001), and NTB and sex F = 8.45 (p < .004). Thus, the Nehrke scale modification displayed some slight age sensitivity with a broad enough sample. Two-way analysis of variance confirmed that both main effects were significant and not just statistical artifacts caused by, say, more of the older subjects being male.

We did a factor analysis of the data from this second sample using the varimax procedure and found four main factors: 1) fear of isolation and immobility (51.7% of the variance); 2) fear of pain (11.8%); 3) fear of the finality of death (16.5%); and 4) fear of burial and decomposition (12.7%). The complete factor matrix for these data is reported in Marshall's review chapter (1982).

In that second study (Thorson & Perkins, 1977), we suggested that the sense of the NTB scale seemed to be skewed more toward claustrophobia and isolation than actual death anxiety, and we made recommendations for a revision that might lower the percentage of the variance accounted for by fear of isolation and increase the variance associated with fear of pain. We also sought to add items related to the fear of loss of control, a concept that we felt was closely associated with death anxiety, and to eliminate several items that loaded across several factors or that were double-barrelled.

We reported on the development and factor analysis of a revised scale in another paper several years later (Thorson & Powell, 1984). The revision had eliminated or rephrased a number of the NTB items, and it included several of our own construction. Subsequently, we have been asked to provide information so that this 25-item revised scale can be placed on file with the Psychosocial Instruments database maintained by the Behavioral Measurement Database Service in Pittsburgh; such a listing requires that the instrument have a name, so for lack of a better one we are calling it the Revised Death Anxiety Scale (RDAS), although that terminology does not appear in any of our studies published prior to 1991.

The third sample (Thorson & Powell, 1984) consisted of 599 students and adults (92 males, 486 females, 21 not indicated; ages 16–19 = 101, ages 20–29 = 228, ages 30–59 = 135, and 60+ = 99). Alone among our samples, this one had a sufficient number of racial minority group members (blacks = 59) to make a meaningful comparison, and whites in this instance did in fact have slightly higher death anxiety scores ($F = 5.19$, $p < .02$) than did black respondents.

The revised scale consisted of 25 true-false items, scored at that time with one point given for responses indicating no anxiety, two for blank items, and three for responses indicating anxiety; thus there was a possible range of 25 to 75, with higher scores indicating higher death anxiety. The Cronbach alpha of reliability calculated for these data was .804.

Again, analysis of variance confirmed higher mean scores for women ($F = 4.72$, $p < .03$), but there was a much greater variance for age ($F = 33.26$, $p < .0001$). Death anxiety was shown to be linear by age with this group, teenagers having the highest and those aged 60 and above the lowest scores; the two groups between ages 20 and 59 were not significantly different. Factor analysis of these data was presented in a four-factor solution, with the first being fear of the uncertainty associated with death, the second was fear of pain, the third factor was related to fear of the dying process, and the fourth clustered items associated with fear of burial and decomposition.

We have since done an expanded analysis of this same information, including another factor analysis not forcing the data into a four-factor solution; the subsequent publication reports a seven-factor structure (Thorson & Powell, 1988). We also reported an item analysis in an effort to determine just which elements of death anxiety were higher among particular groups. That is, given that some people have greater death fear than others, what is it about death that they fear? Women, for example, were found to be significantly higher than men on only four of the 25 items: those relating to fear of pain, dread of an operation, what happens to the body after death, and body decomposition. We thus had some data to confirm Diggory and Rothman's (1961) contention that females have higher anxiety over the loss of bodily integrity associated with death.

However, younger respondents scored significantly higher on fully 13 of the 25 items. These were the ones associated with fears of decomposition, immobility, uncertainty, pain, helplessness, and isolation, for the most part. Interestingly, scores on three of the items were significantly higher among *older* respondents; they were most concerned with loss of control and with two items dealing with existence of an afterlife.

We should note that 399 of these respondents also completed a Lethal Behaviors Scale (LBS). Briefly, the LBS asks for a self-report of subjects' behaviors that might be seen as dangerous (e.g., skydiving and hang gliding, driving a motorcycle, scuba diving, fast driving, use of dangerous drugs, owning a gun, doing dangerous things for the fun of it, and so on) as opposed to their *attitudes* toward lethal behaviors and risk taking. There was no relationship ($r = -.05$, n.s.) found between scores on the LBS and the measure of death anxiety. These data have subsequently appeared in the literature (Thorson & Powell, 1990b).

We have also reported upon use of the Revised Death Anxiety Scale among a sample of medical students (Powell, Thorson, Kara, & Uhl, 1990; Thorson & Powell, 1991a; Thorson, Powell, Kara, & Uhl, 1988). Three freshman classes of students at the Creighton University School of Medicine completed the scale (using the true-false format) during their first year ($N = 277$, males $= 219$, mean age $= 23.7$); a total of 233 again completed it as graduating seniors. Their mean RDAS scores were not significantly different (means for the freshmen and the seniors of 43.47 and 44.44, respectively; $t = 1.51$). Compared to the RDAS mean (47.49) scored by the 599 individuals in the previous sample, however, the medical students both upon entry and upon graduation were significantly *lower* in death anxiety than a sample from the general population ($t = 4.02$, $p < .001$).

The freshman medical students also completed the EPPS as freshmen (but not during their senior year), and two low-level but significant correlations were found: between scores on the RDAS and the EPPS trait of Succorance ($r = .14$, $p < .02$), and between RDAS score and Heterosexuality ($r = .15$, $p = .02$).

The fifth study using this scale was reported in two parts. Observing that the greatest fears among older respondents in the sample of 599 reported above had to do with the uncertainty of an afterlife, we sought to again plow the fertile ground that had been probed so long ago by Hall (1896, 1915) and Scott (1896) and so many others since their time. Seeking to determine whether or not there is a relationship between fear of death and religiosity, we attempted to avoid some of the problems with previous research and minimize the variables to control for age and gender by testing a sample of older men (Thorson & Powell, 1989).

A group of 103 white males ranging in age from 61 to 88 ($M = 70.8$ years) completed the RDAS and the Intrinsic Religious Motivation scale developed by Hoge (1972). In order to improve on the death anxiety scale's sensitivity in this study, we used a five-point Likert response format, scoring $0 =$ least anxiety and $4 =$ most. Contrary to the experience that Nehrke had reported (1973, 1974), the older respondents had no difficulty responding using the Likert, rather than the true-false, format.

Table 2-1   Mean Scores on the Revised Death Anxiety Scale for Respondents of Different Ages ($N = 325$)

Age group	N	RDAS mean	SD
18–20	72	51.85[a]	15.93
21–36	93	48.43[b]	17.83
37–67	74	39.79[c]	14.57
66–88	86	41.22[c]	14.78

Means with different subscripts are significantly different ($p < .05$).

Rather to our surprise, however, the relationship between the RDAS and religiosity was so small with this sample that it could have been found by chance ($r = .11$, n.s.). However, there was some evidence that our hypothesis of a relationship did exist: there were significant correlations between two of the death anxiety items and mean scores on the Intrinsic Religious Motivation Scale: "I am not at all concerned over whether or not there is an afterlife," ($r = -.41$, $p < .001$), and "I am looking forward to a new life after I die," ($r = .55$, $p < .001$). We felt that further inquiry might be justified.

We reasoned that there was a data compaction problem with the homogeneous sample of older men, so we gathered additional data from other groups and combined them (Thorson & Powell, 1990a). The total sample then equalled 346; their ages ranged from 18 to 88 (mean $= 43.6$, SD $= 23.4$); 167 were males. The correlation between RDAS score and sex was slight ($r = .10$, $p < .05$); the difference in mean RDAS score between males and females did not remain significant when tested by analysis of variance. However, as indicated in Table 2-1, there again was a robust difference in death anxiety by age.

The difference in RDAS by age when tested by ANOVA was substantial ($F = 10.1$, $p < .0001$); a Duncan multiple range procedure confirmed that the difference was significant between three of the age groups: the youngest, those 21 to 36, and the two older groups taken together. The Cronbach alpha of reliability of the RDAS in this instance was .83. (Note that, because of the Likert response format, the means reported above for this sample cannot be compared to previous studies using the RDAS with a true-false format.)

Dividing the group, the 40% of this sample highest in death anxiety had significantly lower Intrinsic Religious Motivation (IRM) scores ($t = 3.89$, $p < .01$), and the 40% highest in Intrinsic Religious Motivation had lower RDAS scores ($t = 5.64$, $p < .01$). The relationship between death anxiety and religiosity was not, however, simply a linear one. Those lowest in fear of death, the 136 scoring a mean on the RDAS of 39 or less, demonstrated a meaningful correlation between IRM and RDAS score: $r = -.31$, $p < .001$. That is, as religiosity went up, death anxiety went down among these low death-fear people.

There was no corresponding relationship, though, for those highest in death anxiety; the correlation between IRM and RDAS for the 141 respondents scoring 49 or higher on the death anxiety scale was only .08, which was not significant. Seemingly, the relationship between religiosity and death fear simply did not exist for those scoring highest in death anxiety in this sample.

Similarly, there was a significant correlation ($r = -.36, p < .001$) between IRM and RDAS for the 145 participants scoring 29 or higher on Hoge's Intrinsic Religious Motivation scale; for these individuals, as religiosity went up, death anxiety score went down. However, there again was no relationship for those *low* in IRM (mean score of 24 or less, $N = 137$). The correlation of IRM and RDAS for these low-religiosity individuals was a nonsignificant .11. Again, the relationship between death anxiety and intrinsic religious motivation was absent among these individuals.

So, religiosity and death anxiety had a significant, negative correlation for both those high in religiosity and those low in death anxiety, but there was no meaningful relationship between the two constructs for either those high in death anxiety or those low in religiosity. These complex relationships are probed further in a number of articles appearing in this and in other journals (Powell & Thorson, 1991; Thorson, 1991; Thorson & Powell, 1991b).

Setting aside the concept of religiosity, though, it is apparent from factor analysis of these data that persons who are higher and those who are lower in death anxiety seemingly construe the meaning of death differently. That is, the difference in the way elements of death fear are perceived goes beyond a greater or lesser score on a death anxiety scale.

Data in Table 2-2, for example, represent a four-factor solution for the 141 respondents in the above sample who had mean scores on the RDAS of 49 or higher. The first principal factor clusters items relating to the concept of "not being." The second indicates an association for these high-anxiety individuals of items dealing with fears of pain and helplessness; the third factor clusters life after death and decomposition items; and the fourth factor shows an association of items dealing with control, pain, and afterlife concerns. Theoretically, a different factor structure for data gathered among other individuals would demonstrate different ways of construing death (Conte, Weiner, & Plutchik, 1982).

The data in Table 2-3 demonstrate that the 136 persons in this sample whose mean score was 39 or less on the RDAS seemingly have a different perspective on death than do those high-anxiety respondents whose data was presented in Table 2-2. For those low in death anxiety, uncertainty seems to be the predominant theme of the items that cluster in the first factor. Afterlife concerns make up the second. The third factor deals with helplessness and bodily integrity items, and two items that deal with the fear of pain load in the fourth factor. Determining whether differences in these data indicate true differences in the way death is conceptualized, or if they simply can be explained by differences in age (the high-RDAS group's mean age was 36.4 years, while the low-RDAS group's

Table 2-2 Varimax Rotated Factor Matrix: Constructions of Death Anxiety for Those Highest in Death Anxiety ($\bar{X} > 48$, $N = 141$)

RDAS item	Factor			
	I	II	III	IV
1. I fear dying a painful death.				.771
2. Not knowing what the next world is like troubles me.	.638			
3. The idea of never thinking again after I die frightens me.	.673			
4. I am not at all anxious about what happens to the body after burial				.777
5. Coffins make me anxious.			.516	
6. I hate to think about losing control over my affairs after I am gone.	.535			
7. Being totally immobile after death bothers me.	.604			
8. I dread to think about having an operation.				.818
9. The subject of life after death troubles me greatly.			.523	
10. I am not afraid of a long, slow dying.		.765		
11. I do not mind the idea of being shut into a coffin when I die.		.401		
12. I hate the idea that I will be helpless after I die.	.522			
13. I am not at all concerned over whether or not there is an afterlife.			.436	
14. Never feeling anything again after I die upsets me.	.604			
15. The pain involved in dying frightens me.		.474		.452
16. I am looking forward to new life after I die.			.888	
17. I am not worried about ever being helpless.		.721		
18. I am troubled by the thought that my body will decompose in the grave.			.652	
19. The feeling that I will be missing out on so much after I die disturbs me.	.511			
20. I am worried about what happens to us after we die.	.664			
21. I am not at all concerned with being in control of things.		.541		
22. The total isolation of death is frightening to me.	.589		.457	
23. I am not particularly afraid of getting cancer.		.718		
24. I will leave careful instructions about how things should be done after I am gone.				.633
25. What happens to my body after I die does not bother me.			.635	
Eigenvalue	4.29	2.78	1.76	1.62

Table 2-3 Varimax Rotated Factor Matrix: Constructions of Death Anxiety for Those Lowest in Death Anxiety ($\bar{X} < 40$, $N = 136$)

RDAS item	Factor I	II	III	IV
1. I fear dying a painful death.				.777
2. Not knowing what the next world is like troubles me.	.561			
3. The idea of never thinking again after I die frightens me.	.682			
4. I am not at all anxious about what happens to the body after burial	–			
5. Coffins make me anxious.	.441			
6. I hate to think about losing control over my affairs after I am gone.	.504			
7. Being totally immobile after death bothers me.	.468			
8. I dread to think about having an operation.	–			
9. The subject of life after death troubles me greatly.	.448			
10. I am not afraid of a long, slow dying.			.491	
11. I do not mind the idea of being shut into a coffin when I die.				–
12. I hate the idea that I will be helpless after I die.	.575			
13. I am not at all concerned over whether or not there is an afterlife.		.476		
14. Never feeling anything again after I die upsets me.		.725		
15. The pain involved in dying frightens me.				.681
16. I am looking forward to new life after I die.		.731		
17. I am not worried about ever being helpless.			.619	
18. I am troubled by the thought that my body will decompose in the grave.	.599			
19. The feeling that I will be missing out on so much after I die disturbs me.	.489			
20. I am worried about what happens to us after we die.	–			
21. I am not at all concerned with being in control of things.			.431	
22. The total isolation of death is frightening to me.	.511			
23. I am not particularly afraid of getting cancer.			.524	
24. I will leave careful instructions about how things should be done after I am gone.	–			
25. What happens to my body after I die does not bother me.			.467	
Eigenvalue	3.36	1.95	1.78	1.77

mean age was 49.7), or by some other variable, will require additional research and analysis. Nevertheless, the implication that different conceptual elements make up the meaning of death for different individuals that is suggested here is supported by some of our previous research (Thorson & Powell, 1990a).

Given that the data in Tables 2-2 and 2-3 are differentiated by how persons high and low in religiosity construe death, we would point the reader interested in the general factor structure of the RDAS itself to the information previously published on a sample of 599 adults (Thorson & Powell, 1988). It indicates a factor structure of: 1) fear of uncertainty and missing out on things, 2) fear of the pain associated with death, 3) concern over disposition of one's body, 4) fear of helplessness and loss of control, 5) afterlife concerns, 6) fear of decomposition, and 7) concerns over leaving instructions on how things should be done after one's death.

CONCLUSIONS

We have previously suggested (Thorson & Powell, 1988) that instruments such as the Death Attitude Repertory Test (Neimeyer, Bagley, & Moore, 1986) may provide more appropriate means for sorting out the complex individual frameworks of orientations toward death than do the various questionnaires designed to assess death anxiety. Psychological scales such as the RDAS, however, do have the virtue of convenience of administration with large samples, and they provide a means of assessing differences and making comparisons between and within groups.

Information has been presented on the development and factor analysis of a Revised Death Anxiety Scale, a 25-item device that has been used both with true-false and five-point Likert response formats. Acceptable levels of reliability have been achieved in its use among several large, diverse samples. The scale has been shown to be age-sensitive, and it has been utilized in several studies demonstrating differences in the elements that make up the construct of death anxiety.

REFERENCES

Becker, E. (1973). *The denial of death*. New York: Free Press.

Bengtson, V. L., Cuellar, J., & Ragan, P. (1977). Stratum contrasts and similarities in attitudes toward death. *Journal of Gerontology, 32*, 76–88.

Boyar, J. I. (1964). *The construction and partial validation of a scale for the measurement of the fear of death*. Unpublished doctoral dissertation, University of Rochester.

Butler, R. N. (1963). The life review: An interpretation of reminiscence in old age. *Psychiatry, 26*, 65–76.

Conte, H. R., Weiner, M. B., & Plutchik, R. (1982). Measuring death anxiety: Conceptual psychometric and factor analytic aspects. *Journal of Personality and Social Psychology, 43*, 775–785.

Diggory, J. C., & Rothman, D. (1961). Values destroyed by death. *Journal of Abnormal and Social Psychology, 63*, 205–210.

Edwards, A. L. (1959). *Edwards Personal Preference Schedule Revised Manual*. New York: The Psychological Corporation.

Epting, F., & Neimeyer, R. A. (1984). *Personal meanings of death*. Washington, DC: Hemisphere.

Hall, G. S. (1896). Study of fears. *American Journal of Psychology, 8*, 147–249.

Hall, G. S. (1915). Thanatophobia and immortality. *American Journal of Psychology, 26*, 550–613.

Hoge, D. R. (1972). A validated intrinsic religious motivation scale. *Journal for the Scientific Study of Religion, 11*, 369–391.

Kalish, R. (1986). Cemetery visits. *Death Studies, 10*, 55–58.

Lonetto, R., & Templer, D. I. (1986). *Death anxiety*. Washington, D.C.: Hemisphere.

Marshall, V. W. (1982). Death and dying. In D. Mangen & W. Peterson (Eds.), *Research instruments in social gerontology, Volume 1: Clinical and social psychology* (pp. 303–381). Minneapolis: University of Minnesota Press.

Moore, M. K., & Neimeyer, R. A. (1991). A confirmatory factor analysis of the Threat Index. *Journal of Personality and Social Psychology, 60*, 122–129.

Momeyer, R. W. (1986). Fearing death and caring for the dying. *Omega, 16*, 1–9.

Nehrke, M. (1973). *Perceived generational differences in attitudes toward death*. Paper presented at the 26th annual scientific meeting of the Gerontological Society, Miami Beach, FL.

Nehrke, M. (1974). *Actual and perceived attitudes toward death and self concept in three-generational families*. Paper presented at the 27th annual scientific meeting of the Gerontological Society, Portland, OR.

Nehrke, M. F., Bellucci, G., & Gabriel, S. J. (1978). Death anxiety, locus of control, and life satisfaction in the elderly: Toward a definition of ego-integrity. *Omega, 8*, 359–368.

Nehrke, M. F., Morganti, J. B., Willrich, R., & Hulicka, I. M. (1979). Health status, room size, and activity level: Research in an institutional setting. *Environment and Behaviour, 11*, 451–463.

Neimeyer, R. A. (1988). Death anxiety. In H. Wass, F. M. Berardo, & R. A. Neimeyer (Eds.), *Dying: Facing the facts*. Washington, DC: Hemisphere.

Neimeyer, R. A., Bagley, K., & Moore, M. K. (1986). Cognitive structure and death anxiety. *Death Studies, 10*, 273–288.

Neimeyer, R. A., & Moore, M. K. (1989). Assessing personal meanings of death. *Death Studies, 13*, 227–245.

Powell, F. C., & Thorson, J. A. (1991). Constructions of death among those high in intrinsic religious motivation: A factor-analytic study. *Death Studies, 15*, 131–138.

Powell, F. C., Thorson, J. A., Kara, G., & Uhl, H. S. M. (1990). Stability of medical students' attitudes toward aging and death. *Journal of Psychology, 124*, 339–342.

Scott, C. A. (1896). Old age and death. *American Journal of Psychology, 8*, 550–613.

Templer, D. I. (1970). The construction and validation of a death anxiety scale. *Journal of General Psychology, 82*, 165–177.

Thorson, J. A. (1977). Variations in death anxiety related to college students' sex, major field of study, and certain personality traits. *Psychological Reports, 40,* 857–858.

Thorson, J. A. (1991). Afterlife constructs, death anxiety, and life reviewing: Importance of religion as a moderating variable. *Journal of Psychology and Theology, 19*(3) 278–284.

Thorson, J. A., & Perkins, M. (1977). *A factor-analytic study of a scale designed to measure death anxiety.* Paper presented at the 30th annual scientific meeting of the Gerontological Society, San Francisco.

Thorson, J. A., & Powell, F. C. (1984). *Revision and factor analysis of a death anxiety scale.* Paper presented at the 37th annual scientific meeting of the Gerontological Society, San Antonio.

Thorson, J. A., & Powell, F. C. (1988). Elements of death anxiety and meanings of death. *Journal of Clinical Psychology, 44,* 691–701.

Thorson, J. A., & Powell, F. C. (1989). Death anxiety and religion in an older male sample. *Psychological Reports, 64,* 985–986.

Thorson, J. A., & Powell, F. C. (1990a). Meanings of death and intrinsic religiosity. *Journal of Clinical Psychology, 46,* 379–391.

Thorson, J. A., & Powell, F. C. (1990b). To laugh in the face of death: The games that lethal people play. *Omega, 21,* 225–239.

Thorson, J. A., & Powell, F. C. (1991a). A cross-sequential study of medical students' attitudes towards ageing and death. *Medical Education, 25,* 32–37.

Thorson, J. A., & Powell, F. C. (1991b). Life, death, and life after death: Meanings of the relationship between death anxiety and religion. *Journal of Religious Gerontology, 8*(l) 41–56.

Thorson, J. A., Powell, F. C., Kara, G., & Uhl, H. S. M. (1988). *Personality correlates and changes in medical students' attitudes toward old people and death.* Paper presented at the 45th annual scientific meeting of the American Geriatrics Society, Anaheim, CA.

APPENDIX 2-1: Scoring the Revised Death Anxiety Scale (RDAS)

The RDAS is a scale with 25 statements, 17 phrased positively and eight negatively (see Table 2-2). Respondents are asked to agree or disagree with the statements on a five-point Likert format: items are scored with the value 0 given for least anxiety and 4 for highest death anxiety; responses to negatively-phrased items are reversed in the scoring process. Thus, the possible range of an individual respondent's total score is from 0 (lowest) to 100 (highest possible score). Note that some earlier articles using these items had a true-false format; we now recommend using the Likert response format with the RDAS.

Simply score the following values for the responses indicated on the positively phrased items (Numbers 1, 2, 3, 5, 6, 7, 8, 9, 12, 14, 15, 16, 18, 19, 20, 22, and 24): strongly agree = 4; agree = 3; neutral = 2; disagree = 1; strongly disagree = 0. And, score the following values for the items that are phrased negatively (Numbers 4, 10, 11,

13, 17, 21, 23, and 25): strongly agree = 0; agree = 1; neutral = 2; disagree = 3; strongly disagree = 4. Count any items left blank as neutrals (score = 2). Then, just add up the assigned item scores to get a respondent's total score.

Other researchers may use the RDAS, provided they cite this text as the source.

Respondents were also asked to give their sex and their age.

Chapter 3

The Collett–Lester
Fear of Death Scale

David Lester

Although the Collett–Lester Fear of Death Scale (Collett & Lester, 1969) was reported in 1969, it has never been published and has been available only from the authors. This chapter publishes the scale (Appendix 3-1), critically reviews the published research using the scale, and presents a revised version of the scale (Appendix 3-2).

THE ORIGINAL COLLETT–LESTER FEAR OF DEATH SCALE

The Collett–Lester Fear of Death Scale (Collett & Lester, 1969) was developed to eliminate the problem of heterogeneity of item content in the scales used to measure fear of death at the time. First, Collett and Lester eliminated items about funerals and cemeteries completely. (D. Lester and Blustein, 1980, devised a scale for these items.) Second, they distinguished between death and dying and between the self and others, giving four separate subscales: Fear of Death of Self, Fear of Death of Others, Fear of Dying of Self, and Fear of Dying of Others.

A minor problem with this original scale was that each subscale contained a different number of items (9, 10, 6, and 11 items, respectively), reflecting the difficulty of writing items for the Fear of Dying of Self subscale. Another problem with the scale is that reports of its use have indicated that it may have been misscored. For example, Dickstein (1977–78) reported mean scores of 1.9 for Death of Self, 3.4 for Fear of Death of Others, 0.8 for Fear of Dying of Self, and −5.5 for Fear of Dying of Others, scores similar to those D. Lester (1974) obtained when he derived the scale. Scores on the Fear of Dying of Others subscale are usually the lowest. In contrast, Hayslip and Stewart-Bussey (1986–87) obtained scores of 32.9, 33.5, 18.5, and 46.7, respectively, which clearly deviate from the range of scores obtained by other investigators and are not in the commonly reported rank order.

RESEARCH ON THE COLLETT–LESTER SCALE

Reliability

Test–Retest Reliability　Only one test–retest reliability study has appeared. Rigdon and Epting (1985) reported 7-week test–retest correlations averaging 0.55. They did not report separate correlations for each subscale.

Factor Analyses　Livneh (1985a) conducted an SAS factor analysis of the responses of 200 college students to the Collett–Lester items and identified 5 factors: General Fear of Death of Self, Interaction with Dying Friends, Death of a Friend, Avoiding Meeting Dying Friends, and Attitudes Toward One's Potential Death. D. Lester (1974), however, using the University of California, Los Angeles, Biomed Statistical Program BMD03M on the responses of 241 female college students, found 11 factors, only 2 of which matched the subscales as labeled by Collett and Lester (1969).

Schultz (1977) reported a multidimensional scaling and cluster analysis of the items in the scale, using the responses of 264 randomly sampled adults in a small semirural community. He presented the results in a series of two-dimensional maps that represented the degree of similarity between the items. Two features stood out in the maps: The clustering of items was different for men and women, and the evaluation (classified by Schultz as positive or negative) of some items also differed between the sexes.

It appears from these three studies that the factorial structure of the Collett–Lester scale is complex and does not match the structure hypothesized on the basis of the content of the items.

Validity

Concurrent Validity with Other Fear of Death Scales　Many researchers have reported positive correlations between the Collett–Lester subscales and other fear of death scales (Bailis & Kennedy, 1977; Dickstein, 1977–78; Durlak, 1972; Hayslip & Stewart-Bussey, 1986–87; Howells & Field, 1982; D. Lester, 1974; Neimeyer, 1985; Neimeyer, Bagley, & Moore, 1986; Neimeyer & Dingemans, 1980–81; Vargo, 1980). These studies support the validity of the Collett–Lester scale.

In some instances, correlation with the Collett–Lester scale permits some conclusions to be drawn about a scale. For example, four studies have correlated scores on the Lester Attitude Toward Death Scale (D. Lester, 1967) with scores on the Collett–Lester scale (Durlak, 1972; Durlak & Kass, 1981–82; D. Lester, 1974; Neimeyer & Dingemans, 1980–81). The median correlations out of 12 reported sets were .57 for Fear of Death of Self, .05 for Fear of Death of Others, .29 for Fear of Dying of Self, and .17 for Fear of Dying of Others. These averages suggest that the Attitude Toward Death Scale is primarily a measure of the fear of one's own death.

Six studies have correlated scores on Templer's (1970) Death Anxiety Scale with scores on the Collett–Lester scale (Dickstein, 1977–78; Durlak & Kass, 1981–82; Neimeyer, 1985; Neimeyer & Dingemans, 1980–81; Vargo, 1980). The medians of the seven sets of correlations available were .55 for Fear of Death of Self, .48 for Fear of Death of Others, .53 for Fear of Dying of Self, and .40 for Fear of Dying of Others. Thus, the Templer scale appears to assess all four aspects of the fear of death and dying, quite different from the Lester Attitude Toward Death Scale.

The scores of various fear of death scales were factor-analyzed in two studies (Durlak & Kass, 1981–82; Rigdon & Epting, 1981–82). The results indicated three to five factors, depending on the type of factor analysis conducted. The Collett–Lester scales loaded on three of the five factors for the five-factor solution and on two of the three factors for the three-factor solution. These results suggest that either a battery of fear of death scales or a multicomponent scale (such as the Collett–Lester scale) should be used to ensure adequate assessment of attitudes toward death.

Nine studies have between them provided 18 sets of correlations between the subscales of the Collett–Lester scale (Dickstein, 1977–78; Durlak & Kass, 1981–82; Hayslip & Stewart-Bussey, 1986–87; D. Lester, 1974; Neimeyer, 1985; Neimeyer et al., 1986; Neimeyer & Dingemans, 1980–81; Shursterm & Sechrest, 1973; Vargo, 1980). The median correlations were as follows: .36 between Fear of Death of Self and Fear of Death of Others, .50 between Fear of Death of Self and Fear of Dying of Self, .30 between Fear of Death of Self and Fear of Dying of Others, .26 between Fear of Death of Others and Fear of Dying of Self, .32 between Fear of Death of Others and Fear of Dying of Others, and .36 between Fear of Dying of Self and Fear of Dying of Others. Being positive and moderate, these correlations suggest that the four fears measured by the Collett–Lester scale are not independent, but rather moderately associated.

Concurrent Validity with Other Death-Related Variables   Hayslip (1986–87) found that fears of the death and dying of others were associated with anxiety about talking about dying. Stoller (1980–81) found that the fear of others' dying predicted the responses of nurses in hospital situations, such as provision of care to and interaction with a dying patient. Rigdon and Epting (1985) found no association between Collett–Lester scores and having had a brush with death.

Collett–Lester scores for fear of death of self and dying of self were found to correlate with subjective estimates of life expectancy (Neimeyer et al., 1986) and with having negative images of death (McDonald & Hilgendorf, 1986).

Scores on the Collett–Lester scale do not appear to be related to measures of covert death anxiety. G. Lester and D. Lester (1970) found no associations between Collett–Lester scores and the speed of recognition of indistinct words concerned with death (used as a measure of unconscious death anxiety). Hayslip and Stewart-Bussey (1986–87) found negative correlations between the Collett–Lester subscales and a measure of covert death anxiety.

Correlations between the Collett–Lester scale and the Threat Index appear to be inconsistent (Neimeyer, 1985; Neimeyer et al., 1986; Rigdon & Epting, 1985; Rigdon, Epting, Neimeyer, & Krieger, 1979; Robinson & Wood, 1983, 1984–85).

Shursterm and Sechrest (1973) found no associations between nurses' scores on the Collett–Lester subscales and their self-confidence in the care of dying patients, their satisfaction with the nursing profession's standard of care for dying patients, or the death rate in the unit in which they worked.

Thus some associations between Collett–Lester scores and death-related variables have been found. It is easier to interpret these results in terms of construct validity (i.e., whether scores on the Collett–Lester scales show the associations one would expect) than as directly relevant to concurrent validity, because the measures used are quite different from the Collett–Lester fear of death items. Furthermore, the lack of consistent associations between the Collett–Lester scale and certain measures, such as the Threat Index, indicate that the measures are quite different and thus each is potentially useful. If two death-related measures correlated strongly, one could argue that they measure a similar quality and two measures of that quality are unnecessary.

Social Desirability   Dickstein (1977–78) reported that the total score from all four Collett–Lester subscales was negatively related to scores on a scale of social desirability ($r = -.23$ for male students and $-.27$ for female students). Hayslip and Stewart-Bussey (1986–87) also reported significant negative correlations, but, as noted earlier, their scoring of the Collett–Lester scales appears to have been deviant. This negative association raises questions about the validity of the Collett–Lester scale, although some other fear of death scales fare no better in this respect (Dickstein, 1977–78). There has been much discussion in the literature on psychological testing about whether social desirability scales measure actual social desirability (thereby impugning the validity of inventory scores with which their scores correlate) or particular personality traits, thereby providing construct validity for the inventory scores.

Correlates of Collett–Lester Scores

Occupation Hunt, Lester, and Ashton (1983) reported that firefighters and police officers had higher fears of death and dying than did students and faculty. Lattanner and Hayslip (1984–85) found that firefighters and funeral personnel had higher fears of death of self than did secretaries, teachers, and accountants. On the other hand, Ford, Alexander, and Lester (1971) found no differences between police officers and mail carriers in fear of death. On the whole, however, it appears that those in dangerous or death-related occupations do have higher fears of death and dying than those in other occupations.

Sundin, Gaines, and Knapp (1979) found that dental students had higher Collett–Lester scores for fear of death while medical students had a higher fear of dying. Fang and Howell (1976) found that medical students had a higher fear of dying of others than did law students. Scores did not vary with year in school for either group. B. S. Linn, Moravec, and Zeppa (1982) reported differences, by specialty, in the fear of death scores of junior-year medical students. Jordan, Ellis, and Grallo (1986) found that counseling students had higher Collett–Lester fears than did medical students. On the whole, there is no conclusive evidence from these studies that medical students have a significantly higher fear of death and dying than do other students.

D. Lester, Getty, and Kneisl (1974) found that Collett–Lester scores decreased with year at nursing school, with faculty members having the lowest scores. Area of specialization was not related to Collett–Lester scores. Stoller (1980–81) found no differences between licensed practical nurses and registered nurses.

D. Lester (1971a) found no differences in Collett–Lester scores between workers at a suicide prevention center and matched controls at other agencies. However, Neimeyer and Dingemans (1980–81) found higher scores for fear of death of self (but not others) in suicide prevention workers.

Alexander and Lester (1972) found no differences between sky divers and controls in fears of death and dying.

Thus few differences in fears of death and dying between professionals in various occupations have been found. This is surprising, but perhaps it is a result of the fact that the Collett–Lester scale, like other fear of death scales, taps only conscious fears of death.

Illness and Disease Robinson and Wood (1983) found no differences in fear of death between patients with arthritis, diabetes, or cancer and healthy controls. D'Amanda, Plumb, and Tantor (1977) studied heroin addicts and found that those who had also sniffed glue had lower scores on Fear of Dying of Self than did those who did not sniff glue.

Changes in Fear of Death   Testa (1981) found that various treatment plans designed to reduce death anxiety had no effect on the Collett–Lester scores of nurses, and Bohart and Bergland (1979) found no effects of such plans in college students. Carrera and Elenewski (1980) found no changes in Collett–Lester scores after a treatment program for insomnia. Rigdon and Epting (1985) found that writing an obituary did not change Collett–Lester scores.

Leviton and Fretz (1978–79) found that a death education course reduced fears of death of self and dying of others in one of two studies that they conducted. M. W. Linn, Linn, and Stein (1983) found that after a training program, nursing home staff had more fear of death of self but less fear of dying of others. Vargo and Batsel (1984) found that experiential training in a death anxiety reduction program reduced fear of death of self, but didactic training had no impact. McDonald and Hilgendorf (1986) found that a thanatology course raised fears of dying of self, whereas an introductory psychology course raised fears of dying of others. B. S. Linn et al. (1982) found that the fear of death of others decreased in medical students after they served surgical clerkships.

In contrast, Hayslip and Walling (1985–86) found that a course on death anxiety increased fear of death of others in hospice volunteers and in control subjects. Similarly, Bailis and Kennedy (1977) found that a death education course increased high school students' Collett–Lester scores, but, as noted earlier, these authors may have misscored their questionnaires.

Hart (1978–79) found that Collett–Lester scores were related to people's responses to a training program on euthanasia and shifts in their attitudes toward euthanasia.

In sum, reports of changes in fears of death and dying after training programs have been few and inconsistent.

Parents and Children   Fretz and Leviton (1979) found that parents of mildly dysfunctional children had lower Collett–Lester scores than did parents of normal children.

D. Lester (1970c) found that the Collett–Lester scores of mothers and daughters were positively associated, but daughters' and fathers' scores were not. The scores of mothers and fathers were also positively associated.

McNeil (1983) had mothers talk to their children about death and found that the mothers' style of talking about death was not related to their Collett–Lester scores.

Other Correlates   No sex differences in Collett–Lester scores were found by Dickstein (1977–78), Fang and Howell (1976), D. Lester (1972, 1984–85), or Loo (1984b). However, Livneh (1985b), Neimeyer et al. (1986), and Rigdon and Epting (1985) found higher scores for women.

The elderly have lower Collett–Lester scores (Kurlychek & Trepper, 1982; Nehemkis & Charter, 1983–84). In younger subjects, D. Lester (1972) found no variation of Collett–Lester scores with age. In nurses, age and experience were found to be negatively correlated with Collett–Lester scores (Shursterm & Sechrest, 1973).

Collett–Lester scores have correlated with trait anxiety (Dickstein, 1977–78; Loo, 1984b), state anxiety (in women only) (Dickstein, 1977–78), an external locus of control (Hayslip & Stewart-Bussey, 1986–87; Hunt et al., 1983), depression (for fear of death of self only) (D. Lester, 1985), femininity (Templer, Lester, & Ruff, 1974), psychoticism and neuroticism (Loo, 1984b), rigidity (B. S. Linn et al., 1982), attitude toward aging (Hayslip & Stewart-Bussey, 1986–87), self/ideal self discrepancy (D. Lester & Collett, 1970; Neimeyer & Chapman, 1980–81), self-actualization (D. Lester & Colvin, 1977; Robinson & Wood, 1984–85), liberalism and working for a political candidate (Peterson, 1985–86), religiosity (Kraft, Litwin, & Barber, 1987; Kurlychek, 1976; Livneh, 1985b), the use of seat belts (Loo, 1984a), assertiveness (Kraft et al., 1987), and attitude toward physically disabled persons (Livneh, 1985a; although Livneh, 1983, found no association).

No associations have been found between scores on the Collett–Lester scale and hopelessness (D. Lester, 1985); preferred method for suicide (D. Lester, 1979); attitude toward suicide (D. Lester, 1971b); extraversion (Loo, 1984b); manifest anxiety (Shursterm & Sechrest, 1973); religious affiliation (Fang & Howell, 1976; D. Lester, 1970a); religiosity (D. Lester, 1970a; Smith, Nehemkis, & Charter, 1983–84); belief in animism (D. Lester, 1970b); anomie, self-esteem, distrust of government, political interest or information, participation in political protests, or voting behavior (Peterson, 1985–86); androgyny (D. Lester, 1984–85); education (Smith et al., 1983–84); nightmare and dream frequency (D. Lester, 1969); attitude toward euthanasia (Slezak, 1982); or attitude toward funerals (D. Lester & Blustein, 1980).

The associations that have been reported between psychological test scores and scores on the Collett–Lester fears of death and dying subscales have involved primarily measures of anxiety and psychological health. More anxious people and those with more psychological disturbance appear to have stronger fears of death and dying.

A REVISED COLLETT–LESTER SCALE

As mentioned in the Introduction, a revision of the Collett–Lester scale seems needed for two main reasons: The subscales of the original scale have unequal numbers of items, and some users have had difficulty scoring the subscales.

Accordingly, I have prepared a revised version of the Collett–Lester scale (see Appendix 3-2).

In the revised scale, the items are separated into the four subscales. I believe this will help subjects analyze their attitudes more coherently. It will also simplify scoring. In addition, all items are keyed the same way, and the scale has been changed from a 6-point ($-3-+3$) system to a 5-point (1–5) system, again for simplicity in scoring. Finally, each subscale now has the same number of items (eight).

Reliability

Test–Retest Reliability   I administered the revised scale to 27 anonymous college students enrolled in psychology courses to determine 2-day test–retest reliability. Test–retest Pearson correlations were .85 for Fear of Death of Self, .79 for Fear of Dying of Self, .86 for Fear of Death of Others, and .83 for Fear of Dying of Others. Spearman-Brown correlations were .91, .90, .72, and .88, respectively. Further test–retest studies are needed, especially for time intervals longer than 2 days.

Internal Consistency   I administered the revised scale to 73 anonymous adults working at a developmental center for profoundly and severely retarded men. The 22 men and 51 women had a mean age of 35.9 years ($SD = 9.7$). Cronbach's alphas were .91, .89, .72, and .87, respectively, for Fear of Death of Self, Fear of Dying of Self, Fear of Death of Others, and Fear of Dying of Others.

Item–Total Correlations   The item–total correlations, based on the 73 adults, for the items in each of the subscales (in which the total scores were the totals for the remaining seven items in the subscale) ranged from .36 to .78 (median correlation = .62). I modified two items that had particularly low item–total correlations.

A factor analysis using the Statistical Package for the Social Sciences with a PC extraction and a varimax rotation identified seven orthogonal factors with values greater than 1 (see Table 3-1). Factor 1 had high loadings (>0.40) from 7 of the 8 items on the Fear of Death of Self subscale. Factor 2 had loadings from 9 of the 16 items on the two subscales concerned with others. Factor 4 had loadings from 6 of the items of the self-oriented subscales and one from the other-oriented subscales. The other factors were mixed. Thus, the results of the factor analysis are not supportive of the content validity of the items on the subscales. Further studies of the factor structure of the scale items using larger numbers of subjects are needed.

Table 3-1   Results of Factor Analysis of the Revised Collett–Lester Fear of Death and Dying Scale (*N* = 73)

Subscale/item	Factor						
	1	2	3	4	5	6	7
Death of Self							
1	65*	08	30	44*	11	10	−03
2	76*	11	20	16	16	16	−02
3	83*	06	04	03	09	16	18
4	76*	22	12	08	10	25	−06
5	54*	21	49*	41*	−02	−05	−13
6	77*	13	18	23	16	−03	19
7	12	15	60*	11	32	−09	−51*
8	60*	09	43*	41*	01	−01	−11
Dying of Self							
1	12	24	11	21	81*	10	12
2	27	26	04	24	69*	16	01
3	12	01	02	48*	35	−01	49*
4	15	34	16	39	22	10	66*
5	16	25	03	77*	33	10	03
6	27	16	03	76*	17	15	16
7	36	08	52*	13	39	08	37
8	05	39	54*	12	40*	−03	25
Death of Others							
1	28	75*	19	06	13	12	03
2	36	44*	37	−13	−06	41*	−01
3	29	58*	11	13	36	−18	−19
4	13	14	61*	37	14	11	−09
5	07	16	35	26	61*	05	16
6	25	27	72*	06	−01	−24	09
7	35	69*	22	08	03	−05	14
8	37	03	72*	−10	02	25	11
Dying of Others							
1	15	17	13	14	25	79*	03
2	35	13	28	20	03	73*	11
3	12	56*	−14	−05	50*	34	−13
4	−07	68*	−04	16	34	33	−02
5	−02	65*	01	13	36	28	02
6	05	74*	39	27	−06	02	−01
7	06	75*	18	21	20	08	30
8	30	30	24	64*	11	23	12

Note. Decimal points are omitted from the loadings. Items are identified in Appendix B.
*Loading greater than .40.

Construct Validity

I also gave the 73 adults working at the developmental center for retarded men the short version of the Maudsley Personality Inventory (Jensen, 1958) to measure correlations between scores on the revised Collett–Lester scale and neuro-

Table 3-2   Pearson Correlations Among Collett–Lester Subscales for Neuroticism and Extraversion (N = 73)

| | Men | | Women | |
Subscale	Extra-version	Neuroticism	Extra-version	Neuroticism
Death of Self	41*	.54**	.18	.43***
Dying of Self	.31	.30	.18	.45***
Death of Others	.44*	.36*	.09	.45***
Dying of Others	.44*	.26	.20	.40**

*One-tailed $p < .05$.
**One-tailed $p < .01$.
***One-tailed $p < .001$.

ticism and extraversion. For both men and women, neuroticism correlated significantly with fears of death and dying (see Table 3-2); for men, extraversion also correlated with fears of death and dying.

CONCLUSION

The Collett–Lester Fear of Death and Dying Scale was devised to provide a measure of death anxiety that distinguished between the fear of death and the fear of dying and between fears for oneself and fears for others.

Over the years, although it remained unpublished, many researchers have used the scale. On the basis of the present review of these studies, I conclude that the scale has reasonable reliability, validity, and usefulness.

I publish the scale here for the first time, enabling any researcher who so desires to use it. Problems with the original scale have led me to revise it. This revised scale is also published here, together with supporting reliability and construct validity data.

REFERENCES

Alexander, M., & Lester, D. (1972). Fear of death in parachute jumpers. *Perceptual & Motor Skills, 34*, 338.

Bailis, L. A., & Kennedy, W. R. (1977). Effects of a death education program upon secondary school students. *Journal of Educational Research, 72*, 63–66.

Bohart, J. B., & Bergland, B. W. (1979). The impact of death and dying counseling groups on death anxiety in college students. *Death Education, 2*, 382–391.

Carrera, R. N., & Elenewski, J. J. (1980). Implosive therapy as a treatment for insomnia. *Journal of Clinical Psychology, 36*, 729–734.

Collett, L. J., & Lester, D. (1969). The fear of death and the fear of dying. *Journal of Psychology, 72*, 179–181.

D'Amanda, C., Plumb, M. M., & Tantor, Z. (1977). Heroin addicts with a history of glue sniffing. *International Journal of the Addictions, 12*, 255–270.

Dickstein, L. D. (1977–78). Attitudes toward death anxiety, and social desirability. *Omega, 8,* 369–378.

Durlak, J. A. (1972). Measurements of the fear of death. *Journal of Clinical Psychology, 28,* 545–547.

Durlak, J. A., & Kass, R. A. (1981–82). Clarifying the measurement of death attitudes. *Omega, 12,* 129–141.

Fang, B., & Howell, K. A. (1976). Death anxiety among graduate students. *Journal of the American College Health Association, 25,* 310–313.

Ford, R. W., Alexander, M., & Lester, D. (1971). Fear of death of those in a high stress occupation. *Psychological Reports, 29,* 502.

Fretz, B., & Leviton, D. (1979). Life and death attitudes of parents of midly dysfunctional children. *Omega, 6,* 161–170.

Hart, E. J. (1978–79). The effects of death anxiety and mode of "case study" presentation on shifts of attitudes toward euthanasia. *Omega, 9,* 239–244.

Hayslip, B. (1986–87). The measurement of communication apprehension regarding the terminally ill. *Omega, 17,* 251–261.

Hayslip, B., & Stewart-Bussey, D. (1986–87). Locus of control–levels of death anxiety. *Omega, 17,* 41–50.

Hayslip, B., & Walling, M. L. (1985–86). Impact of hospice volunteer training on death anxiety and locus of control. *Omega, 16,* 243–254.

Howells, K., & Field, D. (1982). Fears of death and dying among medical students. *Social Science and Medicine, 16,* 1421–1424.

Hunt, D. M., Lester, D., & Ashton, N. (1983). Fear of death, locus of control and occupation. *Psychological Reports, 53,* 1022.

Jensen, A. R. (1958). The Maudsley Personality Inventory. *Acta Psychologica, 14,* 314–325.

Jordan, T. J., Ellis, R. R., & Grallo, R. (1986). A comparison of levels of anxiety of medical students and graduate counselors about death. *Journal of Medical Education, 57,* 684–691.

Kraft, W. A., Litwin, W. J., & Barber, S. E. (1987). Religious orientation and assertiveness. *Journal of Social Psychology, 127,* 93–95.

Kurlychek, R. T. (1976). Level of belief in afterlife and four categories of fear of death in a sample of 60+ year olds. *Psychological Reports, 38,* 228.

Kurlychek, R. T., & Trepper, T. S. (1982). Accuracy of perception of attitude. *Perceptual & Motor Skills, 54,* 272–274.

Lattanner, B., & Hayslip, B. (1984–85). Occupation-related differences in level of death anxiety. *Omega, 15,* 53–66.

Lester, D. (1967). The Lester Attitude Toward Death Scale. Pomona, NJ: Richard Stockton State College.

Lester, D. (1969). Fear of death and nightmare experiences. *Psychological Reports, 25,* 427–438.

Lester, D. (1970a). Religious behavior and the fear of death. *Omega, 1,* 181–188.

Lester, D. (1970b). Correlates of animism in adults. *Psychological Reports, 27,* 806.

Lester, D. (1970c). Relation of fear and death in subjects to fear of death in their parents. *Psychological Record, 20,* 541–543.

Lester, D. (1971a). Attitudes toward death held by staff of a suicide prevention center. *Psychological Reports, 28,* 650.

Lester, D. (1971b). Attitudes toward death and suicide in a non-disturbed population. *Psychological Reports, 29,* 386.

Lester, D. (1972). Studies in death attitudes. *Psychological Reports, 30*, 440.

Lester, D. (1974). *The Collett–Lester Fear of Death Scale: A Manual.* Pomona, NJ: Richard Stockton State College.

Lester, D. (1979). Preference for method of suicide and attitudes toward death in normal people. *Psychological Reports, 45*, 638.

Lester, D. (1984–85). The fear of death, sex and androgyny. *Omega, 15*, 271–274.

Lester, D. (1985). Depression and fear of death in a normal group. *Psychological Reports, 56*, 882.

Lester, D., & Blustein, J. (1980). Attitudes toward funerals. *Psychological Reports, 46*, 1074.

Lester, D., & Collett, L. J. (1970). Fear of death and self–ideal discrepancy. *Archives of the Foundation of Thanatology, 2*, 130.

Lester, D., & Colvin, L. M. (1977). Fear of death, alienation and self-actualization. *Psychological Reports, 41*, 526.

Lester, D., Getty, C., & Kneisl, C. R. (1974). Attitudes of nursing students and faculty toward death. *Nursing Research, 23*, 50–53.

Lester, G., & Lester, D. (1970). The fear of death, the fear of dying and threshold differences for death words and neutral words. *Omega, 1*, 175–179.

Leviton, D., & Fretz, B. (1978–79). Effects of death education on fear of death and attitudes toward death and life. *Omega, 9*, 267–277.

Linn, B. S., Moravec, J., & Zeppa, R. (1982). The impact of clinical experience on attitudes of junior medical students about death and dying. *Journal of Medical Education, 57*, 684–691.

Linn, M. W., Linn, B. S., & Stein, S. (1983). Impact on nursing home staff of training about death and dying. *Journal of the American Medical Association, 250*, 2332–2335.

Livneh, H. (1983). Death anxiety and attitudes toward disabled persons. *Psychological Reports, 53*, 359–363.

Livneh, H. (1985a). Brief note on the structure of the Collett–Lester Fear of Death Scale. *Psychological Reports, 56*, 136–138.

Livneh, H. (1985b). Death attitudes and their relationship to perceptions of physically disabled persons. *Journal of Rehabilitation, 51*(1), 38–41, 80.

Loo, R. (1984a). Correlates of reported attitudes towards and use of seat belts. *Accident Analysis & Prevention, 16*, 417–421.

Loo, R. (1984b). Personality correlates of the fear of death. *Journal of Clinical Psychology, 40*, 120–122.

McDonald, R. T., & Hilgendorf, W. A. (1986). Death imagery and death anxiety. *Journal of Clinical Psychology, 42*, 87–89.

McNeil, J. N. (1983). Young mothers' communication about death with their children. *Death Education, 6*, 323–339.

Neimeyer, R. A. (1985). Actualization, integration and fear of death. *Death Studies, 9*, 235–244.

Neimeyer, R. A., Bagley, K. J., & Moore, M. K. (1986). Cognitive structure and death anxiety. *Death Studies, 10*, 273–288.

Neimeyer, R. A., & Chapman, K. M. (1980–81). Self–ideal discrepancy and fear of death. *Omega, 11*, 233–240.

Neimeyer, R. A., & Dingemans, P. M. (1980–81). Death orientation in the suicide intervention worker. *Omega, 11*, 15–23.

Peterson, S. A. (1985–86). Death anxiety and politics. *Omega, 16*, 169–174.

Rigdon, M. A., & Epting, F. R. (1981–82). Reclarifying the measurement of death anxiety. *Omega, 12*, 143–146.

Rigdon, M. A., & Epting, F. R. (1985). Reduction in death threat as a basis for optimal functioning. *Death Studies, 9*, 427–448.

Rigdon, M. A., Epting, F. R., Neimeyer, R. A., & Krieger, S. R. (1979). The Threat Index. *Death Education, 3*, 245–270.

Robinson, P. J., & Wood, K. (1983). Fear of death and physical illness. *Death Education, 7*, 213–228.

Robinson, P. J., & Wood, K. (1984–85). The Threat Index. *Omega, 15*, 139–144.

Schultz, C. M. (1977). Death anxiety and the structuring of a death concerns cognitive domain. *Essence, 1*, 171–188.

Shursterm, L. R., & Sechrest, L. (1973). Attitudes of registered nurses toward death in a general hospital. *International Journal of Psychiatry in Medicine, 4*, 411–426.

Slezak, M. E. (1982). Attitudes toward euthanasia as a function of death fears and demographic variables. *Essence, 5*, 191–197.

Smith, D. K., Nehemkis, A. M., & Charter, R. A. (1983–84). Fear of death, death attitudes and religious conviction in the terminally ill. *International Journal of Psychiatry in Medicine, 13*, 221–232.

Stoller, E. P. (1980–81). The impact of death-related fears on attitudes of nurses in a hospital work setting. *Omega, 11*, 85–96.

Sundin, R. H., Gaines, W. G., & Knapp, W. B. (1979). Attitudes of dental and medical students toward death and dying. *Omega, 10*, 77–86.

Templer, D. I. (1970). The construction and validation of a death anxiety scale. *Journal of General Psychology, 82*, 165–177.

Templer, D. I., Lester, D., & Ruff, C. F. (1974). Fear of death and femininity. *Psychological Reports, 35*, 530.

Testa, J. R. (1981). Group systematic desensitization and implosive therapy for death anxiety. *Psychological Reports, 48*, 376–378.

Vargo, M. E. (1980). Relationship between the Templer Death Anxiety Scale and the Collett–Lester Fear of Death Scale. *Psychological Reports, 46*, 561–562.

Vargo, M. E., & Batsel, W. M. (1984). The reduction of death anxiety. *British Journal of Medical Psychology, 57*, 334–337.

APPENDIX 3-1: Original Collett–Lester Fear of Death and Dying Scale

Here is a series of general statements. You are to indicate how much you agree or disagree with them. Record your opinion in the blank space in front of each item according to the following scale.

+ 1 slight agreement	− 1 slight disagreement
+ 2 moderate agreement	− 2 moderate disagreement
+ 3 strong agreement	− 3 strong disagreement

Read each item and decide *quickly* how you feel about it; then record the extent of your agreement or disagreement. Put down your first impressions. Please answer *every* item.

_____	1. I would avoid death at all costs.
_____	2. I would experience a great loss if someone close to me died.
_____	3. I would not feel anxious in the presence of someone I knew was dying.
_____	4. The total isolation of death frightens me.
_____	5. I am disturbed by the physical degeneration involved in a slow death.
_____	6. I would not mind dying young.
_____	7. I accept the death of others as the end of their life on earth.
_____	8. I would not mind visiting a senile friend.
_____	9. I would easily adjust after the death of someone close to me.
_____	10. If I had a choice as to whether or not a friend should be informed he/she is dying, I would tell him/her.
_____	11. I would avoid a friend who was dying.
_____	12. Dying might be an interesting experience.
_____	13. I would like to be able to communicate with the spirit of a friend who has died.
_____	14. I view death as a release from earthly suffering.
_____	15. The pain involved in dying frightens me.
_____	16. I would want to know if a friend were dying.
_____	17. I am disturbed by the shortness of life.
_____	18. I would not mind having to identify the corpse of someone I knew.
_____	19. I would never get over the death of someone close to me.
_____	20. The feeling that I might be missing out on so much after I die bothers me.
_____	21. I do not think of dead people as having an existence of some kind.
_____	22. I would feel uneasy if someone talked to me about the approaching death of a common friend.
_____	23. Not knowing what it feels like to be dead does not bother me.
_____	24. If I had a fatal disease, I would like to be told.
_____	25. I would visit a friend on his/her deathbed.
_____	26. The idea of never thinking or experiencing again after I die does not bother me.
_____	27. If someone close to me died, I would miss him/her very much.
_____	28. I am not disturbed by death being the end of life as I know it.
_____	29. I would feel anxious if someone who was dying talked to me about it.
_____	30. The intellectual degeneration of old age disturbs me.
_____	31. If a friend were dying, I would not want to be told.
_____	32. I could not accept the finality of the death of a friend.
_____	33. It would upset me to have to see someone who was dead.
_____	34. If I knew a friend were dying, I would not know what to say to him/her.
_____	35. I would not like to see the physical degeneration of a friend who was dying.
_____	36. I am disturbed by the thought that my abilities will be limited while I lie dying.

Scoring Key for the Original Collett–Lester Scale

The items for each subscale are positive or negative. The scores of the negative items must be reversed before summing the scores on the subscale, that is, a $+3$ changed to a -3, and vice versa.

	Item	
Subscale	Positive	Negative
Death of Self	1, 4, 17, 20	6, 14, 23, 26, 28
Death of Others	2, 13, 19, 27, 32, 33	7, 9, 18, 21
Dying of Self	5, 15, 30, 36	12, 24
Dying of Others	11, 22, 29, 31, 34, 35	3, 8, 10, 16, 25

The final score on each subscale has meaning only relative to someone else's score on the subscale. Scores on different subscales cannot be compared. Furthermore, a positive score does not indicate a fear of death, and a negative score does not indicate no fear of death.

APPENDIX 3-2: Revised Collett–Lester Fear of Death and Dying Scale

How disturbed or made anxious are you by the following aspects of death and dying? Read each item and answer it quickly. Don't spend too much time thinking about your response. We want your first impression of how you think right now. Circle the number that best represents your feeling.

	Very	Somewhat			Not
Your Own Death					
1. The total isolation of death	5	4	3	2	1
2. The shortness of life	5	4	3	2	1
3. Missing out on so much after you die	5	4	3	2	1
4. Dying young	5	4	3	2	1
5. How it will feel to be dead	5	4	3	2	1
6. Never thinking or experiencing	5	4	3	2	1
7. The possibility of pain and punishment during life-after-death	5	4	3	2	1
8. The disintegration of your body after you die	5	4	3	2	1

	Very	Somewhat			Not
Your Own Dying					
1. The physical degeneration involved	5	4	3	2	1
2. The pain involved in dying	5	4	3	2	1
3. The intellectual degeneration of old age	5	4	3	2	1
4. That your abilities will be limited as you lie dying	5	4	3	2	1
5. The uncertainty as to how bravely you will face the process of dying	5	4	3	2	1
6. Your lack of control over the process of dying	5	4	3	2	1
7. The possibility of dying in a hospital away from friends and family	5	4	3	2	1
8. The grief of others as you lie dying	5	4	3	2	1
The Death of Others					
1. Losing someone close to you	5	4	3	2	1
2. Having to see the person's dead body	5	4	3	2	1
3. Never being able to communicate with the person again	5	4	3	2	1
4. Regret over not being nicer to the person when he or she was alive	5	4	3	2	1
5. Growing old alone without the person	5	4	3	2	1
6. Feeling guilty that you are relieved that the person is dead	5	4	3	2	1
7. Feeling lonely without the person	5	4	3	2	1
*8. Envious that the person is dead	5	4	3	2	1
The Dying of Others					
1. Having to be with someone who is dying	5	4	3	2	1
2. Having the person want to talk about death with you	5	4	3	2	1
3. Watching the person suffer from pain	5	4	3	2	1
4. Having to be the one to tell the person that he or she is dying	5	4	3	2	1
5. Seeing the physical degeneration of the person's body	5	4	3	2	1
6. Not knowing what to do about your grief at losing the person when you are with him or her	5	4	3	2	1
7. Watching the deterioration of the person's mental abilities	5	4	3	2	1
8. Being reminded that you are going to go through the experience also one day	5	4	3	2	1

*Recent examination of this item indicates that its score should be reversed.

Chapter 4

The Threat Index and Related Methods

Robert A. Neimeyer

In some respects, research on the psychology of death and dying has been impressive, generating a burgeoning empirical literature on the topic of death attitudes alone (R. A. Neimeyer, 1988). If only as a result of the sheer volume of this work, we now know more than we once did about the demographic, situational, and personality correlates of death fear and anxiety, and we are beginning to recognize that individuals' fears of death are not easily altered by even well-intentioned educational interventions (for reviews, see R. A. Neimeyer, 1988; Pollak, 1980). But contemporary psychological research on attitudes toward death also can be criticized on several levels. On the theoretical level, reviewers argue that the majority of studies to date are both conceptually impoverished in their definitions of death attitudes (Kastenbaum & Costa, 1977; Pollak, 1980) and grossly overestimated in their significance (Simpson, 1980). At a scientific level, methodologists note that investigators continue to rely on instruments that have dubious validity and reliability (Durlak, 1982; Lester, 1967; R. A. Neimeyer, 1988; Simpson, 1980) and tend to pursue random, opportunistic studies rather than coherent research programs (Kalish, 1988). Finally, at the level of praxis, critics point to the scant implications of existing studies for applied contexts and the failure of mainstream research to focus on existential concerns, such as fostering the individual's confrontation with death as a means of reaffirming the value of human life (Warren, 1989).

In the context of these recurring criticisms, personal construct theory (Kelly, 1955) has made a sustained contribution to improving the caliber of research on the psychology of death and dying. In contrast to most studies of death attitudes, those using the Threat Index (TI) are conceptually grounded in a comprehensive model of human functioning, specifically operationalizing the concept of death threat in terms that are compatible with Kelly's theory. Methodologically, the TI represents the best validated measure of death attitudes in the literature, with a 20-year history of psychometric refinement that has continued to the present. Finally, the TI and related research tools developed within personal construct psychology have been applied to a widening range of practical problems, as well as to the promotion of personal awareness of death in the context of death education. As a result of this long and multifaceted research program, I share the optimistic appraisal of independent reviewers, such as Kastenbaum and Costa (1977), who described early investigations using the TI as "an example of sophisticated research which might be taken as a model in the field of death concern" (p. 236). Similarly, summarizing the state of the art in death attitude research approximately a decade ago, Simpson (1980) noted,

> So far, the limitations of our understanding of the relevant phenomena have perhaps been more the result of the conceptual poverty of the simplistic rating systems and categorizations used and of the excessive concentration on anxiety, fear, and blanket denial instead of a more comprehensive range of responses, than the result of the inherent difficulties of the subject. It is surprising that more sophisticated and adaptable models like those provided by personal construct psychology have been so little used. . . . Certainly the personal construct methodology offers a better chance of delineating the personal meaning of death for each subject, with less distortion by the experimenter's preconceptions and more sensitivity to the influence of each subject's personality structure. (pp. 142–143)

As I hope this chapter will convey, a great deal of research has been conducted on personal meanings of death from a personal construct perspective since Simpson's (1980) remarks, and I am confident that this research program will continue to diversify in the future. In the pages that follow, I first review the extensive psychometric literature on the validity and reliability of the TI and then discuss a few recent extensions of personal construct methods that promote their use in clinical and research settings. Finally, to convey a sense of the TI's utility in various substantive areas of study, I summarize some illustrative areas of research using the TI. My overall aim is to describe the versions of the instrument currently available and its possible areas of application, so that readers can intelligently use it in their own assessment or research efforts.

DEVELOPMENT OF THE THREAT INDEX

Of the numerous measures of death attitudes currently in use, only the TI is grounded in an overarching theory of personality, the psychology of personal constructs (Kelly, 1955). The guiding assumption of personal construct theory is that human beings literally construct the meaning of their own lives, by devising, testing, and continously revising personal theories that help them anticipate their experience. Each personal theory, termed a *construct system*, comprises an indefinite number of personal constructs that help people differentiate, integrate, and predict events. Personal constructs may be highly idiosyncratic or widely shared and may vary in terms of how central or important they are in construing one's life.

Kelly (1955) referred to our most central dimensions of meaning as *core constructs*, those that govern one's identity and existence (p. 482). When these are challenged, we experience threat, defined as "the awareness of imminent comprehensive change in one's core role structures" (Kelly, p. 489). Kelly cited death as the prototypical example of the threatening event, because most individuals are aware that they will encounter it and see it as bringing about sweeping changes in their identity as living beings. Nonetheless, death may pose differential degrees of threat for different people, with some possibly seeing it as more compatible with the meaning of their lives than others.

Structured-Interview Form

To assess death threat, Krieger, Epting, and Leitner (1974) devised the TI on the basis of Kelly's (1955) repertory grid technique. In its original structured-interview format, the TI consists of two phases: construct elicitation and element placement. In the first phase, the interviewer presents the respondent with a triad of three cards, each carrying a brief description of a situation. For example, the subject might be presented with three situations: "You discover you have leukemia and have only a few weeks to live," "A terminally ill patient dies after months of unrelievable pain," and simply "Death," which is included in each triad to keep the subject focused on death-relevant themes (Table 4-1 presents several situations that have been used to elicit constructs in previous studies). The interviewer then asks the respondent to state "some important way in which any two of the situations are alike and different from the third." The subject's response (e.g., "These two seem unpredictable, but this one seems predictable") is then recorded as one important construct by which he or she construes death. Further constructs are elicited using new triads, as described in the manual provided by R. A. Neimeyer, Epting, and Rigdon (1984), until a total of 30 different original death-relevant constructs are obtained.

In the element placement phase of administration the TI, the interviewer asks respondents to consider each of their constructs in turn and to designate the side of the construct they more closely associate with themselves or their life, their ideal self or ideal life, and their death. For example, the interviewer might ask, "Do you see yourself [or your current life] more as predictable or as seeming

Table 4-1 Elements Used in Several Studies to Elicit Constructs for Repertory Grids on Death Attitudes

1. You discover you have leukemia and have only a few weeks to live.[a,b,c]
2. Your closest friend is killed in a plane crash.[a,b,c]
3. Your grandmother dies in her sleep.[a,b,c]
4. You run over and kill a young child.[a,b,c]
5. A homicidal maniac is on the loose and has already viciously mutilated six people in your town.[a,b,c]
6. Your father drowns while trying to save another person from drowning.[a,c]
7. A divorced mother of two dies of an overdose.[a,c]
8. A genetically deformed baby is allowed to die in the hospital.[a,c]
9. A terminal patient dies after months of unrelievable pain.[a,c]
10. Three children die when a tornado hits their elementary school.[a,c]
11. An old man becoming senile starves himself to death in order not to burden his family.[a]
12. Medical staff at a hospital decide to allow a patient to die rather than employ "extraordinary means" to preserve his life.[a]
13. Your own death, as you would expect it to occur if it happened at this time in your life.[a,b,c]
14. Your own life, as it currently is.[a,b,c]
15. Your own life, as you would *ideally* like it to be.[a,b,c]
16. President Kennedy's assassination.[b]
17. A Buddhist monk burns himself to protest the war in Indochina.[b]
18. A baby dies of lead poisoning from eating chips of paint.[b]
19. Capital punishment.[b]

Note. Just as the content of these elements has been updated across time, it can be modified to suit the purposes of the investigator. For example, the evaluator might provide a variety of hospital deaths, deaths from various diseases (e.g., acquired immune deficiency syndrome or heart failure), deaths that raise ethical issues, and scenarios involving protagonists who differ in age or other characteristics and then elicit constructs specific to the domain being assessed.

[a]Used by R. A. Neimeyer, Bagley, and Moore (1986).
[b]Used by Krieger, Epting, and Leitner (1974) and R. A. Neimeyer, Dingemans, and Epting (1977).
[c]Used by Rainey and Epting (1977).

unpredictable?"[1] After recording respondents' answers, the interviewer poses similar questions to elicit the meanings respondents attach to their ideal self or ideal life and their death, thinking about it as if it were to occur in the near future. Death threat is indicated by the extent to which the respondent cognitively splits the self (or life) and death elements by construing them in polar opposition on a number of personal constructs, such as when the self and ideal self are seen

[1]Chambers (1986) has criticized the presumed equivalence of self and current life in these instructions, arguing that the two ratings are qualitatively different and that self–death splits could mean something quite different from life–death splits. However, I (R. A. Neimeyer, 1986) examined the question empirically using a modified TI and discovered that the two split scores had a correlation of .94. Thus, the standard instructions requesting a rating of "yourself or your current life" seem merely to reflect the psychological equivalence of these concepts in the minds of actual subjects. It is also questionable whether separating self and life elements enriches the interpretation of the TI, insofar as self–life splits correlate highly (.84) with self–ideal splits, which are routinely calculated from the traditional TI.

as predictable and personal death as unpredictable. The higher the percentage of such splits on an individual's sample of relevant constructs, the greater his or her death threat is considered to be.

This structured-interview form of the TI was used in a series of studies through the 1970s (Krieger et al., 1974; Krieger, Epting, & Hays, 1979; R. A. Neimeyer, Dingemans, & Epting, 1977), the focus of which was to establish the psychometric soundness of the method as a measure of death threat. The results of these studies are summarized in Table 4-2. These data generally indicate that the TI procedure possessed satisfactory internal consistency and test–retest reliability, at least over periods of up to 4 weeks. Unlike other death attitude measures, it appeared to be unconfounded by social desirability response bias, and it showed good convergence with other self-reported fear of death measures. Finally, the TI met preliminary criteria for construct validity: Subjects with fewer splits were better able to conceive of their own death, the constructs elicited by the interview method seemed more intensely meaningful to subjects than standardized semantic differential scales, and the split configuration correlated highly with what subjects considered terrifying in their lives. This degree of concern over the psychometric soundness of an interview method for the assessment of death anxiety is rare in the literature, considering that most investigators have displayed a naive willingness to assume that face-to-face interviews yield automatically valid and reliable reflections of a client's death anxiety (R. A. Neimeyer, 1988).

Standardized (Provided) Form

Despite its initial promise (cf. Kastenbaum & Costa, 1977; Pollak, 1980), the original TI suffered from limitations inherent in its interview-based format. The most serious of these was its time-intensive administration, requiring 60–90 min for the assessment of a single subject (R. A. Neimeyer, Epting, & Rigdon, 1984). Although the idiosyncratic constructions of death elicited in this format offer a rich perspective on an individual's death concerns that could be of particular relevance in a clinical context, the original version of the instrument was simply too unwieldy to encourage its widespread use in psychological research on death attitudes. For this reason, Krieger et al. (1979) developed a self-administered form of the TI, consisting of the most popular constructs (e.g., *predictable–random* and *feels bad–feels good*) elicited during the original interview studies. Instructions require placement of the self, ideal self, and death elements on these dimensions, and splits are calculated in the same fashion as in the original procedure. However, the streamlined format circumvents the lengthy construct elicitation phase of the interview version, reducing the length of administration to 15–30 min. More important, it eliminates the need for a trained interviewer, permitting the instrument to be used in group administrations and anonymous surveys. In this more convenient form, the TI has proven more

Table 4-2 Reliability and Validity of the Interview Version of the Threat Index (TI)

Subjects	Correlation	Study
Split-half reliability		
13 College students	.93	Krieger, Epting, & Leitner (1974)
32 College students	.80	Krieger et al. (1974)

Subjects	Correlation	Time	Study
Test–retest reliability			
12 College students	.73	3 weeks	Krieger et al. (1974)
32 College students	.82	3 weeks	Krieger et al. (1974)

Subjects	Instrument	Correlation	Study
Discriminant validity			
32 College students	Social Desirability Scale	.06	Krieger, Epting, & Hays (1979)
43 College students	Frequency of Death Thoughts	.06	Krieger et al. (1974)

Subjects	Instrument	Correlation	Study
Convergent validity			
43 College students	Self-Report Fear of Death (FOD)	.42	Krieger et al. (1974)
57 College students	Self-Report FOD	.51	Krieger et al. (1974)
57 College students	Lester FOD Scale	.67	Krieger et al. (1974)
57 College students	Death Anxiety Scale	.12	Krieger et al. (1974)
38 College students	Lester FOD Scale	.38	R. A. Neimeyer, Dingemans, & Epting (1977)
32 College students	Self-Report FOD	.38	Krieger et al. (1979)

Subjects	Finding	Study
	Construct validity	
43 College students	Low-threat subjects were better able to conceive of their own death	Krieger et al. (1974)
56 College students	Low-threat subjects were better able to conceive of their own death	Krieger et al. (1974)
38 College students	TI rated more meaningfully by subjects than semantic differential scales	R. A. Neimeyer et al. (1977)
32 College students	*Comfortable* elements were rated like self and ideal self *Terrifying* elements were rated like death (Supports validity of splits as measures of threat)	Krieger et al. (1979)

attractive to researchers, making it the second most popular measure of death attitudes in the published literature of the last 10 years (R. A. Neimeyer, 1988).

Table 4-3 summarizes the extensive data now available on the reliability and validity of the self-administered form of the TI. A number of studies have demonstrated its high internal consistency and considerable stability for periods of up to 9 weeks. A broad nomothetic net of relationships to other commonly used measures of death concern supports the instrument's convergent validity, especially as an index of apprehension regarding personal mortality. The provided form of the TI also appears to be substantially independent of the social desirability bias that contaminates other established death anxiety measures. Finally, considerable evidence has accrued with respect to its construct validity, as a result of its use in numerous predictive studies with a wide range of populations.[2] As the most carefully validated measure of death attitudes available in

---

[2] Recently, Chambers, Miller, and Mueller (1992) published a second critique of the TI based on a mixed group of students and human immunodeficiency virus (HIV)-infected respondents. They first administered a TI-like task that required respondents to rate their "self at present" and their "death as if it were to happen at this time" on 30 bipolar adjectives and then indicate whether they viewed each of the resulting splits or matches as threatening. They found that approximately 25% of the splits, compared with approximately 12% of the matches, were perceived as threatening by subjects across the two groups. Chambers et al. interpreted this as an indictment of the validity of the TI, insofar as "little evidence supports the claim that splits are by definition threatening while matches are inherently nonthreatening" (p. 490).

Although this procedure requesting a self-report of threat implied by splits or matches is interesting, several difficulties arise in determining the implications of this study for research using the TI. First, the rationale of the TI does not require that respondents consciously perceive certain discrepancies between the self and death as threatening. Indeed, research comparing the TI with various conscious and nonconscious measures of death attitudes has indicated that the TI correlates not only with conscious, but also with midlevel (fantasy) measures of fear of death (Epting, Rainey, & Weiss, 1979), a factor that may help account for its freedom from a social desirability confound (Dattel & Neimeyer, 1990; Krieger et al., 1979). Moreover, this same research suggests that the majority of subjects deny fearing death at a conscious level (perhaps leading them to downplay the threat implied by self–death splits) but are significantly more ambivalent in their midlevel and nonconscious attitudes. Therefore, it is altogether possible that the split configuration does indeed reflect threat, but at levels that are more often tacitly experienced rather than explicitly formulated by the subject.

A second difficulty with interpreting Chambers et al.'s (1992) findings derives from their apparent inconsistency with numerous other studies indicating the validity of the TI (see Tables 4-2 and 4-3). In particular, studies that have used procedures similar to those used by Chambers et al. have reached opposite conclusions. For example, Krieger et al. (1979) requested subjects to rate self-designated *threatening* and *comfortable* events on the constructs of the TI, along with the conventional self and death elements. Subjects showed a strong tendency to align the *comfortable* element with self and preferred self, and the *threatening* element with death, a result that reinforces the essential validity of the threat configuration. The apparent inconsistency in these findings deserves attention in future research.

A third ambiguity in Chambers et al.'s (1992) research derives from their own results, which indicated that subjects were likely to view splits as threatening as they were to view matches as threatening. Chambers et al. dismissed this finding as a reflection of the content of the constructs on which the ratings were performed, but it could equally well be interpreted as indirect evidence for the validity of the split configuration as a measure of threat, insofar as a split was perceived as threatening twice as often as the match configuration was. From this standpoint, splits would not have to be a perfect measure of threat on an item-by-item basis in order for the overall instrument

the literature, the TI has been used in a number of medical, educational, and research contexts, some of which are described later. The instrument is presented in Appendix 4-1.

NEW DIRECTIONS IN THE ASSESSMENT OF DEATH ORIENTATION

Dimensionality of the Threat Index

As the psychological study of death attitudes has become more sophisticated, so has the level of criticism it draws. From a psychometric standpoint, greater concern has been expressed about the possible multidimensionality of theoretically unidimensional instruments. For example, Durlak (1982) has expressed serious reservations about continued use of Templer's (1970) popular Death Anxiety Scale (DAS), because factor-analytic studies have indicated that it actually measures not one, but several factors, which shift in number and composition from one study to the next (see also Lonetto & Templer, 1986). The difficulty is not that the instrument is multidimensional, but rather that the dimensions it does assess have not reliably been established. As a result, it is impossible to determine whether two respondents who have the same overall score on the scale have comparable or radically different varieties of death anxiety.

Like the DAS and most other dealth attitude instruments, the self-administered form of the TI was originally conceptualized as a unidimensional assess-

---

to be useful, as long as splits provided a more valid reflection of threat than matches.

Finally, it is questionable whether the findings reported by Chambers et al. (1992) can be generalized to the TI at all. Although they stated that their "subjects first completed the 30-item Threat Index" (p. 489) and cited Epting and Neimeyer (1984) as the source of the instrument, in fact none of the four constructs they cited as examples of items used appears in the 30-item version of the TI or any other published version that I could locate. Two of the items they cited (*meaningful–meaningless* and *purposeful–random*) overlap partially with actual TI items (*empty–meaningful* and *predictable–random*), whereas two others (*rotten–fresh* and *filthy–clean*) bear no similarity to any version of the TI used in the literature. Chambers et al. did not report the other 26 items they used. At the very least, these deviations from the TI content used elsewhere in the published literature caution against reading Chambers et al.'s findings as an indictment of the TI procedure, just as a researcher purporting to assess the validity of the Minnesota Multiphasic Personality Inventory but using a psychometrically unvalidated parallel form with occasionally bizarre content would make a dubious contribution to the understanding of the advantages or disadvantages of the standard measure. Collectively, Chambers et al.'s uncertain assumption about the critical role of conscious self-report of threat, the inconsistency between their conclusions and those of a large number of studies by other investigators, plausible reinterpretations of their actual findings, and the unexplained modification or replacement of an untold number of TI items make generalizing from their results extremely hazardous. The research conducted by Chambers et al. does, however, serve as a reminder that further examination of the TI's rationale using novel methods is feasible. Certainly, any existing measure is subject to continued criticism, whose value grows to the extent that it is carefully reasoned, contextualized within the relevant tradition of research, clear in its interpretation, and unambiguous in its methodology.

Table 4-3 Reliability and Validity of the Self-Administered Version of the Threat Index (TI)

Subjects	Correlation	Method	Study
		Internal consistency	
32 College students	.96	Split-half reliability	Krieger, Epting, & Hays (1979)
244 Mixed adults	.92	Split-half reliability	MacInnes & Neimeyer (1980)
95 College students	.90	Split-half reliability	Krieger, Epting, & Leitner (1974)
810 College students	.88	Cronbach's alpha	Moore & Neimeyer (1991)

Subjects	Correlation	Time	Study
		Test–retest reliability	
29 College students	.86	45 min	R. A. Neimeyer, Dingemans, & Epting (1977)
25 College students	.87	9 weeks	Rainey & Epting (1977)
32 College students	.90	4 weeks	Krieger et al. (1979)
96 College students	.73	7 weeks	Rigdon & Epting (1974)
810 College students	.64	4 weeks	Moore & Neimeyer (1991)

Subjects	Instrument	Correlation	Study
	Discriminant validity		
32 College students	Social Desirability Scale	–.08	Krieger et al. (1979)
117 Mixed adults	Social Desirability Scale	–.07	Dattel & Neimeyer (1990)
810 College students	Minnesota Multiphasic Personality Inventory Lie Scale	–.01	Moore & Neimeyer (1991)

Subjects	Instrument	Correlation	Study
	Convergent validity		
38 College students	TI interview form	.45	R. A. Neimeyer et al. (1977)
32 College students	Self-Report Fear of Death (FOD)	.48	Krieger et al. (1979)
60 High school and college students	Feifel FOD measure	.58	Epting, Rainey, & Weiss (1979)
116 Crisis workers and controls	Death Anxiety Scale	.28	R. A. Neimeyer & Dingemans (1980)
	Lester FOD Scale	.46	
	Collett–Lester (CL) total scale	.40	
	CL Death of Self	.33	
	CL Dying of Self	.32	
108 College students	Death Concern Scale	.30	Tobacyk & Eckstein (1980)
32 College students	Death Anxiety Scale	.56	Wood & Robinson (1982)
	CL total scale	.54	
	CL Death of Self	.42	
	CL Death of Others	.35	
	CL Dying of Self	.52	
	CL Dying of Others	.51	
100 Adults of varying health status	Death Anxiety Scale	.22	Robinson & Wood (1984)
	CL total scale	.22	
	CL Dying of Self	.21	
73 Adults from various community groups	CL total scale	.23	R. A. Neimeyer (1985)
	CL Dying of Self	.23	
	CL Death of Self	.22	
228 College students and 117 mixed adults	Death Anxiety Scale	.30	Patterson, Gates, & Faulkender (1988)
	Death Anxiety Scale	.21	Dattel & Neimeyer (1990)
145 Nursing home staff and 130 controls	Multidimensional Fear of Death Scale	.16	DePaola, Neimeyer, Lupfer, & Fiedler (Chapter 11 in this volume)

(Continued)

Table 4-3   Reliability and Validity of the Self-Administered Version of the Threat Index (TI) *(Continued)*

Subjects	Finding	Study
	Construct validity	
38 College students	TI rated subjects more meaningfully than semantic differential	R. A. Neimeyer et al. (1977)
24 Death education students and 25 controls	Students had fewer splits than controls	Rainey & Epting (1977)
57 Death preplanners	Adults who made arrangements for body disposal had less threat	Rainey & Epting (1977)
32 College students	*Comfortable* elements were rated like self and ideal self *Terrifying* elements were rated like death	Krieger, Epting, & Hays (1979)
30 Death education students and 78 controls	Students had fewer splits than controls	Tobacyk & Eckstein (1980)
120 College students	Low-split subjects scored lower on all CL subscales	Robinson & Wood (1984)
78 College students	Traditional religious orientation was only dimension of paranormal beliefs that correlated with lower threat	Tobacyk (1984)
25 Neonatal physicians	High-threat doctors were likely to engage in denial strategies when confronted with patient death	Neimeyer et al. (1984)
103 Medical students	High-threat subjects were likely to consider more factors before informing terminal patient of diagnosis	Eggerman & Dustin (1985)
84 College students	Split scores increased after cognitive description of funerals	Lantzy & Thornton (1982)
30 Hospice patients, 22 cancer patients, and 30 nonterminal patients	Hospice patients displayed dramatically lower threat scores than comparison groups	Hendon & Epting (1989)

ment of death concern, that is, as an assessment of the degree of threat implied by the respondent's conceptualization of death. However, it is possible that the TI may actually be multidimensional, with subgroups of the constructs it contains clustering into different, empirically distinguishable factors. Thus, research was needed to determine whether the instrument yielded a pure, unambiguous measure of death threat or required a revised scoring procedure in line with its factorial complexity.

Ongoing research has attempted to address this issue. R. A. Neimeyer, Moore, and Bagley (1988) used factor-analytic procedures to explore the factor structure of the 30-item, self-report version of the TI, as completed by a heterogeneous sample of more than 400 adult respondents. Rather than relying on conventional exploratory factor-analytic methods, they used the LISREL VI program, which permits a test of the goodness of fit of various user-defined models. On the basis of the high estimates of internal consistency of the TI found in previous studies, R. A. Neimeyer et al. hypothesized that one general factor (i.e., a "G model") would best fit the data. However, the results of this analysis disconfirmed the G model hypothesis as a workable fit for the full 30-item TI. Instead, the analysis suggested the possible presence of minor subfactors that were too weak or obscure to emerge fully from the data set. As an alternative, we attempted to prune the TI by retaining only those items with the highest communalities, resulting in a factorially pure 7-item version of the TI for which a simple G model provided an excellent fit (see Appendix for a copy of this instrument). The number of self–death splits on this abbreviated form of the instrument correlated highly ($r = .80$) with the number of self–death splits on the full 30-item scale from which it was derived, providing a preliminary indication of the short form's validity. Similarly, initial data on the reliability of the short form were also promising, yielding a Cronbach's alpha of .813. Subsequently, some investigators (e.g., Greyson, in Chapter 8) have begun to use the short form of the TI as a "factorially unambiguous" version of the instrument.

Despite the possible utility of the 7-item TI as a screening measure for death threat, interest remained in developing a factor structure that encompassed more of the original pool of items and captured more of the complexity of respondents' death attitudes. To pursue this question, Moore and R. A. Neimeyer (1991) conducted an exploratory factor analysis of a 40-item TI administered to a new sample of 405 respondents and then attempted to confirm this model with a second sample of 405 respondents using the LISREL procedure. In addition, new scaling metrics for the TI were tried, in an attempt to increase its sensitivity as a measure of death threat .and improve its factorability. For example, the reliability and interpretability of a standardized Euclidean distance score were examined by calculating the discrepancy between self and death ratings on 7-point Likert scales flanked by personal construct poles and comparing the distance score with the simple split score used in previous studies. Use of this metric and the larger sample of 40 items produced a reliable hierarchical G + 3 factor

Table 4-4   Final LISREL VI Standardized Solution for G + 3 Standardized Euclidean Distance Model of the Threat Index– Factor Loading (Lambda) Matrix (N = 810)

Threat Index Construct	Factor			
	Global Threat	Threat to Well-Being	Uncertainty	Fatalism
Healthy–sick	.180	.616		
Strong–weak	.256	.598		
Existence–nonexistence	.079	.555		
Open–closed	.396	.473		
Mentally healthy–crazy	.276	.469		
Happy–sad	.390	.468		
Competent–incompetent	.262	.456		
Feels good–feels bad	.438	.434		
Secure–insecure	.530	.381		
Concrete–abstract	.203		.595	
Conforming–nonconforming	.212		.557	
Changing–static	.212		.557	
Specific–general	.241		.511	
Objective–subjective	.221		.490	
Predictable–random	.150		.457	
Animate–inanimate	.204		.454	
Easy–hard	.421		.360	
Learning–not learning	.113			.792
Hope–no hope	.310			.629
Useful–useless	.451			.617
Productive–unproductive	.296			.604
Peaceful–violent	.394			.383
Alive–dead	.346			.369
Understanding–not understanding	.482			.337
Helping others–being selfish	.494			.325

model that retained 25 items and showed excellent goodness of fit with the data. The constructs included in the new TI-25, along with their LISREL factor load-ings, appear in Table 4-4. These results suggest that the TI can be decomposed for clinical or research purposes into three component factors, interpreted as Threat to Well-Being, Uncertainty, and Fatalism, or can be considered collec-tively as a measure of Global Threat. Use of this version of the TI in future studies should further improve the instrument's utility and precision.

The Structure of Death Attitudes

As central as the experience of anxiety or threat may be to the human encounter with death, it clearly represents only part of humans' death orientation. Our cultural, philosophic, and religious institutions embody more or less coherent belief systems for giving meaning to death, and our own experiences with death over the course of our lives lead us to construct idiosyncratic views of different ways of dying. Illuminating the larger cultural context of our belief systems may require us to move beyond psychology, but psychologists should be able to help us understand the richness and complexity of such belief systems on an individual level.

In fact, the interview form of the TI was developed in just such an attempt to elucidate the meaning structures individuals use to construe death. However, this original version of the instrument was limited not only by its cumbersome individual administration, but also by its exclusive focus on a single aspect of cognitive structure (the self–death split) and its inability to analyze the content of death-relevant constructs (on anything other than a clinical or impressionistic basis). Moreover, refinements in the standardized, self-administered version of the instrument, although increasing its reliability and precision, actually imposed more constraints on it as an idiographic assessment technique. Thus, what seemed necessary was an elaboration of the basic TI method that would permit a more encompassing assessment of the complexity of death orientation.

Drawing on Kelly's (1955) repertory grid technique (see also Fransella & Bannister, 1977; G. J. Neimeyer & Neimeyer, 1981), some investigators (e.g., Ingram & Leitner, 1989; Meshot & Leitner, 1993; Rigdon & Epting, 1985; Warren & Parry, 1981) have attempted to construct methods capable of assessing subtle structural features of death attitudes. One such method, termed the Death Attitude Repertory Test (DART), retains some of the personalism of the original TI while permitting the convenience of small-group administration (R. A. Neimeyer, Bagley, & Moore, 1986). It also yields indices of at least three aspects of cognitive structure concerning death and dying.

The DART is essentially a concept formation task, in which the respondent is presented with brief descriptions of death-related situations and is asked to compare and contrast them in a systematic way. In this respect, it is like the structured interview form of the TI, except that instructions are given in written form and clarified verbally by the experimenter. In the first phase of the DART procedure, the respondent is presented with a list of 15 situations pertaining to life and death (e.g., "A genetically deformed baby is allowed to die in the hospital" and "A divorced mother of two dies of an overdose"; see Table 4-1). These situations represent a broad sampling of "ways of death" and include the self-relevant elements "Your own death, as you would expect it to occur at this time in your life," "Your own life, as it currently is," and "Your own life, as you would ideally like it to be." Pairs of these situations are presented on a separate response sheet, with the instruction that the respondent describe "some important way in which the two situations are either alike or different." For example, a respondent who is asked to compare the situations involving the baby and the divorced mother might respond that in the latter case, the mother made a decision to die, whereas in the former instance, the baby had no choice. This

ELEMENTS	You have leukemia	Close friend killed	Grandmother dies in sleep	You run over child	Maniac Loose	Father drowns	Divorced mother overdoses	Deformed baby dies	Terminal patient dies	Tornado kills children	Old man starves himself	Euthanasia	Your own death	Self	Ideal Self	Column 2
Column 1 -6 -5 -4 -3 -2 -1	1	2	3	4	5	6	7	8	9	10	11	12	13	14	15	+1 +2 +3 +4 +5 +6
1 Pain	-5	-3	+6	-5	-5	-4	+3	+2	+4	-6	-3	+3	+5	+3	+5	Painless 1
2 Confusion	-6	-3	+2	-5	-6	-4	+2	-1	+4	-6	-2	-2	-3	+3	+5	Organized 2
3 Peaceful	+4	+3	-6	+6	+6	+5	-1	-5	-5	+5	+4	-3	-5	-4	-5	Unrest 3
4 Independence	+5	-1	0	+2	+5	+4	+4	+3	-4	0	-6	-6	-5	-1	-4	Dependency 4
5 Tragic	-6	-6	+6	-6	-6	-6	-4	+5	+3	-6	-6	-2	-6	+4	+5	Peaceful 5
6 Blessing	+4	+5	-4	+6	+6	+5	-1	-6	-6	+5	+4	+2	+5	-3	-3	Catastrophe 6
7 Panic	-4	-4	+4	-5	-5	-6	-4	+4	+2	-5	-5	+2	-4	+4	+6	Calm 7
8 Random	-5	-4	-2	-6	+4	-5	+3	-1	+2	-5	+3	+1	-5	-2	-3	Premeditated 8
9 Irregular	-6	-3	+3	-5	-5	-6	+2	-2	+3	-5	-4	+1	-4	-2	+1	Straight 9
10 Kindness	+3	-1	-3	+2	+5	-3	+2	-5	-2	+4	+5	-1	+3	-4	-5	Hatred 10
11 Shocking	-6	-6	+2	-5	-6	-6	-4	+3	+4	-6	-6	-3	-5	+3	+4	Expected 11
12 Predictable	+4	+5	-3	+4	+4	+3	+3	+2	-3	+5	+4	-3	+4	0	-4	Confusing 12
13 Grief	-6	-6	-3	-6	-6	-6	-3	-3	+4	-6	-4	-3	-6	+2	+5	Happy 13
14 Natural	+2	+2	-6	+2	+1	+2	+2	+2	-3	+3	+3	-5	+5	-3	-6	Fake 14
15 Relief	+2	0	-1	+1	+4	+3	-2	-3	-6	+3	-5	-5	+3	-3	+4	Anxiety 15

Figure 4-1 Completed Death Attitude Repertory Test for Anne.

dimension (making a decision vs. having no choice) would be recorded as one important construct that the respondent used to interpret situations regarding death and dying. Additional dimensions would be elicited through presentation of new pairs of situations, until a total of 15 constructs was recorded.

The second phase of DART administration involves the rating of each of the 15 situations on each of the 15 construct scales, using 13-point Likert scales (ranging from -6 to $+6$) flanked by the poles of each dimension. For example, a respondent might rate the first situation, "You discover you have leukemia and have only a few weeks to live," as a $+5$ on the *making a decision–having no choice* dimension, indicating that he or she sees it as a situation involving very little choice. Similar ratings are made of each of the other situations on each construct, yielding a grid of 225 ratings. Figure 4-1 provides an example of a DART completed by a 34-year-old nurse named Anne, who was enrolled in a continuing education course on the psychology of death and dying.

To an even greater extent than the original interview form of the TI, repertory grid tasks like the DART elicit a detailed snapshot of the respondent's views of death at a given point in time. Reading down the columns of Figure 4-1, one gains an impression of the way Anne construed various kinds of death in her own terms. Thus, she viewed a situation involving passive euthanasia as relatively painless, peaceful, very natural, and a considerable relief, but also as somewhat shocking, confusing, and tragic. Above all, she regarded it as the ultimate form of independence, perhaps because of the absolute form of self-determination it implies. In contrast, she associated the potential drowning of her father with considerable pain and unrest and as essentially tragic and random. In addition, she rated it as involving intense grief and considerable dependency. It is also possible, by reading across the rows in the grid, to consider how she used each construct to organize her perceptions of the different modes of death. For instance, one might be interested in which kinds of death she associates with the greatest degree of grief. Scanning across the columns for construct 13 (*grief–happy*), it appears that she construed all deaths that threaten to touch her life or those she loves, as well as any deaths of children, as involving equally intense grieving. Only the death of a terminal patient after months of unrelievable pain was considered a happy event. If Anne were to seek counseling for stresses associated with the emotional impact of working in an intensive-care setting, a task of this kind could provide a valuable starting point for therapeutic discussion of the types of deaths she had witnessed in the hospital and their similarity to or differences from those with which she was familiar in daily life.

One of the difficulties with the idiographic richness of such data is that they can be difficult to integrate into a coherent picture; with 15 constructs and 15 situations, the interpreter of the grid has to consider no less than 225 discrete ratings! For this reason, a number of statistical approaches have been devised to reduce such data matrices to a more manageable form, ranging from simple correlational techniques to elaborate tree diagrams (Bell, 1990; Bringmann, 1992).[3] One familiar method, principal components analysis, can be used to disclose the subjective relationships among the elements rated, in this case, those representing aspects of Anne's self and various ways of death, including her own.

Figure 4-2 displays a two-dimensional plot of the principal components of Anne's grid. The construct space of the grid has been reduced to two axes by collapsing the 15 separate constructs Anne produced during the construct elicitation task to those accounting for most of the variation in her ratings of elements. Thus, these two axes can be seen as the two primary dimensions she uses to understand death and dying and its relevance to the self. The first of these contrasts modes of death that are peaceful and painless with those that are catastrophic and associated with unrest; the second contrasts deaths that are

---

[3]Several statistical packages and computer programs are now available to analyze the results of repertory grids (for a review, see Sewell, Adams-Webber, Mitterer, & Cromwell, 1992). Issue 1 of volume 5 of the *International Journal of Personal Construct Psychology* was devoted entirely to developments in grid technique, most of which can be generalized to the study of death attitudes as advocated in this article. The journal also provides periodic updates of new programs that may be useful to researchers interested in the structure of personal attitudes.

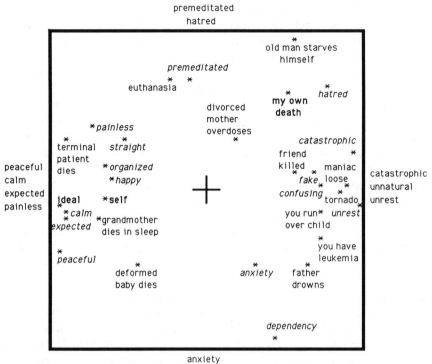

Figure 4-2 Plot of principal components analysis of Anne's repertory grid. Selected situations involving death appear in roman, constructs in italics, and self elements in bold.

premeditated or involve hatred with those that arouse anxiety or dependency. Within the plot formed by these two dimensions, selected situations involving death are presented in roman text, construct poles are in italics, and self elements are in boldface.

This graph facilitates interpretation of the grid, insofar as concepts that are closer together in the plot are construed as more similar by Anne and those that are at greater distance are viewed as more dissimilar. The plot reveals two major clusters of types of death along the first axis. The first contrasts the death of the terminal patient, the grandmother, and the deformed baby (which are viewed as relatively painless, calm, and expected) with a cluster of more violent deaths caused by a tornado, a homicidal maniac, or a car accident (which are viewed as confusing, catastrophic, and causing unrest). Significantly, Anne placed both herself and her ideal self close to the elements in the first cluster (construing both as relatively happy, organized, and calm) but placed the prospect of her own death by leukemia in the second cluster (near the constructs indicating unrest and anxiety). Asked to rate her own death as she would expect it to occur in her life, she also placed it on the more negative side of the plot, close to the construct having to do with hatred. This configuration of elements not only points to the high degree of threat Anne associates with the prospect of imminent death (represented visually on the plot by the splitting of the self and own-death elements into very distinct clusters), but also provides considerable idiographic detail regarding the meanings she attaches to each type of death and its relation to the self. Such plots can be used in death education or counseling contexts to enhance students' or clients' awareness of their views of death or to trace changes in these views across the course of a class or psychotherapy.

For research purposes, nomothetic measures of cognitive structure can also be derived from grids of this kind. For example, R. A. Neimeyer et al. (1986) have experimented with measures that reflect the coherence or complexity of a person's construing of death-related situations, the flexibility of his or her interpretations of death, and the degree of uncertainty implicit in his or her construct system regarding dying (all of which were derived from Landfield's, 1983, Reptest Scoring Program). An individual's system would be considered complex if the various death-relevant situations in the DART were rated in relatively distinct (uncorrelated) ways and as coherent if the ratings were highly similar across situations. Flexibility would be reflected by the respondent's use of many scale points to rate the elements and rigidity by the all-or-nothing use of only a few scalar positions (e.g., by marking all situations as $+6$ or -6 on the construct scales). Uncertainty would be indicated by the percentage of zero ratings in the matrix, suggesting that the respondent was unable to describe a number of death-related situations using either pole of his or her constructs. Traditional threat scores based on splits between current life and death could also be calculated, as could identification scores reflecting the perceived similarity of the respondent's own imagined death with the other ways of dying described in the situations. Pilot research using some of these measures with allied health professionals suggests that subtle structural changes may occur in our cognitive frameworks for interpreting death across the course of adult life. For example, older respondents tend to construe death-related situations in more coherent ways, and more highly educated individuals display greater flexibility and less uncertainty in their views of life and death than their less educated peers (Neimeyer et al., 1986). The meaningful relationship between such structural features and demographic variables, combined with these variables' apparent independence from traditional death anxiety measures, suggests that further refinements of the DART methodology or related repertory grid measures may open new horizons in the assessment of death attitudes (cf. Warren, 1989).

The Content of Personal Meanings of Death

Another methodological development that complements the structural analyses derived from the DART matrix is the "Manual for Content Analysis of Death Constructs" devised by R. A. Neimeyer, Fontana, and Gold (1984). The coding manual was constructed to permit more systematic assessment of a hitherto neglected aspect of death attitudes—the actual content of an individual's constructs pertaining to death. For example, some people interpret death-related situations in terms of the purposefulness or purposelessness of the deaths themselves, whereas others focus on the degree of suffering experienced by the dying person or the degree of choice the person had in bringing about the end. Similarly, individuals may differ markedly in the degree to which their constructs reflect an understanding or acceptance of death or focus on its emotional implications or certainty. The coding manual contains a total of 26 such content categories, with an average interjudge reliability of more than 87% (see Table 4-5).

Although the coding system was devised to permit analysis of the constructs elicited by the DART or structured-interview versions of the TI, it can also be used in clinical contexts to score a patient's verbal response to specific probes, such as ''What is your personal view of death at this point in your illness?'' (cf. Viney, 1984). Recordings of an individual's responses to such questions can be transcribed for subsequent analysis. The applicability of the manual to free-response descriptions of death written by more than 500 respondents was recently tested in analyses of the content of the narratives for subject sex, health status, previous history of suicide attempts or ideation, and degree of death threat and anxiety (Holcomb, Neimeyer, & Moore, 1993). Respondents were instructed to write a brief (5-min) response to the question ''What does death mean to you?'', and responses were segmented and coded using the manual, which includes definitions of coding categories and a dictionary of approximately 1,500 constructs with appropriate codes.

As an example, the following is the response of one female student (codes in parentheses):

> Death to me is the ending (*nonexistence*); someone has fulfilled their lives to its possible extent (*purposeful*). Death hurts a lot of people (*high suffering*), leaving them feeling empty (*purposeless* and *high impact*) and lonely (*negative emotional state*). I think it is one of the worst emotional experiences (*negative emotional state* and *high impact*) in life, one that everybody has to go through (*high certainty*) whether they want to face it or not (*low choice*).

Not surprisingly, given the predominant content of her narrative description, this respondent also showed elevated death fear on Hoelter's (1979) Multidimensional Fear of Death Scale (MFODS). In contrast, consider the following narrative of another female student, whose MFODS score suggested an extremely low level of death anxiety:

> Death is the beginning of a better life in another world (*purposeful* and *existence*). You leave your mortal life and join the Father in heaven (*purposeful* and *existence*). You leave all the pain and suffering behind (*low suffering*).

Table 4-5   Categories and Definitions in the "Manual for Content Analysis of Death Constructs" (R. A. Neimeyer, Fontana, & Gold, 1984)

1. *Purposefulness*
   a. Purposeful: constructs dealing with meaningfulness of the death, its having some justification ethically, psychologically, or naturally.
   b. Purposeless: constructs suggesting the meaninglessness of the death, its being unjustified or unnecessary.
2. *Evaluation*
   a. Positive: constructs expressing an evaluation of death as "good" or valued.
   b. Negative: constructs having to do with an evaluation of the death as nonvalued or "bad."
3. *Emotional State*
   b. Negative: constructs suggesting negative emotional state.
4. *Acceptance*
   b. Low: constructs depicting the death as something to be rejected or resisted.
5. *Understanding*
   a. High: constructs indicating achievement of some understanding of the death.
   b. Low: constructs expressing lack of understanding of the death.
6. *Suffering*
   a. High: constructs suggesting that the death is painful or induces suffering.
   b. Low: constructs implying that death is painless or produces minimal suffering.
7. *Personal Involvement*
   a. High: constructs connoting personal involvement in the death.
   b. Low: constructs depicting the death as remote or not pertaining to the self.
8. *Temporal Expectation*
   a. Long range: constructs suggesting that death is anticipated.
   b. Short range: constructs implying that death is unanticipated.
9. *Certainty*
   a. High: constructs having to do with certain death.
10. *Existence*
    a. Existence: constructs having to do with continued life, as in afterlife.
    b. Nonexistence: constructs having to do with the finality of death.
11. *Choice*
    a. High: constructs emphasizing a degree of personal choice involved in the death.
    b. Low: constructs stressing the absence of personal choice.
12. *Specificity*
    a. Specific: constructs pertaining to the uniqueness of death.
    b. General: constructs suggesting the generality of death.
13. *Impact*
    a. High: constructs dealing with the impact of death.
    b. Low: constructs implying that death has minimal impact.
14. *Causality*
    a. Known: constructs suggesting that the physical cause of death is known or explained.
    b. Unknown: constructs implying that the physical cause of death is nonspecific or unknown.

(Continued)

Table 4-5 Categories and Definitions in the "Manual for Content Analysis of Death Constructs" (R. A. Neimeyer, Fontana, & Gold, 1984) *(Continued)*

15. *Wishful Thinking*
    Constructs suggesting an optimistic portrayal of death, but one that is qualified in such a way that this positive portrayal seems to be at odds with the subject's true beliefs, feelings, or fears.

Note. Categories 1–14 derive from Neimeyer, Fontana, and Gold (1984). Category 15 was suggested by Holcomb, Neimeyer, and Moore (1993), in an effort to refine the manual and increase its utility in coding free-response data in the form of written narratives. Extensive examples of constructs that fit each category are included in the original sources.

Although the overall positive and negative tones of these two descriptions are obvious, coding makes possible a more systematic examination of people's views of death, permitting the comparison of large numbers of subjects. In our initial study, for example, subjects who had a history of suicide attempts were distinguished by their tendency to view death as something that had low impact on them or others, suggesting one cognitive risk factor associated with a greater degree of suicide risk. Distinctive personal meanings of death also characterized high and low death anxiety in subjects, as measured by the MFODS. Compared with less anxious subjects, those who reported more global death fear tended to write narratives containing more references to the negative emotional states engendered by a confrontation with death and tended to interpret death less in terms of some form of continued existence or afterlife. Content analysis was even more informative regarding the connotations that death carried for subjects who reported fears specifically associated with the hereafter. Those who were more fearful about what lay beyond the threshold of death less often viewed death in terms of a continued existence or a purposeful event and more often wrote narratives suggesting little understanding of death, meaninglessness, and nonexistence. Reliable differences in construct content also appeared between men and women, healthy and ill subjects, and those who reported having worked out a satisfactory philosophy of death and those who had not (see below). After appropriate modification to suit the coding of free-response data, the coding system was found to be a flexible tool for extending the study of death attitudes beyond the constraints of forced-choice questionnaires. Thus, the system should allow researchers to capture more of the richness of human belief systems regarding death, without sacrificing the precision of quantitative analysis.

ILLUSTRATIVE AREAS OF RESEARCH

In addition to the persistent concern with methodological development, personal construct research on death attitudes has focused on a number of substantive topics, ranging from the nomothetic investigation of the relationship between birth order and death threat (Eckstein & Tobacyk, 1979) to the idiographic case study of a serious suicide attempt (Rigdon, 1983). In this section, several areas in which programmatic research has been done are reviewed. For the sake of balance, these areas are equally divided between those having a more theoretical emphasis (i.e., sex differences in death anxiety and the relationships between death threat and religiosity and self-actualization and fear of death) and those carrying more immediate practical implications (i.e., the death attitudes of helping professionals, death threat in individuals with physical illness, and death education). In each of these areas, personal construct research has made a tangible contribution to the empirical literature on death attitudes.

Sex Differences in Death Anxiety

In his review of the death anxiety literature through the late 1970s, Pollak (1980) noted that the majority of the earlier work indicated that women reported more fear of death than men, with virtually all of the remaining studies demonstrating no differences between the sexes. Studies suggesting that men had higher death anxiety were rare. Research conducted since that time using the TI reinforces this conclusion and provides a somewhat more refined view of this possible sex difference in death concern (R. A. Neimeyer, 1988).

The most commonly used instrument in the study of these sex differences is Templer's (1970) DAS, a 15-item true/false questionnaire containing simple statements such as "I am very much afraid to die" and "I am often distressed by the way that time flies so very rapidly." Much of the research using this questionnaire supports the conclusion that female respondents have more death anxiety than do male respondents, whether the population being studied consists of college students (Davis, Bremer, Anderson, & Tramill, 1983; Lonetto, Mercer, Fleming, Bunting, & Clare, 1980; MacDonald, 1976; Sadowski, Davis, & Loftus-Vergari, 1979), rural high school students (Young & Daniels, 1980), or the elderly (Sanders, Poole, & Rivero, 1980). Moreover, female subjects' greater death anxiety seems to be a fairly universal phenomenon, insofar as it appears to extend to Eastern as well as Western cultures (McMordie & Kumar, 1984).

But research using the TI places limits on the generality of sex differences in death attitudes. In contrast to studies using the DAS, only one study using the TI has suggested that female respondents display higher death threat than male respondents (Rigdon & Epting, 1985). Instead, the majority of research using the TI has discovered no sex difference in the threat implied by personal death (Eggerman & Dustin, 1985; Krieger et al., 1974, Study 2; R. A. Neimeyer et al., 1977), and one study has even suggested that male subjects indicate greater threat than female subjects (Krieger et al., 1974, Study 1).

In attempting to understand, rather than simply document, the presence or absence of sex differences on these two instruments, personal construct researchers have designed studies to test plausible explanations for the preceding pattern of results. In one experiment, Lantzy and Thornton (1982) hypothesized that death concern, although present for members of both sexes, would be experienced and expressed differently. Specifically, they predicted that women would respond to death stimuli more emotionally, as reflected in the DAS, whereas men would respond more cognitively, as measured by the TI. To test this rationale, they randomly assigned male and female subjects to one of two conditions, in which they completed the two death concern measures before and after an audiotaped presentation on the topic of one's own death. However, for half the subjects of each sex, the presentation was abstract and intellectual, whereas for the remaining half it was concrete and emotionally evocative. Contrary to their predictions, no interaction between subject sex and response to the two tapes was observed on either measure; instead, both sexes showed elevations on the TI after viewing the cognitive tape, and neither showed significant change on the DAS in either condition. Results of the study were thus inconclusive, pointing only to the sensitivity of the TI to changes in death threat in conducive circumstances.

A second attempt to clarify the existence of sex differences in death attitudes was conducted by Dattel and Neimeyer (1990). One popular explanation for the discrepancy in death anxiety scores presumes that women simply are more likely to disclose personal feelings that men are less likely to share openly (Stillion, 1985). This emotional expressiveness hypothesis is compatible with the tendency for women to score higher on feeling-oriented questionnaires like the DAS than on more abstract measures like the TI. To test the viability of this hypothesis, Dattel and Neimeyer administered both death attitude measures to a racially and occupationally diverse adult population, along with the Jourard Self-Disclosure Questionnaire and the Marlowe–Crown Social Desirability Scale. As predicted, women outscored men on the DAS but not on the TI. However, this sex difference persisted even when self-disclosure and social desirability scores were statistically controlled, casting doubt on the adequacy of the emotional expressiveness hypothesis as an explanation of this phenomenon. Instead, it appears that women's greater death anxiety may stem from other uninvestigated factors, such as locus of control, which may correlate with both sex and fear of death (R. A. Neimeyer, 1988).

More subtle differences between the sexes in conceptualizations of death were reported by Holcomb et al. (1993). In content analysis of free-response descriptions of death written by men and women, they discovered that women were more likely to invoke references to negative emotional states than men, but they were also more likely to describe death in evaluative terms, both positive and negative. Death, for female respondents, was more likely to be viewed in terms suggesting high certainty, but also some form of continued existence in the hereafter. By comparison, male respondents viewed death in more abstract, general terms, as something having less personal impact on them. The different socialization experiences of men and women deserve more systematic attention as possible contributions to these different perspectives on death.

Relationship Between Religiosity and Death Threat

Research on the relationship between religious beliefs and death attitudes has been so inconsistent and confusing that some reviewers have chosen to ignore it (e.g., Pollak, 1980). Studies in which personal construct methods were used reflect these inconsistencies in the general literature, and some recent attempts have been made to clarify them through the use of more sophisticated instruments and designs. Typically, earlier researchers tended to measure religiosity in a simple unidimensional fashion, identifying it with membership in a religious group (e.g., R. A. Neimeyer et al., 1977) or a single aspect of religious conviction, such as belief in an afterlife. Unfortunately, these studies often yielded conflicting results. For example, Krieger et al. (1974) found no relationship between belief in an afterlife and scores on the TI, whereas Rigdon and Epting (1985) found that subjects who reported strong beliefs in an afterlife, frequent church attendance, and religious reading were less threatened by death than were comparison subjects.

Fortunately, the adoption of improved methodologies for the assessment of religious orientation seems to be clarifying its relationship to death threat. Administering a broad-ranging scale for the assessment of nonscientific beliefs, Tobacyk (1984) discovered that only beliefs that corresponded to traditional religious doctrines were negatively correlated with death threat, whereas beliefs in witchcraft, extrasensory perception, extraterrestrials, and other paranormal phenomena were unrelated to scores on the TI. Support for this conclusion was recently provided by Ingram and Leitner (1989), who assessed death threat using both the standardized TI and a repertory grid, which permitted subjects to compare self and death elements on a sample of personally meaningful constructs relevant to their social lives, rather than to their death per se. Death threat as measured by both instruments was negatively correlated with several subscales of Putney and Middleton's (1961) Dimensions of Religious Ideology Scale, although, like Tobacyk, Ingram and Leitner found the dimension assessing religious orthodoxy to be the best single predictor of death threat. Interestingly, a second instrument, Faulkner and DeJong's (1965) Religiosity Scale, correlated only with threat scores derived from the interpersonal repertory grid and not with those calculated from the TI. This suggests that general interpersonal constructs may prove more useful than constructs specific to death, when one is trying to assess how death fits into the context of individuals' daily life. Moore and Neimeyer (1993) are currently attempting to replicate and extend some of Ingram and Leitner's findings, by first clarifying the factor structure of these psychometrically problematic religiosity questionnaires and then comparing them with subscales of the factor-analyzed TI discussed earlier, using a large and representative national sample.

Although current evidence points to a positive relationship between orthodox religious beliefs and death acceptance, this conclusion should be tempered by several considerations. First, Tobacyk and Driggers (1989) reported that the negative correlation between religiosity and death threat held only for low self-monitors, that is, individuals who tend to show behavioral consistency across social contexts and act in ways that are compatible with a stable set of beliefs. In contrast, high self-monitors, who strategically present different aspects of themselves depending on the social context, showed no such correlation. This suggests that various personality factors may moderate the impact that religious beliefs have on death concern, highlighting the importance of more sophisticated multivariate research designs.

Second, studies to date have tended to focus on Christian ideology, leaving largely unexplored the relationship between death attitudes and other (especially non-Western) religious systems. Recent suggestive findings by Holcomb et al. (1993) indicate that individuals who profess a personal philosophy of death are more likely to see it as purposeful and to construe it in terms that imply greater understanding, acceptance, and personal involvement than are subjects who lack such a personal philosophy. However, because the sample was predominantly Christian, it is unclear whether these meanings of death correlate with Christian theology only or would hold for any subject who possessed a meaningful philosophy, whether Christian or Jewish, theistic or atheistic. Such questions can be answered only by extending research on the relationship between religiosity and death concern beyond the relatively narrow samples that are studied by most investigators.

Third, it is not yet clear whether it is the content or the strength of a person's religious beliefs that is the best predictor of death acceptance. Ingram and Leitner's (1989) finding that death threat was positively correlated with ambivalence of belief reinforces this concern. It may be that individuals who unambivalently reject a Christian ideology are as untroubled by the prospect of death as those who wholeheartedly embrace it, whereas those who vacillate in their belief regard it with the most apprehension. To test this hypothesis, Moore and Neimeyer (1993) are currently comparing the death orientation of devout Christians and equally devout atheists, predicting that both groups will show lower degrees of death threat than will respondents whose religious views are uncertain. This pattern of findings suggests that philosophic integrity, rather than religiosity per se, allows an individual to construe death as a nonthreatening personal reality.

Finally, it should be mentioned that religion may have other effects on an individual's attitudes, aside from simply influencing them to be positive or negative. For example, R. A. Neimeyer et al. (1986) found that those who believed in an afterlife displayed more coherent and less uncertain understandings of death-related situations on the DART, irrespective of their positivity, than did persons who did not believe in an afterlife. Thus, future work on the psychology of religion could include more sophisticated assessments of the structure of belief systems about death, which may vary considerably within as well as between members of particular denominations.

Relationship Between Self-Actualization and Fear of Death

Existential philosophy argues that human beings are unique largely because of their capacity for self-creation; humans are thought to consolidate the essential meaning of their lives by positing unique projects or goals that they strive to actualize. Sartre contended that it is through active investment in such goals that individuals evolve substantial identities for themselves. Death, however, destroys all human projects, negating the anticipated realization of possibilities. Thus death confers on the individual a final and absolute identity, defining the individual entirely as what he or she *has been*. Because the essence or significance of a person's life becomes crystallized at the moment of death, an existentially oriented thanatologist would predict that death would be threatening to a person whose primary life projects were incomplete or unfinished. In contrast, for the individual whose primary life projects have been fulfilled, death would be a source of less anxiety, appropriately punctuating a life that has permitted the individual to approximate his or her chosen ideals (R. A. Neimeyer & Chapman, 1980). Moreover, individuals' sense of resolution about their life may be enhanced by genuine confrontation with the prospect of their death. As Gamble and Brown (1981) have argued, "an actualized and authentic existence is possible only when the individual has come to terms with the fact of personal mortality" (p. 8).

R. A. Neimeyer and Chapman (1980) attempted to test this existential hypothesis by deriving a self–ideal discrepancy rating from the TI, instead of the more commonly derived self–death discrepancy score. A self–ideal discrepancy was reasoned to reflect the extent to which respondents construed themselves as distant from their ideal self and thus to predict level of apprehension about death. That is, less actualized respondents (those with higher self–death discrepancy) would show greater apprehension about personal death. This hypothesis was supported by the results from a heterogenous adult population. As expected, less actualized subjects scored higher on Templer's (1970) DAS as well as the Collett–Lester Death of Self, Death of Others, and Dying of Others subscales. Actualization was unrelated to scores on the fourth Collett–Lester subscale, Fear of Dying of Self, which focuses on the pain and debilitation of the dying process. Use of the traditional self–death split (threat) score on the TI as a further dependent variable in the study was avoided, out of the concern that the contribution of the self rating to both the self–ideal discrepancy and self–

death split scores might introduce a methodological confound that could obscure results.

In their extension of this research program, Wood and Robinson (1982) proposed an "additive model" that considered the role of actualization (the inverse of self–ideal discrepancy) and integration (the inverse of self–death splits) together in shaping death attitudes. Specifically, they noted that many highly actualized subjects nonetheless had difficulty integrating the concepts of self and death (i.e., they scored high in death threat), and they hypothesized that such individuals would experience more death fear and anxiety than similarly actualized individuals who had higher levels of self–death integration. Testing this model with a college population, they were able to replicate R. A. Neimeyer and Chapman's (1980) findings that more actualized subjects displayed less fear of death on subscales of the Collett–Lester scale, although not on the DAS. A second study with a sample of college students (Robinson & Wood, 1984a) provided additional replication of the additive model: Highly actualized and highly integrated subjects scored lower than all other groups on the same set of measures used by R. A. Neimeyer and Chapman.

Subsequent research, however, has failed to corroborate the additive model, although it has provided consistent support for the existential hypothesis relating actualization to lower levels of apprehension about death. For example, in a study of physically ill and healthy individuals, Robinson and Wood (1984b) found that although both actualization and integration were correlated with various measures of death fear and anxiety, they made no independent contribution to the prediction of death attitudes. Similarly, I (R. A. Neimeyer, 1985) studied a diverse group of non-college-educated adults and failed to find any interaction between integration and actualization and scores on a range of measures of death concern, although each score derived from the TI was significantly related to different facets of death fear and anxiety. Thus, it appears that individuals' level of actualization (or the degree to which they have attained their ideals) is a robust predictor of death acceptance, but an interaction of this factor with self–death integration occurs only within narrowly defined college student populations.

Death Attitudes of Helping Professionals

When he first surveyed the literature on the relationship between occupational status and death attitudes 25 years ago, Lester (1967) could find little sense in investigators' choice of vocational categories for comparison. In contrast, the recent personal construct research in this area is much more focused, concentrating on helping professionals who encounter death or its possibility as part of their work. For example, R. A. Neimeyer and Dingemans (1980) reported that suicide intervention personnel displayed greater death threat than comparison subjects on the TI, although a follow-up study by R. A. Neimeyer and Neimeyer (1984) called into question whether this higher level of death concern could be replicated using other measures of death attitude or a broader sample of crisis counselors. Similarly, Ingram and Leitner (1989) were unable to detect significant differences in death threat between a group of Protestant ministers and religious laypersons and DePaola and his colleagues (Chapter 11) of this volume did not find nursing home personnel to have higher death threat or anxiety than matched controls. Thus, it should not be assumed that functioning in an occupational role in which one confronts human suffering and death necessarily is associated with greater personal death threat.

A more promising approach to studying the relationship between death attitudes and occupation is to examine the impact of personal death orientation on helping professionals' work-related decisions and behaviors. Eggerman and Dustin (1985) took this approach in studying medical students' levels of death threat and found that those who were most personally threatened were also most likely to consider multiple factors before informing a patient of a terminal diagnosis. Moreover, they reported that practicing physicians with higher TI scores showed a related tendency to take into account psychological factors before they raised the topic of dying with a seriously ill patient.

Further evidence for a relationship between physicians' personal death orientation and their professional behaviors was provided by G. J. Neimeyer, Behnke, and Reiss (1984). Administering scenarios that depicted different forms of patient death to a group of neonatal residents, they discovered that those who were highly threatened by death were more likely to cope by resorting to avoidance strategies such as throwing themselves into their work or avoiding the patient's funeral. Those who responded with less meaningful or clear-cut ratings of death threat on the TI were more likely to acknowledge the use of drugs or alcohol in an attempt to shake off the impact of patient death. DePaola et al. (Chapter 11) have investigated similar issues regarding the impact of nursing home personnel's levels of death threat, fear, and personal anxiety about aging on their work with the elderly. Results indicated that subjects with elevated death threat and fear were more anxious about their own aging and those with greater fear of aging and death also displayed more negative attitudes toward the elderly. Ultimately, a clearer understanding of the complex ramifications of the helping professional's constructions of death for the way he or she intervenes in human life may form the basis for a patient-centered approach to education in the allied health professions, as Rainey's (1984) preliminary work has suggested.

Death Threat in the Physically Ill

In conjunction with the relatively recent upsurge of interest in behavioral medicine, personal construct researchers have begun to study the constructions of death held by people whose lives have been touched by physical illness or anticipated death. An early study in this vein (Rainey & Epting, 1977) indicated that healthy subjects who accepted the eventuality of their own death by preplanning for the burial or disposal of their body showed much lower scores on the TI than did comparison subjects who had not made such arrangements. Higher levels of death acceptance also characterized the mothers of children with cystic fibrosis in a study by Lewis (1981): As a group, such mothers reported less personal death threat than did mothers of healthy children. Mothers of children with chronic asthma scored in the intermediate range on the TI and could not be reliably distinguished from either group. Finally, Hendon and Epting (1989) have studied the emotional adjustment of terminal cancer patients being treated in a hospice whose staff was explicitly committed to a care rather than cure orientation. Comparing these patients with remitted cancer patients and patients experiencing brief hospitalizations for transient illness, Hendon and Epting found the hospice sample to be dramatically lower in death threat than either control group. Moreover, the fact that the hospice patients acknowledged greater depression than the remitted group argues against the interpretation that their lower death threat was simply a function of their level of palliative medication. Instead, it appears that personal factors and the institutional setting in which the hospice patients confronted the eventuality of death contributed specifically to greater integration of their concepts of self and death. In general, all of the preceding studies suggest that deeply personal encounters with the prospect of death can help alleviate the threat associated with personal mortality, at least for many people. This conclusion is also compatible with the results of Greyson's research on people who have had near-death experiences, reported in Chapter 8.

However, it would be dangerous to endorse a uniformity myth implying that all people react similarly to personal illness (Viney, 1984). This is poignantly illustrated by the research of Robinson and Wood (1984b), who studied groups of people who were healthy; undergoing a medical checkup; or suffering from rheumatoid arthritis, diabetes, or cancer. Surprisingly, they found no differences among any of these subject groups on a range of measures of death fear and anxiety. However, apprehension about personal death on a number of questionnaires was consistently related to a measure of self–ideal discrepancy derived from the TI. Thus, it appears that personal factors such as actualization or attainment of projected ideals have a more direct potential relationship to death anxiety or acceptance than medical status per se.

Death Education

As courses concerned with death and dying have secured a place in college curricula, personal construct researchers have become more interested in the impact of death education programs on students' personal meanings of death. In an early study of the impact of death-related audiovisual materials, R. A. Neimeyer et al. (1977) found that subjects showed an increase in death anxiety (as measured by the DAS) but not death threat (as measured by the TI) after watching a film depicting Nazi atrocities in World War II. However, a reanalysis of these data indicated that subjects who initially scored higher on the TI experienced greater anxiety after viewing the film (R. A. Neimeyer, 1978), suggesting that the TI could be useful in predicting the emotional reactions of students to death-oriented presentations. But the potential utility of the TI as a predictor of individual response to death education may not extend to predicting the intellectual processing of course materials. Patterson, Gates, and Faulkender (1988) examined this issue by administering the TI and DAS to a large group of college students, who subsequently watched a film on cultural practices related to death. Contrary to their hypothesis, students who scored high on these measures were no less likely than their less anxious and threatened counterparts to perform well on a recall test after the film.

Overall, the impact of death education and awareness programs on death threat has been consistent from one study to the next. For example, Rigdon and Epting (1985) were unable to demonstrate any impact of participation in a death awareness exercise (e.g., writing one's own obituary and farewell letter), as opposed to a stress reduction workshop, on death fear or threat. In contrast, Tobacyk and Eckstein (1980) found that students enrolled in a semester-long course in death education showed a reliable decrease in death threat compared with controls. Interestingly, the death education students in this study also displayed lower death threat prior to the class than did comparison students, replicating the findings of Rainey and Epting (1977). Nonetheless, the latter investigators failed to find any systematic change in death threat for students in the death and dying class, and instead reported a threefold increase in the variance of TI scores across time. This pattern of results once again points to students' highly individualized reactions to death education experiences, making it impossible to generalize about the impact of such classes on death threat or anxiety.

The assumption that death education should promote greater death acceptance is itself questionable. Warren (1989) has persistently challenged the underlying rationale of this anxiety reduction model. He argues that personal construct tools (particularly repertory grid technique) should be used to sensitize instructors and students alike to their constructions of self and death and to promote an authentic recognition of its unique impact on the individual. In a similar vein, I (Neimeyer, 1988) have recommended the use of the TI as a didactic prompt for discussion in death education classes, and Epting (1990) has used a small-group discussion of participants' TI ratings as a provocative exercise in death and dying workshops.

CONCLUSION

In this chapter, I have surveyed the growing literature on personal construct methods in thanatology, supplementing a review of this research program written more than a decade ago (Rigdon, Epting, Neimeyer, & Krieger, 1979). In the 20 years since the introduction of the TI, an impressive body of evidence has accumulated supporting its psychometric soundness. Equally impressive have been the efforts of several groups of investigators to carry out programmatic series of studies using the instrument, something that is all too rare in the sometimes chaotic mosaic of research on death anxiety (R. A. Neimeyer, 1988).

Undoubtedly, future research will usher in not only new applications of personal construct methods for assessing death orientation, but also innovations in basic methodology. Recent research suggests a few of these innovative methods and applications. For example, it seems likely that future investigators will benefit from the established factor structure for the TI, which permits a finer grained interpretation of an individual's tendency to perceive death as a threat to well-being or with uncertainty or fatalism, as well as measuring more global death threat (Moore & Neimeyer, 1991). The development of new scaling metrics may also yield greater psychometric senstivity to variations in degree of death threat. Because the rationale and interpretation of the TI can only benefit from further scrutiny (see footnote 2), I hope that investigators will continue to conduct the sort of basic research that has distinguished the personal construct approach to the measurement of death attitudes.

One of the most promising areas of future research concerns the connection between death attitudes and interpersonal relationships, not only because of the applied importance of such research but also because it may usher in extensions of methodology. The exploration of repertory grid methodologies that examine the construction of death in the context of an individual's social world (cf. Ingram & Leitner, 1989; Meshot & Leitner, 1993) is a case in point. Meshot and Leitner (1993) have used grid technique to study college students who had experienced the death of a parent during their adolescence. Compared with controls, this bereaved sample showed more tendency to integrate their constructions of the self and death on their interpersonal rep grid, but also displayed a greater need to be noticed by others in adulthood. Also investigating the association between death attitudes and role relationships, Epting, Pritchard, and Beagle (1990) have experimented with a more detailed scoring system for the TI, which takes into account not only the traditional similarity or dissimilarity in ratings of self and death, but also the positivity or negativity of the construing of each element. Early results using this method suggest that subjects with certain profiles (e.g., the depressed configuration, in which both the self and death are construed negatively) display distinctive patterns in their construing of the self and others (e.g., showing the lowest degree of identification with significant others on their repertory grids). Further research in this area may elucidate the ways in which significant interpersonal events (e.g., loss, commitment to a relationship, and birth of a child) can influence our attitudes toward death and, conversely, how our attitudes toward death influence our needs and behaviors in relation to others.

Finally, content analysis of free-response descriptions of death, dying, or serious illness (Holcomb et al., 1993; Viney, 1990) may give more idiographic richness to future studies of the psychology of death and dying, complementing and extending the much broader use of standardized questionnaires. In particular, extensive development and use of reliable coding manuals for death-related constructions could be a salutary trend in the area of death studies, allowing thanatology to benefit from the narrative turn that is transforming much research in the social sciences.

In summary, personal construct theory and its associated methods have made a sustained and substantial contribution to the growing discipline of death studies. I hope that investigators will continue to improve and diversify their repertoire of research tools, so that the personalism and complexity of our encounter with death will eventually be matched by the personalism and complexity of the methods we use to study it.

REFERENCES

Bell, R. (1990). Analytic issues in the use of repertory grid technique. In G. J. Neimeyer & R. A. Neimeyer (Eds.), *Advances in personal construct psychology* (Vol. 1, pp. 25–48). Greenwich, CT: JAI Press.

Bringmann, M. (1992). Computer-based methods for the analysis and interpretation of personal construct systems. In R. A. Neimeyer & G. J. Neimeyer (Eds.), *Advances in personal construct psychology* (Vol. 2, pp. 57–90). Greenwich, CT: JAI Press.

Chambers, W. V. (1986). Inconsistencies in the theory of death threat. *Death Studies, 10*, 165–175.

Chambers, W. V., Miller, D., & Mueller, M. (1992). Validity of the Threat Index. *Psychological Reports, 71*, 488–490.

Dattel, A. R., & Neimeyer, R. A. (1990). Sex differences in death anxiety: Testing the emotional expressiveness hypothesis. *Death Studies, 14*, 1–11.

Davis, S. F., Bremer, S. A., Anderson, B. J., & Tramill, J. L. (1983). The interrelationships of ego strength, self-esteem, death anxiety, and gender in undergraduate college students. *Journal of General Psychology, 108*, 55–59.

Durlak, J. A. (1982). Using the Templer scale to assess "death anxiety": A cautionary note. *Psychological Reports, 50*, 1257–1258.

Eckstein, D., & Tobacyk, J. (1979). Ordinal position and death concern. *Psychological Reports, 44*, 967–971.

Eggerman, S., & Dustin, D. (1985). Death orientation and communication with the terminally ill. *Omega, 16*, 255–265.

Epting, F. R. (1990). *Guidelines for the use of the Threat Index in a death awareness workshop*. Unpublished manuscript, University of Florida, Gainesville.

Epting, F. R., & Neimeyer, R. A. (1984). *Personal meanings of death*. Washington, DC: Hemisphere.

Epting, F. R., Pritchard, S., & Beagle. J. W. (1990, June). *Death threat and interpersonal worlds*. Paper presented at the North American Personal Construct Network Conference, San Antonio, TX.

Epting, F. R., Rainey, L. C., & Weiss, M. J. (1979). Constructions of death and levels of death fear. *Death Education, 3*, 21–30.

Faulker, J. E., & DeJong, G. F. (1965). *Religiosity in 5-D: An empirical analysis*. Paper presented at the annual convention of the American Sociological Association, Chicago.

Fransella, F., & Bannister, D. (1977). *A manual for repertory grid technique*. San Diego, CA: Academic.

Gamble, D. T., & Brown, K. L. (1981). Self-actualization and personal mortality. *Omega, 11*, 341–353.

Hendon, M. K., & Epting, F. R. (1989). A comparison of hospice patients with recovering and ill patients. *Death Studies, 13*, 567–578.

Hoelter, J. W. (1979). Multidimensional treatment of fear of death. *Journal of Consulting and Clinical Psychology, 47*, 996–999.

Holcomb, L. E., Neimeyer, R. A., & Moore, M. K. (1993). Personal meanings of death: A content analysis of free-response narratives. *Death Studies, 17*, 299–318.

Ingram, B. J., & Leitner, L. M. (1989). Death threat, religiosity, and fear of death: A repertory grid investigation. *International Journal of Personal Construct Psychology, 2*, 199–214.

Kalish, R. A. (1988). The study of death: A psychological perspective. In H. Wass, F. Berardo, & R. A. Neimeyer (Eds.), *Dying: Facing the facts* (2nd ed., pp. 55–75). Washington, DC: Hemisphere.

Kastenbaum, R., & Costa, P. T. (1977). Psychological perspectives on death. *Annual Review of Psychology, 28*, 225–249.

Kelly, G. A. (1955). *The psychology of personal constructs*. New York: Norton.

Krieger, S. R., Epting, F. R., & Hays, L. H. (1979). Validity and reliability of provided constructs in assessing death threat. *Omega, 20*, 87–95.

Krieger, S. R., Epting, F. R., & Leitner, L. M. (1974). Personal constructs, threat,and attitudes toward death. *Omega, 5*, 299–310.

Landfield, A. W. (1983). *Reptest scoring program*. Unpublished software, University of Nebraska.

Lantzy, P. & Thornton, G. (1982). Differential effects of the type of death stimuli and sex of subjects on personal death attitudes. In R. A. Pacholski & C. A. Corr (Eds.), *Priorities in death education and counseling* (pp. 215–229). Arlington, VA: Forum for Death Education and Counseling.

Lester, D. (1967). Experimental and correlational studies of the fear of feath. *Psychological Bulletin, 67*, 27–36.

Lewis, B. S. (1982). *Factors affecting psychosocial adjustment in chronically ill children and their parents*. Unpublished doctoral dissertation, University of Florida, Gainesville.

Lonetto, R., Mercer, G. W., Fleming, S., Bunting, B., & Clare, M. (1980). Death anxiety among university students in Northern Ireland and Canada. *Journal of Psychology, 104*, 75–84.

Lonetto, R., & Templer, D. I. (1986). *Death anxiety*. Washington, DC: Hemisphere.

MacDonald, G. W. (1976). Sex, religion, and risk-taking behavior as correlates of death anxiety. *Omega, 7*, 35–44.

MacInnes, W. D., & Neimeyer, R. A. (1980). Internal consistency of the Threat Index. *Death Education, 4*, 193–194.

McMordie, W. R., & Kumar, A. (1984). Cross-cultural research on the Templer/ McMordie Death Anxiety Scale. *Psychological Reports, 54*, 959–963.

Meshot, C. M., & Leitner, L. M. (1993). Death threat, parental loss, and interpersonal style: A personal construct investigation. *Death Studies, 17*, 319–332.

Moore, M. K., & Neimeyer, R. A. (1991). A confirmatory factor analysis of the Threat Index. *Journal of Personality and Social Psychology, 60*, 122–129.

Moore, M. K., & Neimeyer, R. A. (1993). *An empirical investigation of the relationship between religiosity and death concern.* Manuscript in preparation.

Neimeyer, G. J., Behnke, M., & Reiss, J. (1984). Constructs and coping: Physicians' responses to patient death. In F. R. Epting & R. A. Neimeyer (Eds.), *Personal meanings of death* (pp. 159–180). Washington, DC: Hemisphere.

Neimeyer, G. J., & Neimeyer, R. A. (1981). Personal construct perspectives on cognitive assessment. In T. Merluzzi, C. Glass, & M. Genest (Eds.), *Cognitive assessment* (pp. 188–231). New York: Guilford Press.

Neimeyer, R. A. (1978). Death anxiety and the Threat Index: An addendum. *Death Education, 1*, 464–467.

Neimeyer, R. A. (1985). Actualization, integration and fear of death: A test of the additive model. *Death Studies, 9*, 235–250.

Neimeyer, R. A. (1986). The threat hypothesis: A conceptual and empirical defense. *Death Studies, 10*, 177–190.

Neimeyer, R. A. (1988). Death anxiety. In H. Wass, F. Berardo, & R. A. Neimeyer (Eds.), *Dying: Facing the facts* (2nd ed., pp. 97–136). Washington, DC: Hemisphere.

Neimeyer, R. A., Bagley, K. J., & Moore, M. K. (1986). Cognitive structure and death anxiety. *Death Studies, 10*, 273–288.

Neimeyer, R. A., & Chapman, K. M. (1980). Self–ideal discrepancy and fear of death: The test of an existential hypothesis. *Omega, 11*, 233–240.

Neimeyer, R. A., & Dingemans, P. (1980). Death orientation in the suicide intervention worker. *Omega, 11*, 15–23.

Neimeyer, R. A., Dingemans, P., & Epting, F. R. (1977). Convergent validity, situational stability, and meaningfulness of the Threat Index. *Omega, 8*, 251–265.

Neimeyer, R. A., Epting, F. R., & Rigdon, M. A. (1984). A procedure manual for the Threat Index. In F. R. Epting & R. A. Neimeyer (Eds.), *Personal meanings of death* (pp. 235–242). Washington, DC: Hemisphere.

Neimeyer, R. A., Fontana, D. J., & Gold, K. (1984). A manual for content analysis of death constructs. In F. R. Epting & R. A. Neimeyer (Eds.). *Personal meanings of death* (pp. 213–234). Washington, DC: Hemisphere.

Neimeyer, R. A., Moore, M. K., & Bagley, K. (1988). A preliminary factor structure for the Threat Index. *Death Studies, 12*, 217–225.

Neimeyer, R. A., & Neimeyer, G. J. (1984). Death anxiety and counseling skill in the suicide interventionist. *Suicide and Life-Threatening Behavior, 14*, 126–131.

Patterson, K. S., Gates, L. J., & Faulkender, P. J. (1988). Assessment of death attitudes: An empirical approach. *Journal of Psychology, 121*, 475–479.

Pollak, J. M. (1980). Correlates of death anxiety: A review of empirical studies. *Omega, 10*, 97–121.

Putney, S., & Middleton, R. (1961). Dimensions and correlates of religious ideologies. *Social Forces, 39*, 285–290.

Rainey, L. C. (1984). Death education for oncology professionals: A personal construct theory perspective. In F. R. Epting & R. A. Neimeyer (Eds.), *Personal meanings of death* (pp. 195–210). Washington, DC: Hemisphere.

Rainey, L. C., & Epting, F. R. (1977). Death threat constructions in the student and the prudent. *Omega, 8*, 19–28.

Rigdon, M. A. (1983). Death threat before and after attempted suicide: A clinical investigation. *Death Education, 7*, 195–209.

Rigdon, M.A., & Epting, F. R. (1985). Reduction in death threat as a basis for optimal functioning. *Death Studies, 9*, 427–448.

Rigdon, M. A., Epting, F. R., Neimeyer, R. A., & Krieger, S. R. (1979). The Threat Index: A research report. *Death Education, 3*, 245–270.

Robinson, P. J., & Wood, K. (1984a). The Threat Index: An additive approach. *Omega, 15*, 139–144.

Robinson, P. J., & Wood, K. (1984b). Fear of death and physical illness: A personal construct approach. In F. R. Epting & R. A. Neimeyer (Eds.), *Personal meanings of death* (pp. 127–142). Washington, DC: Hemisphere.

Sadowski, C. J., Davis, S. F., & Loftus-Vergari, M. C. (1979). Locus of control and death anxiety: A reexamination. *Omega, 10*, 203–210.

Sanders, J. F., Poole, T. E., & Rivero, W. T. (1980). Death anxiety among the elderly. *Psychological Reports, 46*, 53–56.

Sewell, K. W., Adams-Webber, J., Mitterer, J., & Cromwell, R. L. (1992). Computerized repertory grids: Review of the literature. *International Journal of Personal Construct Psychology, 5*, 1–23.

Simpson, M. A. (1980). Studying death: Problems of methodology. *Death Education, 4*, 139–148.

Stillion, J. M. (1985). *Death and the sexes*. Washington, DC: Hemisphere.

Templer, D. I. (1970). The construction and validation of a death anxiety scale. *Journal of General Psychology, 82*, 165–177.

Tobacyk, J. (1984). Death threat, death concerns, and paranormal belief. In F. R. Epting & R. A. Neimeyer (Eds.), *Personal meanings of death* (pp. 29–38). Washington, DC: Hemisphere.

Tobacyk, J., & Eckstein, D. (1980). Death threat and death concerns in the college student. *Omega, 11*, 139–155.

Viney, L. (1984). Concerns about death among severely ill people. In F. R. Epting & R. A. Neimeyer (Eds.), *Personal meanings of death* (pp. 143–157). Washington, DC: Hemisphere.

Viney, L. (1990). A constructivist model of psychological reactions to physical illness and injury. In G. J. Neimeyer & R. A. Neimeyer (Eds.), *Advances in personal construct psychology* (Vol. 1, pp. 117–151). Greenwich, CT: JAI Press.

Warren, W. G. (1982). Personal construction of death and death education. *Death Education, 6*, 17–28.

Warren, W. G. (1989). *Death education and research: Critical perspectives*. New York: Haworth.

Warren, W. G., & Parry, G. (1981). Personal constructs and death: Some clinical refinements. In H. Bonarius, R. Holland, & S. Rosenberg (Eds.), *Personal construct psychology: Recent advances in theory and practice* (pp. 267–276). New York: Macmillan.

Wood, K., & Robinson, P. J. (1982). Actualization and the fear of death: Retesting an existential hypothesis. *Essence, 5*, 235–243.

Young, M., & Daniels, S. (1980). Born again status as a factor in death anxiety. *Psychological Reports, 47*, 367–370.

APPENDIX 4-1: Provided Form of the 25-Item Threat Index

PART I

You or Your Present Life

INSTRUCTIONS: Below is a list of 25 dimensions, each of which is made up of a pair of opposite constructs. For each dimension, please decide which one of the pair (the left or the right side) describes you or your present life more closely. Then, indicate whether you strongly agree, moderately agree, or mildly agree with the dimension by circling a number. You do not need to circle the dimension, just the number. In a few of the cases, you may feel as if both sides describe you to some degree. If both sides of the dimension describe you equally, then circle the middle response (i.e., the 4). For example, do you see yourself as more healthy or sick? Please circle only one number for each of the 25 dimensions.

1 = Strongly agree with left construct
2 = Moderately agree with left construct
3 = Mildly agree with left construct
4 = Equally agree with both constructs
5 = Mildly agree with right construct
6 = Moderately agree with right construct
7 = Strongly agree with right construct

1	2	3	4	5	6	7	1. Healthy	Sick
1	2	3	4	5	6	7	2. Strong	Weak
1	2	3	4	5	6	7	3. Existence	Nonexistence
1	2	3	4	5	6	7	4. Open	Closed
1	2	3	4	5	6	7	5. Mentally Healthy	Crazy
1	2	3	4	5	6	7	6. Happy	Sad
1	2	3	4	5	6	7	7. Competent	Incompetent

1	2	3	4	5	6	7	8. Feels Good .... Feels Bad
1	2	3	4	5	6	7	9. Secure .... Insecure
1	2	3	4	5	6	7	10. Concrete .... Abstract
1	2	3	4	5	6	7	11. Conforming ....Nonconforming
1	2	3	4	5	6	7	12. Changing .... Static
1	2	3	4	5	6	7	13. Specific ....General
1	2	3	4	5	6	7	14. Objective .... Subjective
1	2	3	4	5	6	7	15. Predictable .... Random
1	2	3	4	5	6	7	16. Animate ....Inanimate
1	2	3	4	5	6	7	17. Easy ....Hard
1	2	3	4	5	6	7	18. Learning .... Not Learning
1	2	3	4	5	6	7	19. Hope .... No Hope
1	2	3	4	5	6	7	20. Useful .... Useless
1	2	3	4	5	6	7	21. Productive ....Unproductive
1	2	3	4	5	6	7	22. Peaceful .... Violent
1	2	3	4	5	6	7	23. Alive .... Dead
1	2	3	4	5	6	7	24. Understanding .... Not Understanding
1	2	3	4	5	6	7	25. Helping Others .... Being Selfish

PART II

Your Ideal Self

INSTRUCTIONS: For each of the 25 dimensions, please decide which one of the pair (the left or the right side) you more closely associate with your ideal self or the way you would prefer to be living. Then, indicate whether you strongly agree, moderately agree, or mildly agree with the dimension by circling a number. You do not need to circle the dimension, just the number. In a few of the cases, you may feel as if both sides describe your ideal self to some degree. If both sides of the dimension describe your ideal self equally, then circle the middle response (i.e., the 4). For example, do you see your ideal self as more healthy or sick? Please circle only one number for each of the 25 dimensions.

1 = Strongly agree with left construct
2 = Moderately agree with left construct
3 = Mildly agree with left construct
4 = Equally agree with both constructs
5 = Mildly agree with right construct
6 = Moderately agree with right construct
7 = Strongly agree with right construct

1	2	3	4	5	6	7	1. Healthy ....Sick
1	2	3	4	5	6	7	2. Strong ....Weak
1	2	3	4	5	6	7	3. Existence .... Nonexistence

1	2	3	4	5	6	7	4. Open ....Closed
1	2	3	4	5	6	7	5. Mentally Healthy ....Crazy
1	2	3	4	5	6	7	6. Happy ....Sad
1	2	3	4	5	6	7	7. Competent .... Incompetent
1	2	3	4	5	6	7	8. Feels Good .... Feels Bad
1	2	3	4	5	6	7	9. Secure .... Insecure
1	2	3	4	5	6	7	10. Concrete .... Abstract
1	2	3	4	5	6	7	11. Conforming ....Nonconforming
1	2	3	4	5	6	7	12. Changing ....Static
1	2	3	4	5	6	7	13. Specific ....General
1	2	3	4	5	6	7	14. Objective .... Subjective
1	2	3	4	5	6	7	15. Predictable .... Random
1	2	3	4	5	6	7	16. Animate ....Inanimate
1	2	3	4	5	6	7	17. Easy ....Hard
1	2	3	4	5	6	7	18. Learning .... Not Learning
1	2	3	4	5	6	7	19. Hope .... No Hope
1	2	3	4	5	6	7	20. Useful ....Useless
1	2	3	4	5	6	7	21. Productive ....Unproductive
1	2	3	4	5	6	7	22. Peaceful .... Violent
1	2	3	4	5	6	7	23. Alive .... Dead
1	2	3	4	5	6	7	24. Understanding .... Not Understanding
1	2	3	4	5	6	7	25. Helping Others .... Being Selfish

PART III

Your Own Death

INSTRUCTIONS: For each of the 25 dimensions, please decide which one of the pair (the left or the right side) you more closely associate with your own death, thinking of your own death as if it were to occur at this time in your life. Then, indicate whether you strongly agree, moderately agree, or mildly agree with the dimension by circling a number. You do not need to circle the dimension, just the number. In a few of the cases, you may feel as if both sides describe your own death to some degree. If both sides of the dimension describe your own death equally, then circle the middle response (i.e., the 4). For example, do you see your own death as more healthy or sick? Please circle only one number for each of the 25 dimensions.

> 1 = Strongly agree with left construct
> 2 = Moderately agree with left construct
> 3 = Mildly agree with left construct
> 4 = Equally agree with both constructs
> 5 = Mildly agree with right construct

6 = Moderately agree with right construct
7 = Strongly agree with right construct

1	2	3	4	5	6	7	1. Healthy .... Sick
1	2	3	4	5	6	7	2. Strong .... Weak
1	2	3	4	5	6	7	3. Existence .... Nonexistence
1	2	3	4	5	6	7	4. Open .... Closed
1	2	3	4	5	6	7	5. Mentally Healthy .... Crazy
1	2	3	4	5	6	7	6. Happy .... Sad
1	2	3	4	5	6	7	7. Competent .... Incompetent
1	2	3	4	5	6	7	8. Feels Good .... Feels Bad
1	2	3	4	5	6	7	9. Secure .... Insecure
1	2	3	4	5	6	7	10. Concrete .... Abstract
1	2	3	4	5	6	7	11. Conforming .... Nonconforming
1	2	3	4	5	6	7	12. Changing .... Static
1	2	3	4	5	6	7	13. Specific .... General
1	2	3	4	5	6	7	14. Objective .... Subjective
1	2	3	4	5	6	7	15. Predictable .... Random
1	2	3	4	5	6	7	16. Animate .... Inanimate
1	2	3	4	5	6	7	17. Easy .... Hard
1	2	3	4	5	6	7	18. Learning .... Not Learning
1	2	3	4	5	6	7	19. Hope .... No Hope
1	2	3	4	5	6	7	20. Useful .... Useless
1	2	3	4	5	6	7	21. Productive .... Unproductive
1	2	3	4	5	6	7	22. Peaceful .... Violent
1	2	3	4	5	6	7	23. Alive .... Dead
1	2	3	4	5	6	7	24. Understanding .... Not Understanding
1	2	3	4	5	6	7	25. Helping Others .... Being Selfish

Scoring Key for the Threat Index

As described in this chapter, the Threat Index has been scored in a number of ways in its 20-year history.

Split Scores

Split scores can be calculated by simply counting the number of instances in which ''you or your present life'' is scored on the opposite side of a construct from ''your ideal self'' (yielding a measure of self–ideal discrepancy or, conversely, actualization) or from ''your own death'' (yielding a measure of death threat or, conversely, integration). For example, if a respondent rates himself as 5, 6, or 7 (the *weak* side) on the *strong–weak* dimension and rates his own death as 1, 2, or 3 (the *strong* side), this would be taken as one split for the purpose of calculating death threat. No split is scored when either element in the pair is rated as 4. Thus, split scores for self–ideal discrepancy and for death threat can range from 1 to 25 on the 25-item version of the Threat Index.

Distance Scores

Distance scores can be calculated by a simple absolute or Manhattan distance procedure, or by more a elaborate standardized Euclidean formula, for both self–ideal discrepancy and death threat (see Moore & Neimeyer, 1991). For example, if a subject rates her own death as 2 on the *strong–weak* dimension and herself as 5, an absolute distance score of 3 would be obtained as a measure of death threat. Distance scores may be more sensitive to nuances of meaning than split scores, although initial studies should use both distance and split scoring procedures to validate the former against the latter, which are more psychometrically established.

Factor Scores

Factor scores can be calculated using either split or distance metrics for the Global Threat factor or the three component factors, Threat to Well-Being, Uncertainty, and Fatalism, as indicated in Table 4-4. Scores are simply tabulated separately for items associated with each factor, and if an index of global threat is desired, they are combined. Because the factor structure was established for self–death ratings only, it cannot be generalized to the self–ideal discrepancy.

Short Form

A brief form of the Threat Index can be administered by investigators interested in using a short, unidimensional form of the instrument. Instructions are identical to those presented above, but only the 7 constructs identified by Neimeyer, Moore, and Bagley (1988) are included in place of the 25 listed earlier in this Appendix. The 7 constructs in the short form are good–bad, existence–nonexistence, understanding–not understanding, healthy–sick, peaceful–violent, hope–no hope, and satisfied–dissatisfied.

Chapter 5

Validity and Reliability of the Multidimensional Fear of Death Scale

Robert A. Neimeyer
Marlin K. Moore

What do we fear when we fear death? Although this question would seem fundamental to the study of death anxiety, it was in fact treated as relatively unproblematic for the first 25 years of empirical research in this area, from the mid-1950s through the late 1970s (Neimeyer, 1988). Although the typical death anxiety questionnaire contained items assessing a broad range of death-related experiences (e.g., avoidance of reminders of death, concern over loss of body integrity, and fear of painful death), these disparate attitudes were simply summed to yield a single measure, interpreted as death fear or death anxiety. The resulting imprecision in measurement, combined with a lack of attention to the validity and reliability of these early measures, contributed substantially to the ambiguity of the resulting literature on the causes, correlates, and consequences of negative attitudes toward death (cf. Kastenbaum & Costa, 1977; Lester, 1967; Levin, 1990; Pollak, 1979; Simpson, 1980).

In response to this problem, Hoelter published in 1979 a 42-item scale designed to measure fear of death, defined as ''an emotional reaction involving subjective feelings of unpleasantness and concern based on contemplation or anticipation of any of several facets related to death'' (1979a, p. 996). Unlike most popular measures of death attitudes, Hoelter's instrument was multidimensional, comprising eight subscales, each of which measured a conceptually distinct aspect of fear of death. Although other multidimensional measures of death attitudes existed and were in common use at the time (e.g., Collett & Lester, 1969; Lester, Chapter 3 this volume), these were based on rational rather than empirical grounds, raising the question of whether respondents actually discriminated death fears into clusters that were similar to those of the tests' authors (Neimeyer, 1988). In contrast, Hoelter (1979a) provided evidence for the coherence and interpretability of his Multidimensional Fear of Death Scale (MFODS) using factor-analytic procedures before it was used in a number of substantive studies. Subsequently, other investigators have also found the MFODS useful as a refined index of fear of death, even though other multidimensional measures of death attitudes recently have been developed (see Chapters 4 and 6).

Our aim in the present chapter is fourfold. First, we summarize the existing literature on the psychometric properties of the MFODS, giving special attention to studies of its factor structure, insofar as this represents the most distinctive feature of the instrument. Second, because this literature has several limitations, we report the results of original research that clarifies the validity and reliability of the scale. Third, we review the attitudinal and behavioral correlates of the various MFODS dimensions, suggesting particularly provocative findings that are in need of replication or further elaboration. Finally, because investigators of death anxiety continue to display an overreliance on potentially less useful unidimensional measures, we include a copy of the MFODS in Appendix 5-1 to encourage its use in future studies.

EXISTING PSYCHOMETRIC DATA ON THE MULTIDIMENSIONAL FEAR OF DEATH SCALE

Factor Structure

In his initial study yielding the MFODS, Hoelter (1979a) administered a questionnaire containing numerous pretested Likert-type items to a sample of 143 male and 232 female college undergraduates. Subjecting the results to a common factor analysis with varimax rotation, he identified eight distinguishable factors, which he labeled as follows:

F1: Fear of the Dying Process (including painful and violent deaths)

F2: Fear of the Dead (including avoidance of both human and animal remains)

F3: Fear of Being Destroyed (including dissection and cremation of the body)

F4: Fear for Significant Others (including apprehension about the impact of the respondent's death on significant others and of their deaths on the respondent

F5: Fear of the Unknown (including fear of nonexistence)

F6: Fear of Conscious Death (including anxieties about falsely being declared dead)

F7: Fear for the Body after Death (including concern about decay and isolation of the body)

F8: Fear of Premature Death (including concern that death will prevent one from accomplishing important life goals or having significant experiences).

Only 4 of the 42 items displayed significant loadings on inappropriate factors (in addition to their appropriate loadings), suggesting a remarkably clear factor structure, at least for a restricted undergraduate population.

Walkey (1982) sought to replicate this factor structure with a sample of 256 students and their families in New Zealand. Using a principal-components factor analysis with varimax rotation, he discovered that the first five factors of Hoelter's (1979a) solution were "almost perfectly reproduced." Only F8 seriously departed from the expected structure, and even it conformed to the hypothesized pattern once a single problematic item was excluded. As was true in Hoelter's study, factor loadings were impressively clear, with only five off-diagonal loadings exceeding .30. This degree of replicability of a factor structure is unusual, especially in light of the variation between the samples of two studies.

A third attempt to replicate the factor structure of the MFODS was less successful. Administering an Arabic translation of the instrument to a group of 84 male Saudis living temporarily in the United States, Long (1985–86) found "little support" for Hoelter's model. Using common factor analysis with varimax rotation, he discovered that only two factors marginally resembled the corresponding dimensions from English-language samples. Instead, the most interpretable solution contained only three factors, which he identified as Fear of Dying and the Dead (eight items), Fear for Significant Others (four items), and Fear of Premature Death (two items). In light of these results, he concluded that many of the specific fears associated with death in a Western, Christian culture (e.g., fears of the unknown or being destroyed) may not be applicable to members of an Islamic society.

In summary, the exploratory factor analyses of the MFODS conducted by Hoelter (1979a) and Walkey (1982) were encouraging, suggesting that the instrument offers a refined and consistent measure of a broad spectrum of death fears, at least for members of Western, Christian societies. Long's (1985–86) results with an Islamic sample, however, should caution investigators against indiscriminate use of American questionnaires with non-Western cultures. Even more generally, the factor structure of the MFODS deserves replication with other large samples, particularly those that are more broadly based than the college student groups that were the primary subject pool for the Hoelter and Walkey samples (cf. Gaudagnoli & Velicer, 1988). Finally, the factor structure of the scale should be more definitively established using contemporary confirmatory procedures, such as LISREL (Joreskog & Sorbom, 1986). A primary

Table 5-1   Internal Consistency Estimates (Cronbach's alpha) for Subscales of the Multidimensional Fear of Death Scale for Two Samples

Subscale	No. of items	Hoelter (1979a; n = 365)	Walkey (1982; n = 256)
F1: Fear of the Dying Process	6	.80	.79
F2: Fear of the Dead	6	.72	.75
F3: Fear of Being Destroyed	4	.81	.80
F4: Fear for Significant Others	6	.76	.79
F5: Fear of the Unknown	5	.73	.65*
F6: Fear of Conscious Death	5	.65	.67
F7: Fear for the Body after Death	6	.82	.80
F8: Fear of Premature Death	4	.72	.80
Mean alpha		.75	.75

*Exclusion of one item, "I am not afraid to meet my creator," improved alpha to .85.

advantage of these state-of-the-art methods is that they permit the user to test the adequacy of the specified model, in this case the eight dimensions of death anxiety hypothesized by Hoelter. In addition, the hierarchical factor-analytic procedures available within the LISREL program enable the identification of a global orthogonal factor, in addition to the discrete dimensions (cf. Moore & Niemeyer, 1991). Such a general factor, if found, could allow for the interpretation of a global death fear factor that transcends the various facets of death concern measured by each subscale, much as an IQ test can be interpreted as reflecting the general construct of intelligence in addition to the particular intellectual skills tapped by its subtests.

Internal Consistency

Once a factor structure is established for a multidimensional instrument such as the MFODS, calculating Cronbach's alpha on the separate subscales provides a useful index of their internal consistency. These internal reliability estimates have been provided by both Hoelter (1979a) and Walkey (1982) and are summarized in Table 5-1. In general, the two sets of coefficients are highly comparable and suggest that each subscale possesses adequate consistency to warrant its interpretation as a coherent factor. However, it is noteworthy that several subjects in the Walkey sample indicated difficulty with one item on F5, which reads, "I am not afraid to meet my creator." Exclusion of this single item increased alpha from .65 to .85, indicating that it should probably be dropped from future applications of the MFODS.

Validity

The development of the MFODS has been in reverse compared with that of most other measures of death attitudes. Whereas the authors of many instruments in this field have established the validity and reliability of their scales in early studies and only later examined their factor structure, early research on the MFODS was almost exclusively concerned with factor analyses and applications of the instrument, so that studies of its validity and temporal stability have lagged behind. Although interest in the factor structure of the MFODS is understandable in light of its distinctive multidimensional construction, face validity of the items and internal consistency of the subscales should not be accepted in lieu of more direct assessments of its validity and reliability.

Hoelter (1979a) tried to provide a starting point for validation of the scale by examining its correlations with measures of religious orthodoxy. However, such data provide only very indirect reflections of an instrument's validity, especially in light of the problematic and ambiguous relationship between religiosity and death anxiety reported in the broader literature (Neimeyer, 1988). For this reason, we defer discussion of the relationship between the MFODS and religious belief and behavior to the Research Applications section and turn now to more direct assessments of the MFODS's validity.

One means of establishing the validity of a new instrument is to demonstrate its convergence with established measures of similar constructs. In the area of death attitudes, the Threat Index (TI) has been the subject of extensive validational studies over a 20-year period (see Chapter 4), providing one possible measure with which to assess the concurrent validity of the MFODS. DePaola, Neimeyer, Lupfer, and Fiedler (Chapter 11 this volume) administered both instruments to 145 nursing home staff and 130 matched controls. As expected, the TI correlated significantly with a number of MFODS dimensions, including F1 ($r = .12$), F2 ($r = .14$), F4 ($r = .21$), and F5 ($r = .13$). The convergence of the two instruments provides some support for the validity of these MFODS dimensions, although the low magnitude of these correlations suggests that the constructs measured by the two scales are substantially different.

Somewhat different data reflecting the validity of the MFODS were provided by Holcomb, Neimeyer, and Moore (1993), who used the instrument in a study of the content of narratives written by 504 college students depicting their "personal meanings of death." Using a reliable system for coding the content of the paragraphs, Holcomb et al. discovered that respondents who scored as more fearful on the various dimensions of the MFODS tended to emphasize distinctive themes in their descriptions of death. For example, those who scored high on F1 wrote narratives that were more likely to associate death with negative emotional states and also were more likely to emphasize elements of personal control over the dying process. Subjects who scored high on F2 likewise wrote of death in terms of negative emotion, as well as more negative evaluation. F3 was associated with descriptions implying high personal involvement, and F4 correlated with use of negative emotional terms in the narratives. Subjects who scored high on F7 expressed low understanding in their paragraphs, and those with high scores on F8 tended to view death as a negative and universal emotional experience. Finally, respondents who expressed elevated fear of the unknown (F5) were unlikely to view death as a transition to some form of continued existence or afterlife, but instead to see it as a purposeless event of which they had little understanding. Only F6 failed to be associated with distinctive meanings of death coded in the narratives. These findings, relating results of the highly structured MFODS to themes analyzed in free-response narratives, provide clear documentation that respondents who score high on the MFODS do indeed have very different death attitudes from those who score low on the measure. In particular, the frequency with which the various MFODS subscales correlated with narrative content reflecting negative states reinforces the validity of the scales as measures of fear of death.

In summary, previous research offers encouraging preliminary support for the validity of the MFODS, in terms of its convergence with an established measure and its relationship to relevant content analysis categories of unstructured narratives on the meaning of death. However, more extensive validation research seems called for if the MFODS is to be used with confidence by future investigators.

SOME NEW DATA

In light of the encouraging but incomplete evidence supporting the psychometric integrity of the MFODS, we undertook a study of the instrument with two large adult samples. In particular, because no previous investigators had examined the test–retest reliability of the instrument and its component subscales, we corrected this important omission. Moreover, we sought to provide additional evidence for the convergent and construct validity of the inventory and to explore relationships between the MFODS factors and basic demographic variables whose relationships with other questionnaires on death attitudes have been documented extensively in the literature.

Test–Retest Reliability

Ironically, although reliability is perhaps the basic desideratum of any psychological test, the temporal stability of the MFODS has yet to be assessed. To address this omission, we recruited 106 undergraduates (49 male and 57 female) ranging in age from 18 to 48 ($M = 21.74$, $SD = 5.47$) and administered the MFODS to them on two occasions over a 3-week period. Pearson reliability coefficients for the eight subscales were as follows: .77 for F1, .77 for F2, .71 for F3, .61 for F4, .72 for F5, .77 for F6, .81 for F7, and .73 for F8. A General factor comprising all items on the MFODS yielded an *r* of .85.[1] In summary, although F4 appeared somewhat less stable than the other subscales on the instrument, the component scales generally displayed good reliability over time. These findings enhance the interpretability of the various subscales of the MFODS, which appear to tap relatively enduring aspects of individuals' fears of death.

Construct Validity and Demographic Correlates

Because fear of death cannot be observed directly but must be inferred from a subject's behavior or responses to a self-report measure, no simple criterion exists against which an instrument can be compared to establish its validity. Instead, the construct validity of any attitude measure is developed gradually across time as the scale demonstrates theoretically predicted relationships with other relevant variables. Thus, we attempted to augment the database supporting the construct validity of the MFODS in three ways: by demonstrating its sensitivity to meaningful group differences and by analyzing its correlations with the TI and an independent self-report fear of death measure. Finally, we considered the MFODS's relationship to basic demographic variables to determine whether it covaried with them in ways that were compatible with the general literature on death anxiety.

One limitation in most studies of attitudes toward death is reliance on relatively small and restricted college student populations. To surmount this limitation, we recruited a large and diverse adult sample through contacts with churches, a senior citizen center, a school of nursing, the American Humanist Organization, three chapters of a grief recovery group, and various social service agencies. Of the 952 subjects who at least partly completed and returned our questionnaire packet, 562 were women and 390 were men. More than 96% of the subjects were white, and they ranged in age from 18 to 92 ($M = 53.9$, $SD = 17.2$). The sample was well educated, with 18.4% holding doctorate degrees, 20.7% having master's degrees, 27.7% being college graduates, 24.9% having some college experience, and 7.9% holding a high school diploma only. Respondents were sent the questionnaire packets (containing the MFODS, the TI, and a background information form) and returned them anonymously in a stamped, self-addressed envelope.

As an initial test of the validity of the MFODS, we divided the respondents into two groups on the basis of their binary response to the question "Do you feel you have worked out a satisfactory philosophy of life and death?" Because previous research suggests that individuals who have such a personal philosophy

---

[1]The General factor was established through a confirmatory LISREL analysis of nearly 1,000 adult respondents, permitting the more confident interpretation of a second-order factor measuring general fear of death. Prepublication copies of this technical report may be obtained from the authors.

Table 5-2   Mean Scores and Standard Deviations on Subscales of the Multidimensional Fear of Death Scale for Individuals with and Without a Personal Philosophy of Death

Subscale	With (n = 723)	Without (n = 83)	F(1, 804)	p
F1: Fear of the Dying Process				
M	16.18	13.77	14.44	.0002
SD	5.92	5.10		
F2: Fear of the Dead				
M	21.68	19.18	23.08	.0001
SD	4.83	4.98		
F3: Fear of Being Destroyed				
M	14.95	13.73	5.89	.02
SD	4.62	4.40		
F4: Fear for Significant Others				
M	15.36	12.73	23.30	.0001
SD	5.07	4.19		
F5: Fear of the Unknown				
M	13.86	11.01	35.11	.0001
SD	4.47	4.00		
F6: Fear of Conscious Death				
M	23.60	22.80	2.16	ns
SD	5.03	4.91		
F7: Fear for Body after Death				
M	25.79	23.41	25.14	.0001
SD	4.26	5.49		
F8: Fear of Premature Death				
M	12.85	11.16	13.52	.0003
SD	4.14	4.33		
General (total)				
M	139.63	124.16	38.99	.0001
SD	21.32	21.89		

Note: Higher scores indicate lower fear of death.

view death with greater equanimity (Holcomb et al., 1993), the MFODS should be able to discriminate between the two groups, with those who possessed a meaningful personal philosophy expressing lower levels of death fear.

Table 5-2 displays the results of this analysis. As predicted, respondents who believed they had worked out a satisfactory philosophy of death scored as less fearful on the overall MFODS and on each of the component subscales than those who had not, with the single exception of F6 (Fear of Conscious Death). The MFODS's ability to detect theoretically hypothesized differences in death attitudes for the two groups therefore contributes to its construct validation.

As a second reflection of the construct validity of the MFODS, we sought to replicate and extend its correlations with an established instrument, the TI, as

Table 5-3 Pearson Correlations Between Subscales of the Multidimensional Fear of Death Scale and Threat Index Factors and Self-Report of Death Concern

Subscale	Threat Index ($n = 672$)				Death concern ($n = 205$)
	Global Threat	Threat to Well-Being	Uncertainty	Fatalism	
F1: Fear of the Dying Process	.20	.20	.11	.17	.32
F2: Fear of the Dead	.07	.09	ns	.08	.29
F3: Fear of Being Destroyed	−.14	−.12	−.19	ns	.12
F4: Fear for Significant Others	.19	.19	.10	.23	.34
F5: Fear of the Unknown	.22	.22	.22	.06	.17
F6: Fear of Conscious Death	ns	ns	.12	ns	.14
F7: Fear for Body after Death	ns	ns	.13	ns	.27
F8: Fear of Premature Death	.22	.23	.12	.17	.35
General (total)	.16	.19	ns	.14	.43

Note. Signs have been reversed for ease of interpretation. In reality, high scores on the Threat Index indicate greater death threat, whereas high scores on the MFODS indicate less death fear. All coefficients are significant at $p < .05$ or better, except as noted.

reported by DePaola et al. (1992). In addition, because a confirmatory factor analysis of the TI has recently been reported (Moore & Neimeyer, 1991), we explored the correlations of the MFODS subscales with both the Global Threat factor of the TI, representing the total score on the instrument, and its three component factors, Threat to Well-Being, Uncertainty, and Fatalism. The results of this analysis (based on the Manhattan distance scoring of the TI described by Moore and Neimeyer, 1991) appear in Table 5-3.

In general, a low but significant pattern of correlations emerged between the MFODS and the TI, suggesting that individuals who scored as more fearful of the various aspects of death and dying also experienced greater degrees of death threat. The most consistent correlations occurred between the TI and F1, F4, F5, and F8 of the MFODS. In contrast, F6 and F7 of the MFODS were substantially unrelated to scores on the TI. Curiously, F3 was significantly but inversely correlated with death concern as measured by the TI. Thus, this analysis of the convergence between the two independent scales provides some validational support for five of the MFODS factors, four of which had also shown significant correlations with the TI in the DePaola et al. study (Chapter 11 this volume). The pattern of correlations also suggests that death threat, as defined in the personal construct literature (Epting & Neimeyer, 1984), covaries with more abstract fears about dying (e.g., premature death, fear of the unknown, and fear for significant others), but not with a morbid preoccupation with bodily disintegration or being buried alive.

As a final reflection of convergent validity, we also compared scores on the MFODS with responses to a single self-report item: ''How much does the idea

Table 5-4   Sex Differences in Fear of Death by Subscale of the Multidimensional Fear of Death Scale

Subscale	Men (n = 483)		Women (n = 331)		F(1, 812)	p
	M	SD	M	SD		
F1: Fear of the Dying Process	16.70	5.74	14.87	5.96	21.67	.0001
F2: Fear of the Dead	22.62	4.48	19.71	5.02	84.28	.0001
F3: Fear of Being Destroyed	15.57	4.36	13.77	4.74	35.33	.0001
F4: Fear for Significant Others	16.16	4.85	13.62	4.95	59.37	.0001
F5: Fear of the Unknown	12.57	4.53	14.93	4.11	64.29	.0001
F6: Fear of Conscious Death	23.84	4.84	23.03	5.26	5.81	.02
F7: Fear for Body after Death	26.17	4.19	24.61	4.67	27.94	.0001
F8: Fear of Premature Death	12.87	4.14	12.34	4.22	3.58	ns
General (total)	141.70	21.24	132.66	21.84	34.79	.0001

Note: Higher scores indicate lower fear of death.

of your death bother you?'' Responses ranged from ''I am very strongly bothered by the idea'' to ''I am never bothered by the idea,'' with ratings being performed on a 6-point Likert scale. The results of this analysis also appear in Table 5-3. Correlations between this item and the MFODS subscales were typically higher than those between the MFODS and TI, which may reflect the explicit design of the MFODS and death concern item as measures of conscious death concern (cf. Hoelter, 1979a). In contrast, evidence suggests that the TI is responsive to preconscious death concerns as well (Epting, Rainey, & Weiss, 1979), a factor that may attenuate its correlation with measures that require conscious self-awareness of death anxiety.

Finally, we explored the relationship between the MFODS and the basic demographic background of subjects, including sex and age. A review of the general literature on death anxiety demonstrates that women fairly consistently report greater fear of death than men (Neimeyer, 1988), a finding that seems to persist even when sex differences in self-disclosure and social desirability are controlled (Dattel & Neimeyer, 1990). As Table 5-4 indicates, women in the present sample reported greater fear of death than men on the general MFODS factor, as well as on six of the eight subscales. In some cases (e.g., F6), the magnitude of these sex differences was slight, but in others (e.g., F2 and F4) it was substantial. Thus, research using the MFODS with a large and diverse adult sample replicates the general finding of women's elevated death concern, adding detail to the aspects of death that women find more disturbing. Interestingly, however, one strong sex difference showed the opposite trend: Women showed significantly less apprehension about what lies after death than men (F5). Because this factor was influenced by religious conviction about the nature of an afterlife, it suggests that further study of the relationship between religiosity and death concern is warranted.

Finally, scores on the MFODS and its component factors were correlated with age of subjects, in view of the broad range of ages in the present sample. As is true in the general literature on death anxiety (Neimeyer, 1988), more mature respondents indicated less fear of death in general ($r = .22, p < .001$), of the dying process ($.14, p < .001$), of the dead ($.19, p < .001$), of personal destruction ($.13, p < .001$), and of bodily disfigurement after death ($.09, p < .05$). Older respondents were even less likely to report fears about premature death ($.29, p < .001$) or concerns for significant others ($.33, p < .001$). However, a reverse trend occurred for MFODS F5, with older subjects expressing more, rather than less, fear of the unknown ($-.22, p < .001$). No age differences were detected in a final MFODS subscale concerned with fear of conscious death ($r = .03$, n.s.).

In summary, new data collected on two large samples provide the first evidence of the test–retest reliability of the MFODS and reinforce its construct validity by demonstrating its ability to discriminate relevant groups and converge with alternative measures of death concern. Moreover, general trends in the literature associating death anxiety with subject sex and age can be replicated and extended using the MFODS. Collectively, these findings and those of previous investigators clarify the psychometric properties of the MFODS as a measure of fear of death, permitting more confident interpretation of substantive research using the instrument. We conclude this chapter by summarizing and evaluating this research.

RESEARCH APPLICATIONS

Although the majority of research to date using the MFODS has been methodological rather than substantive, a handful of applied studies have appeared. We present a survey of the results of these investigations, attempting to provide recommendations for future research where possible.

Relationship Between Religiosity and Fear of Death

One of the most confusing and controversial topics in the literature of death attitudes is the relationship between religiosity and fear of death (Pollak, 1979). The conflicting results regarding the impact of religious belief on death anxiety stem from many factors, among them the reliance on simplistic and potentially invalid measurements of religiosity and the overuse of unidimensional, omnibus measures of death concern (Neimeyer, 1988). Research using the MFODS, although preliminary, has begun to make a healthy contribution to this literature by addressing both shortcomings.

Hoelter (1979a) initiated interest in the religious correlates of the MFODS by analyzing the scale's relationship to an established measure of religious orthodoxy. He found that more orthodox college students (presumably Christians) showed substantially less fear of the unknown ($r = -.64$ with MFODS F5) but actually tended to show slightly higher levels of fear for significant others, fear of conscious death, fear of being destroyed, and fear for their bodies after death. Thus, it may be that whereas orthodoxy may inoculate believers against some anxieties surrounding death, it may sensitize them to others. Generalization of this finding to a broader population should be attempted only cautiously, however, until studies of more heterogeneous adult samples are completed.

Long's (1985–86) research on Saudi Arabians temporarily residing in the United States provided an interesting lesson in cultural relativism. Translating the MFODS into Arabic, he discovered that the factor structure for the instrument departed substantially from that reported for Western respondents and suggested that fear of the unknown, fear of being destroyed, and fear of being conscious during burial may not be salient for Islamic fundamentalists. Further analyses of these data by Long and Elghanemi (1987) indicated that nearly all Saudi respondents responded extremely to the religiosity measures used in the study, indicating little variation in strength of religious conviction or performance of relevant behaviors (e.g., mosque attendance). The resulting range restriction may well have accounted for the relatively small and generally nonsignificant correlations between religiosity and fear of death as measured by the MFODS. Only two negative relationships were evident: Fear of premature death was lower for individuals who frequently attended mosque ($-.16$), and fear for significant others was lower for individuals who perceived themselves as more devout ($-.28$). Perhaps the most intriguing findings from a Western perspective were adventitious. Several respondents either refused to participate in the study or took offense at the questionnaires for "challenging their religious devotion." One even refused to touch the questionnaires because they contained holy words, and he had unclean hands. This underscores the need for cultural sensitivity if research on the relationship between religion and death attitudes is to move beyond the American college environment.

Relationship Between Fertility and Death Anxiety

Some theorists have conjectured that one impetus for human beings to reproduce is the fear of death, insofar as this confers on individuals a kind of symbolic immortality through their children (Kastenbaum, 1974). A few authors have attempted to test this proposition empirically by examining the relationship between attitudes toward fertility and death concerns as measured by the MFODS.

Hoelter, Whitlock, and Epley (1979) administered the MFODS and a fertility attitude scale to a large undergraduate sample. Only 12% of their respondents agreed with the belief that having children helped one face death, whereas 44%

disagreed with this statement. However, subjects who were more fearful of death were more likely to endorse this statement, as indicated by the low but positive correlations between endorsement of this opinion statement and several MFODS subscales. Different aspects of the fear of death seemed related to fertility beliefs for male and female respondents: Men who expected to have more children reported more fear of the unknown, and women with a similar expectation acknowledged greater fear of the death of significant others. Overall, a multiple correlation indicated that fear of death related moderately to expected number of children for the whole sample.

Subsequent research by Dixon and Kinlaw (1981–82) called this conclusion into question. Examining the death anxieties and fertility beliefs of a large group of churchgoers and students in North Carolina, they first partialed out the effects of age and education and then analyzed the resulting correlations between the two sets of measures. Contrary to the results of Hoelter et al. (1979), the total score on the MFODS and seven of the nine subscales showed inverse relationships with actual and desired fertility. Thus, their data provided a strong argument against the hypothesis that fear of death and the urge to have offspring are positively related, at least within the general population.

Influence of Attitude Toward Death on Acceptability of Suicide

Hoelter (1979b) conducted a preliminary study of the influence of attitude toward death on belief in the acceptability of suicide. On the basis of a "cognitive dissonance theory of suicide," he reasoned that social and personal factors could impel an individual to consider suicide, if he or she saw such a course of action as the least drastic of the effective measures available to terminate the stress. However, various countervailing factors could militate against the acceptability of suicide, including fear of death. Administering the MFODS to a group of approximately 200 students, he discovered that several factors, including fears of the dead, conscious death, and bodily destruction, showed slight but negative relationships with the acceptability of suicide. A multiple correlation of .41 between the various subscales and endorsement of suicide as a viable alternative suggests that death anxieties may be one factor to consider in diagnosing the lethality of a self-destructive individual in clinical contexts.

Attitudes Toward Aging

DePaola et al. (Chapter 11 this volume) recently examined the role of death anxiety in mediating the attitudes of nursing home staff and controls working in other occupations toward aging and the elderly. Although nursing staff displayed less fear of the dead and fewer concerns for death of significant others than did controls, death-anxious respondents in both groups reported more anxiety about their personal aging than did those who were less fearful of death. Perhaps more disturbingly, subjects who had higher levels of death fear as measured by the MFODS also tended to devalue elderly people, a factor that could be detrimental to caregiving in a nursing home setting.

CONCLUSIONS

As research on death attitudes has developed, so has the quality of the methods used to study them. Early use of idiosyncratic, face-valid, and unidimensional assessments of fear of death has gradually yielded to reliance on standardized, psychometrically sound, and more comprehensive measures of death attitudes. Viewed in this context, the MFODS represents an important addition to the thanatologist's methodological resources. Data provided by both previous investigators and our own research indicate that the MFODS is an internally consistent, reliable, valid, and multifaceted measure of fear of death, one that could clarify some of the ambiguity in the death concern literature attributable to overuse of inferior measures.

Although the research reviewed in this chapter is encouraging, further methodological work on the MFODS is in order. It is possible that the internal consistency of some subscales could be improved by pruning less relevant items, and a final factor structure could be established more definitively and convincingly through the use of state-of-the-art confirmatory and hierarchical factor-analytic procedures. The stability of the scale over longer periods of time also should be documented, and its promising evidence of construct validity should be extended in studies of its convergence with other instruments and its ability to corroborate theoretically sound predictions. Equally important, the MFODS should be adopted in a broader range of research applications, beyond the early forays into the areas of religiosity, fertility, and suicide acceptability pioneered by Hoelter (1979b; Hoelter et al., 1979). If incorporated into methodologically sound and clinically useful research efforts, the MFODS could help shed light on one of the more obscure but fascinating areas of human psychology: our complex and multifaceted reactions to death.

REFERENCES

Collett, L. J., & Lester, D. (1969). The fear of death and the fear of dying. *Journal of Psychology, 72*, 179–181.

Dattel, A. R., & Neimeyer, R. A. (1990). Sex differences in death anxiety: Testing the emotional expressiveness hypothesis. *Death Studies, 14*, 45–55.

Dixon, R. D., & Kinlaw, B. J. R. (1981–82). Fear of death and fertility: New evidence. *Omega, 12*, 151–164.

Epting, F. R., & Neimeyer, R. A. (1984). *Personal meanings of death*. Washington, D.C.: Hemisphere.

Epting, F. R., Rainey, L. C., & Weiss, M. J. (1979). Constructions of death and levels of death fear. *Death Education, 3*, 21–30.

Guadagnoli, E., & Velicer, W. F. (1988). Relation of sample size to the stability of component patterns. *Psychological Bulletin, 103*, 265–275.

Hoelter, J. W. (1979a). Multidimensional treatment of fear of death. *Journal of Consulting and Clinical Psychology, 47*, 996–999.

Hoelter, J. W. (1979b). Religiosity, fear of death, and suicide acceptability. *Suicide and Life-Threatening Behavior, 9*, 163–172.

Hoelter, J. W., Whitlock, J. L., & Epley, R. J. (1979). Fertility attitudes and the fear of death. *Psychological Reports, 45*, 795–800.

Holcomb, L. E., Neimeyer, R. A., & Moore, M. K. (1993). Personal meanings of death: A content analysis of free-response narratives. *Death Studies, 17*, 299–318.

Joreskog, K. G., & Sorbom, D. (1986). *LISREL: Analysis of linear structural relationships by the method of maximum likelihood.* Mooresville, IN: Scientific Software.

Kastenbaum, R. (1974). Fertility and fear of death. *Journal of Social Issues, 30*, 63–78.

Kastenbaum, R., & Costa, P. T. (1977). Psychological perspectives on death. *Annual Review of Psychology, 28*, 225–249.

Lester, D. (1967). Experimental and correlational studies of the fear of death. *Psychological Bulletin, 67*, 27–36.

Levin, R. (1990). A reexamination of the dimensionality of death anxiety. *Omega, 20*, 341–349.

Long, D. D. (1985–86). A cross-cultural examination of fears of death among Saudi Arabians. *Omega, 16*, 43–50.

Long, D. D., & Elghanemi, S. (1987). Religious correlates of fear of death among Saudi Arabians. *Death Studies, 11*, 89–97.

Moore, M. K., & Neimeyer, R. A. (1991). A confirmatory factor analysis of the Threat Index. *Journal of Personality and Social Psychology, 60*, 122–129.

Neimeyer, R. A. (1988). Death anxiety. In H. Wass, R. Berardo, & R. A. Neimeyer (Eds.), *Dying: Facing the facts* (2nd ed., pp. 97–136). Washington, DC: Hemisphere.

Pollak, J. M. (1979). Correlates of death anxiety: A review of empirical studies. *Omega, 10*, 97–121.

Simpson, M. A. (1980). Studying death: Problems of methodology. *Death Education, 4*, 139–148.

Walkey, F. H. (1982). The Multidimensional Fear of Death Scale: An independent analysis. *Journal of Consulting and Clinical Psychology, 50*, 466–467.

APPENDIX 5-1: Multidimensional Fear of Death Scale

INSTRUCTIONS: Listed below are death-related events and circumstances that some people find to be fear-evoking. Indicate the extent to which you agree or disagree with each statement by circling one number for each item. Do not skip any items if you can avoid it.

1 = Strongly agree
2 = Mildly agree
3 = Neither agree nor disagree
4 = Mildly disagree
5 = Strongly disagree

1	2	3	4	5	1. I am afraid of dying very slowly.
1	2	3	4	5	2. I dread visiting a funeral home.
1	2	3	4	5	3. I would like to donate my body to science.
1	2	3	4	5	4. I have a fear of people in my family dying.
1	2	3	4	5	5. I am afraid that there is no afterlife.
1	2	3	4	5	6. There are probably many people pronounced dead that are really still alive.
1	2	3	4	5	7. I am afraid of my body being disfigured when I die.
1	2	3	4	5	8. I have a fear of not accomplishing my goals in life before dying.
1	2	3	4	5	9. I am afraid of meeting my creator.
1	2	3	4	5	10. I am afraid of being buried alive.
1	2	3	4	5	11. I dread the thought of my body being embalmed some day.
1	2	3	4	5	12. I am afraid I will not live long enough to enjoy my retirement.
1	2	3	4	5	13. I am afraid of dying in a fire.
1	2	3	4	5	14. Touching a corpse would not bother me.
1	2	3	4	5	15. I do not want medical students using my body for practice after I die.
1	2	3	4	5	16. If the people I am very close to were to die suddenly, I would suffer for a long time.
1	2	3	4	5	17. If I were to die tomorrow, my family would be upset for a long time.
1	2	3	4	5	18. I am afraid that death is the end of one's existence.
1	2	3	4	5	19. People should have autopsies to ensure that they are dead.
1	2	3	4	5	20. The thought of my body being found after I die scares me.
1	2	3	4	5	21. I am afraid I will not have time to experience everything I want to.
1	2	3	4	5	22. I am afraid of experiencing a great deal of pain when I die.
1	2	3	4	5	23. Discovering a dead body would be a horrifying experience.
1	2	3	4	5	24. I do not like the thought of being cremated.
1	2	3	4	5	25. Since everyone dies, I won't be too upset when my friends die.
1	2	3	4	5	26. I would be afraid to walk through a graveyard, alone, at night.
1	2	3	4	5	27. I am afraid of dying of cancer.

1	2	3	4	5	28.	It doesn't matter whether I am buried in a wooden box or a steel vault.
1	2	3	4	5	29.	It scares me to think I may be conscious while lying in a morgue.
1	2	3	4	5	30.	I am afraid that there may not be a Supreme Being.
1	2	3	4	5	31.	I have a fear of suffocating (including drowning).
1	2	3	4	5	32.	It would bother me to remove a dead animal from the road.
1	2	3	4	5	33.	I do not want to donate my eyes after I die.
1	2	3	4	5	34.	I sometimes get upset when acquaintances die.
1	2	3	4	5	35.	The thought of being locked in a coffin after I die scares me.
1	2	3	4	5	36.	No one can say, for sure, what will happen after death.
1	2	3	4	5	37.	If I die, my friends would be upset for a long time.
1	2	3	4	5	38.	I hope more than one doctor examines me before I am pronounced dead.
1	2	3	4	5	39.	I am afraid of things which have died.
1	2	3	4	5	40.	The thought of my body decaying after I die scares me.
1	2	3	4	5	41.	I am afraid I may never see my children grow up.
1	2	3	4	5	42.	I have a fear of dying violently.

Scoring Key for the Multidimensional Fear of Death Scale

To obtain subscale scores for the following factors, simply sum the respondent's ratings on the relevant items. Lower scores on each subscale reflect higher fears of death. Note that items followed by an asterisk are reverse-scored to reduce response bias, such that responses should be recoded prior to analysis ($1 = 5$, $2 = 4$, $4 = 2$, and $5 = 1$). Also, in order to mitigate the formation of response sets, items from the various scales have been interspersed, so that item numbers do not correspond to those listed in Hoelter's (1979a) or Walkey's (1982) reports.

F1: Fear of the Dying Process: 1, 13, 22, 27, 31, 42
F2: Fear of the Dead: 2, 14*, 23, 26, 32, 39
F3: Fear of Being Destroyed: 3*, 15, 24, 33
F4: Fear for Significant Others: 4, 16, 17, 25*, 34, 37
F5: Fear of the Unknown: 5, 9*, 18, 30, 36
F6: Fear of Conscious Death: 6, 10, 19, 29, 38
F7: Fear for the Body after Death: 7, 11, 20, 28*, 35, 40
F8: Fear of Premature Death: 8, 12, 21, 41

Chapter 6

Death Attitude Profile–Revised: A Multidimensional Measure of Attitudes Toward Death

Paul T. P. Wong
Gary T. Reker
Gina Gesser

In the mid-1960s, when Templer began research on the concept of death anxiety, death was a taboo topic with behavioral scientists and mental health professionals (Templer, 1970). Much has changed since. Kübler-Ross's (1969) book on death and dying played a pivotal role in the growing popularity of death awareness. According to Feifel (1990), the events of World War II and the impact of humanistic/existential psychology have helped thrust death research to the forefront.

The study of death is now a fertile ground for research. Various instruments have been developed to assess death attitudes (e.g., Collett & Lester, 1969; Gesser, Wong, & Reker, 1987–88; Hooper & Spilka, 1970; Marshall, 1981; Neimeyer, Dingemans, & Epting, 1977). In terms of applications, the emphasis has been on death education for health and hospice professionals (Amenta, 1984; Kalish, 1976; Wass, Corr, Pacholski, & Forfar, 1985).

Death anxiety has been by far the dominant theme in empirical studies on death. The inadequacy of research on other types of death attitudes becomes

Gina Gesser died unexpectedly, shortly after collecting the data for this chapter. This chapter is dedicated to her in memory of her contributions to research on death attitudes.

conspicuous when one contrasts this research with the number of instruments and studies focused on death anxiety (Marshall, 1981). Moreover, empirical studies have outstripped theoretical developments in death research. Very few studies have been theoretically motivated. There has been a lack of overarching theory, although an approach based on Kelly's (1955) personal construct theory and focusing on the cognitive structure of death anxiety holds promise (Epting & Neimeyer, 1984; Neimeyer, 1988).

We address these issues in death attitude research in this chapter. First, we develop an existential view of death attitudes and argue that both death acceptance and death fear are related to the pursuit of personal meaning. Second, we examine the different ways in which individuals come to terms with their mortality, and we propose a three-component model of death acceptance. Third, we provide the rationale for developing the Death Attitude Profile–Revised (DAP–R), a multidimensional measure of death acceptance and avoidance as well as fear of death (see Appendix 6-1). Fourth, we review the literature on the relationships between death attitudes and well-being and present predictions regarding correlations between psychological well-being and the various dimensions of the DAP–R. Finally, we present the results of a test of our predictions and data on the psychometric properties of the DAP–R.

AN EXISTENTIAL VIEW OF DEATH ATTITUDES

Fear of Death

The terms *fear of death* and *death anxiety* are used interchangeably in the literature, but it may be helpful to regard fear of death as specific and conscious and death anxiety as more generalized and perhaps inaccessible to awareness. One needs to be cautious in accepting at face value the degree of fear of death verbalized at the conscious level (Feifel & Branscomb, 1973).

It is commonly believed that fear of death is universal and that its absence may reflect denial of death (Bakan, 1971; Becker, 1973; Marshall, 1980). However, fear of death is not a unitary construct (Collett & Lester, 1969; Littlefield & Fleming, 1984), and issues related to death and dying are complex (Kastenbaum & Costa, 1977; Wass, 1979).

Death is feared for different reasons. The loss of self, the unknown beyond death, pain and suffering, lost opportunity for atonement and salvation, and the welfare of surviving family members are just some of the sources of fear of death (Feifel, 1977; Feifel & Nagy, 1981; Fry, 1990). Furthermore, in growing up we are imbued with the importance of achievement and self-worth; in growing old, we realize our impotence in the face of death, which threatens to terminate all that we hold dear in life (Wass, Berardo, & Neimeyer, 1988). Another pervasive source of fear of death is not so much the awareness of our finitude as our failure to lead meaningful lives (Butler, 1975; Erikson, 1963).

Relationship Between Fear of Death and Personal Meaning

Our research on death attitudes is derived from an existential perspective, which posits that individuals are motivated to pursue personal meaning (Frankl, 1965; Reker, Peacock, & Wong, 1987; Reker & Wong, 1988; Wong, 1989). A corollary from this proposition is that fear of death stems from the failure to find personal meaning for one's life and death.

This existential emphasis is consistent with Erikson's (1963) view that individuals in their last stage of developement have to come to terms with death by resolving the crisis of integrity versus despair. Integrity is a state of mind—the conviction that life has been worthwhile and meaningful and the reconciliation of the discrepancy between reality and the ideal. Individuals who are able to achieve integrity can face death without fear. Individuals who feel they have wasted their life and it is too late to start life anew are likely to experience despair and fear death. Therefore, whether one fears or accepts death depends to a large extent on whether one has learned to accept one's only life cycle.

A similar view was advocated by Butler (1963, 1975). He proposed that people are more afraid of a meaningless existence than of death. Individuals who see their lives as fulfilling and meaningful should show less death anxiety and more death acceptance (Lewis & Butler, 1974).

Studies on the relationship between life review and death attitudes tend to support Butler's view. For example, Georgemiller and Maloney (1984) reported that life review participants showed a decrease in death denial compared with the alternative-activity control group. Flint, Gayton, and Ozmon (1983) found a significant correlation between subjective satisfaction with one's past life and death acceptance. More recently, Wong and Watt (1991) reported that seniors who revealed integrity in their reminiscence were more likely to be healthier and happier than those who did not. A number of investigators have also found a relationship between death anxiety and lack of meaning in life. Durlak (1972) reported that subjects who had purpose and meaning in their lives tended also to have less fear of death and more positive and accepting attitudes toward death. Quinn & Reznikoff (1985) found that subjects who lacked a sense of purpose and direction in their lives reported high levels of death anxiety. In sum, there is sufficient evidence supporting the existential view that whether one fears or accepts death depends on whether one has found meaning in life and achieved integrity.

It should now be clear to the reader that death anxiety and death acceptance are intimately related. Death anxiety cannot be fully understood without an understanding of death acceptance. We agree with Ray and Najman (1974) that death acceptance is not the categorical opposite of death fear. It is more likely that fear and acceptance coexist in an uneasy truce (Feifel, 1990). Even individuals who cognitively accept the inevitability and "goodness" of their mortality may still not be completely free from an uneasiness about personal death and its aftermath. Similarly, no matter how dreadful death appears, all individuals have to learn to accept their mortality in some fashion. In the following section, we examine the various ways of preparing oneself psychologically before the final exit.

A CONCEPTUAL ANALYSIS OF DEATH ACCEPTANCE

Death Acceptance Defined

Kübler-Ross (1969) considered acceptance to be the last stage of dying. For her, it was resignation to the inevitability of death after denial, anger, bargaining, and depression. Her conception of acceptance was primarily based on observation of the dying processes of terminally ill patients. In this chapter, we are concerned with the psychological preparations of normal, functioning individuals for the prospect of personal demise. Therefore, death acceptance may be broadly defined as being psychologically prepared for the final exit. It is likely that those who have already come to terms with death prior to the diagnosis of terminal illness may bypass the stages of dying as described by Kübler-Ross.

Our insights on death acceptance came from our research on successful aging. Having worked with the elderly for many years, we could not help but be impressed by their willingness to talk about death and by their apparent lack of death anxiety. This observation corroborates the general finding that the majority of older adults are not afraid of death and like to talk about it (Kastenbaum & Aisenberg, 1972; Wass et al., 1988). In some cases, we even detected an eager anticipation to be finally freed from the bondage and burden of a frail body. Therefore, we became convinced that low death anxiety does not necessarily reflect denial mechanisms and that acceptance seems to be the prominent death attitude among the elderly.

Klug and Sinha (1987) regarded death acceptance as "being relatively at ease with one's awareness of personal mortality" (p. 229). They defined death acceptance as "the deliberate, intellectual acknowledgment of the prospect of one's own death and the positive emotional assimilation of the consequences" (p. 230). Thus, death acceptance consists of two components: cognitive awareness of one's own finitude and a positive (or at least neutral) emotional reaction to this cognizance.

Measurements of Death Acceptance

Although death acceptance has received increasing attention, issues regarding conceptualization and measurements have not been adequately addressed. Kurlychek (1976) made a preliminary proposal to measure death acceptance. Ray and Najman (1974) developed the seven-item Death Acceptance Scale, which consists of heterogenous items, including denial ("Death is not something terrible"), death as an escape ("Death is merely relief from pain"), and positive attitudes ("Death is a friend"). This may account for the scale's low alpha coefficient (.58).

As mentioned earlier, Klug and Sinha (1987) conceptualized death acceptance as consisting of two components: confrontation of death and integration of death. Confrontation, the cognitive component, is facing up to one's own death; it suggests cognizance of mortality as a fact of life (Weisman, 1974). Integration is the positive affective reaction to confrontation. To measure these two components, Klug and Sinha developed the 16-item Death Acceptance Scale. Unfortunately, the items have questionable face validity. Most of the Confrontation items concern avoidance, such as "I avoid discussion of death when the occasion presents itself" and "If possible, I avoid friends who are grieving over the loss of someone." It is debatable whether negation of avoidance means positive acceptance. There is only one item stated in the positive—"I am willing to discuss death with a dying friend"—but this item is about another person's death, rather than personal death. Still another Confrontation item—"After discussing the subject of death, I feel depressed"—measures affective reaction rather than cognition.

The Integration items are equally problematic. Most measure the consequence of rather than affective reactions to death acceptance. Statements such as "I enjoy life more as a result of facing the fact of death," "Accepting death helps me to be more responsible for my life," and "My life has more meaning because I accept the fact of my own death" do not measure positive affective reactions per se, but rather the positive impact of death acceptance on one's life.

Flint et al.'s (1983) death acceptance measure was primarily based on the Death Concern Scale developed by Klug and Boss (1977). The psychometric properties of Flint et al.'s acceptance scale have not been reported. Flint et al. found a positive relationship between life satisfaction and death acceptance when they administered it to an elderly sample.

Three-Component Model of Death Acceptance

On the basis of our conceptual analysis of death attitudes, we have identified three distinct types of death acceptance: neutral, approach, and escape acceptance.

Neutral Acceptance   Death is an integral part of life. To be alive is to live with death and dying (Armstrong, 1987; Kübler-Ross, 1981; Saunders & Baines,

1983; Morison, 1971). One neither fears death nor welcomes it; one simply accepts it as one of the unchangeable facts of life and tries to make the best of a finite life. Therefore, it implies an ambivalent or indifferent attitude, similar to that measured by the Indifference Toward Death subscale of Hooper and Spilka's (1970) Death Perspective Scale (DPS).

A basic tenet of humanistic/existential psychology is that self-actualization is possible only when the individual has come to terms with the fact of personal mortality (Bugental, 1965; Feifel, 1990; Maslow, 1968; May, Angel, & Ellenberger, 1958). Therefore, an actualized adult is not threatened by personal death. Frankl (1965) also believed that finding a meaning in life removes an individual's fear of death and increases his or her well-being. Alexander and Adlerstein (1959) reported that nonreligious subjects who see death as the natural end of life may plunge themselves into the rewards of living. Bregman (1989) remarked that if death is natural, as Kübler-Ross insisted that it is, then acceptance of death is a moral good, and denial is a violation of this good. This ethical naturalism is independent of particular beliefs in the afterlife.

Approach Acceptance   Approach acceptance implies belief in a happy afterlife (Dixon & Kinlaw, 1983). It is similar to what is tapped by the Death as an Afterlife of Reward subscale of the DPS. It has been well documented that belief in an afterlife is related to religious beliefs and practices. Jeffers, Nichols, and Eisdorfer (1961) found that individuals with strong religious commitments were more likely to believe in an afterlife and more likely to show less fear of death. Berman (1974) observed that belief in an afterlife was closely tied to degree of religious involvement. Aday (1984) found that belief in an afterlife was primarily a function of religion and not a direct correlate of fear of death. In a discriminant analysis of belief in heaven and an afterlife, Hertel (1980) found that religious affiliation was the only significant predictor of this belief. Peterson and Greil (1990) found that belief in an afterlife was significantly related to various measures of religiosity. They also found that death experience positively correlated with religiosity, suggesting that experiences with death incline people toward greater religious involvement. Klenow and Bolin (1989) found that religion and church attendance were the only significant discriminating variables of belief in an afterlife. The results also indicated that the majority of adults in the United States believe in a life after death.

In view of the evidence that belief in afterlife is rooted in religiosity, it seems logical to deduce that religious individuals should experience less death anxiety. However, the relationship between religious beliefs and fear of death remains inconclusive. Although most researchers have reported a negative relationship between the two (e.g., Feifel & Nagy, 1981; Gibbs & Achterbery-Lawlis, 1978; Hooper & Spilka, 1970; Jeffers et al., 1961; Martin & Wrightsman, 1965; Stewart, 1975; Templer, 1972), some researchers have found no relationship (Feifel, 1974; Kalish, 1963; Templer & Dodson, 1970), and others have even found a positive relationship (Templer & Ruff, 1975; Young & Daniels, 1981).

It has also been noted that the relationships found between belief in an afterlife and death anxiety have tended to be small or nonsignificant, depending on the measure of death anxiety used (Berman & Hays, 1975). The disparity among the studies may be due to different conceptualizations and measures of religiosity and death anxiety (Schultz, 1978).

There is also some evidence that fear of death is lowest in people who have either strong faith or no faith (e.g., McMordie, 1981; Smith, Nehemkis, & Charter, 1983–84; Williams & Cole, 1968). It appears that people who are firm believers in either afterlife or nonexistence beyond death have less fear than those who are uncertain. This raises the possibility that firm believers, in contrast to those who are uncertain, may have acquired a sense of symbolic immortality (the ability to symbolize death and life continuity) that helps them cope with the fear of death (Drolet, 1990). Drolet (1990) reported a negative relationship between death anxiety and purpose in life and a positive relationship between purpose in life and a sense of symbolic immortality. Steinitz (1980) found that belief in an afterlife was associated with optimism and meaningfulness. Therefore, considering all the findings on religiosity and belief in afterlife, it appears that firm believers tend to have less death anxiety and to enjoy a higher level of personal meaning and well-being.

Escape Acceptance   When life is full of pain and misery, death may be a welcome alternative. Vernon (1972) suggested that the fear of living under certain conditions may be stronger than the fear of death. When people are overwhelmed by suffering and pain, and there is little likelihood of relief, death seems to offer the only escape. Therefore, in escape acceptance the positive attitude toward death is based not on the inherent "goodness" of death, but on the "badness" of living. Typically, people exhibit escape acceptance because they can no longer effectively cope with the pain and problems of existence.

In sum, there are three different routes through which individuals come to terms with personal death. Although various investigators have alluded to these three types of death acceptance, these concepts had never been clearly defined and measured until the Death Attitude Profile was developed.

RATIONALE FOR THE DEATH ATTITUDE PROFILE-REVISED

The DAP–R is a revision of the DAP, a multidimensional measure of attitudes toward death developed by Gesser et al. (1987–88). The DAP consisted of four factorially derived dimensions: (a) Fear of Death/Dying (negative thoughts and feelings about the state of death and process of dying), (b) Approach Acceptance (the view of death as a gateway to a happy afterlife), (c) Escape Acceptance (the view of death as escape from a painful existence), and (d) Neutral Acceptance (the view of death as a reality that is neither feared nor welcomed).

In our research on the DAP with college students and middle-aged adults, we discovered that some of them would rather avoid the topic of death. Although a negative attitude is implied by both death fear and death avoidance, a distinction needs to be made between the two. In death fear, a person confronts death and the feelings of fear it evokes. In death avoidance, a person avoids thinking or talking about death in order to reduce death anxiety. Thus, death avoidance is a defense mechanism that keeps death away from one's consciousness. In other words, two persons may both have a negative attitude toward death, but one shows a high degree of fear of death, whereas the other shows a high level of avoidance of death. This consideration led to the inclusion of the seven-item Death Avoidance subscale in the DAP–R.

Because we are interested primarily in attitudes toward death, we eliminated items related to dying in the Fear of Death/Dying dimension of the DAP, added new fear of death items, and shortened the name of this dimension to Fear of Death. Additional items were also added to the three acceptance subscales. As a result, the original 21-item DAP was expanded to 36 items.

To determine empirically the face validity of the five dimensions in the DAP–R, we asked 10 young, 10 middle-aged, and 10 elderly subjects to place each item into what they believed was the most conceptually appropriate category. All 36 items reached our criterion of 70% agreement in classification. In fact, most of the items exceeded the 90% agreement level.

Although the DAP is adequate psychometrically, the DAP–R is more comprehensive and is conceptually purer. The data we have collected thus far convince us that the DAP–R is indeed superior to the original DAP (some of these data are presented later). A clear advantage of the DAP–R is that it represents a broad spectrum of death attitudes, ranging from avoidance to neutral acceptance to approach acceptance. We are pleased that some nursing schools have already used the DAP–R to educate students about the varieties of death attitudes and their implications for well-being.

CORRELATES OF DEATH ATTITUDES

We have shown that how individuals view life affects their attitudes toward death. The converse is also true: How people view death affects how they conduct their lives. Feifel (1959) wrote, "We are mistaken to consider death as a purely biological event. The attitudes concerning it and its meaning for the individual can serve as an important organizing principle in determining how he conducts himself in life" (p. 128). Basically, there are two different views about death— either it is the end of one's identity or it is a doorway to another life (Epting & Neimeyer, 1984). Individuals who view death as the end of existence are likely to live for the here and now. Persons who view death as a passage to another life must live with the next life in mind. Kalish (1981) also proposed that these different conceptions about death affect our present lives: "Many individuals derive both comfort and strength from a deeply held belief that some form of personal self-aware existence will follow death. Others appear to find equivalent satisfaction from believing death leads to total extinction" (p. 231).

We made some predictions about the relationships between the five different death attitudes measured by the DAP–R and psychological well-being and tested them in the present study. We hypothesized that fear of death and death avoidance would be negatively related to psychological well-being and positively related to depression, whereas neutral acceptance and approach acceptance would be positively related to psychological well-being and negatively related to depression.

Because neutral acceptance reflects a mature outlook on life and death and may motivate individuals to lead a full life, we expected it to be positively related to perceived physical well-being. Escape acceptance was predicted to correlate negatively with perceived physical and psychological well-being, because it is an attempt to escape from physical and psychological pain.

Differential predictions were also made for the five dimensions of the DAP–R. We predicted that Fear of Death would be positively related to Templer's (1970) Death Anxiety Scale (DAS) but negatively related to semantic differential (SD) ratings of life and death. Avoidance of thinking of death reflects a negative attitude toward death, but individuals may maintain a positive attitude toward life by not thinking about death. Therefore, we predicted that Death Avoidance would be unrelated to SD ratings of life but negatively related to SD ratings of death. Neutral Acceptance was expected to be positively related to Hooper and Spilka's (1970) Indifference Toward Death subscale. Approach Acceptance was predicted to relate positively to Hooper and Spilka's Death as an Afterlife of Reward subscale and to SD ratings of life and death. Because Escape Acceptance reflects a negative view toward life and a positive view toward death, it was predicted to relate negatively to the DAS and to SD ratings of life but positively to SD ratings of death. This complex pattern of predictions permitted us to determine the convergent and discriminant validity of the DAP–R.

To test our predictions, we administered Reker and Wong's (1984) Perceived Well-Being Scale (PWB), which measures both perceived physical and psychological well-being, and Zung's (1965) Depression Scale to subjects. They were also given SD ratings designed to measure attitudes toward life and death; a high score always reflects a positive attitude. In addition, a subset of the subjects completed the DAS as well as Hooper and Spilka's (1970) Death as an Afterlife of Reward and Indifference Toward Death subscales. Another subset of the subjects were readministered the DAP–R in order to determine its temporal stability.

In addition to investigating the psychological correlates of the DAP–R, we were interested in examining age and gender differences in death attitudes. By administering the DAP–R to young, middle-aged, and older adults, we were able to investigate how different death attitudes were related to these demographical variables.

Age Differences

Life span psychologists (Kastenbaum, 1979; Levinson, 1977; Neugarten, 1968) have postulated that different age groups vary in their attitudes toward death, partly because of their differential proximity and exposure to death. Past research has focused mainly on age differences in fear of death. Although Templer, Ruff, and Franks (1971) found no relationship between age and death anxiety, other researchers have found that older adults have less fear of death (Feifel & Branscomb 1973; Iammarino, 1975; Wass & Myers, 1982).

With a multidimensional approach to death attitudes, the picture is more complex. Keller, Sherry, and Piotrowski (1984) measured three separate dimensions of death attitudes: Evaluation of Death in General, Belief in the Hereafter, and Death Anxiety Related to Self. With respect to Evaluation of Death in General, middle-aged adults were less anxious than the old and young adults. The oldest group had greater belief in an afterlife than did the middle-aged, but they were not significantly different from the young adults. The oldest group showed significantly less anxiety toward death of self than did the two younger groups.

Reduction of death anxiety in old age should be accompanied by an increase in death acceptance. Erikson (1963) suggested that the major developmental task in old age is to accept one's past life and the reality of death. Thus, older adults should show greater neutral acceptance. Indeed, Gesser et al. (1987) found this type of acceptance to increase with age.

It has been reported that elderly adults tend to be more religious and have stronger beliefs in an afterlife than either middle-aged or young adults (Bengtson, Cuellar, & Ragan, 1977). Although it is questionable whether this difference reflects true developmental stages or simply cohort effects, it seems reasonable to predict that approach acceptance will be higher among the elderly. Keller et al. (1984) have provided some support for this hypothesis.

Older people are more likely to be beset by personal losses and physical illness. Their inability to carry on with many of the activities and roles that used to give them meaning and fulfillment, coupled with social isolation and loneliness, may further increase their longing to be delivered from a painful existence. Therefore in the present study, we predicted that escape acceptance would be higher for the elderly than for the middle-aged and young subjects, a prediction that has received some support (Gesser et al., 1987).

Gender Differences

In his review of the correlates of death anxiety, Pollak (1979) found that most researchers reported a higher level of fear of death in women. Although some studies failed to find a gender difference (Aronow, Rauchway, Peller, & DeVito, 1980; Conte, Weiner, & Plutchik, 1982; Mullins & Lopez, 1982; Viney, 1984) and still others found that men had higher anxiety than women (Cole, 1978; Robinson & Wood, 1984), most of the recent work has confirmed Pollak's observation (Lonetto, Mercer, Fleming, Bunting, & Clare, 1980; McMordie, 1978; Neimeyer, Bagley, & Moore, 1986; Neimeyer et al., 1977; Wass & Myers, 1982). In fact, this difference has been found in other cultures (Lonetto et al., 1980; McMordie & Kumar, 1984).

Again, the picture becomes more complicated when a multidimensional approach is used. For example, Neimeyer et al. (1986) found that women scored higher on the Collett–Lester Fear of Dying of Self subscale, but not on Fear of Death of Self, Fear of Death of Others, or Fear of Dying of Others. Dattel and Neimeyer (1990) gave a racially heterogeneous group of adults the DAS, the Threat Index, the Jourard Self-Disclosure Questionnaire (JSDQ), and a measure of social desirability. Women displayed greater death anxiety than men on the DAS but not on the Threat Index. Their greater death anxiety remained on the DAS even when the effects of self-disclosure and social desirability were statistically controlled. The results discredit the suggestion that the greater death anxiety reported by women is due to their tendency to disclose their fears and anxiety (Stillion, 1985). Dattel and Neimeyer concluded that the weight of evidence suggests that women do have a higher tendency to report more death anxiety, especially about their own dying.

With respect to belief in an afterlife, most of the findings again show that women tend to score higher. Klenow and Bolin (1989) found that women were more likely than men to be believers in an afterlife, and Berman and Hays (1975) found that women tended to have a higher belief in an afterlife and lower scores in death anxiety than men.

On the basis of the literature on age and gender differences in death attitudes, we predicted that older adults would show less death fear and more death acceptance than the two younger groups. We also predicted that women would score higher then men in fear of death and approach acceptance.

AN EMPIRICAL STUDY OF THE DEATH ATTITUDE PROFILE–REVISED

Method

Subjects One hundred young adults (55 males and 45 females; mean age = 23.3, range = 18–29 years), 100 middle-aged adults (47 males and 65 females; mean age = 41.8, range = 30–59 years), and 100 older adults (35 males and 65 females; mean age = 72.9, range = 60–90 years) served as subjects. They were recruited from the community through various means, including poster notices, newspaper advertising, contacts with community agencies, and word of mouth. Subjects represented a cross-section of residents of a mid-sized city of 65,000.

Instruments   In addition to the DAP–R, the following instruments were administered.

Death Anxiety Scale   The DAS (Templer, 1970) is a 15-item true/false measure of verbalized death anxiety that addresses death, thoughts of death, disease, and time perspective. Templer (1970) reported a 3-week stability coefficient of .83 for a group of college students. The DAS correlates .74 with Boyar's (1964) Fear of Death Scale; moderate correlations with a number of relevant subscales of the Minnesota Multiphasic Personality Inventory have also been reported (Templer, 1970).

Death Perspective Scale   The DPS (Hooper & Spilka, 1970) is a 60-item multidimensional measure of perspectives on death. Eight scales are based on items rated on a 6-point Likert-type scale from *strongly disagree* (1) to *strongly agree* (6). Two subscales, Death as an Afterlife of Reward (6 items) and Indifference Toward Death (5 items), were used in the present study. Coefficient alphas are reported to be .92 for Death as an Afterlife of Reward and .71 for Indifference Toward Death. Construct validity has been supported by moderate intercorrelations of the scales with measures of religiosity (Spilka, Stout, Minton, & Sizemore, 1976).

Semantic Differential   Two measures consisting of twelve 7-point bipolar adjectives (e.g., *pleasant–unpleasant*, *meaningful–meaningless*, and *satisfying–dissatisfying*) were constructed to assess attitudes toward life and death. A high score on each measure is indicative of a positive attitude. Alpha coefficients were found to be .93 and .95 for the life and death measures, respectively.

Perceived Well-Being Scale   The PWB (Reker & Wong, 1984) is a 14-item, 7-point Likert scale of psychological and physical well-being. Psychological Well-Being is a 6-item index of the presence of positive emotions such as happiness, joy, and peace of mind and the absence of negative emotions such as fear, anxiety, and depression. The alpha coefficient was found to be .82 in a sample of 238 older adults. Test–retest correlation over a 2-year period was .79. Psychological well-being is correlated positively with happiness and negatively with depression.

Physical well-being is an eight-item measure of self-rated physical health and vitality coupled with perceived absence of physical discomforts. Internal consistency and 2-year stability estimates are .78 and .65, respectively. Physical well-being is correlated positively with happiness and negatively with depression and physical symptoms.

Zung Depression Scale The Zung Depression Scale (Zung, 1965) is a 20-item, 4-point measure of self-reported depression during the past week. Response options range from "a little of the time" to "most of the time." The scale measures the presence of pathological disturbances or changes in four areas: somatic, psychological, psychomotor, and mood. Knight, Waal-Manning, and Spears (1983) reported an alpha coefficient of .79. The scale has been shown to discriminate between depressed and nondepressed psychiatric patients and normal subjects (Zung & Wonnacott, 1970) and is unaffected by demographic factors including age, sex, marital status, financial status, and educational level (Zung, 1967).

Procedure The DAP–R, the SD ratings of life and death, the PWB, and the Zung Depression Scale were administered in counterbalanced order to all subjects. In addition, the DAS and the Death as an Afterlife of Reward and Indifference Toward Death subscales of the DPS were administered to a subsample of 83 respondents. Four weeks later, a random sample of 30 subjects was drawn from each of the three age groups and retested on the DAP–R.

RESULTS AND DISCUSSION

Factor Structure The responses to the 36-item DAP–R were subjected to principal-components factor analysis. Consistent with our theoretical formulation, five components were extracted and rotated to an orthogonal (varimax) solution. The five components accounted for 63.1% of the variance.

All 36 items loaded .40 or greater on at least one component. Only one item, "Death is the worst thing that could possibly happen to me," was factorially complex, loading .40 or greater on two components. The five components clearly represented the Approach Acceptance, Fear of Death, Death Avoidance, Escape Acceptance, and Neutral Acceptance theoretical scales. The first component contained all 10 of the items from the Approach Acceptance scale (29.5% of the variance). The second component contained all 8 of the items from the Fear of Death scale plus 2 negatively loading items from the Neutral Acceptance scale (13.8% of the variance). The third component was represented by 5 of the 5 Death Avoidance items plus one item from the Fear of Death scale (8.5% of the variance). The fourth component contained 5 of the 6 Escape Acceptance items (6.0% of the variance), and the fifth component contained 5 of the 7 Neutral Acceptance items plus 1 Escape Acceptance item (5.3% of the variance).

Given the extremely good empirical fit to the theoretically derived DAP–R scales, we eliminated the factorially complex item and the 3 intrusion items and refactored the remaining 32 items. The resulting factor structure is presented in Table 6-1. The final DAP–R consists of 10 Approach Acceptance items (33.3% of the variance), 7 Fear of Death items (13.4% of the variance); 5 Death Avoid-

Table 6-1   Rotated Component Structure of the Death Attitude Profile–Revised

Item no.	Loading	Item
		Component 1: Approach Acceptance
16.	.90	Death brings a promise of a new and glorious life.
25.	.90	I see death as a passage to an eternal and blessed place.
15.	.89	Death is a union with God and eternal bliss.
22.	.86	I look forward to a reunion with my loved ones after I die.
28.	.84	One thing that gives me comfort in facing death is my belief in the afterlife.
4.	.84	I believe that I will be in heaven after I die.
31.	.83	I look forward to a life after death.
8.	.80	Death is an entrance to a place of ultimate satisfaction.
13.	.80	I believe that heaven will be a much better place than this world.
27.	.73	Death offers a wonderful release of the soul.
		Component 2: Fear of Death
32.	.76	The uncertainty of not knowing what happens after death worries me.
18.	.76	I have an intense fear of death.
21.	.75	The fact that death will mean the end of everything as I know it frightens me.
7.	.71	I am disturbed by the finality of death.
2.	.71	The prospect of my own death arouses anxiety in me.
20.	.69	The subject of life after death troubles me greatly.
1.	.44	Death is no doubt a grim experience.
		Component 3: Death Avoidance
19.	.83	I avoid thinking about death altogether.
12.	.82	I always try not to think about death.
26.	.81	I try to have nothing to do with the subject of death.
3.	.73	I avoid death thoughts at all cost.
10.	.69	Whenever the thought of death enters my mind, I try to push it away.
		Component 4: Escape Acceptance
29.	.80	I see death as a relief from the burden of life.
23.	.77	I view death as a relief from earthly suffering.
9.	.75	Death provides an escape from this terrible world.
11.	.74	Death is deliverance from pain and suffering.
5.	.68	Death will bring an end to all my troubles.
		Component 5: Neutral Acceptance
24.	.83	Death is simply a part of the process of life.
14.	.81	Death is a natural aspect of life.
6.	.70	Death should be viewed as a natural, undeniable, and unavoidable event.
30.	.49	Death is neither good nor bad.
17.	.40	I would neither fear death nor welcome it.

Table 6-2 Intercorrelations of the Dimensions of the Death Attitude Profile–Revised

Dimension	Death Avoidance	Neutral Acceptance	Approach Acceptance	Escape Acceptance
Fear of Death	.47***	−.12*	−.40***	−.28**
Death Avoidance		.02	−.20**	−.10
Neutral Acceptance			−.07	−.03
Approach Acceptance				.57***
Escape Acceptance				

*p < .05.
**p < .01.
***p < .001.

ance items (7.7% of the variance), 5 Escape Acceptance items (6.0% of the variance), and 5 Neutral Acceptance items (5.7% of the variance). The five components account for 66.2% of the variance.

The results of the factor analysis make it quite clear that the five dimensions are relatively independent. The high loading of each item on the theoretically appropriate factor demonstrate that the factors are pure and internally consistent.

The intercorrelation matrix for the DAP–R dimensions is presented in Table 6-2. Of note is the moderate positive association between Approach Acceptance and Escape Acceptance and the moderate negative association between Approach Acceptance and Fear of Death. The Death Avoidance dimension correlated positively with Fear of Death, accounting for 22% of the variance, and negatively with Approach Acceptance (4% of the variance). Thus, we have replicated the results of Gesser et al. (1987–88) and have demonstrated that death avoidance is relatively distinct from fear of death. It is surprising that death avoidance has never been investigated in its own right, given the enormous amount of work already done on death anxiety. A great deal of additional research is needed to understand how death avoidance and fear of death are related to each other and to determine what variables are related to these two different manifestations of the same uneasiness about personal mortality.

One important observation is that people's death attitudes tend to be a mixed bag, with conflicting attitudes that counterbalance each other in the service of adaptation (Feifel, 1990). Therefore, in death education and counseling, it is important that individuals are made aware of the diverse attitudes they may have and how these attitudes together determine the way they conduct their lives.

Reliability of the Death Attitude Profile–Revised Alpha coefficients of internal consistency and 4-week test–retest coefficients of stability are presented in Table 6-3. Alpha coefficients ranged from a low of .65 (Neutral Acceptance) to a high of .97 (Approach Acceptance); stability coefficients ranged from a low

Table 6-3   Reliability of the Death Attitude Profile–Revised

Dimension	Alpha coefficient	4-Week test–retest reliability ($n = 90$)
Fear of Death	.86	.71
Death Avoidance	.88	.61
Neutral Acceptance	.65	.64
Approach Acceptance	.97	.95
Escape Acceptance	.84	.83

of .61 (Death Avoidance) to a high of .95 (Approach Acceptance). Taken together, the DAP–R scales have good to very good reliability.

Convergent–Discriminant Validity   The correlations pertaining to the convergent–discriminant validity of the DAP–R are presented in Table 6-4. Fear of Death was positively related to the DAS and negatively related to SD ratings of life and death. Death Avoidance was negatively related to SD ratings of death but not significantly related to SD ratings of life. Neutral Acceptance was positively related to the Indifference Toward Death subscale of the DPS and to SD ratings of life, but it was unrelated to SD ratings of death. Approach Acceptance was positively related to the Death as an Afterlife of Reward subscale of the DPS and to SD ratings of life and death. Finally, Escape Acceptance was positively correlated with SD ratings of death, but, contrary to prediction, it was unrelated to SD ratings of life.

The fact that nearly all of the predicted correlations were confirmed attests to the construct validity of the five dimensions. The finding that Escape Acceptance was negatively related to perceived physical well-being (see Table 6-7) but not to SD ratings of life attitude suggests that poor physical health might be the main reason for escape acceptance of death.

Table 6-4   Correlates of the Death Attitude Profile–Revised

Dimension	DAS	Death as an Afterlife of Reward	Indifference Toward Death	Semantic differential Life	Semantic differential Death
Fear of Death	.61***	−.33***	−.07	−.25***	−.61***
Death Avoidance	.16	−.02	−.01	−.11	−.32***
Neutral Acceptance	−.34***	.03	.27***	.20***	−.08
Approach Acceptance	−.27**	.82***	.15	.20***	.59***
Escape Acceptance	−.25**	.28**	.23*	.01	.42***

Note. DAS = Templer's (1970) Death Anxiety Scale; Death as an Afterlife of Reward and Indifference Toward Death are subscales of Hooper and Spilka's (1970) Death Perspective Scale.
*$p < .05$.
**$p < .01$.
***$p < .001$.

Table 6-5 Death Attitude Means and Standard Deviations as a Function of Age

| Death attitude dimension | Age groups | | | | Tukey's honestly significant difference | | |
	1 18–29	2 30–59	3 60–90	F (2, 294)	1 vs. 2	2 vs. 3	1 vs. 3
Fear of Death							
M	3.25	3.10	2.72	3.42*			*
SD	1.3	1.1	1.3				
Death Avoidance							
M	2.84	2.89	2.93	<1.00			
SD	1.2	1.4	1.5				
Neutral Acceptance							
M	5.31	5.59	5.80	8.55***			**
SD	0.9	0.9	0.8				
Approach Acceptance							
M	4.84	4.70	5.38	2.86+		*	
SD	1.7	1.8	1.5				
Escape Acceptance							
M	4.06	4.15	5.20	14.76***		**	**
SD	1.7	1.6	1.2				
Multivariate				5.46***			

Note. n = 100 for each age group.
+ p < .06.
*p < .05.
**p < .01.
***p < .001.

Age and Gender Differences   The death attitude ratings of the young, middle-aged, and older adults were subjected to a 3 (age group) × 2 (sex) multivariate analysis of variance (MANOVA). Only the main effects of age and sex were significant.

Age Differences   Age group means (averaged over the total number of items for each scale), standard deviations, and F ratios are presented in Table 6-5. Consistent with our predictions, there was a significant multivariate effect for age, $F(10, 580) = 5.46$, $p < .001$. Univariate F tests revealed significant differences for the Fear of Death, $F(2, 294) = 3.42$, $p < .05$; Neutral Acceptance, $F(2, 294) = 8.55$, $p < .001$; and Escape Acceptance, $F(2, 294) = 14.76$, $p < .001$, dimensions. A marginal level of significance was found for Approach Acceptance, $F(2, 294) = 2.86$, $p < .06$. Noteworthy is the greater variability in approach acceptance in all age groups. This suggests that opinions were more sharply divided with respect to beliefs in a afterlife.

Subsequent post hoc Tukey comparisons of the means showed that the older adults were significantly less afraid of death and more accepting of death as a reality compared with the young adults, but not the middle-aged adults. Older adults were significantly more likely to accept death as an escape from life than were both the middle-aged and younger adults. Older adults were also more accepting of life after death, particularly in comparison with middle-aged adults.

Kalish (1976) proposed several explanations for older adults' decreased fear of death. First, elderly individuals may believe they have already had their fair share of life and feel ready to die. In contrast, young adults have not yet fulfilled their life goals and therefore may fear that death may cut short what is rightfully theirs (Diggory & Rothman, 1969). There is evidence that fear of death is relatively high at this stage of life (Birren, Kinney, Schaie, & Woodruff, 1981).

Another plausible interpretation is that elderly persons have become socialized to death, because they have survived the death of so many friends and loved ones (Kalish, 1976). It is also possible that they have lost interest in life because of physical decline, illness, and personal losses. From an existential perspective, many elderly persons may believe they have completed their missions in life and feel ready to die.

Our finding regarding escape acceptance is consistent with the notion that elderly individuals are willing to be freed from the infirmities of the body. Decreased opportunities for engaging in meaningful activities and increased isolation may also contribute to the increase in escape acceptance with advancing age.

The results regarding approach acceptance are more complex. As predicted, older adults indeed showed the highest scores on the Approach Acceptance dimension. However, although they differed significantly from the middle-aged adults, they did not differ significantly from the young adults. This finding replicates the result of Keller et al. (1984). One plausible interpretation is that young adults may still have residues of beliefs in heaven from childhood. Such beliefs are eroded in middle life but revived in old age.

Gender Differences   A MANOVA revealed a significant multivariate effect for gender, $F(5, 290) = 2.48$, $p < .05$. Univariate F tests showed significant differences between men and women on the Death Avoidance, Approach Acceptance, and Escape Acceptance dimensions. Gender means, standard deviations, and F ratios are presented in Table 6-6. Examination of the means shows that women were significantly more accepting of life after death and of death as an escape from life than were men. Men, on the other hand, were significantly more prone to avoid all thoughts of death than were women.

Death Attitudes and Well-Being   Of interest is the relationship between death attitudes and well-being. Most of our predictions were supported by the results, which are presented in Table 6-7. The bottom panel shows the results for the total sample.

Fear of death was associated with psychological distress and depression. The associations, however, held only for the older adults. Templer (1971) re-

Table 6-6 Death Attitude Means and Standard Deviations as a Function of Gender

Death attitude dimension	Men ($n = 137$)	Women ($n = 163$)	$F(1, 298)$
Fear of Death			
M	3.13	2.93	<1.00
SD	1.3	1.3	
Death Avoidance			
M	3.07	2.74	4.82*
SD	1.3	1.4	
Neutral Acceptance			
M	5.61	5.53	2.22
SD	0.8	1.0	
Approach Acceptance			
M	4.66	5.23	7.04**
SD	1.7	1.6	
Escape Acceptance			
M	4.19	4.70	4.08*
SD	1.6	1.6	
Multivariate			2.48*

*$p < .05$.
**$p < .01$.

ported that death anxiety is a common component of depression. Such anxiety is alleviated when depression lessens.

Death avoidance was associated with psychological distress, but significant associations were found only for the middle-aged and older adults. For older adults, death avoidance was also related to depression. It is possible that death avoidance prevents individuals from dealing with thoughts and feelings of death that exist below conscious awareness but nonetheless affect behavior. Failure to deal with these thoughts and feelings creates psychological discomfort.

Neutral acceptance was positively related to psychological and physical well-being and negatively related to depression, particularly for the young and middle-aged adults. Respondents who accepted death as an inevitable reality of life appeared to enjoy physical and mental health. It is likely that individuals with this attitude are motivated to make life as full and meaningful as possible.

Approach acceptance was positively associated with subjective well-being, but this was found only for the older adults. The older adults who were more accepting of life after death experienced greater psychological well-being and lower depression.

Escape acceptance was associated with reduced physical well-being. This relationship was strongest for young adults. Young adults whose lives are filled with pain, illness, and suffering are probably more likely to long for an escape.

Table 6-7   Death Attitudes and Well-being by Age Group

Death attitude dimension	Well-being		
	Psychological	Physical	Depression
Young adults (n = 100)			
Fear of Death	−.15	−.16	.18
Death Avoidance	−.19	−.11	.03
Neutral Acceptance	.10	.28**	−.28**
Approach Acceptance	.08	−.05	.01
Escape Acceptance	−.11	−.26**	.15
Middle-aged adults (n = 100)			
Fear of Death	−.11	.02	.03
Death Avoidance	−.20*	−.01	.04
Neutral Acceptance	.31**	.31**	−.13
Approach Acceptance	−.04	−.02	−.01
Escape Acceptance	−.17	−.12	.09
Elderly adults (n = 100)			
Fear of Death	−.31**	−.22*	.24*
Death Avoidance	−.22*	−.08	.24*
Neutral Acceptance	.15	.15	−.14
Approach Acceptance	.20*	.08	−.30**
Escape Acceptance	−.03	−.07	.00
All subjects (N = 300)			
Fear of Death	−.20***	−.09	.12*
Death Avoidance	−.20***	−.07	.08
Neutral Acceptance	.21***	.21***	−.17**
Approach Acceptance	.11*	−.03	−.06
Escape Acceptance	−.08	−.20***	.07

$*p < .05.$
$**p < .01.$
$***p < .001.$

Considering all the correlations between neutral acceptance of death and well-being and depression, it is clear that this attitude toward death is most adaptive. This result reinforces our earlier suggestion that when individuals come to terms with death as an inevitable fact of life, they are more likely to make the best use of their lives. It is also consistent with the reasoning that people who believe they have led a meaningful, fulfilling life are more likely to accept death without fear. In either event, the beneficial effects of neutral acceptance on mental health are quite convincing.

The benefits of approach acceptance seem to be limited to older adults. As the end of our earthly journey approaches and we have to let go all the things that are dear to us, belief in a happy afterlife may indeed be a powerful source of hope and comfort. Little wonder that such belief was negatively related to feelings of depression and positively related to perceived psychological well-being in our older subjects. A combination of neutral and approach acceptance seems to be the best antidote to depression and fear of death.

CONCLUSION

To our knowledge, the DAP–R is the only instrument that measures a broad spectrum of death attitudes. We believe that a better understanding of the fear of death can be achieved only in the context of an understanding of other death attitudes. It would not be fruitful to study fear of death in isolation. It is possible that the same level of fear of death may reflect very different death attitudes. For example, the person with a low fear of death and a high escape acceptance is very different from the person with the same low fear of death and a high neutral acceptance. The former is probably sick and tired of living; the latter may be highly motivated to complete his or her life tasks before it is too late. Therefore, it is the patterns of different death attitudes rather than the magnitude of a single death attitude that best captures individual differences.

The findings on the relative magnitude of death attitudes reinforce our observation that death acceptance is more salient than death anxiety. The scores for both fear of death and death avoidance tended to be around the midpoint of the 7-point scale, reflecting uncertainty. All scores for the three acceptance scales reflected high endorsement. Sooner or later, all individuals must in their own way come to terms with their personal mortality. Therefore, it is important to study how individuals psychologically prepare themselves for the final exit and to measure the different routes toward acceptance of death.

The existential emphasis that people need a sense of meaning in order to survive and face death offers a useful conceptual framework for integrating various patterns of death attitudes. Individuals who feel that they have led a productive, meaningful life should be high in neutral acceptance and low in fear of death, death avoidance, and escape acceptance. Individuals who derive meaning and optimism from the belief in a happy afterlife should be high in approach acceptance and low in fear of death, death avoidance, and escape acceptance. We can also predict that those who find life devoid of meaning because of an incurable disease may be high in escape acceptance and low in fear of death and death avoidance. In short, the meaning construct is relevant to many different constellations of death attitudes. Future research should focus on individual differences in patterns of death attitudes.

Existential theory provides us with an integrating conceptual framework, and the DAP–R promises to be a valid and reliable instrument. Armed with these two tools, we are better equipped to grapple with the complex issues surrounding attitudes toward death.

REFERENCES

Aday, R. H. (1984). Belief in afterlife and death anxiety: Correlates and comparisons. *Omega, 15*, 67–75.

Alexander, I. E., & Adlerstein, A. M. (1959). Death and religion. In H. Feifel (Ed.), *The meaning of death*. New York: McGraw-Hill.

Amenta, M. D. (1984). Death anxiety, purpose in life and duration of service in hospice volunteers. *Psychological Reports, 54*, 979–984.

Armstrong, D. (1987). Silence and truth in death and dying. *Social Science and Medicine, 24*, 651–657.

Aronow, E., Rauchway, A., Peller, M., & DeVito, A. (1980). The value of the self in relation to fear of death. *Omega, 11*, 37–44.

Bakan, D. (1971). *Disease, pain, and sacrifice: Toward a psychology of suffering*. Boston: Beacon Press.

Becker, E. (1973). *The denial of death*. New York: Free Press.

Bengtson, V. L., Cuellar, J. B., & Ragan, P. K. (1977). Stratum contrasts and similarities in attitudes towards death. *Journal of Gerontology, 32*, 76–88.

Berman, A. (1974). Belief in afterlife, religion, religiosity and life-threatening experiences. *Omega, 5*, 127–135.

Berman, A., & Hays, J. E. (1975). Relation between death anxiety, belief in afterlife, and locus of control. *Journal of Consulting and Clinical Psychology, 41*, 318–321.

Birren, J. E., Kinney, D. K., Schaie, K. W., & Woodruff, D. S. (1981). *Developmental psychology: A life-span approach*. Boston: Houghton-Mifflin.

Boyar, J. I. (1964). *The construction and partial validation of a scale for the measurement of the Fear of Death*. Doctoral dissertation, University of Rochester (Microfilms 64-9228).

Bregman, L. (1989). Dying: A universal human experience? *Journal of Religion and Health, 28*(1), 58–69.

Bugental, J. F. T. (1965). *The search for authenticity: An existential analytic approach to psychotherapy*. New York: Holt, Rinehart & Winston.

Butler, R. N. (1963). The life review: An interpretation of reminiscence in the aged. *Psychiatry, 26*, 65–76.

Butler, R. N. (1975). *Why survive? Being old in America*. New York: Harper & Row.

Cole, M. A. (1978). Sex and marital status differences in death anxiety. *Omega, 9*, 139–147.

Collett, L., & Lester, D. (1969). The fear of death and fear of dying. *Journal of Psychology, 72*, 179–181.

Conte, H. R., Weiner, M. B., & Plutchik, R. (1982). Measuring death anxiety: Conceptual psychometric and factor analytic aspects. *Journal of Personality and Social Psychology, 43*, 775–785.

Dattel, A. R., & Neimeyer, R. A. (1990). Sex differences in death anxiety: Testing the emotional expressiveness hypothesis. *Death Studies, 14*, 1–11.

Diggory, J., & Rothman, D. (1969). Values destroyed by death. *Journal of Abnormal and Social Psychology, 63*, 205–210.

Dixon, R., & Kinlaw, B. (1983). Belief in the existence and nature of life after death: A research note. *Omega, 13*, 287–292.

Durlak, J. A. (1972). Relationship between individual attitudes toward life and death. *Journal of Consulting and Clinical Psychology, 38*, 463.

Drolet, J. L. (1990). Transcending death during early adulthood: Symbolic immortality, death anxiety, and purpose in life. *Journal of Clinical Psychology, 46*, 148–160.

Epting, F. R., & Neimeyer, R. A. (Eds.). (1984). *Personal meanings of death: Applications of personal construct theory to clinical practice.* Washington, DC: Hemisphere.

Erikson, E. (1963). *Childhood and society* (2nd ed.). New York: Norton.

Feifel, H. (Ed.) (1959). *The meaning of death.* New York: McGraw-Hill.

Feifel, H. (1974). Religious conviction and fear of death among the healthy and terminally ill. *Journal for the Scientific Study of Religion, 13*, 353–360.

Feifel, H. (1990). Psychology and death. *American Psychologist, 45*, 537–543.

Feifel, H., & Branscomb, A. B. (1973). Who's afraid of death? *Journal of Abnormal Psychology, 81*, 282–288.

Feifel, H., & Nagy, V. T. (1981). Another look at fear of death. *Journal of Consulting and Clinical Psychology, 49*, 278–286.

Flint, G. A., Gayton, W. F., & Ozmon, K. L. (1983). Relationship between life satisfaction and acceptance of death by elderly persons. *Psychological Reports, 53*, 290.

Frankl, V. E. (1965). *The doctor and the soul.* New York: Knopf.

Fry, P. S. (1990). A factor analytic investigation of home-bound elderly individuals' concerns about death and dying and their coping responses. *Journal of Clinical Psychology, 46*, 737–748.

Georgemiller, R., & Maloney, H. N. (1984). Group life review and denial of death. *Clinical Gerontologist, 2*(4), 37–49.

Gesser, G., Wong, P. T. P., & Reker, G. T. (1987). Death attitudes across the life-span: The development and validation of the Death Attitude Profile (DAP). *Omega, 18*, 109–124.

Gibbs, H. W., & Achterbery-Lawlis, J. (1978). Spiritual values and death anxiety: Implications for counseling with terminal cancer patients. *Journal of Counseling Psychology, 25*, 563–569.

Hertel, B. R. (1980). Inconsistency of beliefs in the existence of heaven and afterlife. *Review of Religious Research, 21* (Spring), 171–183.

Hooper, T., & Spilka, B. (1970). Some meanings and correlates of future time and death among college students. *Omega, 1*, 49–56.

Iammarino, N. K. (1975). Relationship between death anxiety and demographic variables. *Psychological Reports, 17*, 262.

Jeffers, F. C., Nichols, C. R., & Eisdorfer, C. (1961). Attitudes of older persons toward death. A preliminary study. *Journal of Gerontology, 16*, 53–56.

Kalish, R. A. (1963). Some variables in death attitudes. *Journal of Social Psychology, 59*, 137–145.

Kalish, R. A. (1976). Death and dying in a social context. In R. H. Binstock & G. Shanas (Eds.), *Handbook of aging in the social sciences* (pp. 483–507). New York: Van Nostrand Reinhold.

Kalish, R. A. (1981). Coping with death. In P. Ahmed (Ed.), *Living and dying with cancer* (pp. 223–237). New York: Elsevier.

Kastenbaum, R. (1979). *Human developing: A lifespan perspective.* Boston: Allyn & Bacon.

Kastenbaum, R., & Aisenberg, R. (1972). *The psychology of death.* New York: Springer.

Kastenbaum, R., & Costa, P. T. (1977). Psychological perspectives on death. *Annual Review of Psychology, 28,* 225–249.

Keller, J. W., Sherry, D., & Piotrowski, C. (1984). Perspective on death: A developmental study. *Journal of Psychology, 116,* 137–142.

Kelly, G. A. (1955). *The psychology of personal constructs.* New York: Norton.

Klenow, D. J., & Bolin, R. C. (1989). Belief in an afterlife: A national survey. *Omega, 20,* 63–74.

Klug, L., & Boss, M. (1977). Further study of the validity of the Death Concern Scale. *Psychological Report, 40,* 907–910.

Klug, L., & Sinha, A. (1987). Death acceptance: A two-component formulation and scale. *Omega, 18,* 229–235.

Knight, R. G., Waal-Manning, H. J., & Spears, G. F. (1983). Some norms and reliability data for the State-Trait Anxiety Inventory and the Zung Self-Rating Depression Scale. *British Journal of Clinical Psychology, 22,* 245–249.

Kübler-Ross, E. (1969). *On death and dying.* New York: Macmillan.

Kübler-Ross, E. (1981). *Living with death and dying.* New York: Macmillan.

Kurlychek, R. T. (1976). Assessment of death acceptance: A proposed scale. *Psychology, 13*(1), 19–20.

Levinson, D. J. (1977). The mid-life transition: A period of adult psychosocial development. *Psychiatry, 40,* 99–112.

Lewis, M. I., & Butler, R. N. (1974). Life-review therapy: Putting memories to work in individual and group psychotherapy. *Geriatrics, 29*(11), 165–173.

Littlefield, C., & Fleming, S. (1984). Measuring fear of death: A multidimensional approach. *Omega, 15,* 131–138.

Lonetto, R., Mercer, G. W., Fleming, S., Bunting, B., & Clare, M. (1980). Death anxiety among university students in Northern Ireland and Canada. *Journal of Psychology, 104,* 75–82.

Marshall, V. W. (1980). *Last chapters: A sociology of aging and dying.* Monterey, CA: Brooks/Cole.

Marshall, V. W. (1981). Death and dying. In D. Mangen & W. Peterson (Eds.), *Research instruments in social gerontology* (pp. 303–381). Minneapolis: University of Minnesota Press.

Martin, D., & Wrightsman, L. S. (1965). The relationship between religious behavior and concern about death. *Journal of Social Psychology, 65,* 317–323.

Maslow, A. H. (1968). *Toward a psychology of being* (2nd ed.). Princeton, NJ: Van Nostrand.

May, R., Angel, E., & Ellenberger, H. F. (Eds.). (1958). *Existence: A new dimension in psychiatry and psychology.* New York: Basic Books.

McMordie, W. R. (1978). Improving measurement of death anxiety. *Psychological Reports, 44,* 975–980.

McMordie, W. R. (1981). Religiosity and fear of death: Strength of belief system. *Psychological Reports, 49,* 921–922.

McMordie, W. R., & Kumar, A. (1984). Cross-cultural research on the Templer/McMordie Death Anxiety Scale. *Psychological Reports, 54,* 959–963.

Mullins, L. C., & Lopez, M. A. (1982). Death anxiety among nursing home residents: A comparison of the young-old and old-old. *Death Education, 6,* 75–86.

Neimeyer, R. A. (1988). Death anxiety. In H. Wass, F. M. Berardo, & R. A. Neimeyer (Eds.), *Dying: Facing the facts* (2nd ed., pp. 97–136). Washington, DC: Hemisphere.

Neimeyer, R. A., Bagley, K. J., & Moore, M. K. (1986). Cognitive structure and death anxiety. *Death Studies, 10,* 273–288.

Neimeyer, R. A., Dingemans, P., & Epting, F. R. (1977). Convergent validity, situational stability, and meaningfulness of the Threat Index. *Omega, 8,* 251–265.

Neugarten, B. (1968). *Middle-age and aging.* Chicago: University of Chicago Press.

Peterson, S. A., & Greil, A. L. (1990). Death experience and religion. *Omega, 21,* 75–82.

Pollak, J. M. (1979). Correlates of death anxiety: A review of empirical studies. *Omega, 10,* 97–121.

Quinn, P. K., & Reznikoff, M. (1985). The relationship between death anxiety and the subjective experience of time in the elderly. *International Journal of Aging and Human Development, 21,* 197–209.

Ray, J. J., & Najman, J. (1974). Death anxiety and death acceptance: A preliminary approach. *Omega, 5,* 311–315.

Reker, G. T., Peacock, E. J., & Wong, P. T. P. (1987). Meaning and purpose in life and well-being. A life-span perspective. *Journal of Gerontology, 42,* 44–49.

Reker, G. T., & Wong, P. T. P. (1984). Psychological and physical well-being in the elderly: The Perceived Well-Being Scale. *Canadian Journal on Aging, 3,* 23–32.

Reker, G. T., & Wong, P. T. P. (1988). Aging as an individual process: Towards a theory of personal meaning. In J. E. Birren, & V. L. Bengtson (Eds.), *Emergent theories of aging* (pp. 214–246). New York: Springer.

Robinson, P. J., & Wood, K. I. (1984). Fear of death and physical illness: A personal construct approach. In F. Epting & R. A. Neimeyer (Eds.), *Personal meanings of death.* Washington, DC: Hemisphere.

Saunders, C., & Baines, M. (1983). *Living with dying.* London: Oxford University Press.

Schultz, R. (1978). *The psychology of death, dying and bereavement.* Reading, MA: Addison-Wesley.

Smith, D. K., Nehemkis, A. M., & Charter, R. A. (1983–84). Fear of death, death attitudes, and religious conviction in the terminally ill. *International Journal of Psychiatry in Medicine, 13,* 221–232.

Spilka, B. L., Stout, L., Minton, B., & Sizemore, D. (1976). *Death perspectives, death anxiety, and form of personal religion.* Paper presented to the Society for the Scientific Study of Religion, Philadelphia.

Steinitz, L. Y. (1980). Religiosity, well-being, and weltanschauung among the elderly. *Journal of the Scientific Study of Religion, 19,* 60–87.

Stewart, D. W. (1975). Religious correlates of the fear of death. *Journal of Thanatology, 3,* 161–164.

Stillion, J. M. (1985). *Death and the sexes.* Washington, DC: Hemisphere.

Templer, D. (1970). The construction and validation of the Death Anxiety Scale. *Journal of General Psychology, 82,* 165–177.

Templer, D. (1971). Death anxiety as related to depression and health of retired persons. *Journal of Gerontology, 26,* 521–523.

Templer, D. (1972). Death anxiety in religiously very involved persons. *Psychological Reports, 31,* 361–362.

Templer, D., & Dodson, E. (1970). Religious correlates of death anxiety. *Psychological Reports, 26,* 895–897.

Templer, D., & Ruff, C. (1975). The relationship between death anxiety and religion in psychiatric patients. *Journal of Thanatology, 3,* 165–168.

Templer, D., Ruff, C., & Franks, C. (1971). Death anxiety: Age, sex, and parental resemblance in diverse populations. *Developmental Psychology, 4,* 108.

Vernon, G. (1972). Death control. *Omega, 3,* 131–138.

Viney, L. L. (1984). Concerns about death among severely ill people. In F. R. Epting & R. A. Neimeyer (Eds.), *Personal meanings of death* (pp. 143–158). Washington, DC: Hemisphere/McGraw-Hill.

Wass, H. (Ed.). (1979). *Dying: Facing the facts.* New York: McGraw-Hill.

Wass, H., Berardo, F., & Neimeyer, R. A. (Eds.). (1988). *Dying: Facing the facts* (2nd ed.). Washington, DC: Hemisphere.

Wass, H., Corr, C. A., Pacholski, R. A., & Forfar, C. S. (1985). *Death education II: An annotated resource guide.* Washington, DC: Hemisphere.

Wass, H., & Myers, J. E. (1982). Psychosocial aspects of death among the elderly: A review of the literature. *Personnel and Guidance Journal, 61,* 131–137.

Weisman, A. D. (1974). *The realization of death.* New York: Jason Aronson.

Williams, R. L., & Cole, S. (1968). Religiosity, generalized anxiety and apprehension concerning death. *Journal of Social Psychology, 75,* 111–117.

Wong, P. T. P. (1989). Successful aging and personal meaning. *Canadian Psychology, 30,* 516–525.

Wong, P. T. P., & Watt, L. (1991). What types of reminiscence are associated with successful aging? *Psychology and Aging, 6,* 272–279.

Young, M., & Daniels, S. (1981). Religious correlates of death anxiety among high school students in the rural South. *Death Education, 5,* 223–233.

Zung, W. W. K. (1965). A self-rating depression scale. *Archives of General Psychiatry, 12,* 63–70.

Zung, W. W. K. (1967). Factors influencing the self-rating depression scale. *Archives of General Psychiatry, 16,* 543–547.

Zung, W. W. K., & Wonnacott, T. H. (1970). Treatment prediction in depression using a self-rating scale. *Biological Psychiatry, 2,* 321–329.

APPENDIX 6-1: Death Attitude Profile– Revised

Age: _____   Sex: M _____ F _____

This questionnaire contains a number of statements related to different attitudes toward death. Read each statement carefully, and then indicate the extent to which you agree or disagree. For example, an item might read: "Death is a friend." Indicate how well you agree or disagree by circling one of the following; SA = strongly agree; A = agree; MA = moderately agree; U = undecided; MD = moderately disagree; D = disagree; and SD = strongly disagree. Note that scales run both from *strongly agree* to *strongly disagree* and from *strongly disagree* to *strongly agree.*

If you strongly agreed with the statement, you would circle SA. If you strongly disagreed you would circle SD. If you are undecided, circle U. However, try to use the Undecided category sparingly.

It is important that you work through the statements and answer each one. Many of the statements will seem alike, but all are necessary to show slight differences in attitudes.

1.	Death is no doubt a grim experience.	SD	D	MD	U	MA	A	SA
2.	The prospect of my own death arouses anxiety in me.	SA	A	MA	U	MD	D	SD
3.	I avoid death thoughts at all costs.	SA	A	MA	U	MD	D	SD
4.	I believe that I will be in heaven after I die.	SD	D	MD	U	MA	A	SA
5.	Death will bring an end to all my troubles.	SD	D	MD	U	MA	A	SA
6.	Death should be viewed as a natural, undeniable, and unavoidable event.	SA	A	MA	U	MD	D	SD
7.	I am disturbed by the finality of death.	SA	A	MA	U	MD	D	SD
8.	Death is an entrance to a place of ultimate satisfaction.	SD	D	MD	U	MA	A	SA
9.	Death provides an escape from this terrible world.	SA	A	MA	U	MD	D	SD
10.	Whenever the thought of death enters my mind, I try to push it away.	SD	D	MD	U	MA	A	SA
11.	Death is deliverance from pain and suffering.	SD	D	MD	U	MA	A	SA
12.	I always try not to think about death.	SA	A	MA	U	MD	D	SD
13.	I believe that heaven will be a much better place than this world.	SA	A	MA	U	MD	D	SD
14.	Death is a natural aspect of life.	SA	A	MA	U	MD	D	SD
15.	Death is a union with God and eternal bliss.	SD	D	MD	U	MA	A	SA
16.	Death brings a promise of a new and glorious life.	SA	A	MA	U	MD	D	SD
17.	I would neither fear death nor welcome it.	SA	A	MA	U	MD	D	SD
18.	I have an intense fear of death.	SD	D	MD	U	MA	A	SA
19.	I avoid thinking about death altogether.	SD	D	MD	U	MA	A	SA
20.	The subject of life after death troubles me greatly.	SA	A	MA	U	MD	D	SD
21.	The fact that death will mean the end of everything as I know it frightens me.	SA	A	MA	U	MD	D	SD
22.	I look forward to a reunion with my loved ones after I die.	SD	D	MD	U	MA	A	SA
23.	I view death as a relief from earthly suffering.	SA	A	MA	U	MD	D	SD
24.	Death is simply a part of the process of life.	SA	A	MA	U	MD	D	SD
25.	I see death as a passage to an eternal and blessed place.	SA	A	MA	U	MD	D	SD
26.	I try to have nothing to do with the subject of death.	SD	D	MD	U	MA	A	SA
27.	Death offers a wonderful release of the soul.	SD	D	MD	U	MA	A	SA

28. One thing that gives me comfort in facing   SD D MD U MA A SA
    death is my belief in the afterlife.
29. I see death as a relief from the burden of   SD D MD U MA A SA
    this life.
30. Death is neither good nor bad.   SA A MA U MD D SD
31. I look forward to life after death.   SA A MA U MD D SD
32. The uncertainty of not knowing what hap-   SD D MD U MA A SA
    pens after death worries me.

Scoring Key for the Death Attitude Profile–Revised

Dimension	Items
Fear of Death (7 items)	1, 2, 7, 18, 20, 21, 32
Death Avoidance (5 items)	3, 10, 12, 19, 26
Neutral Acceptance (5 items)	6, 14, 17, 24, 30
Approach Acceptance (10 items)	4, 8, 13, 15, 16, 22, 25, 27, 28, 31
Escape Acceptance (5 items)	5, 9, 11, 23, 29

Scores for all items are from 1 to 7 in the direction of *strongly disagree* (1) to *strongly agree* (7). For each dimension, a mean scale score can be computed by dividing the total scale score by the number of items forming each scale.

Chapter 7

Death Competency: Bugen's Coping with Death Scale and Death Self-Efficacy

Rosemary A. Robbins

Both the professional (Lonetto & Templer, 1986; Schulz, 1978) and popular (Becker, 1973) literatures on death concern have dealt almost entirely with death anxiety and fear of death. Although it is indisputable that humans fear death at least sometimes in their lives, it is not certain what an understanding of this fear will provide in dealing with the reality of our existential condition. Might it not be more useful to note that humans also cope with death, and have done so in their own sometimes bungling ways since time immemorial? In American culture, it is often health care providers who must not only cope with death themselves on a daily basis, but also assist patients and their loved ones in coping with it. Kübler-Ross (1969) described normal reactions to death in terminal patients and their families and showed that health care professionals can help these individuals by understanding their experiences (whether or not they occur in stages). Her efforts were aimed at teaching professionals who deal with dying patients how to be effective in the face of the emotional and physical processes that precede death. Since Kübler-Ross first drew our attention to this issue, some headway has been made in dealing with dying patients.

Evidence of this is the hospice movement, which is predicated on the assumption that people deserve to die with as much dignity and control as possible. Hospice care has been reported by patients and their families to be much more satisfying than the medical care received previously in curative settings (Godkin,

Krant, & Doster, 1983–84). Hospices provide patients and families with an alternative to the "preserve life at all costs" approach of technological medicine. On the surface this may seem defeatist, as though it encourages giving up rather than fighting death. But when one explores further, it becomes apparent that hospices are promoting competency in dealing with death. Typical hospice professional and volunteer training develops not only skills at communicating about death and providing emotional support for patients and families, but also very practical skills and information, such as funeral service information and training in the physical care of the dying. This emphasis on competency may be critical in understanding death concern and may lead professionals to more effective strategies for intervention as well.

A competency emphasis also may be important in evaluating the results of death education. Many researchers have relied on dependent measures designed to assess anxiety instead of looking at skills attained, and these very dependent measures have made interpretation of their findings difficult (Peal, Handal, & Gilner, 1981–82; White, Gilner, Handal, & Napoli, 1983–84). Other researchers have focused on skill training programs rather than on decreasing anxiety. Given the hospice movement's commitment to effectiveness in the face of death it is not surprising that the first psychometric measure of death competency, Bugen's (1980–81) Coping with Death Scale, should have emerged from this context. Bugen provided a skills-oriented training for hospice volunteers and devised his scale to include specific competencies that volunteers believed they could display after training. He offered this measurement approach as a means of (a) measuring valid death education gains, (b) monitoring the effectiveness of a death education seminar, and (c) emphasizing coping as a desirable outcome of a death education experience.

Another potentially useful approach is based on Bandura's (1977, 1982, 1986) social/cognitive learning theory. Bandura has shown that humans learn not only through reinforcement but also and principally through imitation. Research by Bandura and his colleagues has shown that phobic anxieties can be reduced by demonstrating appropriate behavior and having learners perform the behavior themselves. Shifts in behavior are accompanied in the learner by shifts in what Bandura calls *perceived self-efficacy*, the belief in one's capacity to perform a particular behavior. As ability to perform a skill increases, so does perceived self-efficacy, and vice versa. A learner's best sources of information on his or her degree of self-efficacy are performance attainments and vicarious experience; verbal persuasion is less informative, and anxiety or arousal is the least informative (Bandura, 1986). Thus an intervention strategy based on demonstration followed by active participation by the learner (participant modeling in Bandura's scheme) should lead to more powerful outcomes than an intervention based on reducing anxiety. This assertion has been supported in the work of Bandura and his colleagues. This is not to say that fear or anxiety are not experienced, only that training in specific behaviors, through modeling and participation, results in a more powerful, skill-based outcome that may also reduce anxiety.

Bandura's (1977, 1982) measurement philosophy follows his theory. He engages in what he calls *microanalysis* of skills and beliefs, looking for the specific elements that are relevant rather than attempting to generalize about people's beliefs in their own capabilities. For example, in the case of spider or snake phobia, learners are asked about their self-efficacy in performing a series of increasingly difficult skills in approaching the feared creatures and then are tested on the skills. Measurement of self-efficacy consists of first asking subjects whether they believe they can perform each task in a graded series of tasks and then asking them to rate on a scale from 0 to 100 how certain they are that they can. It is noteworthy that as actual attainments increase, so does perceived self-efficacy, whereas one's level of anxiety or arousal bears a less clear relationship to effective behavior.

Might this approach be applied to dealing with death? Perhaps death competency could be thought of as perceived self-efficacy in confronting death and a measurement strategy similar to Bandura's used. Such an approach might provide an operational alternative that is conceptually parallel to Bugen's coping with death, giving individuals increased access to death competency.

In this chapter, I report my efforts to apply a competency model in the area of death concern. Many of the same theoretical issues were addressed in each study, including the relationship between death competency and self-actualization, the relationship between death competency and death-preparation behaviors, and strategies for increasing death competency. However, organizing the findings in a chronology, or series of studies, appeared to be the most understandable approach. In the summary, the findings from the studies are integrated.

STUDY 1: DEATH COMPETENCY IN COLLEGE STUDENTS

My effort to obtain an understanding of death competency (Robbins, 1990–91) began with a study of 94 undergraduate and graduate students designed to further evaluate the notion of coping with death using Bugen's (1980–81) Coping with Death scale as an operational definition of this construct (see Appendix 7-1). Although Bugen had devised his scale using self-reports of participants in a death education seminar and had shown that many of the items discriminated between trainees and controls, further study of the psychometric properties of the scale was required. Initially, efforts were aimed at determining whether this instrument was reliable as a measure of death competency. It was determined that it was both internally consistent ($\alpha = .89$, $p < .001$) and stable over a 2-week time period ($r = .91$, $p < .001$), so it could be considered a reliable scale of death competency. Bugen had begun validating the Coping with Death Scale by testing it on a new group of hospice volunteers and finding that it discriminated between trainees and controls. In Study 1, I pursued the issue of validity by relating the scale to reports of death-preparation behaviors as well as reports of self-actualization. The scale correlated significantly with four death-preparation behaviors, including writing a will, planning one's estate, planning one's funeral, and signing an organ donor card. Bugen's scale had higher correlations with the first three behaviors than did scales of death anxiety, but both Templer's (1970) Death Anxiety Scale (DAS) and the Collett–Lester Fear of Death and Dying Scales (Lester, 1974) were equally useful as predictors of donor card signing.

Students were also asked several questions designed to assess their commitment to self-actualizing values. Because of time limitations, these values were operationalized as single items rated on 7-point Likert scales. The items were ''I feel very competent to handle my life,'' ''I am deeply committed to my work,'' ''I am very assertive,'' ''I am very certain about my purpose in life,'' and ''I am deeply committed to my family.'' Bugen's scale correlated significantly with all of these items except the one concerning work. However, trait and state anxiety as measured by the State–Trait Anxiety Inventory (Spielberger, 1983), a reliable and valid measure of general anxiety, was found to account for this variance, because partial correlations controlling for trait and state anxiety resulted in nonsignificant correlations between Coping with Death and these self-actualization items.

Overall, Study 1 demonstrated that Bugen's scale is both internally consistent and reliable. In addition, some evidence was gathered that coping with death is related to other sorts of death competencies besides capacity to do hospice volunteer work.

STUDY 2: DEATH COMPETENCY IN HOSPICE VOLUNTEERS

Study 2 was designed to explore further the death-related competencies required in hospice work. Although it was clear that hospice volunteer trainees showed gains on the Coping with Death Scale, other death-related competencies that might exist in individuals who can cope with their own death remained unclear. In addition to talking with or caring for a dying patient, could hospice volunteers also write their own wills, prepay their funerals, and sign organ donor cards? Perhaps those who develop hospice-related skills are also more likely to develop personal death-related competencies. Thus in addition to exploring Bugen's scale further, I wished to determine whether the concept of perceived self-efficacy is useful in understanding the complex of death-related competencies. In cooperation with one of the participating hospices, the Death Self-Efficacy Scale (Robbins, 1992) was developed, which taps hospice-related competencies as well as self-efficacy regarding death-preparation behaviors and coping with and handling the deaths of loved ones and other losses (see Appendix 7-2). Of course, people's beliefs in their ability to prepare for death or handle the loss of loved ones were expected to be based on their actual experiences with death preparation and coping with loss.

Study 2 further explored the reliability and validity of the Coping with Death scale. At the same time, the psychometric soundness of the Death Self-Efficacy Scale was evaluated. Both scales were compared with McMordie's (1979, 1982) revision of the DAS, the former being a Likert version of the latter that is somewhat more reliable.

A sample of 320 volunteers (272 women and 48 men) from six hospices in Pennsylvania completed the Coping with Death Scale, the Death Self-Efficacy Scale, and McMordie's revison of the DAS as part of their participation in the hospice program. Seventy-eight of these subjects served as controls (26 patient care volunteers from hospital settings and 52 non-patient-care volunteers from hospice settings, who did not differ on demographic variables or variables of interest). The remaining subjects were 242 individuals who provided direct care to hospice patients (52 trainees, 94 medium-term [2–42 months] volunteers, and 96 long-term [48 months or more] volunteers).

As in Study 1, the Coping with Death scale, administered to the entire sample, was found to be internally consistent ($a = .90, p < .001$). The Death Scale-Efficacy Scale was also found to be internally consistent ($a = .94, p < .001$) for the overall group. Because the Death Self-Efficacy Scale was new, its test–retest reliability was assessed on a separate sample of 39 undergraduates, and adequate stability was demonstrated over a 2-week period ($r = .91, p < .001$).

An attempt was made to replicate Bugen's (1980–81) finding that hospice training participants demonstrated gains on the Coping with Death Scale, with the other two scales also considered. A small subsample of 13 hospice volunteer trainees completed all three scales before training and immediately after completing their training. A repeated measures multivariate analysis of variance (MANOVA) was performed for pre- versus post-testing for the three tests. The overall effect demonstrated a trend toward a two-way interaction (Wilks's $\lambda = .61, p = .069$). Perhaps with a larger sample the training effect on death competency variables might have been demonstrated; however, Bugen's finding was not replicated in this study.

Attention was then turned to differences among the three groups of patient care volunteers (trainees and medium- and long-term volunteers) and the control group. Preliminary analyses revealed that the four groups did not differ in terms of gender, education, occupation, marital status, or religion. However, substantial differences were noted among these groups based on age, $F(3, 316) = 11.80, p < .001$, with Scheffé subgroup comparisons revealing that the controls ($m = 54.9$ years) and long-term volunteers ($m = 55.8$ years) were significantly older than the trainees ($m = 44.1$ years) and medium-term volunteers ($m = 49.3$ years). Thus age was dealt with as a possible confound in other analyses.

A MANOVA was then performed on the four groups' scores on the three scales: the Coping with Death Scale, McMordie's revision of the DAS, and the

Death Self-Efficacy Scale, using age as a covariate. The overall Group $\times$ Test effect was significant (Wilks's $\lambda = .94, p < .002$), as was the covariate effect, $F(1, 315) = 6.12, p < .05$. Group comparisons for each dependent variable were then conducted using one-way analyses of variance (ANOVAs) and analyses of covariance (ANCOVAs) excluding age. Table 7-1 displays the cell means and standard deviations, as well as F values and probabilities. The groups differed significantly on the Coping with Death Scale in both the ANOVA and ANCOVA, with medium-term and long-term volunteers scoring significantly higher than trainees and controls. The groups also differed significantly on the Death Self-Efficacy Scale in both analyses, with all three hospice patient care groups scoring higher than controls. No differences were noted among groups on McMordie's verison of the DAS, however.

The most intriguing findings were the differences noted between the groups on the measures of coping with death and death self-efficacy. The medium-term and long-term volunteers scored higher on the former than did the other groups, suggesting a greater perceived power to cope with death among experienced volunteers. It would be useful to study the Coping with Death Scale longitudinally to determine the effects of training and experience on scores on this measure. Scores on the Death Self-Efficacy Scale revealed a somewhat different pattern, discriminating all three hospice patient care groups from controls. This suggests that even trainees come to hospice work feeling more self-efficacious in dealing with death than do other volunteers, leading to speculation that the Death Self-Efficacy Scale might make a useful selection tool for hospice trainees. Of course, further research would be needed to assess the appropriateness of its use in this fashion.

One assertion of existential theory is that if a person confronts mortality, he or she will be capable of living life more fully (Yalom, 1981). Although some researchers have studied the relationship between death anxiety and self-actualization, no one has yet studied how this construct might relate to coping with death or death self-efficacy. In Study 2 I undertook to do this, operationalizing self-actualization by using the Personal Orientation Inventory (POI; Shostrom, 1974), a well-designed measure of Maslow's (1970) concept of self-actualization with demonstrated reliability and validity.

The correlation between each of the scales of death concern and the subscales of the POI for the entire sample are reported in Table 7-2. As may be seen, both the Coping with Death Scale and the Death Self-Efficacy Scale correlated positively with 11 of the 12 POI subscales, the sole exception being Synergy. These relationships also held when partial correlations removing the effects of age were combined. Although McMordie's revision of the DAS demonstrated some correlations with the POI subscales, the relationships were less consistent than those between the death competency scales and the POI subscales. Possibly, the notion of death competency provides better access than the notion of death anxiety to the aspects of confrontation with mortality that are related to self-actualization.

Table 7-1   Differences Among Volunteer Groups on Death Anxiety and Death Competency Variables, with Results of Analyses of Variance (ANOVAs) and Covariance (ANCOVAs) Excluding Age

	Group				ANOVA	ANCOVA		Scheffé
Measure	1. Trainees (n = 52)	2. Medium term (n = 94)	3. Long term (n = 96)	4. Controls (n = 78)	F groups	F groups	F age	group comparison
Coping with Death								
M	154.77	161.02	163.12	151.51	5.10*	5.18*	10.73**	2, 3 > 1, 4
SD	20.47	18.38	22.26	25.01				
McMordie revision of Templer Death Anxiety Scale								
M	54.23	55.51	52.13	56.09	ns			
SD	10.35	10.56	12.62	10.85				
Death Self-Efficacy Scale								
M	83.92	84.47	85.57	78.33	8.26**	8.20**	ns	1–3 > 4
SD	8.09	8.21	10.24	13.07				

*p < .01.
**p < .001.

155

Table 7-2 Correlations Between Scores on the Personal Orientation Inventory/Numbers of Death-Related Experiences and Scores on Scales of Death Concern, Including Pearson *r* and Partial Correlations Excluding the Effects of Age for the Hospice and Other Volunteer Sample (*N* = 320)

Measure	Coping with Death		Death Self-Efficacy		McMordie's version of Templer's Death Anxiety Scale	
	Age included	Age excluded[a]	Age included	Age excluded[b]	Age included	Age excluded[c]
Personal Orientation Inventory						
Time Competence	.29***	.29***	.25***	.25***	−.24***	−.24***
Inner-Directed	.25***	.27***	.29***	.29***	−.16**	−.17**
Self-Actualizing Value	.16***	.17***	.16***	.16***	−.08	−.08
Existentiality	.19***	.20***	.16**	.16**	−.13**	−.13**
Feeling Reactivity	.13**	.19***	.26***	.27***	−.02	−.04
Spontaneity	.18***	.20***	.26***	.26***	−.12*	−.13**
Self-Regard	.30***	.31***	.28***	.28***	−.19***	−.19***
Self-Acceptance	.22***	.21***	.19***	.20***	−.19***	−.19***
Nature of Man Constructive	.13**	.14**	.17***	.17***	−.06	−.07
Synergy	.08	.07	.08	.08	−.06	−.05
Acceptance of Aggression	.16***	.25***	.19***	.20***	−.06	−.07
Capacity for Intimacy	.28***	.30***	.29***	.29***	−.11*	−.12*
Experiences						
Total death-preparation behaviors	.17***	.12*	.17***	.19***	−.07	−.05
Total deaths of loved ones	.18***	.12*	.13**	.17***	−.08	−.06

[a]Correlation between age and Coping with Death Scale = .15 (*p* < .01).
[b]Correlation between age and Death Self-Efficacy Scale = −.02 (*ns*).
[c]Correlation between age and McMordie revision of the Death Anxiety Scale = −.05 (*ns*).
*p < .05.
**p < .01.
***p < .001.

Also presented in Table 7-2 are the correlations between the three scales of death concern and death-related experiences. As may be noted, the Coping with Death and Death Self-Efficacy scales correlated with total number of death-preparation behaviors as well as total number of deaths of loved ones experienced, whereas the McMordie version of the DAS bore no relation to these factors. These are only correlational findings, but they do further elaborate a picture of people who deal effectively with death. In the present study, these people had experienced more deaths of loved ones and engaged in more death-preparation behaviors, reported large numbers of death-related competencies, and held a large number of self-actualization values.

STUDY 3: SELF-EFFICACY IN ORGAN DONATION

In Study 1, signing an organ donor card or donating organs was considered a death-preparation behavior. It was expected that all death-preparation behaviors would be related to both death anxiety and coping with death. Surprisingly, however, most of the death-preparation behaviors were associated with coping with death but not with death anxiety. The exception was organ donation, which was related to both coping and anxiety. Thus it appeared that both competency and anxiety were at work in people's decisions about donation. Further analysis of the data from the sample of 94 students revealed, not surprisingly, that donors were higher on self-efficacy for signing a donor card. Furthermore, when the subjects were regrouped on the basis of whether they believed in donation, nondonors who believed they should donate were intermediate in self-efficacy between donors and those who had no interest in donating (Robbins, 1990).

The next step was to research the process of organ donation more directly, guided in part by the self-efficacy conceptualization. A study (Robbins, McLaughlin, & Nathan, 1991) was begun at health fairs in the region in an attempt to approach this topic in a naturalistic setting. Because the data on card signing and self-efficacy were self-report data from undergraduate students, it was particularly important to address the issue in the way it might be presented to the public in the real world. Thus the health-fairs study examined how both death competencies and death anxieties were related to card signing in the general public. A brief interview questionnaire (18 items) was devised that could be completed verbally in less than 5 min. and included the opportunity to sign a card. Items included self-efficacy ratings of the ability to sign a donor card and the ability to talk to families about donation, expectation ratings of the effectiveness of donation, measures of anxieties and concerns, and knowledge items about brain death. Three hundred five attendees at health fairs completed the interview. Findings suggest that although people did report anxiety regarding signing a card and anxiety did enter the final regression equation in a minor way, the major portion of the variance in card signing was accounted for by self-efficacy for signing. This may have major implications for encouraging donation, because appeals in the past have tended to focus on people's fears rather than their competencies. Perhaps more emphasis needs to be placed on people's power and capability to make a difference through donation. Having the courage to contemplate one's own death long enough to plan to donate one's organs and sign a card to this effect may be seen as an aspect of death competency.

STUDY 4: DEATH COMPETENCY IN OFFERING THE OPPORTUNITY FOR ORGAN DONATION

Although members of the general public may express their wish to donate their organs posthumously by signing a card, the actual opportunity for donation ordinarily takes place in a medical context. Thus it was believed to be particularly important to attempt to apply the death competency model to the training of health care workers who offer patients the opportunity for donation. A local foundation provided independent funding for a project that was designed to increase organ donation in regional hospitals. Core teams of health care workers (primarily nurses) were formed who had an interest in and a commitment to increasing donor referrals and successful donations from their hospitals. The transplant coordinator for the region, training and development specialists from each of three hospitals, and I provided training to these teams that was based in part on Bandura's theoretical position, taking into account how people increase their perceived self-efficacy and success in performing a target behavior. It was necessary, of course, to present didactic material regarding donation and transplantation in the initial portion of the training. This segment also included a heavy emphasis on the service provided to the donor family by offering the opportunity to donate, with the trainers citing research that indicates that family members of the donor feel that the opportunity to donate helps them mourn and make meaning out of their loss. However, the central focus of the training was talks by individuals with whom core team members could empathize and identify, people who had lived through the experience of organ donation and transplantation. The mother of an organ donor, who was also a registered nurse, shared her experience of donating her son's kidneys 9 years previously. In addition, a woman who was the recipient of a combined kidney/pancreas transplant shared her experience of waiting for and then receiving her transplant, as well as the vast improvement in the quality of her life since that time. Both of these women were effective in helping team members understand the real-life experience of transplantation from both sides of the process. Trainees then observed possible approaches to offering the opportunity to the donor family. Finally, they were given a chance to practice how they might do this. This paradigm is consistent with Bandura's participant modeling intervention, designed for optimal increase in self-efficacy and in effective behavior.

Forty-eight core team members from three hospitals participated. Their average age was 37 ($SD = 8.7$), and 3 of them were men. Twenty team members were chaplains, social workers, or administrators; the remaining 28 were nurses. They had spent an average of 14.9 years ($SD = 9.2$) working in their fields and had participated in an average of three donor situations ($SD = 3.8$). All subjects were tested before and again after training. Test materials included a 13-item organ donation self-efficacy questionnaire (see Appendix 7-3) and several single-item questions about fears and concerns about donation. The self-efficacy questionnaire, which was found to be internally consistent ($\alpha = .90$), included items designed to measure perceived capacity to talk to the family of a potential donor, to understand and assist with donation, and to deal with donation as a personal issue. Whereas no changes were noted in levels of anxiety from pre- to post-testing, average self-efficacy values increased from 72.9 ($SD = 18.7$) to 82.3 ($SD = 17.2$), $t(47) = 7.42, p < .001$.

Thus, as a result of training, core team members increased their perceived self-efficacy for offering the opportunity of donation and for dealing with donation as a personal issue. Most important, the interventions also resulted in increased donation-related behavior. Before training, 21 subjects had signed or wished to sign donor cards; after training 32 of these subjects had signed cards. The training sessions appeared to affect actual donations from these hospitals as well. In the 9 months preceding the training sessions, a total of 20 organs and tissues had been recovered from these three hospitals, whereas in the 9 months after training, organ and tissue donations totaled 43. This represents a 115% increase in donation, compared with the 25% increase in donation for the region as a whole. Thus it appears that the training was useful in increasing both psychological and behavioral self-efficacy regarding organ donation.

The main focus of Study 4 was the use of a competency model to intervene in death-avoidant behavior. Core team members had been hesitant to speak with families about donation, feeling that they might increase the grief these families feel. However, once they were made aware that they were serving the families and experienced the training aimed at increasing their competency, they were able to be effective at dealing with and communicating about a very difficult death-related situation.

STUDY 5: DEATH COMPETENCY IN A RELIGIOUS CONTEXT

The training provided for health care workers in Study 4 was presented in a modified form for the clergy in the community in Study 5. After the training, one pastor invited me to help plan a course entitled "End-of-Life Decisions" for the adult Sunday School at her church. This was undertaken as a pilot project to experiment with ways of presenting death-related issues to the general public, under the assumption that people may deal with these issues more easily in a religious context. Nine sessions addressed the following topics: Death—What Is It?; Living Wills; Hospice Care; Wills and Estates; Funeral Options; Organ

Donation and Transplantation; Christian Funeral; Near Death Experiences; and Grief, Grieving, and Support Groups. The format included a moderator from the congregation, guest speakers who were experts on each of the topics and who shared their personal experiences, and interaction with the audience. Although attendance varied from 40 to 75 adults at the sessions, feedback questionnaires handed out at the last session were collected from only 26 participants, making our findings suggestive only. Participants were asked to rate the usefulness of each session on a scale of 1 to 5. All nine sessions were rated above 4, and subjective feedback indicated that the series was one of the most useful ever presented at the Sunday School. Many of the participants planned to take actions consistent with the subjects of the sessions, but few had completed these actions at the time of the follow-up questionnaire. Social learning theory (Bandura, 1986) suggests that the verbal persuasion used in these sessions should have been coupled with participant modeling to assist the participants to take action rather than simply express an interest in doing so. However, many people were sufficiently affected by the presentations to undertake self-exploration and make plans for specific actions.

SUMMARY

Death competency is a construct that represents a range of human skills and capabilities in dealing with death, as well as our beliefs and attitudes about these capabilities. In the present studies, the notion of death competency was operationalized psychometrically as Bugen's (1980–81) Coping with Death Scale, the Death Self-Efficacy Scale (Robbins, 1990–91), and a scale of self-efficacy related to organ donation. All three measures were found to have internal consistency, and the first two were found to be stable on retest. The Coping with Death Scale related to completion of a hospice volunteer training program, experience working as a hospice volunteer, self-actualizing values, and completion of death-preparation behaviors. The Death Self-Efficacy Scale related to willingness to serve as a hospice volunteer, death-preparation behaviors, and self-actualization values. The questionnaire on organ donation self-efficacy reflected increased self-efficacy in health care providers, as a function of participation in an organ donation training program. Furthermore, it was shown to be related to increases in the numbers of donor cards signed and donations from target hospitals. Thus, in addition to its correlations with other factors, the concept of death competency was useful in designing a program that resulted in increases in effective death-related behaviors. Viewing humans' relationships with death from the perspective of death competency may help health care professionals give patients and families greater access to their own effectiveness in this regard.

ACKNOWLEDGMENTS

The research on organ donation hospital core teams was supported in part by a grant from the Whitaker Foundation, Mechanicsburg, PA, and conducted with the cooperation of the Delaware Valley Transplant Program and the hospitals of the Pennsylvania Capital Region. The cooperation of Forbes Hospice, Hospice of Berks County, Hospice of Central Pennsylvania, Hospice of Lancaster County, Professional Hospice Care, and Wissahickon Hospice is also gratefully acknowledged.

REFERENCES

Bandura, A. (1977). Self-efficacy: Toward a unifying theory of behavioral change. *Psychological Review, 84*, 191–215.

Bandura, A. (1982). Self-efficacy mechanism in human agency. *American Psychologist, 37*, 122–147.

Bandura, A. (1986). *Social foundations of thought and action*. Englewood Cliffs, NJ: Prentice-Hall.

Becker, E. (1973). *The denial of death*. New York: Free Press.

Bugen, L. A. (1980–81). Coping: Effects of death education. *Omega, 11*, 175–183.

Godkin, M. A., Krant, M. J., & Doster, N. J. (1983–84). The impact of hospice care on families. *International Journal of Psychiatry in Medicine, 13*, 153–165.

Kübler-Ross, E. (1969). *On death and dying*. New York: Macmillan.

Lester, D. (1974). *The Collett–Lester Fear of Death Scale: A manual*. Unpublished manuscript, Stockton State College, Pomona, N.J.

Lonetto, R., & Templer, D. I. (1986). *Death anxiety*. Washington, DC: Hemisphere.

Maslow, A. H. (1970). *Motivation and personality* (rev. ed.). New York: Harper & Row.

McMordie, W. R. (1979). Improving measurement of death anxiety. *Psychological Reports, 44*, 975–980.

McMordie, W. R. (1982). Concurrent validity of Templer and Templer/McMordie death anxiety scales. *Psychological Reports, 51*, 265–266.

Peal, R. D., Handal, P. J., & Gilner, F. H. (1981–82). A group desensitization procedure for the reduction of death anxiety. *Omega, 12*, 61–70.

Robbins, R. A. (1990–91). Bugen's Coping with Death Scale: Reliability and further validation. *Omega, 22*, 287–299.

Robbins, R. A. (1990). Signing an organ donor card: Psychological factors. *Death Studies, 14*, 219–229.

Robbins, R. A. (1992). Death competency: A study of hospice volunteers. *Death Studies, 16*, 557–567.

Robbins, R. A., McLaughlin, N. R., & Nathan, H. M. (1991). Using self-efficacy theory to predict organ donor card signing. *Journal of Transplant Coordination, 1*(111).

Schulz, R. (1978). *The psychology of death, dying and bereavement*. Reading, MA: Addison-Wesley.

Shostrom, E. L. (1974). *Manual for the Personal Orientation Inventory*. San Diego, CA: Educational and Industrial Testing Service.

Spielberger, C. D. (1983). *Manual for the State–Trait Anxiety Inventory*. Palo Alto, CA: Consulting Psychologists Press.

Templer, D. I. (1970). The construction and validation of a death anxiety scale. *Journal of General Psychology, 82*, 165–177.

White, P. D., Gilner, F. H., Handal, P. J., & Napoli, J. G. (1983–84). A behavioral intervention for death anxiety in nurses. *Omega, 14*, 33–42.

Wilkinson, H. J., & Wilkinson, J. W. (1986–87). Evaluation of a hospice volunteer training program. *Omega, 17*, 263–275.

Yalom, I. (1981). *Existential psychotherapy*. New York: Basic Books.

APPENDIX 7-1: Bugen's (1980–81) Coping with Death Scale

Please rate, on a scale from 1 to 7, how much you agree with each statement.

1	2	3	4	5	6	7
Do not agree at all			Neutral			Agree completely

Rating

_____ 1. Thinking about death is a waste of time.

_____ 2. I have a good perspective on death and dying.

_____ 3. Death is an area that can be dealt with safely.

_____ 4. I am aware of the full array of services from funeral homes.

_____ 5. I am aware of the variety of options for disposing of bodies.

_____ 6. I am aware of the full array of emotions that characterize human grief.

_____ 7. Knowing that I will surely die does not in any way affect the conduct of my life.

_____ 8. I feel prepared to face my death.

_____ 9. I feel prepared to face my dying process.

_____ 10. I understand my death-related fears.

_____ 11. I am familiar with funeral prearrangement.

_____ 12. Lately I find it O.K. to think about death.

_____ 13. My attitude about living has recently changed.

_____ 14. I can express my fears about dying.

_____ 15. I can put words to my gut-level feelings about death and dying.

_____ 16. I am making the best of my present life.

_____ 17. The quality of my life matters more than the length of it.

_____ 18. I can talk about my death with family and friends.

_____ 19. I know who to contact when death occurs.

_____ 20. I will be able to cope with future losses.

_____ 21. I feel able to handle the death of others close to me.

_____ 22. I know how to listen to others, including the terminally ill.
_____ 23. I know how to speak to children about death.
_____ 24. I may say the wrong thing when I am with someone mourning.
_____ 25. I am able to spend time with the dying if I need to.
_____ 26. I can help people with their thoughts and feeling about death and dying.
_____ 27. I would be able to talk to a friend or family member about his or her death.
_____ 28. I can lessen the anxiety of those around me when the topic is death and dying.
_____ 29. I can communicate with the dying.
_____ 30. I can tell people, before I or they die, how much I love them.

Scoring Key for the Coping with Death Scale

Scores are obtained for the Coping with Death Scale by first reversing items 13 and 24 and then totaling all items. Wilkinson and Wilkinson (1986–87) scored the values of the items in the opposite direction, leading to an inverted overall score.

APPENDIX 7-2: Hospice-Related Death Self-Efficacy Scale

For each of the items below, rate how certain or uncertain you are that you can perform each one, using this scale (in units of 10):

0	10	20	30	40	50	60	70	80	90	100
Highly uncertain					Moderately certain					Completely certain

Rating

_____ 1. Understand the limits of your role as a volunteer.
_____ 2. Be sensitive to the needs of the patient and his or her family.
_____ 3. Buy life insurance.
_____ 4. Allow the patient and his or her family to support you.
_____ 5. Handle the death of a grandparent.
_____ 6. Listen to the concerns of a dying patient.
_____ 7. Listen to the family of a dying patient.
_____ 8. Touch a dead body.
_____ 9. Identify the concerns of a dying patient and his or her family.

_____ 10. Communicate with the hospice team about your patient(s).

_____ 11. Get a medical checkup.

_____ 12. Handle the illness of your child.

_____ 13. Handle knowing that a family member has a fatal condition.

_____ 14. Provide physical care for a hospice patient.

_____ 15. Assist in transporting a hospice patient.

_____ 16. Prepare your will.

_____ 17. Run errands for a patient.

_____ 18. Listen to a news report of multiple deaths.

_____ 19. Communicate with a dying patient.

_____ 20. Ask someone close to you if he or she has a terminal illness.

_____ 21. Allow a patient to communicate fully.

_____ 22. Purchase your own cemetery plot.

_____ 23. Cope with the death of your mother.

_____ 24. Ask whether you have a terminal illness.

_____ 25. Cope with the death of your father.

_____ 26. Visit a dying friend.

_____ 27. Provide emotional support for the patient's family.

_____ 28. Care for the patient so that the family can have some respite.

_____ 29. Go to a morgue.

_____ 30. Write a Living Will.

_____ 31. Understand the philosophy of hospice.

_____ 32. Plan your funeral service.

_____ 33. Sign a card to be an organ donor.

_____ 34. Attend a funeral or wake in which the casket is open.

_____ 35. Understand bereavement and grief.

_____ 36. Cope with the death of your child.

_____ 37. Handle the death of your spouse.

_____ 38. Cope with the death of a friend the same age as you.

_____ 39. Tolerate spiritual and religious differences.

_____ 40. Cope with the death of a pet.

_____ 41. Care for yourself if you are experiencing stress in caring for a dying patient.

_____ 42. Be with a person at the time of death.

_____ 43. Be with a person experiencing unpleasant physical symptoms.

_____ 44. Prepay your funeral.

APPENDIX 7-3: Organ Donation Self-Efficacy Scale

For each of the items below, rate how certain or uncertain you are that you *can perform* each one, using this scale (in units of 10):

0	10	20	30	40	50	60	70	80	90	100

| Highly | | | | Moderately | | | | | Completely |
| uncertain | | | | certain | | | | | certain |

Rating

_____ 1. Offer the opportunity for donation to the family of a potential donor.

_____ 2. Time your discussions of donation with the family appropriately.

_____ 3. Take the time to contact the organ procurement organization.

_____ 4. Refer an organ or tissue donor to the organ procurement organization.

_____ 5. Make time to spend with the family of a patient who is a potential organ or tissue donor.

_____ 6. Ask a family whether they have talked about donation.

_____ 7. Understand brain death criteria and the process of procurement.

_____ 8. Talk to your next-of-kin about donation.

_____ 9. Get your next-of-kin to witness your signature on a donor card.

_____ 10. Offer your family members the opportunity to sign a donor card.

_____ 11. Sign a donor card yourself.

_____ 12. Consent to the donation of the organs or tissues of a family member if asked.

_____ 13. Offer to donate the organs or tissues of a family member before being asked by medical personnel.

Part III

Applications

Chapter 8

Reduced Death Threat in Near-Death Experiencers

Bruce Greyson

Near-death experiences (NDEs) are profound subjective events with transcendental or mystical elements that are reported by about one third of people who have been close to death (Gallup & Proctor, 1982; Greyson & Stevenson, 1980; Sabom & Kreutziger, 1977). These experiences typically include enhanced cognitive functioning, including a life review; strong positive affect, often associated with an encounter with ineffable light; apparent paranormal elements, including an out-of-body experience; and a sense of being in an unearthly realm or dimension of being (Greyson, 1983b). Though their etiology has yet to be established conclusively, NDEs have been shown to precipitate a wide variety of pervasive and long-lasting personality transformations (Flynn, 1982; Greyson, 1983a; Noyes, 1980; Ring, 1984).

The attitude changes most consistently reported after NDEs have been dramatic reductions in death anxiety and fear of death. In coining the term "near-death experience," Moody (1975) wrote that almost every "near-death experiencer" (NDEr) had expressed in some form or another the thought of being no longer afraid of death. Moody attributed this nearly universal decrease in fear of death to NDErs' disavowal of the concept of death as annihilation, in favor of a model of death as transition to another state of being.

Noyes (1980) regarded reduced fear of death as the most striking effect of NDEs, and wrote that it seemed to contribute to the NDErs' subsequent health and well-being. He reported that 41% of survivors of life-threatening accidents or illnesses claimed that their fear of death had been reduced, and that resignation in the face of death often brought a sense of peace and tranquility. Noyes's subjects described this resignation as the most remarkable aspect of their experience and linked it to their subsequent reduction in fear of death. Many of his interviewees claimed a greater awareness of death, and felt their NDEs not only brought death closer but integrated it more fully into their lives, the increased awareness of death adding zest to life.

Ring (1980) reported that of 49 NDErs he interviewed, 80% claimed their fear of death had decreased or vanished entirely, as opposed to 29% of a control sample of 38 nonNDErs who had been close to death. Ring's subjective impression from these interviews was that loss of fear of death was one of the strongest effects differentiating NDErs from nonNDErs.

Sabom (1982), in a study of patients who had had a life-threatening cardiac arrest, noted that those whose arrest precipitated an NDE lost much of their fear of dying immediately after the event, in contrast to those who did not have NDEs. Of 61 patients who reported NDEs, 82% claimed their fear of death had decreased, 18% claimed it had not changed, while none reported an increase. On the other hand, of 45 patients who did not report NDEs, 2% claimed their fear of death had decreased, 87% claimed it had not changed, and 11% claimed it had increased.

Six months after his initial interviews with these subjects, Sabom mailed them the Death Anxiety Scale (Templer, 1970) and the Death Concern Scale (Dickstein, 1972). The 26 NDErs who returned these questionnaires scored significantly lower than did the 18 nonNDErs, on both the Death Anxiety Scale (NDErs' mean = 3.62; nonNDErs' mean = 6.39) and the Death Concern Scale (NDErs' mean = 58.1; nonNDErs' mean = 68.6).

A nationwide Gallup poll (Gallup & Proctor, 1982), which unfortunately did not consistently differentiate NDEs from other near-death events, reported that more than one third of individuals with "near-death encounters" said their fear of death had decreased as a result. Ring (1984) called NDErs' permanent loss of fear of death one of the most consistent findings to emerge from near-death research. His studies corroborated Moody's impression that NDErs tend to see death not as annihilation, but as a transitional event between life before and after what we call death.

Flynn (1986) reported that of 21 NDErs, 100% claimed their fear of death had decreased. By contrast, of 12 survivors of close brushes with death who did not have NDEs, 42% claimed their fear of death had decreased, 25% reported it had not changed, and 33% claimed it had increased. Flynn's further investigations of these subjects suggested that this decreased fear of death among NDErs left them indifferent to the negative immortality striving that leads to selfish pursuit of unlimited wealth and competitive striving to achieve at others' expense.

While these studies are unanimous in reporting decreased death anxiety or fear of death after the NDE, they share two methodological limitations. First, with the exception of Sabom's (1982) use of the Death Anxiety Scale and Death Concern Scale, these researchers have relied on subjects' spontaneous descriptions of death attitudes or their responses to a single question regarding fear of death. Secondly, they have treated NDErs as a homogeneous group and not considered "depth" of the NDE as a possible influence on death attitudes.

Reliance on subjects' spontaneous expressions of death attitudes or direct inquiry about those attitudes has been criticized by Krieger, Epting, and Leitner (1974) as likely to yield superficial responses distorted by ego defense maneuvers and response sets. Those authors developed the Threat Index as a measure of the threat posed by the idea of an individual's imminent personal death. Death threat is a comparatively stable cognitive orientation toward death, in contrast to death anxiety and fear of death, which are more conditional affective orientations toward death. The Threat Index (TI) was based on Kelly's (1955) psychology of personal constructs, which postulates that each individual develops a system of bipolar personal constructs to organize and attribute meaning to the world. Constructs are dimensions on which things can be judged as alike or different from each other, such as the dichotomies "predictable/random," "easy/hard," and "sick/healthy."

Kelly (1955) speculated that death would be a threat to most people because they view it as likely to cause drastic changes in them, but he did not see death as intrinsically threatening to life. Rather he argued that life and death can be construed as validating each other, so that living well and dying well go hand in hand (Kelly, 1961). Krieger, Epting, and Leitner (1974) suggested that the degree of threat presented by death would be proportional to the disparity between the individual's constructions of self and death. Individuals who describe both themselves and their imminent deaths similarly on many of their bipolar personal constructs would regard death as less of a change from their current status and therefore less threatening.

For the TI, death threat is operationalized as the respondents' reluctance to place both themselves and their imminent death on the same poles of a group of bipolar personal constructs relevant to the concept of death (Rigdon, Epting, Neimeyer, & Krieger, 1979). In the most common form of the TI, the TI-30, respondents are asked to rate "yourself" and then "your own imminent death" on each of 30 provided death-relevant constructs. Placement of self and death on opposite poles of a construct is called a "split," and the total number of such splits is the death threat score. Inability to place death on either pole of a bipolar construct is considered to indicate threat, and is therefore counted as a split (Krieger, Epting, & Leitner, 1974; Rigdon, Epting, Neimeyer, & Krieger, 1979).

A second scoring procedure has been developed for the TI that involves tabulating the number of splits between ratings of "yourself" and "your ideal or preferred self,'' as a measure of self/ideal self discrepancy or, inversely, actualization (Neimeyer & Chapman, 1981; Neimeyer, Epting, & Rigdon, 1983). It has been hypothesized that individuals who have failed to actualize their ideals and have more self/ideal self splits would be more fearful of death; Robinson and Wood (1984–85) posited that both actualization (few self/ideal self splits) and integration of death into the personal construct system (few self/ death splits) decrease fear of death in an additive fashion, although empirical support for that interaction is lacking (Neimeyer, 1985).

An exploration of the factor structure of the TI with state-of-the-art factor analytic procedures (Neimeyer, Moore, & Bagley, 1988) failed to find a satisfactory model to account for all of the variance, but did identify a factorially "pure" 7-item subset of the TI. Since death threat scores on this factorially pure 7-item subset, the TI-7, correlate highly with scores on the TI-30, the TI-7 is recommended as a factorially unambiguous and less "contaminated" measure of death threat.[1]

TI scores have been shown to be stable over time and despite attempted experimental manipulation of death threat (Neimeyer, Dingemans, & Epting, 1977; Rigdon & Epting, 1985; Rigdon, Epting, Neimeyer, & Krieger, 1979). Rigdon and Epting (1985) concluded that, in contrast to the situational changes that can be experimentally induced in death anxiety and fear of death, meaningful changes in attitudes as complex as death orientation may require a more powerful intervention over a longer period of time.

Studies of the after-effects of near-death experiences suggest that an NDE might be a powerful enough experience to affect death threat. Neimeyer, Dingemans, and Epting (1977) had reported that previous closeness to dying in itself was not significantly associated with TI scores. In a post hoc analysis, Rigdon and Epting (1985) found that subjects reporting a previous close brush with death tended to have lower TI scores than those who did not report having been close to death, although that difference was not significant. They hypothesized retrospectively that near-death experiencers would be likely to view self and death as compatible and show less death threat, but they did not in fact determine whether their subjects who reported previous close brushes with death also reported NDEs.

Near-death experiences can be identified from among reports of close brushes with death, and their "depth" quantified, by the NDE Scale, a 16-item multiple-choice instrument that is a reliable and valid measure of the occurrence and depth of an NDE (Greyson, 1983b) and that significantly differentiates NDEs from other near-death events (Greyson, 1990). For research purposes, a score of 7 or more points (out of a possible 32) on the NDE Scale has been recommended as the criterion for labeling an experience an NDE (Greyson, 1983b).

[1]Subsequent research by Moore and Neimeyer (1991) has established a confirmed factor structure for 25 items on the Threat Index, which can be interpreted as Threat to Well-Being (F1), Uncertainty (F2), and Fatalism (F3), in addition to an overall Global Threat factor.

The present study was designed to explore the influence of near-death experiences, and of close brushes with death that are not accompanied by NDEs, on death threat, and secondarily on actualization, as measured by the TI. Two hypotheses suggested by previous research on NDEs are testable with the TI. The first hypothesis is that NDErs would show less death threat than would either nonNDErs who had come close to death or subjects who had never come close to death, as measured by self/death splits on the TI-30 and its more unambiguous subset, the TI-7. The second hypothesis is that NDErs would show greater actualization than either control group, as measured by fewer self/ideal self splits on the TI-30 and derivative TI-7.

METHOD

Subjects

Subjects were recruited through advertisements in the newsletter of the International Association for Near-Death Studies, an organization founded to promote research into NDEs. Respondents were asked whether they had personally had a close brush with death; and if so, they were asked whether they had had an NDE as a result of that near-death event and were asked to complete the NDE Scale to determine "depth" of NDE.

Included for analysis in this sample were 290 respondents: 135 individuals claimed to have had NDEs and described experiences that met the NDE Scale criterion for an NDE; 43 individuals denied having had an NDE and described experiences that did not meet the NDE Scale criterion for an NDE; and 112 individuals denied ever having been near death.

These three groups differed somewhat in age and gender. The mean age of the NDErs was 49.3 years ($SD = 12.6$); of the nonNDErs, 54.8 years ($SD = 14.2$); and of the subjects who had never been near death, 46.0 years ($SD = 13.0$). This age difference was significant ($F = 7.38; df = 2, 287; p = .0011$). The percent of NDErs who were female was 67.4; of nonNDErs, 55.8; and of subjects who had never been near death, 45.5. These gender ratios were also significantly different ($\chi^2 = 12.01; df = 2; p = .0025$).

In addition to the 290 subjects described above, there were 30 respondents who were excluded from analysis: 11 individuals claimed to have had NDEs but reported experiences that did not meet the NDE Scale criterion for an NDE ("false positives"); and 19 individuals denied having had an NDE but nevertheless reported experiences that did meet the NDE Scale criterion for an NDE ("false negatives").

MATERIALS AND PROCEDURE

Subjects were mailed questionnaires, which they completed and returned identified only by anonymous subject number. All subjects completed the TI-30, from which TI-7 scores were also derived; those who acknowledged having come close to death also completed the NDE Scale describing their near-death event. Subjects reporting more than one close brush with death were asked to complete one copy of the NDE Scale for each near-death event, and the one with the highest score was used for that subject.

NDE Scale scores were used, along with respondents' claims, to assign subjects to the NDEr or nonNDEr group, based on whether or not their experiences scored 7 or greater; NDE Scale scores were also used to measure relative depth of each NDE.

For each subject, the number of splits between self and death elements on the TI-30 was computed as a measure of death threat; and splits between self and death elements on the TI-7 subset of the TI-30 were also computed as a factorially purer measure of death threat.

Two analyses of variance, one for TI-30 scores and one for TI-7 scores, were used to compare self/death splits of NDErs, nonNDErs who had been close to death, and subjects who denied ever having been close to death, in order to assess whether those groups differ from each other in death threat. Pearson's correlation coefficient was used to compare death threat scores with NDE Scale scores of NDErs only, in order to assess whether depth of NDE was inversely related to death threat.

The number of splits between self and ideal self elements on the TI-30 and on the TI-7 was also computed as a measure of self/ideal self discrepancy, or inversely, actualization. As with the death threat scores, two analyses of variance, one for TI-30 scores and one for TI-7 scores, were used to compare self/ideal self splits of NDErs, nonNDErs who had been close to death, and subjects who denied ever having been close to death, in order to assess whether these groups differ from each other in actualization. Pearson's correlation coefficient was used to compare self/ideal self splits with NDE Scale scores of NDErs only, in order to assess whether depth of NDE was negatively related to self/ideal self discrepancy or actualization.

RESULTS

Death Threat Scores

The mean number of splits between self and death elements on the TI-30 for the entire pool of 290 subjects was 9.29 ($SD = 6.96$). The mean number of splits between self and death elements on the TI-30 for the three study groups was as follows: for NDErs, 7.85 ($SD = 6.06$); for nonNDErs who had been close to death, 10.12 ($SD = 6.79$); and for subjects never close to death, 10.71 ($SD = 6.49$). This difference was statistically significant ($F = 6.67$; $df = 2, 287$; $p = .0019$). That is, NDErs showed significantly less death threat than did nonNDErs or subjects who had never been near death.

For the 135 NDErs, there was a moderate but statistically significant negative correlation between self/death splits and NDE Scale scores ($r = -.187; p = .0289$). That is, among NDErs, deeper NDEs were associated with less death threat.

The mean number of splits between self and death elements on the factorially purer TI-7 for the entire pool of 290 subjects was 2.04 ($SD = 2.08$). The mean number of splits between self and death elements on the TI-7 for the three study groups was as follows: for NDErs, 1.57 ($SD = 1.86$); for nonNDErs who had been close to death, 2.35 ($SD = 2.41$); and for subjects never close to death, 2.47 ($SD = 2.17$). This difference also was statistically significant ($F = 6.46$; $df = 2, 287; p = .0022$). That is, NDErs again showed significantly less death threat than did nonNDErs or subjects who had never been near death.

For the 135 NDErs, there was again a moderate but statistically significant negative correlation between self/death splits and NDE Scale scores ($r = -.173$; $p = .0455$). That is, among NDErs, deeper NDEs were associated with less death threat.

Self/Ideal Self Discrepancy Scores

The mean number of splits between self and ideal self elements on the TI-30 for the entire pool of 290 subjects was 4.55 ($SD = 5.01$). The mean number of splits between self and ideal self elements on the TI-30 for the three study groups was as follows: for NDErs, 4.53 ($SD = 5.10$); for nonNDErs who had been close to death, 4.19 ($SD = 5.43$); and for subjects never close to death, 4.72 ($SD = 4.76$). This difference was not significant ($F = 0.18; df = 2, 287$).

For the 135 NDErs, there was a nonsignificant negative correlation between self/ideal self splits and NDE scores ($r = -.111$). That is, among NDErs, deeper NDEs tended to be associated with less self/ideal self discrepancy, or with greater actualization, but that tendency did not reach significance.

The mean number of splits between self and ideal self elements on the TI-7 for the entire pool of 290 subjects was 0.82 ($SD = 1.29$). The mean number of splits between self and ideal self elements on the TI-7 for the three study groups was as follows: for NDErs, 0.88 ($SD = 1.35$); for nonNDErs who had been close to death, 0.77 ($SD = 1.44$); and for subjects never close to death, 0.76 ($SD = 1.14$). This difference also was not significant ($F = 0.31; df = 2, 287$).

For the 135 NDErs, there was again a nonsignificant negative correlation between self/ideal self splits and NDE scores ($r = -.108$). That is, among NDErs, deeper NDEs tended to be associated with greater actualization, but again not to a significant degree.

DISCUSSION

Representative scores for the various formats of the TI have been published (Rigdon, Epting, Neimeyer, & Krieger, 1979); for the 30-item provided-constructs form used in this study, the mean number of self/death splits for a heterogenous sample was 10.00 (*SD* = 7.00). The nonNDErs who had been close to death in this study (mean = 10.12, *SD* = 6.79) and the subjects who had never come close to death (mean = 10.71, *SD* = 6.49) produced comparable scores, while the NDErs (mean = 7.85, *SD* = 6.06) showed significantly less death threat. Thus the decreased death threat shown by NDErs compared to control subjects in this study can be reasonably attributed to their lower degree of death threat and not to the control samples' unusually high levels of death threat.

Previous investigators have generally found that TI scores are not consistently or significantly influenced by age (Rainey & Epting, 1977; Rigdon, Epting, Neimeyer, & Krieger, 1979), though some samples have shown a modest decline in death threat with age (Neimeyer, Moore, & Bagley, 1988). NDErs in this study were between the two control groups in age, and significantly younger than the nonNDErs who had been close to death. Thus their lower death threat scores cannot be attributed to age.

Nor can the NDErs' lower death threat scores be attributed to their greater ratio of women to men (which was not significantly different from the ratio among nonNDErs who had been close to death); gender has not consistently been shown to correlate with TI scores, and most studies revealed no evidence of sex differences (Neimeyer, Moore, & Bagley, 1988; Rigdon, Epting, Neimeyer, & Krieger, 1979).

These data support Rigdon and Epting's (1985) hypothesis that NDErs would find death less threatening than control subjects. That effect, however, clearly was not related to the close brush with death in itself; subjects who reported close brushes with death without NDEs showed as much death threat as did subjects who had never come close to death. Of course, since this association between NDEs and low death threat was demonstrated for subjects only after the near-death event, it does not allow us to differentiate whether NDEs decrease death threat or whether low death threat might predispose toward an NDE. However, there are theoretical arguments supporting the former hypothesis.

Moody (1975) and Ring (1984) attributed NDErs' decreased fear of death to their conviction that they would survive bodily annihilation. Bannister and Mair (1968), echoing Kelly's description of death as the ultimate threat in that it is likely to cause drastic changes in core constructs, added that death should be less threatening when the fundamental meaning of life is not affected by it, such as would be the case with a strong conviction in an afterlife. However, type of belief in an afterlife (personal annihilation, personal transition, or uncertainty) has not been found to be significantly associated with TI scores (Krieger, Epting, & Leitner, 1974; Neimeyer, Dingemans, & Epting, 1977).

Testing Becker's (1973) hypothesis that the purpose of religious belief is to decrease death threat by positing an afterlife, Tobacyk (1983) found that traditional religious beliefs showed a significant, though modest, negative correlation with TI scores, although he failed to find significant associations between TI scores and paranormal beliefs more directly bearing on an afterlife. Tobacyk concluded that traditional religious beliefs, unlike paranormal beliefs, have the institutionalized social support system needed to decrease death threat. Other researchers, however, have reached conflicting conclusions about the role of religious beliefs on death orientation (Rigdon & Epting, 1985).

This study does not directly address the problematic relation of afterlife beliefs to death threat. However, given that NDErs' conviction in an afterlife is derived from personal experience and not from traditional religious training, these data do not support Tobacyk's hypothesis that an institutional social support system is necessary for afterlife beliefs to influence death threat.

There is some evidence that a positive acceptance of death is associated with a healthy approach to life (Rigdon & Epting, 1985), although which attitude is cause and which is effect is problematic. It is reasonable that satisfaction with life, a sense of having actualized ideals, would decrease fear of death. It is also reasonable that acceptance of death would reduce anxiety over unmet goals and enhance satisfaction with life. Existential theorists have suggested that the importance of life is often discovered through an encounter with the prospect of personal death, and personal construct psychologists hold that the meaning of life cannot be construed independently of the meaning of death.

This study did not provide evidence that NDErs are more actualized than control subjects. Though they did have fewer self/death splits, indicating a lower degree of death threat, they had, compared to control subjects, a similar number of self/ideal self splits, indicating a comparable degree of self/ideal self discrepancy or, inversely, actualization. Thus, actualization as measured by fewer self/ideal self splits on the TI did not seem to be associated with NDEs nor with decreased levels of death threat.

This study suggests that all encounters with imminent death are not equally influential and that experiencing an NDE in the face of death may be the critical factor in altering death orientation. Noyes (1980) and Flynn (1982) both reported that NDErs' decreased fear of death led to altered life goals and values and to enhanced health, well-being, tranquility, and zest for life. Thus, despite the indication in this study that NDErs are equivalent to others in terms of approximation to their ideal selves, given prior near-death researchers' findings and this study's evidence of reduced death threat following NDEs, further exploration is warranted into NDErs' attitudes toward life and its meaning as they relate to changes in death orientation.

REFERENCES

Bannister, D., & Mair, J. (1968). *The evaluation of personal constructs*. New York: Norton.

Becker, E. (1973). *The denial of death*. New York: Free Press.

Dickstein, L. (1972). Death concern: Measurement and correlates. *Psychological Reports, 30,* 563–571.

Flynn, C. P. (1982). Meanings and implications of near-death experiencer transformations. *Anabiosis, 2,* 3–14.

Flynn, C. P. (1986). *After the beyond: Human transformation and the near-death experience.* Englewood Cliffs, NJ: Prentice-Hall.

Gallup, G., & Proctor, W. (1982). *Adventures in immortality: A look beyond the threshold of death.* New York: McGraw-Hill.

Greyson, B. (1983a). Near-death experiences and personal values. *American Journal of Psychiatry, 140,* 618–620.

Greyson, B. (1983b). The Near-Death Experience Scale: Construction, reliability, and validity. *Journal of Nervous & Mental Disease, 171,* 369–375.

Greyson, B. (1990). Near-death encounters with and without near-death experiences: Comparative NDE Scale profiles. *Journal of Near-Death Studies, 8,* 151–161.

Greyson, B., & Stevenson, I. (1980). The phenomenology of near-death experiences. *American Journal of Psychiatry, 137,* 1193–1196.

Kelly, G. A. (1955). *The psychology of personal constructs.* New York: Norton.

Kelly, G. A. (1961). Suicide: The personal construct point of view. In N. Farberow & E. Shneidman (Eds.), *The cry for help* (pp. 255–280). New York: McGraw-Hill.

Krieger, S. R., Epting, F. R., & Leitner, L. M. (1974). Personal constructs, threat and attitudes toward death. *Omega, 5,* 299–310.

Moody, R. A. (1975). *Life after life.* Covington, GA: Mockingbird Books.

Moore, M. K., & Neimeyer, R. A. (1991). A confirmatory factor analysis of the Threat Index. *Journal of Personality and Social Psychology, 60,* 122–129.

Neimeyer, R. A. (1985). Actualization, integration, and fear of death: A test of the additive model. *Death Studies, 9,* 235–244.

Neimeyer, R. A., & Chapman, K. M. (1981). Self-ideal discrepancy and fear of death: The test of an existential hypothesis. *Omega, 11,* 233–240.

Neimeyer, R. A., Dingemans, P. M. A. J., & Epting, F. R. (1977). Convergent validity, situational stability and meaningfulness of the Threat Index. *Omega, 8,* 251–265.

Neimeyer, R. A., Epting, F. R., & Rigdon, M. A. (1983). A procedure manual for the Threat Index. *Death Education, 7,* 321–327.

Neimeyer, R. A., Moore, M. K., & Bagley, K. J. (1988). A preliminary factor structure for the Threat Index. *Death Studies, 12,* 217–225.

Noyes, R. (1980). Attitude change following near-death experiences. *Psychiatry, 43,* 234–242.

Rainey, L. C., & Epting, F. R. (1977). Death threat constructions in the student and the prudent. *Omega, 8,* 19–28.

Rigdon, M. A., & Epting, F. R. (1985). Reduction in death threat as a basis for optimal functioning. *Death Studies, 9,* 427–448.

Rigdon, M. A., Epting, F. R., Neimeyer, R. A., & Krieger, S. R. (1979). The Threat Index: A research report. *Death Education, 3,* 245–270.

Ring, K. (1980). *Life at death: A scientific investigation of the near-death experience.* New York: Coward, McCann & Geoghegan.

Ring, K. (1984). *Heading toward omega: In search of the meaning of the near-death experience.* New York: William Morrow.

Robinson, P. J., & Wood, K. (1984–85). The Threat Index: An additive approach. *Omega, 15,* 139–144.

Sabom, M. B. (1982). *Recollections of death: A medical investigation.* New York: Harper & Row.

Sabom, M. B., & Kreutziger, S. (1977). The experience of near death. *Death Education, 1,* 195–203.

Templer, D. I. (1970). The construction and validation of a death anxiety scale. *Journal of General Psychology, 82,* 165–177.

Tobacyk, J. (1983). Death threat, death concerns, and paranormal belief. *Death Education, 7,* 115–124.

Chapter 9

Death Threat, Parental Loss, and Interpersonal Style: A Personal Construct Investigation

Christopher M. Meshot
Larry M. Leitner

In personal construct theory (Kelly, 1955), highly intimate relationships (ROLE relationships; see Leitner, 1985) are based on core role constructs. Briefly, constructs are the lenses through which we see the world and anticipate events; they are the result of the construing process of seeing how things are alike and different from other things. Bipolar, dichotomous constructs result from the process and provide meaning for the individual interpreter. Thus, the process of construing allows the individual to extract meaning from the world that can be highly personal and unique. Some personal constructs, core role constructs, govern and maintain a person's sense of social identity and existence in the world. ROLE relationships involve understanding the other person's core role constructs and engaging in interpersonal actions based on that understanding. In order to distinguish between the traditional use of role (as mere social prescriptions of behaviors) and Kelly's notion of relationships based on core role constructs, Leitner (1985) has adopted the use of all capitals (ROLE). Such relationships are not entered into lightly; it is through ROLE relationships that we define who we are and who we would like to be. ROLE relationships are not simply following socially prescribed roles given to us by society.

ROLE relationships may be seen as central to psychological well-being (Button, 1983, 1985; Epting & Amerikaner, 1980; Leitner & Pfenninger, 1990), and any loss of an intimate relationship may affect a person's well-being and future ROLE relationships. Loss of a ROLE relationship affects a person's sense of personal and social identity. Loss of an intimate relationship means the loss of a major source of validation and of opportunities to elaborate one's personal construct system, especially core ROLE constructs. For example, some bereavement studies (e.g., Parkes, 1972; Parkes & Weiss, 1983; Sanders, 1989) have shown how grief-stricken people may have auditory and visual hallucinations of a person who died and continue to anticipate future events as if the person were still alive. These people may be continuing to seek validation from someone who no longer can provide such service. ROLE relationships place a person in a dialectical position between "the safety-yet-meaninglessness of limiting involvement in such relationships versus the potential terror-yet-meaningfulness of engaging in such relationships" (Leitner & Dill-Standiford, 1993, p. 2). If severe psychological injury occurs, ROLE relationships may be construed as too terrifying, and massive avoidance of ROLE relationships may result.

The death of a parent often is an immensely painful loss of a ROLE relationship. The death of a parent during adolescence is perhaps one of the most tragic losses. Therefore, it might be expected that the death of a parent would adversely affect the development of ROLE relationships. Several studies (e.g., Dietrich, 1984; Hepworth, Ryder, & Dreyer, 1984; Jacobson & Ryder, 1968; Murphy, 1986–87; Silverman, 1987), not based on a personal construct perspective, have studied the effects of death on interpersonal relationships for people who have lost a parent to death while they were adolescents. While some studies (e.g., Silverman, 1987) report that subjects see no connection between the death of their parent and their intimate relationships, other studies have shown such an effect. For example, Taylor (1983-84) found that people who had had a parent die viewed relationships as risky and threatening. Jacobson and Ryder (1968) established that intimate relationships were longed for by those who had a parent die. Thus, subsequent intimate relationships may be terrifying and in jeopardy.

These studies have not sought to understand *how* the personal meaning of death may affect the person's attitude and style toward future relationships. How a person integrates death into the core may moderate the impact of an experience of death on a person's ROLE relating. In this regard, personal construct researchers have developed an extensive literature on death threat (for a review, see Neimeyer & Epting, 1992). Threat, as defined by Kelly (1955), is "the awareness of imminent comprehensive change in one's core structures" (p. 489). To the extent that a person has not integrated death into the core construct system (those constructs that maintain a person's sense of identity and continuity in existence), death will be experienced as threatening. Furthermore, contained within the core construct system are core role constructs that guide ROLE relationships (Leitner, 1985). Thus, the experience of death may affect not only a person's sense of identity (core constructs) but his or her interpersonal style of engaging others in highly intimate relationships. However, since Kelly fundamentally views all people as actively involved in creating the world in which they live, any event, experience, thing, or person is open to a multitude of interpretations. Thus, even the experience of death may be construed in such a way that a person's interpersonal style and core may not be radically affected.

Typically, personal construct researchers have used some form of the Threat Index (TI) to measure death threat. Recently, Ingram and Leitner (1989) have used an alternate elicitation process, the Interpersonal Repertory Grid (IRG), to measure death threat. The IRG elicits constructs derived from a person's interpersonal world rather than constructs derived from the construing of death-relevant situations as with the TI. Thus, because this study focused both on death and interpersonal style, it was appropriate to use both measures of death threat.

In the present study, young adults who had never experienced parental death, divorce, or separation (the control group) were compared to young adults who had experienced the death of a parent while they were adolescents (death-loss group). It was hypothesized that losing a parent to death would lead to problems in interpersonal relationships. In addition, since the death-loss group had experienced significant loss, it is highly probable that they would have integrated the experience in their cores. Therefore, it was hypothesized that the death-loss group would tend to have lower death threat scores than the control group. Furthermore, it was hypothesized that, for both groups, the personal meaning of death would mediate the relationship between the effects of having a death loss (or not) and interpersonal style. Specifically, the personal meaning of death should accentuate or suppress the relationship between the experience of loss and interpersonal style.

METHOD

Research Participants

Death-loss group. The death-loss group was composed of 20 young adults who, between the ages of 12 and 18 years, had a parent die ($M = 15.7$, $s = 2$). The group (10 females and 10 males) ranged in age from 18 to 27 years old ($M = 19.8$, $s = 2.4$). The age of the parent who died ranged from 37 to 61 years old ($M = 50$, $s = 7.3$). The time since the parent's death ranged from 1 to 9 years ($M = 4.6$, $s = 2$). Fifteen people saw the death of their parent as a "sudden" event while five reported they had "expected" it to happen.

Control group. The control group consisted of 22 young adults (20 females, 2 males) whose ages ranged from 18 to 22 years old ($M = 19$, $s = 1$). The control group had more females than the death-loss group, $\chi^2(1) = 8.65$, $p <$ .005. The parents of the group members were married and had never been divorced or separated. Also, all siblings were alive.

Measures

Threat Index. The provided form of the Threat Index (Neimeyer, Epting, & Rigdon, 1984), using 40 bipolar constructs (TIp), was used. The TIp consists of 40 bipolar constructs obtained from participants in earlier research by means of a form of the Threat Index in which constructs were elicited from each subject (TIe; see Krieger, Epting, & Leitner, 1974).

1 predictable—random
2 empty—meaningful
3 lack of control—control
4 satisfied—dissatisfied
5 relating to others—not relating to others
6 pleasure—pain
7 feels bad—feels good
8 objective—subjective
9 alive—dead
10 helping others—being selfish
11 specific—general
12 kind—cruel
13 incompetent—competent
14 insecure—secure
15 static—changing
16 unnatural—natural
17 sad—happy
18 personal—impersonal
19 purposeful—not purposeful
20 responsible—not responsible
21 bad—good
22 not caring—caring
23 crazy—healthy
24 conforming—not conforming
25 animate—inanimate
26 weak—strong
27 useful—useless
28 closed—open
29 peaceful—violent
30 freedom—restriction
31 nonexistence—existence
32 understanding—not understanding
33 calm—anxious

34 easy—hard
35 productive—unproductive
36 learning—not learning
37 sick—healthy
38 stagnation—growth
39 abstract—concrete
40 hope—no hope

From a personal construct theory perspective, threat is the awareness of imminent comprehensive change in one's core structures. Death would be threatening depending upon the amount of reorganization of the core structure a person would need to do in order to construe death as a personal reality (i.e., as part of the "self"). Threat can be viewed as the reluctance of a person to subsume his or her present self, preferred or ideal self, and death together as elements under the same construct. Thus, the participants rated the self, preferred self, and "my own death" on each provided construct on 13-point scales, ranging from 1 to 6 in each direction, with 0 as the mid-point. A threat score was calculated assessing self-preferred self/death (S-PS/D) splits (i.e., the number of instances the respondent places the self and preferred self on the opposite pole of a construct from the rating of death). This threat score, commonly used in death threat research (Neimeyer, Epting, & Rigdon, 1984), can range from 0 to 40. Ratings of 0 (neutral) mark were disregarded when computing the threat score. Past research (see Rigdon, Epting, Neimeyer, & Krieger, 1979) indicates no sex differences with the Threat Index.

Interpersonal Repertory Grid (IRG).   Fifteen bipolar constructs used in construing one's interpersonal environment were elicited using Landfield's (1971) role specification list. Each research participant described 15 people in his or her life, one person at a time. An opposite was elicited for each description. Because these 15 elicited constructs are unique to each participant, reporting these constructs for each participant would go beyond the scope of this article. The self, preferred self, and own death were rated on each of the 15 constructs using a 13-point scale. The threat score (S-PS/D) was computed in the same manner as the TIp and could range from 0 to 15.

Fundamental Interpersonal Orientation-Behavior (FIRO-B).   Schutz (1966, 1978) offers a theory of interpersonal behavior dividing human interaction into three fundamental dimensions: inclusion, control, and affection. Schutz developed the Fundamental Interpersonal Orientation-Behavior (FIRO-B), 54 self-report items that measure these three areas. Each area is subdivided into Expressed and Wanted behaviors. Typically, scores for six scales (Expressed-Inclusion, Wanted-Inclusion, Expressed-Control, Wanted-Control, Expressed-

Affection, and Wanted-Affection) are reported for the FIRO-B. Scores for each scale can range from 0 to 9.

Inclusion refers to one's general social orientation; it indicates the degree of social involvement with which a person is comfortable. Inclusion is defined as the need to establish and maintain a satisfactory feeling of mutual interest between one's self and other people. This means taking an interest in people and letting other people take an interest in oneself. Extreme types of behavior are termed undersocial (introverted and withdrawn) and oversocial (extroverted, narcissistic, and superficial). Schutz (1966) says that inclusion is related to feelings of self-worth; it is the need to feel worthwhile and significant. Undersocial people feel that no one is interested in them; they feel socially abandoned, uninvolved, and not committed. In order to boost self-worth, oversocial people seek to focus attention on themselves, to be prominent, to be listened to, to make people notice them. Thus, a high score on the Expressed-Inclusion scale would indicate that someone is oversocial; he or she would be extraverted. A high score on the Wanted-Inclusion scale signifies someone who is shy, withdrawn, and introverted.

Control behavior refers to influencing others as well as allowing others to influence you, especially with respect to decision-making processes. Having control leads to a sense of responsibility and competence. The issue of power is relevant to this need for control: control over others allows one to have control over one's future while being under the control of others allows the secure feeling of being protected by the other. The abdicrat is a person who tends toward submission, avoids responsibility and control, and allows others to take control in making decisions. He or she wants to be relieved of obligations and is characterized as a "follower." The autocrat tends toward domination in interpersonal behavior. She or he is a power seeker and feels a strong need to be in control of people and situations at all times. As with the undersocial and oversocial behaviors, the abdicrat and autocrat are viewed as rigid, compulsive interpersonal behavior styles. The moderate position is flexibility: to be able to be either in control or allow others to have control as the circumstance dictates. High scores on the Expressed-Control indicate autocrats; those people who seem inflexible and want to take control of situations all of the time. For the Wanted-Control scale, high scores indicate abdicrats—people who tend to be submissive.

Affection refers to the level of personal closeness or intimacy one finds comfortable in relationships (Schutz, 1966). One's feeling of lovability is closely tied to affection. Affectionate behavior always occurs in at least a two-person, dyadic relationship. As with inclusion and control, individuals may have problems with either of two extremes of affection. The underpersonal type avoids close personal ties with other people and rigidly avoids close relations with others. The person who prefers close relations with everyone (seemingly) is called overpersonal. Both of these types are viewed as rooted in the fear that one is fundamentally unlovable (Schutz, 1966). Underpersonal types score high on the Wanted-Affection scale; they seem shallow, superficial, and distant. Overpersonal types score high on the Expressed-Affection scale. Those described as overpersonal make attempts to become very close to people and want others to treat him or her in the same way.

Schutz's model encompasses both healthy and adaptive interpersonal patterns as well as extreme styles that are less adaptive, more rigid and more compulsive. Undersocial and oversocial styles, in the area of inclusion, express self-worth conflicts. In the area of control, autocrats and abdicrats represent conflicts over competence and control. The underpersonal and overpersonal express conflicts about feelings of lovability in the affection area.

Elaborating on these three areas of interpersonal behavior, Schutz (1966) has included indices of both "Expressed" and "Wanted" behavior within each of the three areas in the FIRO-B. Expressed behavior is how we prefer to behave toward others; wanted behavior is how we prefer others to behave toward us (Schutz, 1967).

Procedure

Research participants were recruited through the psychology department at a midwestern university. Participants were told that the research project was interested in their beliefs and views about death and dying as well as how they typically interacted with others. Research participants completed a personal data form to collect demographic data. This was followed by the TIp, FIRO-B, and IRG.

RESULTS

The data were analyzed using analysis of covariance (ANCOVA) between group membership (death-loss group and control group) and the six scales of the FIRO-B with gender as a covariate. Because there was a disproportionate number of females in the control group relative to the death-loss group, it was possible that gender might affect the results. Results indicate a main effect on the Wanted-Inclusion scale for group membership $[(F(1,39) = 4.95, MS_{error} = 4.75, p < .03]$ with the covariate, gender, not significant $[F(1,39) = 1.2, ns]$. Specifically, the death-loss group $(\overline{X} = 7.3, s = 1.2)$ scored higher on the Wanted-Inclusion scale of the FIRO-B than the control group $(\overline{X} = 5.6, s = 2.7)$. Thus, the death-loss group had an interpersonal style marked by a strong desire that others take interest in them; they wanted to be included by other people. Oversocial people are viewed as superficial, narcissistic, and extraverted.

Results for the Wanted-Affection scale indicate that gender $[F(1,39) = 12.9, MS_{error} = 3.03, p < .001]$ is covarying with group membership $[F(1,39) = 5.1, p < .03]$. Thus, for males, those in the death-loss group $(\overline{X} = 8.1, s = 1.4)$ scored higher than control group members $(\overline{X} = 6.15, s = 1.8)$. Females in the control group $(\overline{X} = 5.50, s = 0.7)$ scored higher than death-loss group females ($\overline{X} = 4.5$, $s = 1.7$). Thus, males in the death-loss group are characterized as overpersonal; they seek close personal ties with everyone. Females in the death-loss group tend to be underpersonal and therefore, avoid close relations.

It was hypothesized that the death-loss group would have lower death-threat scores than the control group. The death-loss group ($\overline{X} = 2.9$, $s = 2.8$) tended to have lower death threat scores, as measured by the IRG, than the control group ($\overline{X} = 4.8$, $s = 3.5$). The point biserial correlation was $r_{pb} = .30$, $p < .05$. This finding did not hold for death threat scores measured with the TIp, $r_{pb} = .17$, ns. Perhaps the experience of the loss of a loved one gave the death-loss group an opportunity to integrate the reality of death and mortality into their core constructs. It appears that the experience of the loss of a loved one through death is integrally tied to interpersonal constructs rather than death-relevant constructs since significant results occurred only for the IRG and not the TIp.

Last, for both groups, it was hypothesized that death threat would suppress or accentuate the relationship between the experience of loss and interpersonal style. Zero-order correlations were calculated between group membership (death-loss or control group) and the FIRO-B scores. The zero-order correlation was compared to the partial correlation between the FIRO-B score and group membership with the death threat score held constant. If death threat is not having an influence, there should be no difference between the partial correlation and the zero-order correlation. In contrast, if death threat does have an influence, there should be a significant difference between the two correlations. No such differences were detected. Therefore, there was no evidence for the role of death threat in mediating the impact of the loss of a parent on interpersonal style.

DISCUSSION

Summarizing the results, the death-loss group scored higher on the Wanted-Inclusion scale of the FIRO-B than the control group. Thus, the death-loss group could be characterized as having an oversocial interpersonal style in which they wanted others to include them. Further, death-loss males tended to be overpersonal while females in the death-loss group were avoidant of close ties. In addition, the death-loss group tended to have lower death threat scores than the control group as measured by the IRG.

The death-loss group had experienced the death of a parent while they were adolescents. Future problems in ROLE relationships is one possible effect of such a trauma. Past research (e.g., Taylor, 1983–84; Jacobson & Ryder, 1969) has examined how the death of a parent can adversely affect future relationships. The data in this study are consistent with this past research and suggest that one possible effect of experiencing this loss is the development of an interpersonal style that is marked by a strong need to have to be included by others. With the experience of the death of the parent, imminent change may be called for in the person's core construct system. The core construct system helps a person maintain a sense of social identity and continuity in existence. Thus, reorganization of this sense of identity is required; this includes core role constructs. One way of understanding this finding is that the trauma of the death of the parent has led these young adults to construe themselves as passive, dependent persons in relationships. In our culture, most people anticipate parental death to occur when the parent is at an advanced age and when the offspring are in middle age. Perhaps this construal of reality is obliterated for the death-loss group when the parent dies. What may replace this construal is that death can happen at any time to any loved ones.

Future problems in relationships for this group may be many. Typically, passive, dependent, submissive individuals tend to have difficulty allowing or expressing anger (Weininger, 1986). Leitner and Pfenninger (1990) suggest that healthy ROLE relationships are characterized by nine aspects of optimal functioning: discrimination, flexibility, creativity, responsibility, openness, commitment, courage, forgiveness, and reverence. People who characteristically interact with others by being superficial and narcissistic would have difficulty sustaining an open, committed, responsible ROLE relationship. ROLE relationships require active participation by both parties in order to encourage the growth of the relationships at deep levels; this comes only through respecting the other's core and being able to be open to both one's own and the other's core.

Kelly (1955) believed that any event or experience is open to reconstruction. Depending upon how the death of the parent is dealt with by the survivor and other intimate friends and family, the effects of the death of the parent may be mediated and mitigated. Gray (1987) found that adolescents who had a good relationship with the surviving parent reported less depression as measured by the Beck Depression Inventory. Though our data do not suggest that death threat may be related to the effects of the loss of the parents on interpersonal style through a partial redundancy model, further research into the causal connection between death threat, loss, and interpersonal style is warranted.

Future research involving a larger sample may provide stronger support for the proposed suppression causal model. Further, an elaborated causal model using other factors (e.g., parental support, prior relationship with deceased, and religious beliefs) may indicate the suppressing effects of the loss on interpersonal style. Last, since our death-loss group was predominately female, future research with a more equitable distribution of males and females is called for.

ACKNOWLEDGMENTS

The authors would like to acknowledge Raymond White, Jr. for his comments.

REFERENCES

Button, E. (1983). Personal construct theory and psychological well-being. *British Journal of Medical Psychology, 56*, 313–321.

Button, E. (Ed.) (1985). *Personal construct theory and mental health*. Bechenham, Kent: Croom Helm.

Dietrich, D. R. (1984). Psychological health of young adults who experienced early parental death: MMPI trends. *Journal of Clinical Psychology, 40*, 901–908.

Epting, F., & Amerikaner, M. (1980). Optimal functioning: A personal construct approach. In A. W. Landfield & L. M. Leitner (Eds.), *Personal construct psychology: Psychotherapy and personality*. NY: Wiley Interscience, pp. 55–77.

Gray, R. E. (1987). Adolescent response to the death of a parent. *Journal of Youth and Adolescence, 16(6)*, 511–525.

Hepworth, J., Ryder, R. G., & Dreyer. A. S. (1984). The effects of parental loss on the formation of intimate relationships. *Journal of Marital and Family Therapy, 10*, 73–82.

Ingram, B., & Leitner, L. M. (1989). Death threat, religiosity, and fear of death: A repertory grid investigation. *International Journal of Personal Construct Psychology 2*, 199–214.

Jacobson, G., & Ryder, R. G. (1968). Parental loss and some characteristics of the early marriage relationship. *American Journal of Orthopsychiatry, 39*, 779–787.

Kelly, G. (1955). *Personal construct theory*. New York: Norton.

Krieger, S. R., Epting, F. R., and Leitner, L. M. (1974). Personal constructs, threat, and attitudes toward death. *Omega, 5*, 299–310.

Landfield, A. W. (1971). *Personal construct systems in psychotherapy*. Chicago: Rand McNally.

Leitner, L. M. (1985). The terrors of cognition: On the experiential validity of personal construct theory. In D. Bannister (Ed.), *Issues and approaches in personal construct theory*. London: Academic Press, pp. 83–104.

Leitner, L. M., & Pfenninger, D. T. (1990, May). Risk and commitment: A constructivistic approach to optimal functioning. Presented at a conference on Constructivism and Psychotherapy, Memphis, TN.

Leitner, L. M., & Dill-Standiford, T. (1993). Resistance in experiential personal construct psychotherapy: Theoretical and technical concerns. In L. M. Leitner & N. G. M. Dunnett (Eds.), *Critical issues in personal construct psychotherapy*. Melbourne, FL: Krieger.

Murphy, P. A. (1986–87). Parental death in childhood and loneliness in young adults. *Omega, 17*, 219–228.

Neimeyer, R. A., & Epting, F. (1992). Measuring personal meanings of death: 20 years of research using the Threat Index. In R. A. Neimeyer & G. J. Neimeyer (Eds.), *Advances in personal construct psychology* (vol. 2). Greenwich, CT, pp. 121–147.

Neimeyer, R. A., Epting, F. R., & Rigdon, M. A. (1984). A procedural manual for the Threat Index. In F. R. Epting & R. A. Neimeyer (Eds.), *Personal meanings of death* (pp. 235–241). Washington: Hemisphere.

Parkes, C. M. (1972). *Bereavement: Studies of grief in adult life*. Madison, CT: International Universities Press.

Parkes, C. M., & Weiss, S. (1983). *Recovery from bereavement*. NY: Basic Books.

Rigdon, M. A., Epting, F. R., Neimeyer, R. A., & Krieger, S. R. (1979). The Threat Index: A research report. *Death Education, 3*, 245–270.

Sanders, C. M. (1989). *Grief: The mourning after.* NY: Wiley & Sons.

Schutz, W. (1966). *The interpersonal underworld: A reprint of FIRO: A three dimensional theory of interpersonal behavior.* Palo Alto: Science and Behavior Books.

Schutz, W. (1978). *The FIRO scales manual.* Palo Alto: Consulting Psychologists Press.

Silverman, P. R. (1987). The impact of parental death on college-age women. *Psychiatric Clinics of North America, 10*, 387–404.

Taylor, D. A. (1983–84). Views of death from sufferers of early loss. *Omega, 14*, 77–82.

Weininger, O. (1986). *The differential diagnostic technique a visual-motor projective test: Research and clinical work.* Springfield, IL: Charles C Thomas.

Chapter 10

Death Depression and Death Anxiety in HIV-Infected Males

Julie Hintze
Donald I. Templer
Gordon G. Cappelletty
Winston Frederick

The purpose of the present research was to determine the death depression and death anxiety in gay men as a function of medical, psychosocial, and subjective state variables. The previous literature suggests that all three categories are important in gay men with AIDS. There is considerable evidence that AIDS patients suffer from a high level of subjective distress such as anxiety, fear, depression, hopelessness, suicidal rumination, and guilt (Baer & Lewitter, 1989; Berube, 1989; Dilley, Pies, & Helquist, 1989; Kooner et al., 1989). Social support would appear to be a very important issue because of the literature that indicates that gay men with AIDS are not infrequently rejected by significant others including their families and by society (Berube, 1989; Cowen & Abramowitz, 1989; Dilley et al., 1989).

Although proximity to death is obviously a death-associated variable, the previous death anxiety literature does not show the strong negative relationship between death anxiety and somatic integrity that one might predict from common sense. Terminal cancer patients have actually demonstrated lower Death Anxiety Scale scores than normal persons (Dougherty, Templer, & Brown, 1986; Gibbs & Achterberg-Lawlis, 1978). Average Death Anxiety Scale scores have been reported with kidney dialysis patients (Blakely, 1975; Lucas, 1974) and Huntington's chorea patients (Gielen & Roche, 1979–1980). And small negative correlations between Death Anxiety Scale score and age have been reported, especially when the subjects included elderly persons (Stevens, Cooper, & Thomas, 1980; Lonetto & Templer, 1986). For this reason, it is important to guard against the assumption that HIV-positive individuals experience uniformly high death anxiety. Thus, this study was undertaken to explore the relationship between death anxiety, subjective distress, medical diagnosis, and awareness of that diagnosis among significant others in a sample of HIV-infected men.

METHOD

Subjects

The 94 HIV-positive gay men ranged in age from 18 to 59 years with a mean of 31.57 years and a standard deviation of 7.03. They ranged in formal education from 10 to 18 years with a mean of 13.67 and a standard deviation of 2.01. Forty (42.6%) of the men were Caucasian; 29 (30.9%), black; 14 (14.9%), Hispanic; 6 (6.4%), Oriental; 4 (4.3%), other; and 1 was American Indian. Thirty-four (36.2%) of the men were HIV positive but asymptomatic, 36 (38.3%) had ARC, and 24 (25.5%) had AIDS.

Research Instruments

All subjects were self-administered the 21-item Beck Depression Inventory (Beck, 1967), the State-Trait Anxiety Inventory (Spielberger, Gorsuch, & Lushene, 1970), the Konofsky Scale (Schag, Heinrich, & Ganz, 1989) of medical debilitation, the Death Anxiety Scale (Templer, 1970), and the Death Depression Scale (Templer, Lavoie, Chalgujian, & Thomas-Dobson, 1990). The last two scales constituted the dependent variables. Although the former instrument has demonstrated good psychometric properties and its construct validity has been developed in scores of studies (Lonetto & Templer, 1986), the Death Depression Scale is acknowledged to be a recently developed and less established instrument. The subjects also completed an information sheet requesting age, sex, ethnicity, education, HIV status, Kanofsky disability category, and the following yes-no questions, "Does your family know the results of your HIV test?", "Are they supportive?", "Does your sex partner(s) know?", "Are they supportive?", and "Do you or have you been involved with IV drug use within the past 6 months?"

Procedure

The principal investigator visited or called testing clinics, physicians, gay newspapers, and various AIDS organizations to obtain permission to approach their clients or advertise for subjects. The testing clinics requested that a flyer be available to potential subjects with the investigator's phone number (to set an appointment at a later time) due to the initial emotional state of receiving testing results. The self-help groups attended had a table containing research news and other topics of interest on which questionnaire packets were left. There was an announcement made about this during the meeting forum. A research assistant was hired to attend support groups, clinics, hospices, and hospital wards to recruit potential subjects. Agencies were visited by the research assistant and asked to participate with the aforementioned procedure by directly filling out the questionnaires and returning them at that time. The subjects were offered $5.00 as an incentive to participate. Confidentiality was assured. The number of people seeing the questionnaires could not be known.

RESULTS

Table 10-1 displays the means and standard deviations for the two dependent variables and for all of the continuous independent variables.

Table 10-2 displays the product moment correlations of the independent variables with the Death Anxiety Scale score and Death Depression Scale score. It is apparent that the highest correlations of the death attitude measures were in the subjective state realm—state anxiety, trait anxiety, and depression. The next highest correlations were with medical status. The men whose condition was the worst, as assessed by HIV severity and Kanofsky score, exhibited the most death anxiety and death depression. Finally, the men whose parents knew about their diagnosis had significantly higher death anxiety and death depression.

Table 10-1   Means and Standard Deviations for Continuous Variables for HIV-positive Men (*n* = 94)

	M	*SD*
Death Attitude (dependent variables)		
Death Anxiety Scale	6.82	4.54
Death Depression Scale	7.87	5.13
Subjective State (independent variables)		
State Anxiety Scale	44.63	18.89
Trait Anxiety Scale	44.47	18.54
Beck Depression Inventory (BDI)	16.52	12.29
BDI without somatic items (14, 16, 17, 18, 19, & 20)	11.20	8.78
Medical status (independent variables)		
HIV severity (HIV + = 1, ARC = 2, AIDS = 3)	1.65	.65
Kanofsky Scale	3.43	2.11

Table 10-2   Correlations Between Death Attitude Measures and Independent Variables for HIV-positive Men

	Total Sample		Less Disabled Subsample	
Independent	Death Anxiety ($n=94$)	Death Depression ($n=94$)	Death Anxiety ($n=75$)	Death Depression ($n=75$)
Subjective state variables				
State anxiety	.76*	.81**	.62**	.68**
Trait anxiety	.76**	.81**	.64**	.68**
Depression	.73**	.74**	.57**	.59**
Depression minus somatic items	.73**	.76**	.54**	.57**
Medical status[a]				
HIV severity	.65**	.62**	.50**	.45**
Kanofsky severity	.71**	.69**	.54**	.47**
Psychosocial variables[b]				
Family knowledge	.47*	.43**	.47**	.41**
Family support	.15	.10	.16	.18
Sex partner knowledge	.18	.18	.28*	.24*
Sex partner support	.07	−.07	−.18	−.16
Age	−.13	−.08	−.19	−.13
Education	−.07	−.01	−.17	−.11

* $p < .05$.   ** $p < .001$
[a] HIV+ = 1, ARC = 2, AIDS = 3.
[b] no = 1, yes = 2.

In order to partially rule out the possibility that neurological and/or other debilitation may have prevented some subjects from validly completing the instruments, correlations were carried out without the 19 persons who endorsed Kanofsky categories 6, 7, 8, or 9. These respective categories are "Require considerable assistance and frequent medical care," "Disabled; require occasional care and assistance," "Severely disabled; hospitalization indicated though death not imminent," and "Very sick; hospitalization necessary, active support treatment necessary." Table 10-3 displays the product-moment correlations between the death attitude measures and independent variables for the designated 75 less disabled subjects. As expected, when group heterogeneity was reduced, correlations between death attitude and medical severity conditions are lower than in the first analysis. The death attitude-subjective state correlations are also lower. However, the fact that the two sets of correlations do not greatly differ suggests that the correlations for all 94 subjects are not considerably influenced by subject incapacitation.

The correlation coefficient between the two death attitude measures is .91, appreciably higher than that found in the previous literature. Because of this high

Table 10-3   Stepwise Multiple Regression with Dependent Variable Death Anxiety, for HIV-positive Men ($n = 94$)

Independent Variable	Multiple Regression				
	r	R	R^2	β	F
State Anxiety	.76	.76	.58	.39	12.28*
Beck Depression	.73	.79	.63	.37	12.51*
Family knowledge	.47	.80	.65	.18	6.71*

* $p < .001$.

correlation, and the fact that the correlations of the independent variables with the two death attitude instruments in Table 10-3 are so similar, it is questionable whether death anxiety and death depression can be considered distinguishable constructs, at least with the present sample. For this reason the following multiple regression was conducted with only the more established instrument, the Death Anxiety Scale, as the dependent variable.

Table 10-3 provides the stepwise multiple-regression summary with the Death Anxiety score as the dependent variable and with all of the designated independent variables in the three realms—medical, subjective state, and psychosocial—as dependent variables. The three variables that predicted higher death anxiety in order of their contribution to the multiple regression equation were higher state anxiety, higher depression, and family having knowledge of the diagnosis.

DISCUSSION

The Death Anxiety Scale correlations with state and trait anxiety were much higher than the death anxiety–general anxiety correlations that are ordinarily reported in the literature (Abdel-Khalek, 1986, 1991; Kuperman & Golden, 1978; Loewen, 1984; Lonetto, Mercer, Fleming, Bunting, & Clare, 1980; Neufeldt & Holmes, 1979; Smith, 1977; Templer, 1970, 1972). Of more specific relevance are previously reported correlations of death anxiety with the State-Trait Anxiety Inventory, which usually displays much lower correlations with the Death Anxiety Scale than the correlations in the present study (Abdel-Khalek, 1986; Gilliland & Templer, 1985-6; Lucas, 1974; Ochs, 1979). Clinically, this may indicate that HIV-positive men experience a global state of anxiety in which death anxiety and more general distress are not easily separated. Whether death-related fears "cause" this general apprehension cannot be determined by correlational findings like those in this study.

The correlation of .91 between the Death Anxiety Scale and the Death Depression Scale is at least as high as the previously reported reliabilities for the separate instruments (Templer, 1969, 1970; Templer, Lavoie, Chalgujian, &

Thomas-Dobson, 1990). This high correlation seems to indicate that in the present study the two death attitude instruments do not tap separate entities. Correlations of .67 (Templer, Lavoie, Chalgujian, & Thomas-Dobson, 1990) and .50 (Alvarado, 1991) have been reported in the previous literature. Thus it would appear that such a high relationship between death depression and death anxiety in the present study is a function of the present population. The positive correlations of seriousness of medical status with death anxiety and death depression could be viewed as congruent with common sense but do not mesh with the previous literature as reviewed above, which typically does not suggest a close relationship between physical and psychological well-being.

The positive correlations of death anxiety with family knowledge and sex partner knowledge of diagnosis were the opposite of what was predicted. In retrospect, however, it would appear that such knowledge was probably related to death attitudes because both are related to severity of medical condition. It is difficult not to know about an HIV-positive condition in advanced cases unless there is no contact whatsoever between patient and significant others. In order to more fully explore such an explanation, partial correlations, controlling for HIV severity and Kanofsky disability, were carried out. For all 94 subjects, the family knowledge partial correlation was .27 ($p < .01$) with death anxiety. The original correlation was .57 ($p < .001$). The sex partner partial correlation was .12. The original correlation was .18. Thus it is apparent that the partial correlations controlling for seriousness of the disorder were lower than the original correlations. However, the fact that knowledge of diagnosis by family and partners continued to correlate positively with subject's death anxiety should caution us against the assumption that informing others necessarily assists the HIV-positive individual in coping with his condition.

REFERENCES

Abel-Khalek, A. M. (1986). Death anxiety in Egyptian samples. *Personality and Individual Differences*, 7, 479–483.

Abel-Khalek, A. M. (1991). Death anxiety among Lebanese samples. *Psychological Reports*, 68, 924–926.

Alvarado, K. (1991). *Death anxiety, death depression, and religion in general population persons, and in clergy and seminarians*. Doctoral dissertation, California School of Professional Psychology, Fresno, CA.

Baer, J., & Lewitter-Koehler, S. (1989, May). *The AIDS patient in psychiatric care: A new challenge*. Kings View Center Symposium, Reedley, CA.

Beck, A. T. (1967). *Depression: Clinical experimental and theoretical aspects*. New York: Harper & Row.

Berube, A. (1989). *AIDS and the meaning of natural disaster*. San Francisco, CA: University of San Francisco, AIDS Health Project, pp. 1–2.

Blakely, K. B. (1975). *Chronic renal failure: A study of death anxiety in dialysis and kidney transplant patients*. Unpublished doctoral dissertation, University of Manitoba, Winnipeg, Manitoba, Canada.

Devins, G. M. (1979). Death anxiety and voluntary passive-euthanasia. *Journal of Consulting and Clinical Psychology*, *17*, 301–309.

Dilley, J. W., Pies, C., & Helquist, M. (1989). *Face to face: A guide to AIDS counseling*. Berkeley, CA: University of California San Francisco, AIDS Health Project.

Dougherty, K., Templer, D.I., & Brown, R. (1986). Psychological states in terminal cancer patients as measured over time. *Journal of Consulting Psychology*, *33*, 357–359.

Gielen, A. C., & Roche, K. A. (1979–1980). Death anxiety and psychometric studies in Huntington's Disease. *Omega*, *10*, 135–145.

Gibbs, H. W., & Achterberg-Lawles, J. (1978). Spiritual value and death anxiety: Implications for counseling with terminally ill cancer patients. *Journal of Counseling Psychology*, *25*, 563–569.

Gilliland, J. C., & Templer, D. I. (1985). Relationship of death anxiety scale factors to the subjective state. *Omega*, *16*, 155–167.

Hartshore, T. S. (1979). *The grandparent and grandchild relationship and life satisfaction, death anxiety, and attitude toward the future*. Unpublished doctoral dissertation, University of Texas at Austin.

Koob, P. B., & Davis, S. F. (1977). Fear of death in military officers and their wives. *Psychological Reports*, *40*, 261–262.

Kooner, R., Perecman, E., Lazar, W., Hainline, B., Kaplan, M. H., Lesser, M., & Beresford, R. (1989). Relation of personality and attentional factors to cognitive deficits in human immunodeficiency virus-infected subjects. *Archives of Neurology*, *46*, 274–277.

Kuperman, S. K., & Golden, S. J. (1978). Personality correlative of attitude toward death. *Journal of Clinical Psychology*, *34*, 661–663.

Loewen, I. L. (1984). *Widowhood: The relationship between religious orientation and adjustment to loss of spouse*. Doctoral dissertation. California School of Professional Psychology, Fresno, CA.

Lonetto, R., & Templer, D. (1986). *Death anxiety*. Washington: Hemisphere.

Lonetto, R., Mercer, G. W., Fleming, S., Bunting, B., & Clare, M. (1980). Death anxiety among university students in Northern Ireland and Canada. *Journal of Psychology*, *104*, 75–82.

Lucas, R. A. (1974). A comparative study of measures of general anxiety and death anxiety among the medical groups including patient and wife. *Omega*, *5*, 233–243.

Neufeldt, D. E., & Holmes, C. B. (1979). Relationship between personality traits and fear of death. *Psychological Reports*, *45*, 907–910.

Ochs, C. E. (1979). *Death orientation, purpose of life and choice of volunteer service*. Unpublished doctoral dissertation, California School of Professional Psychology, Fresno, CA.

Schag, C. C., Heinrich, R. L., & Ganz, P. A. (1984). Kanofsky performance status revisited: Reliability, validity, and guidelines. *Journal of Clinical Psychology*, *2*, 187–193.

Smith, A. H., Jr. (1977). A multivariate study of personality situational and demographic predictors of death anxiety in college students. *Essence*, *1*, 139–146.

Spielberger, C. P., Gorsuch, R. L., & Lushene, R. E. (1970). *Trait Anxiety Inventory (self-evaluation questionnaire)*. Palo Alto, CA: Consulting Psychologists Press.

Stevens, S. J., Cooper, P. E., & Thomas, L. E. (1980). Age norms for Templer's Death Anxiety Scale. *Psychological Reports*, *46*, 205–206.

Templer, D. I. (1969). Death Anxiety Scale. *Proceedings of the 77th Annual Convention of the American Psychological Association*, *4*, 737–738.

Templer, D. I. (1970). The construction and validation of a Death Anxiety Scale. *Journal of General Psychology*, *82*, 165–177.

Templer, D. I. (1972). Death anxiety: Extroversion, neuroticism, and cigarette smoking. *Omega*, *3*, 126–127.

Templer, D. I. (1976). Two factor theory of death anxiety: A note. *Essence*, *2*, 91–94.

Templer, D. I., Lavoie, M., Chalgujian, H., & Thomas-Dobson, S. (1990). The measurement of death depression. *Journal of Clinical Psychology*, *46*, 834–838.

Chapter 11

Death Concern and Attitudes Toward the Elderly in Nursing Home Personnel

Stephen J. DePaola
Robert A. Neimeyer
Michael B. Lupfer
Jayne Fiedler

As longevity increases in the United States, researchers have become interested in the nursing profession's role in providing care for the elderly (Taylor & Harned, 1978). However, the care received by the elderly is often marred by nurses' negative attitudes toward the aged (Martin & Buckwalter, 1984). Such negative attitudes are reflected in the scarcity of geriatric curricula in nursing education and the fact that most nurses choose to work with patients of younger age groups (Burnside, 1981). Similarly, Smith, Jepson, and Perloff (1982) argue that nursing staff at all levels display a lack of concern regarding geriatrics and typically have very little information about the elderly patient. The implication of these assertions is that negative attitudes on the part of nursing staff result in less than adequate care for the elderly (Alford, 1982; Burnside, 1981; Storlic, 1982). Thus, as a first step to improving health care for the aged, it is necessary to explore the underlying influences on nursing staff attitudes.

One important influence on attitudes toward the elderly may be the care-giver's own attitudes toward death. That is, negative attitudes toward the elderly may be mediated by a caregiver's death anxiety (Eakes, 1985; Lester, Getty, & Kneisel, 1974). As a result, the quality of nursing care provided by personnel who hold different attitudes toward death and the aged is of interest for researchers.

The central purpose of this investigation was to assess the relationship between death concern and attitudes toward the elderly held by nursing personnel in geriatric facilities. However, unlike most previous research, the present study employed a matched comparison group of participants who work in non-death-related occupations.

ATTITUDES TOWARD THE ELDERLY IN NURSING HOME PERSONNEL

A few studies have examined the attitudes held by different levels of nursing home personnel—registered nurses (RNs), licensed practical nurses (LPNs), and nurse aides (NAs)—toward elderly patients (Chandler, Rachal, & Kazelskis, 1986; Smith, Jepson, & Perloff, 1982; Taylor & Harned, 1978; Williams, 1982). However, the results of these studies are mixed. For example, Williams (1982), in a survey of more than 100 nurses who supplied different levels of care to the elderly, found that 75% of nurses at all levels demonstrated negative attitudes toward the elderly as measured by Palmore's (1977) Facts on Aging Quiz #1 (FAQ #1). Smith, Jepson, and Perloff (1982) analyzed the attitudes of different nursing personnel toward the elderly and found that attitudes toward the elderly differed for nurses at various levels of training. In addition, the researchers took into account the level of nursing care (skilled, intermediate, or discharge) needed by the elderly patients. Their results indicated that RNs exhibited more positive attitudes toward elderly patients than LPNs or nurse aides. Moreover, patients who were being discharged were viewed more positively by all levels of nursing personnel.

Such attitudes may result from a stereotype of old age or from a reaction to the chronic disorders and impairments suffered by the elderly (Almquist, Stein, Weiner, & Linn, 1981). However, an additional factor that may influence reactions toward the elderly may be the caregiver's own attitudes toward death (Eakes, 1985; Vickio & Cavanaugh, 1985).

DEATH ANXIETY AMONG NURSING HOME PERSONNEL

Several studies have found that nursing home personnel with high levels of death anxiety have significantly more negative attitudes toward the elderly than nursing home personnel with low levels of death anxiety (Vickio & Cavanaugh, 1985; Eakes, 1985). In addition, Vickio and Cavanaugh (1985) reported that increased death anxiety was correlated with greater personal anxiety toward aging. Furthermore, they found that employees who had experienced greater exposure to the deaths of the residents reported more comfort in thinking about and discussing death and dying with the patients. However, this same group of employees did not always have lower scores on Templer's (1970) Death Anxiety Scale (DAS). The researchers speculated that these employees may have had the ability to separate their own death anxiety from their desire to discuss concerns that the residents had about death and dying. In addition, the researchers pointed out that the apparent multidimensionality of the DAS may have obscured the relationship between death experience and death anxiety.

DEATH ANXIETY AND AGE

Another variable that influences the level of death anxiety for an individual is age. Research indicates that age is negatively correlated with death anxiety (Johnson, 1980; Neimeyer, 1985; Nelson, 1979; Stevens, Cooper, & Thomas, 1980). However, in broader samples, a curvilinear trend has sometimes been detected. For example, Gesser, Wong, and Reker (1988) administered the Death Attitude Profile to 50 subjects in three age groups: the young (18–26), the middle-aged (35–50), and the elderly (60 & older). Their results indicated that death anxiety was high in young subjects, highest in middle adulthood, and lowest in the elderly. Thus, it seems important to examine how the age of the caregiver is related to both death concern and possible reactions to the aged.

LIMITATIONS OF PREVIOUS RESEARCH

The research previously discussed is a step toward assessing death anxiety and attitudes held by nursing home personnel. However, there are several method-ological problems represented in previous research and there are a number of questions yet to be answered.

One limitation concerns the use of attitude measures of questionable relia-bility, validity (Collette-Pratt, 1976; Green, 1981; McTavish, 1971), and dimen-sionality (Hicks, Rogers, & Shemberg, 1976; Kafer, Rakowski, Lachman, & Hickey, 1980; Weinberger & Millham, 1975). More specifically, several re-searchers have suggested that attitudes toward personal aging should be distin-guished from reactions to the aged as a group (Carp, 1967; Kafer, Rakowski, Lachman, & Hickey, 1980; Kogan & Shelton, 1962). Similarly, there is a growing recognition that attitudes toward death are also multifaceted, requiring more sophisticated assessment (Hoelter, 1979; Neimeyer, 1988).

A second concern is that the Facts on Aging Quizes (1 & 2) are the most commonly used measures to identify positive or negative attitudes toward the elderly (Palmore, 1980; Palmore, 1981). Both scales were designed to assess basic physical, mental, and social facts about aging, rather than attitudes per se. As such, both the FAQ #1 and FAQ #2 are only rough indicators of bias toward the elderly, and Palmore (1980), the author of the instrument, has recommended that they be used only when instruments that measure attitudes toward the elderly in a direct manner are unavailable. In contrast, the Aging Opinion Survey (AOS) (Kafer, Rakowski, Lachman, & Hickey, 1980) was designed specifically to address the issue of multidimensionality when measuring attitudes toward the elderly. Although less frequently used, the AOS measures attitudes toward personal aging, aging of peers, and reactions to the general-other elderly, and it has demonstrated adequate reliability.

A third limitation concerns the psychometric soundness of death concern measures. For example, the death anxiety measure that has been used in all previous studies of death attitudes in relation to attitudes toward the elderly is Templer's Death Anxiety Scale (DAS). But despite its popularity, the DAS has been increasingly criticized on methodological grounds (Neimeyer, 1988). A central problem with the instrument has been its susceptibility to social desirability response bias (Dattel & Neimeyer, 1990), along with its low internal consistency (Devins, 1979; Martin, 1982; Warren & Chopra, 1978). Moreover, the finding that the DAS measures not one, but several dimensions of death attitudes that shift from study to study complicates interpretation of the scale, leading at least one reviewer to recommend that its use be discontinued altogether (Durlak, 1982). Thus, there is a need to replicate the general correlation between death anxiety and negativity toward the elderly with other methodologically sound measures of death concern, such as the Threat Index (Neimeyer & Moore, 1989) or the Multidimensional Fear of Death Scale (Hoelter, 1979). Despite terminological differences, current evidence suggests that death *anxiety* and *fear* are indistinguishable constructs, at least as currently operationalized (Neimeyer, 1988). Both refer to a negative emotional reaction to aspects of death and dying. Death *threat*, on the other hand, can be distinguished from fear and anxiety, since it refers to a cognitive incompatibility between one's view of personal death and one's identity as a living being. For this reason, the present study incorporated psychometrically sound measures of both death fear/anxiety and death threat (collectively described as death concern), to examine their relationship to attitudes toward aging.

A final limitation of previous research is the absence of control groups, which makes any assertions about the negativity of nursing staff attitudes toward aging or death extremely precarious. The use of a control group also would be helpful in determining if the relationship between level of death anxiety and attitudes toward the elderly is a pervasive phenomenon, or if it is distinctive to nursing home personnel.

In summary, the major purpose of the present investigation was to assess the relationship between death concern and attitudes toward the elderly, especially in a relevant occupational group, i.e., staff in nursing homes. However, unlike previous studies, the present study employed a matched comparison group of participants who work in non-death-related occupations to determine whether the responses of nursing staff are distinguishable from those of the general population. In order to ensure comparability of groups, control participants were matched with nursing home personnel on age, sex, race, and educational level.

We hypothesized that when compared to a control group, nursing home personnel would have higher levels of death threat and fear, more negative attitudes toward the elderly, and higher levels of personal anxiety toward aging. We also hypothesized that death fear would be positively associated with the more cognitively oriented death threat score obtained from the Threat Index. Finally, we predicted that age would be negatively correlated with death concern and that more death fearful or threatened subjects would display more negative attitudes toward their own aging and toward the elderly in general.

METHOD

Subjects

The study was conducted in six nursing homes and a number of other worksites in Memphis, Tennessee. Despite efforts to recruit more highly trained personnel, the sample was weighted toward less skilled caregivers. A total of 145 subjects consisting of registered nurses ($n = 4$), licensed practical nurses ($n = 30$), and nurse aides ($n = 111$) working in the six facilities took part in the data collection. In addition, a comparison sample was recruited consisting of 130 participants employed in various non-death-related occupations (e.g., clerical workers and business managers). (See Table 11-1.)

Procedure

The questionnaire packets were administered to nursing home personnel during group sessions. Participants were informed that this was an anonymous survey about personal beliefs and attitudes. Control subjects also completed the questionnaire packets in group sessions at their respective places of employment. The order of presentation of the questionnaires (see below) was the same for both groups of subjects. This order was based on the recommendations of several nursing home directors, who stated that a dissimilar order would provoke discussion among the participants that might influence the results of the study.

Measures

Demographics Form. This was a general information sheet on which the subject provided sociodemographic information needed for the analysis (i.e., age, education, job tenure).

Table 11-1   Demographic and Descriptive Characteristics of Control and Nursing Home Groups

Characteristics	Nursing home (*n* = 145)	Control (*n* = 130)	Test	*p*
Sex				
Male	9 (6%)	17 (13%)	χ^2 = 3.80	*.05
Female	136 (94%)	113 (87%)		
Age (*M*)	35.6	35.6	*t* = −.09	.930
Ethnic status				
Black	108 (74%)	78 (60%)	χ^2 = 6.60	*.010
White	37 (26%)	52 (40%)		
Educational level				
Grade school	26 (18%)	4 (3%)	χ^2 = 16.52	**.000
H. S. graduate	88 (61%)	96 (74%)		
College graduate	31 (21%)	30 (23%)		
Has anyone significant recently died?				
Yes	79 (54%)	62 (48%)	χ^2 = 1.30	.900
No	66 (46%)	68 (52%)		

*p < .05.
**p < .01.

Threat Index (TI)   The TI is the most rigorously validated measure of death orientation published to date (Moore & Neimeyer, 1991; Neimeyer & Epting, 1992; Neimeyer & Moore, 1989). It is also unique in being the only measure of death attitudes derived from a comprehensive theory of personality, the psychology of personal constructs (Kelly, 1955). The TI measures the level of "threat" implied by one's personal death, defined as the subjective incompatibility between one's death and one's identity as a living being (Neimeyer & Epting, 1992).

The TI form used in the present study was the provided construct, 25-item scalar version. On each construct the subject rated three elements (self, preferred self, and my own death). Split scores were calculated on the discrepancy between self and death ratings on 7-point scales, to yield an overall death threat score. A split was defined as any instance in which the subject placed "self" and "own death" elements on opposite poles of a construct. For example, on the TI scale "predictable 1 2 3 4 5 6 7 unpredictable," the subject who rated herself "2" and her death "7" would be said to split on this dimension, whereas the subject who rated herself "1" and death "3" would not. Splits were scored only in those cases in which "self" and "death" ratings were on opposite sides of the central "4" response. Ratings on the four (or neutral) mark were counted as a non-split. Ongoing empirical work supports the reliability and validity of the TI as a measure of death concern (Neimeyer & Epting, 1992). For example, internal reliability coefficients for the scale exceed .93 and test-retest correlation is .87 for a 9-week period. The death threat score derived from the instrument has also demonstrated concurrent and criterion validity in a number of studies (see Neimeyer & Epting, 1992, for review). Lastly, the TI is not biased by social desirability (Dattel & Neimeyer, 1990).

The Multidimensional Fear of Death Scale (MFODS) The MFODS (Hoelter, 1979) was used as the best available multidimensional measure of death fear, thereby broadening the assessment of death concern provided by the Threat Index. The MFODS is a 48-item scale that is composed of eight distinct factors. The eight factors and their alpha coefficients are as follows: fear of the dying process (.80), fear of the dead (.72), fear of being destroyed (.81), fear for significant others (.76), fear of the unknown (.73), fear of conscious death (.65), fear for the body after death (.82), and fear of premature death (.72; Hoelter, 1979; Walkey, 1982).

Social Value of the Elderly Scale (SVES) The SVES (Kafer, Rakowski, Lachman, & Hickey, 1980) is one of the 15-item subscales that comprise the Aging Opinion Survey (AOS; Kafer, Rakowski, Lachman, & Hickey, 1980). The AOS is the only instrument to date that was developed on an multidimensional view of attitudes toward aging and the elderly. The SVES assesses several content areas, generally focusing on interpersonal relations and the place of older persons in the community (e.g., residential segregation, social responsibility, public policy, knowledge). In fact, the SVES scale assesses a factor that has been identified in previous research as being an important component of negative attitudes toward the elderly (Hickey, Bragg, Rakowski, & Hultsch, 1979; Kapos & Smith, 1972). The items focus on perceptions of older persons as a group. Lower scores are indicative of less perceived social value. Coefficient alpha, an index of internal reliability, is .60 for this subscale.

Personal Anxiety toward Aging (PAA) The PAA (Kafer, Rakowski, Lachman, & Hickey, 1980) is a second 15-item subscale of the AOS designed to tap subjects' anxiety and fear concerning their own aging. Previous research has found that fear concerning one's own aging is associated with negative views of the elderly. The items comprising the scale cover a broad range of topic areas (e.g., finances, mobility, friends, family relationships). Lower scores on this scale are indicative of greater anxiety toward personal aging. Coefficient alpha for this subscale is .65.

RESULTS

Overview of Analyses

Descriptive statistics were calculated for both the nursing home and the control groups. Subsequently, a multivariate analysis of covariance (MANCOVA) was conducted on all death orientation measures comparing nursing home personnel with the control group. Next, univariate analyses of covariance (ANCOVAs) were performed on all significant findings. In addition, Pearson correlations were computed on all variables for the combined sample. Finally, a multiple regression analysis of independent variables was conducted to determine the best predictors of negative attitudes toward the elderly.

Descriptive Statistics for Both Groups

Table 11-1 presents means and standard deviations for each demographic variable for the nursing home and control groups. Despite efforts to recruit comparable samples, preliminary analyses indicated that the nursing home sample included more blacks and more females and was somewhat less educated than the control sample. These relatively minor observed differences were controlled in subsequent analyses using appropriate covariance techniques.

Analyses of Covariance on Death Orientation Measures and Attitudes Toward Aging

The MANCOVA for the death orientation scores revealed a significant main effect for group membership (Wilk's λ = .81), $F(9, 262)$ = 6.86, $p < .001$. Subsequently, univariate analyses of covariance (ANCOVAs) were examined for each measure with race, education, and sex as covariates. Table 11-2 presents the adjusted group means, F results, and significance levels for all death attitude measures and attitudes toward aging. Although nursing home and control subjects did not differ in their scores on the Threat Index, differences did emerge on three of the eight subscales of the MFODS. Specifically, the ANCOVA for the fear of the dead subscale revealed a significant main effect for group. Nursing home personnel (M = 16.85) had less apprehension regarding this dimension of death concern when compared to the control group (M = 19.88). The results also indicated a significant difference for the MFODS subscale measuring fear of the impact of one's death on significant others. Again, the control group (M = 23.04) displayed more death concern on this component when compared to nursing home personnel (M = 21.80). Lastly, an ANCOVA found significant differences for the fear of the unknown scale, with nursing home personnel (M = 12.55) exhibiting more concern regarding the ambiguity of death when compared to the control group (M = 10.20).

The ANCOVA on the AOS also revealed a significant effect for group, with nursing home personnel (M = 48.00) displaying higher levels of anxiety regarding their own aging when compared to the control group (M = 45.00). Lastly, the ANCOVA for negative attitudes toward the elderly displayed a significant effect for group. Nursing home personnel (M = 39.50) had more neg-

Table 11-2   Adjusted Means and *F* Results for Nursing Home and Control Groups on Attitude Measures

Characteristic	Nursing home (*n* = 145)	Control (*n* = 130)	*F*	*p*<
Death Threat Score	13.3	13.8	.134	.71
MFODS				
F1 Fear of Dying	21.10	21.27	.048	.826
F2 Fear of the Dead	16.85	19.88	21.81	.00
F3 Fear of Being Destroyed	14.76	14.46	.393	.531
F4 Fear for Significant Others	21.80	23.04	4.31	.038
F5 Fear of the Unknown	12.55	10.20	19.25	.00
F6 Fear of Consciousness When Dead	14.30	13.64	1.186	.277
F7 Fear for Body After Death	14.82	13.80	2.060	.152
F8 Fear of Premature Death	12.48	12.30	.178	.673
Anxiety Toward Aging	48.00	45.00	9.91	.001
Value of the Elderly	39.50	36.50	11.82	.002

Higher scores on the Anxiety Toward Aging Scale and the MFODS factors indicate higher levels of anxiety. A high score on the anxiety toward aging scale indicates more negative attitudes toward the elderly.

ative attitudes toward the elderly when compared to the control group (M = 36.50).

Pearson Correlations Among Death Orientation Measures

Table 11-3 presents the intercorrelations of the death orientation measures, incorporating both the nursing home and control groups.

Death Threat   As expected, death fear as measured by the MFODS was correlated with death threat as assessed by the Threat Index such that individuals with higher death threat scored higher on four of the eight subfactors of the Hoelter measure. Death threat was modestly but significantly correlated with several aspects of personal death anxiety, fear of dying, and fear of facing the unknown. In addition, death threat was associated with fear for the impact of one's death on significant others. This finding provides tentative evidence for the construct validity of both measures. Additionally, death threat was positively correlated with anxiety toward one's own personal aging. Lastly, death threat was not associated with negative views of the elderly.

Personal Anxiety Toward Aging.   As expected, a positive relationship was found between personal anxiety about one's own aging and the total score

Table 11-3 Pearson Correlations of Attitude Measures for Nursing Home and Control Group (*n* = 275)

	Age	DT	Elderly	Aging	MFODS	F1	F2	F3	F4	F5	F6	F7	F8
Age	—	-.14*	-.19**	-.06	-.35**	-.15*	-.30*	-.09	-.24**	-.27**	-.25**	-.26**	-.17**
Death threat (DT)		—	-.01	.13*	.16**	.12*	.14*	-.01	.21**	.13*	-.01	.09	.10
Value of elderly (Elderly)			—	.17**	.12*	-.05	.04	.01	-.05	.29**	.20**	.17**	-.01
Anxiety toward aging (Aging)				—	.40**	.35**	.15*	.14*	.14*	.30**	.23**	.34**	.35**

Note. Reverse scoring of the value of elderly, anxiety toward aging, and the MFODS scales were conducted for interpretive clarity.
F1 Dying; F2 Dead; F3 Destroyed; F4 Significant Others; F5 Unknown; F6 Consciousness; F7 Body; and F8 Premature.
*p < .05, **p < .01, all tests are two-tailed.

on the MFODS. Thus, individuals who had higher levels of death fear were more apprehensive about their own aging. Furthermore, the results indicated that all of the MFODS subscales were positively correlated with personal anxiety about one's own aging. Moderate correlations were found between personal anxiety about growing older and fear of dying, fear of the unknown, fear for the body after death, and fear of premature death.

Attitudes Toward the Elderly. Consistent with past research, negative view of the elderly was significantly (but only weakly) associated with global death fear. The results also indicated that a negative view of the elderly was correlated with fear of the unknown. Individuals who are concerned about the ambiguity of death perceive the elderly as possessing less social value. In addition, both fear of consciousness when dead and fear for the body after death were associated with negative views of the elderly. Lastly, personal anxiety toward one's own aging was correlated with negative views of the elderly.

Prediction of Negative Attitudes Toward The Elderly

Finally, a multiple regression analysis was conducted to identify the statistical model that best explained negative attitudes toward the elderly after controlling for race, education, and sex. In this regression, education, race, and sex were entered first and then a stepwise regression analysis was conducted in which death attitude measures were entered at the first step, followed by personal anxiety toward one's own aging, and lastly, group membership. As shown in Table 11-4, several of the variables were significantly associated with negative

Table 11-4 Multiple Regression Analysis Predicting Perceived Social Value of the Elderly

Variables in the equation	Beta	T^2	Increment in R^2	DF	F
Education	−.17	−2.92			
Race	.01	.217	.08	3,270	7.53**
Sex	.20	3.28			
F5 Fear of the unknown	.23	4.01	.05	1,269	16.10**
Group membership*	−.15	−2.53	.02	1,268	6.40*

Note. At the second and third steps a stepwise regression analysis was conducted.
Total Model Variance = .15.
Model $F(5, 268)$ = 9.45.**
*$p < .05$.
**$p < .01$.

attitudes toward the elderly, accounting for 15% of the variance. Thus, fear of the unknown associated with death and membership in the nursing home group contributed significantly to the prediction of subjects' tendency to devalue the elderly. Personal anxiety toward one's own aging failed to add significantly to the total model.

DISCUSSION

Based on previous research it was expected that nursing home personnel when compared to a control group would have higher levels of death concern and consequently more negative attitudes toward the elderly. Contrary to this hypothesis, nursing home personnel did not display more general death fear or death threat when compared to a group of subjects in non-death-related occupations.

On the contrary, it was found that the control group displayed higher levels of death concern on two dimensions of death fear. Control respondents demonstrated higher levels of fear of the dead, as well as greater fear for the impact of their deaths on significant others. One possible explanation for these findings is that nursing home personnel deal with the dead and dying on a daily basis and may have become desensitized to death and its impact on survivors, at least as observed within the institutional context of the nursing home. However, competing explanations of these results also exist, including the possibility of self-selection for death acceptance in pursuing employment in nursing home settings and acclimation to death as a part of life as a consequence of such employment.

The only dimension of death concern on which nursing home personnel showed more apprehension than controls concerned the uncertainty of death. The items on this scale specifically deal with issues regarding the existence of a life after death. No explanation for their greater anxiety about the existence of an afterlife is readily apparent.

Consistent with the implication of past research, the results of this study revealed that nursing home personnel perceived the elderly as possessing less social value than did controls. It had been expected that negative attitudes toward the elderly would be mediated by the participants' death anxiety. In the present study death anxiety accounted for only a small (albeit significant) proportion of the variance in negative attitudes toward the elderly. However, this proportion of variance was larger than that associated with any other variable. Specifically, fear of the unknown accounted for a larger proportion of variance than either demographic status or occupational group membership.

The findings from the current investigation support previous studies indicating that individuals with higher levels of death threat are also more fearful of death. Moreover, the results from the present study are consistent with past research which indicates that death threat is related to fear of personal death and dying. However, in the present study, these relationships were weaker than those reported in previous studies using the Threat Index in conjunction with other death attitude measures (Neimeyer & Epting, 1992). This lower correlation between the TI and MFODS may result from the heterogeneity of the latter instrument, which measures various aspects of fear of death beyond the discomfort with one's own mortality that is the focus of the TI.

More substantial and consistent relationships were found between death fear and personal anxiety toward one's own aging. All of the MFODS subscales were associated with greater levels of personal anxiety toward one's own aging. Thus, individuals who were more fearful of death were also more anxious about issues related to growing older. One possible interpretation of this finding is that old age may be feared because it represents increasing proximity to death. On the other hand, both fear of death and anxiety about growing older may be the results of a third, unmeasured factor, such as fear of losing one's identity or sense of control.

This study supports the use of a multidimensional definition of death anxiety. A modest significant relationship between global death fear and negative attitudes toward the elderly was found. Further examination of the results indicated that participants who did not accept death as final, who fear the unknown, and who are concerned about their body after death perceive the elderly as possessing less social value. Identifying these dimensions could be useful for developing educational programs aimed at improving attitudes toward the elderly.

The results also indicated that age was negatively associated with seven of the eight subscales on the MFODS. Older respondents in the present sample were less afraid of death than younger respondents. Older respondents also had lower levels of death threat.

One can only speculate on what additional variables influence attitudes toward the elderly. In the present study, only a small (but significant) proportion of the variance was accounted for using death concern measures to predict such attitudes. One possibility is that job satisfaction may mediate negative attitudes toward the elderly, at least in the nursing home group. Nursing staff who are dissatisfied with their jobs may display more negative attitudes toward residents, as a function of lack of institutional support or a reflection of burnout. But in more general terms, it is important to explore the many complex cultural and personal determinants of attitudes toward aging, of which personal levels of death fear and threat are only two examples.

Replication of the present research employing different populations would be beneficial. In particular, a longitudinal design assessing newly employed nursing staff on measures of death anxiety and attitudes toward the elderly would allow observation of actual changes occurring within the subjects with acculturation to that demanding work. In addition, comparing nursing personnel who work with different categories of elderly patients (e.g., physically vs. mentally incapacitated) would be helpful in understanding attitudes toward the elderly in the nursing profession. It is also important to assess nursing staff's attitudes toward the elderly residents they work with rather than assessing their attitudes toward the elderly in general. But even with these acknowledged limitations, the present study suggests the existence of links between personal fear of death and aging and reactions to the elderly that deserve more systematic investigation.

REFERENCES

Alford, D. M. (1982). Tips for teaching older adults. *Nursing Life, 2*, 60–63.

Almquist, E., Stein, S., Weiner, A., & Linn, M. (1981). Evaluation of continuing education for long-term care personnel: Impact upon attitudes and knowledge. *Journal of American Geriatrics Society, 29*, 117–122.

Burnside, I. M. (1981). Psychosocial issues in nursing care of the aged. *Journal of Gerontological Nursing, 7*, 689–693.

Carp, F. M. (1967). The applicability of an empirical scoring standard for a sentence completion test administered to two age groups. *Journal of Gerontology, 22*, 308–312.

Chandler, J. T., Rachal, J. R., & Kazelskis, R. (1986). Attitudes of long-term care nursing personnel toward the elderly. *Gerontologist, 26*, 551–555.

Collette-Pratt, C. (1976). Attitudinal predictors of devaluation of old age in a multigenerational sample. *Journal of Gerontology, 31*, 193–197.

Dattel, A. R., & Neimeyer, R. A. (1990). Sex differences in death anxiety: Testing the emotional expressiveness hypothesis. *Death Studies, 14*, 1–11.

Devins, G. M. (1979). Death anxiety and voluntary passive euthanasia. *Journal of Consulting and Clinical Psychology, 47*, 301–309.

Durlak, J. A. (1982). Using the Templer scale to assess "death anxiety": A cautionary note. *Psychological Reports, 50*, 1257–1258.

Eakes, G. G. (1985). The relationship between death anxiety and attitudes toward the elderly among nursing staff. *Death Studies, 9*, 163–172.

Gesser, G., Wong, P. T. P., & Reker, G. T. (1988). Death attitudes across the life-span: The development and validation of the Death Attitude Profile. *Omega, 2*, 113–128.

Green, S. K. (1981). Attitudes and perceptions about the elderly: Current and future perspectives. *International Journal of Aging and Human Development, 13*, 99–119.

Hicks, D. A., Rogers, C. T., & Shemberg, K. (1976). Attitudes toward the elderly: A comparison of measures. *Experimental Aging Research, 1*, 199–124.

Hickey, T., Bragg, S. M., Rakowski, W., & Hultsch, D. F. (1979). Attitude instrument analysis: An examination of factor consistency across two samples. *International Journal of Aging and Human Development, 9*, 359–375.

Hoelter, J. W. (1979). Multidimensional treatment of fear of death. *Journal of Consulting and Clinical Psychology, 47*, 996–999.

Johnson, J. C. (1980). Death anxiety of rehabilitation counselors and clients. *Psychological Reports, 46*, 325–326.

Kafer, R. A., Rakowski, W., Lachman, M., & Hickey, T. (1980). Aging opinion survey: A report of instrument development. *International Journal of Aging and Human Development, 11*, 319–333.

Kapos, A., & Smith, D. (1972, July). *Identifying standard attitudes toward senescence.* Paper presented at the 9th International Congress of Gerontology, Kiev, U.S.S.R.

Kelly, G. A. (1955). *The psychology of personal constructs.* New York: Norton.

Kogan, N., & Shelton, F. C. (1962). Images of "old people" and "people in general" in an older sample. *Journal of Genetic Psychology, 100,* 3–21.

Lester, D., Getty, C., & Kneisel, C. R. (1974). Attitudes of nursing students and nursing faculty toward death. *Nursing Research, 23,* 50–53.

Martin, T. O. (1982). Death anxiety and social desirability among nurses. *Omega, 13,* 51–58.

Martin, M. E., & Buckwalter, K. C. (1984). New approaches to continuing education for gerontological nursing. *Journal of Continuing Education in Nursing, 15,* 53–57.

McTavish, D. G. (1971). Perceptions of old people: A review of research methodologies and findings. *Gerontologist, 11,* 90–101.

Moore, M. K., & Neimeyer, R. A. (1991). A confirmatory factor analysis of the Threat Index. *Journal of Personality and Social Psychology, 60,* 122–129.

Neimeyer, R. A. (1985). Actualization, integration, and fear of death: A test of the additive hypothesis. *Death Studies, 9,* 235–244.

Neimeyer, R. A. (1988). Death anxiety. In H. Wass, F. Berardo, & R. A. Neimeyer (Eds.), *Dying: facing the facts* (2nd ed.) (pp. 97–136). New York: Hemisphere.

Neimeyer, R. A., & Epting, F. R. (1992). Measuring personal meanings of death: Twenty years of research using the Threat Index. In R. A. Neimeyer & G. J. Neimeyer (Eds.), *Advances in personal construct psychology* (Vol. 2). Greenwich, CN: JAI Press.

Neimeyer, R. A., & Moore, M. K. (1989). Assessing personal meanings of death: Empirical refinements in the Threat Index. *Death Studies, 13,* 227–240.

Nelson, L. D. (1979). Structural conduciveness, personality characteristics and death anxiety. *Omega, 10,* 123–133.

Palmore, E. (1977). Facts on aging: A short quiz. *Gerontologist, 17,* 315–320.

Palmore, E. (1980). The facts on aging quiz: A review of findings. *Gerontologist, 20,* 669–672.

Palmore, E. B. (1981). The facts of aging quiz: Part two. *Gerontologist, 21,* 431–437.

Smith, S. P., Jepson, V., & Perloff, E. (1982). Attitudes of nursing care providers toward elderly patients. *Nursing and Health Care, 3,* 93–98.

Stevens, S. J., Cooper, P. E., & Thomas, L. E. (1980). Age norms for Templer's Death Anxiety Scale. *Psychological Reports, 46,* 205–206.

Storlic, F. J. (1982). The reshaping of the old. *Journal of Gerontological Nursing, 8,* 555–559.

Taylor, K. H., & Harned, T. L. (1978). Attitudes toward old people: A study of nurses who care for the elderly. *Journal of Gerontological Nursing, 4,* 43–47.

Templer, D. I. (1970). The construction and validation of death anxiety scale. *Journal of General Psychology, 82,* 165–177.

Vickio, C. J., & Cavanaugh, J. C. (1985). Relationships among death anxiety, attitudes toward aging, and experience with death in nursing home employees. *Journal of Gerontology, 40,* 347–349.

Walkey, F. H. (1982). The Multidimensional Fear of Death Scale: An independent analysis. *Journal of Consulting and Clinical Psychology, 50,* 446–467.

Warren, W. G., & Chopra, P. N. (1978). Some reliability and validity considerations on Austrian data for the Death Anxiety Scale. *Omega, 9,* 293–299.

Weinberger, L. E., & Millham, J. (1975). Multi-dimensional, multiple method analysis of attitudes toward the elderly. *Journal of Gerontology, 30,* 343–348.

Williams, A. (1982). Nurses' attitudes toward aging and older people. Unpublished doctoral dissertation, University of Denver, CO.

Chapter 12

Psychological Defenses Against Death Anxiety

Robert W. Firestone

When I was 16 years old, I saw the world as turned upside down. I saw people trivializing their lives by bickering, struggling, and dramatizing their experiences while failing to focus on issues of personal identity and ignoring existential reality. I had a strong realization that they were living their lives as though death did not exist and that powerful defenses operated to deny this information. Furthermore, I sensed that this denial played a part in people's insensitivity and inhumanity to other people; their conformity and lack of a definitive point of view; their passive, dulled, paranoid orientation toward life experiences; and their disregard of themselves as unique, feeling entities.

At that time, I was aware of only the most rudimentary defenses against death anxiety, that is, identification with causes or religious ideologies, the imagined continuity of life through one's progeny, and attempts to live on through creative works and contributions that would have everlasting value. Although I was not cognizant of the combined impact and influence of psychological defenses on society and culture, I did recognize that there was collusion among parents and family members to deny death and maintain the defensive process at the expense of children, who expressed a natural curiosity and fear. There was a conspiracy of silence about the subject of death.

After many years of clinical experience, I have come to understand that humans adapt to death anxiety by giving up their life in the face of death, much as prisoners on death row may attempt to take their life. Furthermore, this defense contributes to a withdrawal of feeling from personal relationships, which in turn transforms genuine relating into a fantasy bond of security. The formation of this destructive tie eliminates and destroys the true bond that could exist between people who love one another.

My purpose in this chapter is to describe specific defenses against death anxiety in the context of the cultural framework that supports them. I integrate psychoanalytic and existential thought in explaining how early trauma leads to defense formation and how these defenses are reinforced as the developing child gradually becomes aware of his or her mortality. Thereafter, people adapt to death anxiety through a process of self-denial and withdrawal of interest in life-affirming activities. The denial of death through progressive self-denial leads to premature physical or psychological death; reinforces an antifeeling, antisexual existence; supports the choice of addictive attachment over genuine involvement, love and concern; and predisposes to alienation from others and from personal goals.

By moving out of the familiar safety of this adaptation and expanding their lives, people begin to experience their aloneness, separateness, and existential anxiety; the more invested they are in life, the more they have to lose. Generally, they respond to this anxiety on a preconscious or unconscious level by forming defenses without being aware of them. Paradoxically, patients who progress in psychotherapy place greater value on their lives yet are more apprehensive of death. Without recognition of this underlying pressure, some degree of regression may follow significant improvement. On the basis of extensive clinical data, I have concluded that there is a correlation between the degree of individuation, self-actualization, and life satisfaction of an individual and painful feelings of deep sadness and concern about the finitude of life.[1]

LITERATURE REVIEW

Recent Trends in Existential Thought

Existential philosophers and psychotherapists have written extensively of people's attempts to transcend their dualistic nature and the fact of mortality. However, until recently, fear of death (the complete transformation or termination of one's existence as one knows it) has been almost completely excluded from psychoanalytic theory or has been equated in a reductionistic way with castration and other fears. Regarding this omission, Stern (1972) wrote,

---

[1]The findings that support my thesis were derived in part from data gathered in a nonclinical population composed of high-functioning individuals, colleagues, and associates, who have shared my ongoing interest in and study of resistance in psychotherapy.

> It is surprising that psychoanalytic psychology, despite its characteristic tendency to uncover the hidden truth behind all denials and repressions, nevertheless, in its studies up to this day has rather neglected the fear of death, our steady companion. (p. 901) [Translated by Meyer (1975).]

With few exceptions, most classical psychoanalytic themes of the human response to death have been derived from Freud's (1915/1957b) well-known dictum: "Our unconscious . . . does not know its own death" (p. 296).

In contrast, Becker (1973), Meyer (1975), and Stern (1972) contended that reactions to the realistic fear of death are of the utmost importance in the development and continuation of neurosis. Meyer emphasized that the part played by death and dying in neurosis had "until now barely been considered" (p. xi). Stern argued that working through the fear of death is an indispensable part of every treatment, and the failure of adaptation to this fear, an important cause of neurosis.

Frankl (1946/1959) asserted that individuals have the capacity to transcend tragic aspects of the human condition. He stated,

> I speak of a tragic optimism, that is, an optimism in the face of tragedy and in view of the human potential which at its best always allows for: (1) turning suffering into a human achievement and accomplishment; (2) deriving from guilt the opportunity to change oneself for the better; and (3) *deriving from life's transitoriness an incentive to take responsible action.* (p. 162, emphasis added)

"Healthy" Versus "Morbid" View of Death

There are two views concerning the impact of death anxiety on human affairs. Proponents of the "healthy" view of death assert that the fear of death is not natural and the child who receives good maternal care will develop a sense of basic security and not be subject to morbid fears of losing support, being annihilated, or dying. A corollary from this approach, the "life satisfaction" point of view proposed by Searles (1961), Hinton (1975), Yalom (1980), and others, states that death anxiety is a manifestation of unfulfilled strivings in life and is *"inversely proportional to life satisfaction"* (Yalom, p. 207). They postulate that the fear of living leads to, or is transformed into, the fear of death. However, I believe that it is more logical to consider that the fear of death transforms or alters the life experience.

According to Becker (1973), proponents of the "morbid" view (so named by the proponents of the "healthy" view) claim that although "early . . . experiences may heighten natural anxieties and later fears, . . . nevertheless the fear of death is natural and is present in everyone" (p. 15). Becker, one of the major supporters of this proposition, argued persuasively that the dread of death leads to denial on many levels:

> Everything that man does in his symbolic world is an attempt to deny and overcome his grotesque fate. He literally drives himself into a blind obliviousness with social games, psychological tricks, personal preoccupations so far removed from the reality of his situation that they are forms of madness—agreed madness, shared madness, disguised and dignified madness, but madness all the same. (p. 27)

Becker (1973) did not fail to take into account emotional pain and frustration during childhood that intensify and are equated with death anxiety. He believed that psychological defenses were essential for survival during the formative years, given a child's "precocious or premature" nature and his or her involvement in

> the most unequal struggle any animal has to go through; a struggle that the child can never really understand because he doesn't know what is happening to him, why he is responding as he does, or what is really at stake in the battle. (Becker, p. 29)

The child, facing such a battle, eventually gives up the struggle in despair, building "character" defenses to conceal inner defeat. In another work (Firestone, 1985), I described the crucial point at which the child gives up:

> Soon . . . they [children] learn that they too must die and discover that they cannot sustain their own lives. . . . At this critical "point of futility," their sense of omnipotence is deeply wounded. People rarely recover from this final blow. (p. 242)

Despite the fact that death is inevitable for all human beings, thoughts of dying rarely intrude into the average person's consciousness. By denying death or displacing the fear of death onto other concerns, most people are able to function in their everyday lives without being overwhelmed by anxiety and dread of their anticipated end. Zilboorg (1943) observed this obliviousness to death:

> Therefore in normal times we move about actually without ever believing in our own death, as if we fully believed in our own corporeal immortality. . . . We marshal all the forces which still the voice reminding us that our end must come some day, and we are suffused with the awareness that our lives will go on forever. (p. 468)

Cultural Patterns of Denial

Zilboorg (1943), Becker (1973), Choron (1964), and others have pointed out the vital function that cultural norms, rituals, and institutions serve in anesthetizing people to existential realities. Humans created a social order to help them avoid the fact of their mortality. However, Levin (1951) emphasized that the fear of death is converted into terror through forms of social control that threaten "complete annihilation to those who do not conform" (p. 264) to the standards that restrict life activity. Similarly, in a recent work (Firestone, 1990b), I wrote,

All societies and complex social structures are generally restrictive of individuality and personal expression in the face of existential anxiety, and all cultural patterns or practices represent to some extent a form of adaptation to people's fear of death. (p. 322)

Much of people's destructiveness toward themselves and others can be attributed to the fact that people conspire with one another to create cultural imperatives and institutions that deny the fact of mortality. Becker's (1973) views concerning the incidental destructiveness of defenses and their projection into society are closely aligned with my own thinking. Becker stated,

If we had to offer the briefest explanation of all the evil that men have wreaked upon themselves and upon their world since the beginnings of time right up until tomorrow, it would be not in terms of man's animal heredity, his instincts and his evolution: it would be simply in *the toll that his pretense of sanity takes*, as he tries to deny his true condition. (pp. 29–30)

Death Anxiety and Individuation

A number of theorists subscribe to the view that the process of individuation intensifies the fear of death. Rank (1941/1958) conceptualized neurotic persons as having transformed the fear of death into a fear of living. He wrote extensively about anxiety states aroused by individuation.

In this sense, the individual is not just striving for survival but is reaching for some kind of "beyond," be it in terms of another person, a group, a cause, a faith to which he can submit, because he thereby expands his Self. (Rank, pp. 194–195)

Maslow (1967/1976) agreed with Rank's formulations concerning the close relationship between the fear of death and the fear of standing alone, as an individual, out of the crowd. Maslow believed that this fear manifests itself during a person's most fulfilling or peak experiences, when he or she has a profound sense of being separate from the group:

We fear our highest possibilities (as well as our lowest ones). We are generally afraid to become that which we can glimpse in our most perfect moments. . . . We enjoy and even thrill to the godlike possibilities we see in ourselves in such peak moments. And yet we simultaneously shiver with weakness, awe, and fear before these very same possibilities. (p. 34)

My clinical experience has shown that most individuals live out their lives enmeshed in the kind of "other power" described by Fromm (1941), Maslow, and Rank—in couples, groups, or nationalistic causes—so that they never (or rarely) experience the shiver of weakness to which Maslow alluded. The majority are terrified of differentiating themselves from their original families and of not conforming to accepted cultural norms.

As Becker (1973) succinctly put it in his discussion of the process of individuation,

> Most people play it safe: they choose the beyond of standard transference objects like parents, the boss, or the leader; they accept the cultural definition of heroism and try to be a "good provider" or a "solid" citizen. . . . Almost everyone consents to earn his immortality in the popular ways mapped out by societies everywhere, in the beyonds of others and not their own. (p. 170)

ORIGINS OF THE CORE DEFENSE

Psychological defenses originate before the child develops a concept of death, that is, prior to the experience of death anxiety. However, the way a child is treated within a culture that denies death and the manner in which parents defend themselves against their children play a significant part in the child's development. In attempting to protect themselves against feelings of helplessness and vulnerability in the face of death, many parents unknowingly distance themselves from their children.

> The unwillingness of defended parents to allow repressed emotions to reemerge during tender moments with their children is a major reason those parents find it difficult to sustain loving, affectionate relationships with their children. (Firestone, 1990b, p. 69)

Early frustration and emotional deprivation lead to the formation of a fantasy bond—an imagined connection with the mother—that becomes the core defense. Later, children's discovery of mortality, first their parents' and later their own, destroys their illusion of self-sufficiency and omnipotence and represents the proverbial last straw. This new awareness causes a general tendency to withdraw libido, or genuine feeling for themselves and others, in favor of defenses and self-parenting behaviors that shield them from the consciousness of being alone and exposed to death.

Secondary defenses, including predicting rejection, practicing self-criticism, anticipating negative outcomes, and holding cynical views of the self and others, function to protect the fantasy bond. These views are maintained by the *voice process*—a system of negative thought patterns antithetical to the self and others—that supports every defense against death anxiety. (Internal voices are the incorporation of parents' defenses and their overt and covert negative attitudes and hostility toward the child.) This alienated posture toward the self and others persists into adult life and colors all interactions and pursuits. It is at the core of microsuicidal behavior, self-denial, and self-limitation, instigating and rationalizing methods of accommodation to death.

Children's Reactions to Death

Clinical studies (Anthony, 1971; Lester, 1970; Nagy, 1948/1959; Rochlin, 1967) have shown that a child's denial of the knowledge of death may be almost immediate or may develop gradually. Nagy (1948/1959) conceptualized three stages in children's understanding of death. Rochlin (1967), on the basis of play therapy sessions with children ages 3–5, came to the following conclusion:

> Very young children seem to learn that life ends. They apply this information to themselves. . . . The clinical facts show that the child's views of dying and death are inseparable from the psychological defenses against the reality of death. They form a hard matrix of beliefs which is shaped early and deep in emotional life. It appears not to alter throughout life. (p. 63).

Anthony (1971) reported cases of immediate denial of mortality followed by adverse reactions to the denial:

> Clifford [3 years, 10 months] in his happiest mood . . . suddenly exclaimed "I shall never die!" . . . [However,] both he and Ruth [another child who stoutly denied death] showed anxiety about death during the months following their assertion of immortality. (p. 156)

Anthony also presented numerous examples of children who failed to cope with death anxiety and were assisted in their denial of death by parents who were too threatened to listen to their child's questions or to take them seriously. For example, a mother comforted and reassured her distraught 3-year-old daughter, who had just asked, "Does everyone die?", by telling her that people died when they were old and tired and therefore glad to do so (Anthony, p. 138).

Research studies (Kastenbaum, 1974; Wass et al., 1983) have contributed empirical findings regarding children's reactions to death. Kastenbaum (1974) reported that more than three-fourths of the respondents to a questionnaire expressed the opinion that children "are better off not thinking of death and should be protected from death-relevant situations by their parents" (p. 12).

I have observed numerous children cutting off feeling, becoming inward and distant from others, and manifesting hostility as they went through the process of realization. Their questions indicated a significant increase in anxiety and concern about death.

Many children have nightmares filled with themes about death and indicating feelings of vulnerability about their bodies. These terrifying nightmares seem to occur more frequently in children who have not yet successfully repressed their emotional reactions to the knowledge of death. For example, Ronnie, age 3 years, 3 months, woke up crying from a bad dream in the middle of the night. In tears, he had the following conversation with his mother:

> Ronnie: "I am Ronnie and I am going to be Ronnie when I get big and till I die. Isn't that sad?"
>
> Mother: "What?"
>
> Ronnie: "That I am going to die. Everyone knows that they are going to die, even Doug [a self-assured 5-year-old acquaintance], even strangers. But they pretend they won't. You know why?"
>
> Mother: "Why?"
>
> Ronnie: "Because when you die all your skin peels off and then you're not Ronnie any more."

Another child (age 4 years, 6 months), after learning about death, became increasingly preoccupied with fairy tales about princes and princesses who live forever. She too was often disturbed by nightmares; however, she was unable to recall the contents of her dreams. In general, the frequency of nightmares about death decreases during later childhood and early adolescence, a fact that may indicate preadolescents' (8- to 12-year-olds') increased ability to repress thoughts about death and dying (Firestone, 1985). This notion is supported by several empirical studies. For example, in a large-scale study (McIntire, Angle, & Struempler, 1972) involving 598 children, the 7- and 9-year-olds were the most willing to accept the irreversibility of death and older children showed increasing interest in reincarnation (approaching 20%).

Alexander and Adlerstein (1958/1965), who used a word association test combined with psychogalvanic skin reflex to test children's reactions to death-related words, found that

> two subgroups, 5 through 8 and 13 through 16, show significant decrease in skin resistance. No reliable differences on this measure are found in the 9 through 12 group. (p. 122)

In other words, latency age (9–12 years) children appeared to have less response to death-related words. Meyer (1975) confirmed these findings, writing,

> The fact that death quite early plays a role in the child's life has obviously gone largely unnoticed, as has the fact that death . . . between the eighth year and puberty becomes step by step subject to a process of repression that in many respects runs parallel to the development of sexual taboos. (p. 82)

The apparent tranquility of the latency period may be related more to the repression of death anxiety than to the repression of sexual impulses. Many child developmentalists have commented on the obvious defended attitude of children during this period. For example, Anthony (1971) asserted,

> Denial of personal mortality is only one among several ways in which the child gradually becomes able to assimilate emotionally and intellectually the realities of his physical and social environment. (p. 163)

She went on to describe the latency phase as the "dare stage," in which "children devise a mixture of reality and fantasy in facing their fears" (p. 165). Hall (1915) noted this same issue, but he observed that young children prior to the onset of latency and adolescence were intensely concerned with death. In reflecting on this phenomenon, he wrote,

> During adolescence the death problem becomes a veritable muse, inspiring endless dreads, reveries and perhaps obsessions and complexes of the most manifold kinds. (p. 556)

In addition, Meyer (1975) drew attention to the fact that life and death are central themes in adolescence, "as is clearly shown by the frequency with which young people attempt to commit suicide" (p. 27). Meyer suggested that the loss of a love relationship "may easily cause the adolescent to step across the boundary of the will to survive" (p. 27).

RELATIONSHIP BETWEEN SEPARATION ANXIETY AND FEAR OF DEATH

There are a number of affects common to separation anxiety and the fear of death, as well as certain differences between the two. One affect inherent in both reactions is the fear of being cut off from others, alone and isolated from fellow humans. This fear of object loss recapitulates the infant's anxiety at being separated from the mother.

However, an individual's most profound terror is caused by contemplation of the obliteration of the ego, the total loss of the self. This dread goes beyond separation anxiety. The cessation of the ego's existence in any knowable or recognizable form is terrifying. At the deepest level, any promise of an afterlife, reincarnation, or union with a universal consciousness is unacceptable. The anticipation of the death of the ego is particularly agonizing to a person who lives a happy, fulfilling life; possesses a strong sense of personal identity; and is involved in a mutually rewarding love relationship. These people report that thoughts about dying lead to a painful sense of what their death would mean to significant others.

DEFENSES AGAINST DEATH ANXIETY

In a sense, neurosis can be conceptualized as a reaction to a real fear based on denial and dread of death and the evolution of this defensive process in a cultural framework. Society can be viewed as a social process that represents a pooling of the individual defenses of its members.

Clinicians may find it difficult to identify defenses specifically related to death anxiety, because defenses are instituted before the patient becomes aware of the anxiety on a conscious level. Regressive trends are activated as an individual suppresses death anxiety. There is a retreat to an earlier stage of development, a level at which the individual was not fully aware of death (Firestone, 1990a). These regressive trends may persist throughout a person's life.

The arousal of death anxiety generally leads to an increased reliance on defensive behaviors and self-protective life-styles. Any negative event or reminder of death, such as illness, rejection, accident, or tragedy, can precipitate feelings of death anxiety, which in turn may lead to a retreat to specific, idiosyncratic defenses typically used in times of stress. For example, I treated one young man who, after witnessing his father's sudden collapse from an apparent heart attack (which later was diagnosed as food poisoning), pulled sharply away from his wife and children as well as from his father, for whom he had a great deal of affection. In the months that followed this incident, the young man gained considerable weight and became progressively less efficient at work. These symptoms persisted for well over a year, despite the fact that his father had recovered his health almost immediately after his brief illness.

Basic defenses against death anxiety and their projection into the social structure can be delineated. These defenses are not discrete entities, but they may be categorized for the purpose of clarity as follows.

Self-Nourishing Habits

Self-parenting behaviors are closely tied to children's earliest feelings of omnipotence and self-sufficiency and in adulthood support individuals' illusion of mastery over their world, their life, and their death. Just as the infant and young child partially relieve primitive feelings of hunger by fantasies of connection, thumb-sucking, and masturbation, adults come to use increasingly more sophisticated versions of self-nourishing habits to relieve emotional pain and existential anxiety. Indeed, we are currently in the throes of a drug problem of epidemic proportions in our society, as adolescents and adults strive to obliterate the pain of their existence with every means at their disposal. The United States has become an addictive society, perhaps partly as a response to the anxiety surrounding the possibility of nuclear destruction. As the suicidologist Shneidman (1973) commented,

For the first time in six centuries (since the great European plagues) a generation has been born and raised in a thanatological context, concerned with the imminent possibility of the death of the person, the death of humanity, the death of the universe, and, by necessary extension, the death of God. (p. 189)

Moreover, society as a whole can be seen as moving toward more elaborate and more effective defenses that act to cut off or dull the highs and lows of life, thereby numbing individuals to existential issues. The family—the agent of socialization—encourages children to find ways to suppress feelings and events, rather than discouraging them from adopting painkillers that shelter them from reality. Furthermore, the majority of parents exist in an unfeeling, albeit comfortable, state in which they are removed from genuine emotional contact with their spouses and children. Denying themselves satisfaction in personal interactions, they come to rely on self-nourishing habits and routines as a substitute and, by example, teach a life-style of addiction to their offspring.

The negative thought process, or voice, plays an important role in addictive tendencies, first by seducing the person into indulging the habit, and then by punishing him or her. For example, first it encourages the anxious person to "take one more drink, you need to relax"; then it accuses him or her of having no will power. In an effort to alleviate secondary reactions of guilt and pain, the individual resorts to more painkillers, continuing the cycle.

Interesting studies indicating the relationship between death anxiety and addiction can be found in the work of Rado (1933, 1958) and Meyer (1975). They stressed the obvious indifference to the future in addictive personalities. Death appears to be completely foreign to the conscious thought process of these individuals, who, according to Rado (1933), firmly believe in their personal invulnerability and immortality.

Preoccupation with Pseudoproblems

It is my contention that death anxiety and the fact of death give rise to a basic paranoia that is then projected onto real-life situations. In other words, paranoia is an appropriate reaction to existential realities, inasmuch as powerful forces are operating on humans that are beyond their control, are alien to their physical and mental health, and eliminate all chance of ultimate survival. However, individuals may project this paranoia onto encounters in life that do not justify an intense reaction of helplessness and powerlessness. People often overreact to these events with rage, fear, and panic. Meyer (1975) pointed out that the displacement of problems connected with death is apparent in agoraphobia; fear of cardiac arrest; animal phobias; and, most particularly, claustrophobia. Meyer cited von Gebsattel's (1951) reasoning in relation to the agoraphobic person's defense against annihilation anxiety:

> Where anxiety cannot take on its true meaning, it assumes the form of fear and shifts its true meaning into an apprehensive attitude of fear, in which the threats of daily life play an exaggerated, even an immoderate role. (pp. 37–38)

Most people seem intolerant of a simple, satisfying life and prefer to occupy their minds with melodrama and pseudoproblems while shutting off feeling for real issues in their lives. When preoccupied with these concerns, they are tortured by real-life situations but seem to be immune to death anxiety.

Vanity–Specialness

Vanity may be defined as a fantasized positive image of the self that an individual uses to compensate for deep-seated feelings of inadequacy and inferiority. It represents remnants of the child's imagined invincibility, omnipotence, and invulnerability that live on in the psyche, always available as a survival mechanism at times of great stress or when the person becomes too conscious of the fallibility of the physical nature and the impermanence of life. It expresses itself in the universal belief that death happens to someone else, never to oneself.

Zilboorg (1943) described this defense as "specialness" that sets one apart from one's neighbors and gives one a feeling of immunity from death:

> We must maintain within us the conviction that . . . we, each one of us who speaks of himself in the first person singular, are exceptions whom death will not strike at all. (p. 468)

Soldiers going into battle are well-acquainted with this deep-seated belief that the bullet will not hit them—their comrades may fall to the left and right, yet their life is charmed. The popular novel, *The Right Stuff* (Wolfe, 1983), accurately described this defense as superstition accepted as fact: Test pilots who crashed obviously didn't have "the right stuff," that special combination of masculine strength, courage, and competence that guaranteed survival.

Voices build up an individual's self-importance and support an inflated self-image. Many patients report thoughts about being exceptional, special, and capable of performing at unrealistically high levels. When performance falls short of perfection, severe self-castigation and demoralization can result. However, individuals are willing to accept the tension associated with vanity in a desperate attempt to avoid feeling subject to death, as "ordinary" people are.

A compensatory image of exaggerated self-importance often extends to beliefs about marriage and the family. By being specially chosen, preferred over all other rivals, people convince themselves that this preference guarantees them immortality through specialness. Society's conventions, mores, and institutions support a myth of exclusive and enduring love in couples. Married couples vow to "forsake all others," renounce old friends, and systematically exclude new ones (potential rivals) from their small kingdom in order to preserve the illusion that they are forever preferred. When this illusion is destroyed, there are dire consequences. Many times this fantasy is interrupted by the discovery of the partner's unfaithfulness, leading to catastrophic anxiety.

Male vanity and its corresponding buildup by women are relatively common in our society, perhaps because they are so closely linked to the denial of death. Men implicitly learn in childhood that they are to be the head of a household, the preferred choice of their wives, the great lover, superior to other men. Women are able to control men by manipulating their vanity, by deferring, or by making "their man's" life and interests the center of their universe and themselves the center of his existence. Both roles are damaging to the real feelings that once existed in the relationship. Again, on a societal level, stereotypic views of male superiority and strength and female inferiority and weakness support these unrealistic images.

Addictive Couple Bonds

The impact that defenses against death anxiety have on relationships by perpetuating the formation of destructive bonds has not been fully recognized. One of the things that invariably impresses me as a clinician is the extent to which people appear to want debilitating, conventional forms of safety, security, and "togetherness," yet reject genuine closeness with their loved ones. They tend to relive early, painful experiences from childhood in their present relationships and, at the same time, maintain a fantasy that they somehow can escape death by merging with another person. They fail to realize that to use a relationship to obtain security—that is, to secure a lie about life from another person—is tantamount to losing that relationship. The same is true of sexuality; to use sex to manipulate or to control or for any function other than its natural purposes of pleasure and reproduction bends the individual out of shape psychologically and sexually.

One of the major reasons people are afraid of intimacy is that having a deeply satisfying sexual experience combined with close emotional contact and friendship paradoxically makes people more aware of their separateness. In addition, some persons may become sexually withholding in order to escape an awareness of being connected to their body, which is vulnerable to illness, aging, and death. Regarding people's fears of erotic love and sexual passion, Kernberg (1980) wrote,

> In this connection, orgasm as part of sexual passion also may represent symbolically the experience of dying, of still maintaining self-awareness while being swept into passive acceptance of neuro-vegetative sequences involving excitement, ecstasy, and ending. (p. 292)

Another reason people avoid intimacy and closeness is their fear of losing the partner through rejection or death. The fear of object loss is akin to the fear of losing the self through death and can lead to a withdrawal of loving responses. My clinical experience has shown that any negative event is capable of precipitating this terror or dread that exists usually only on the periphery of conscious awareness. For example, late one evening, a couple watched the story of Lou Gehrig's life on television. The young woman, who was affectionate, outgoing, and very much in love with her husband, identified closely with the wife of the famous baseball player. At the point in the story where Lou Gehrig died, she felt a rush of deep sadness, picturing the emptiness of her life should her husband die. The next morning she was uncharacteristically cool and aloof and pulled away from her husband's embrace. Much later, the woman realized she had reacted adversely to the reminder of death presented in the film.

In another case, one of my clients was delayed by an accident on the freeway while driving home from work one day. As he slowly drove past the scene of the accident, he saw an overturned car by the side of the road and an ambulance attendant covering the face of someone lying on a stretcher. The man felt his heart pounding—what if his wife had been involved in the accident? He could not get the image of the body on the stretcher out of his mind. When he reached home, he was still shaken and tearfully told his wife about the accident and his fears for her safety. Two weeks later, the client suddenly realized that he had not made love to his wife since the night of the accident. In a session, he revealed, "I numbed my feelings of attraction for my wife, trying to somehow erase the image of that accident from my mind."

In distancing themselves to protect against the fear of loss and in using each other for security, men and women essentially give up their real lives together for an illusion that they will be spared death. Consequently, they find their lives increasingly hollow and empty. However, the pull to believe that death can be eluded if one is truly loved by one's beloved is irresistible for most people.

Gene Survival

Most parents believe that their children "belong" to them and experience intense feelings of exclusivity and possessiveness in relation to their offspring. To the extent that children resemble their parents in appearance, characteristics, and behavior, they are their parents' legacy, providing evidence to the world after the parents die that their lives were meaningful (Firestone, 1988). Both parents and children imagine that this "belonging" or merger somehow imbues them with immortality. Rank (1936/1972) intuitively sensed that this belief existed in children and that it led to guilt in separating from their parents and developing their own unique personalities.

The problem of the neurosis itself is a separation problem and as such a blocking of the human life principle, the conscious ability to endure release and separation, first from the *biological power represented by parents,* and finally from *the lived out parts of the self which this power represents* and which obstruct the development of the individual personality. (p. 73, emphasis added)

The "biological power represented by parents" referred to by Rank is the special transcendental quality that parents hold out to their children, that is, the possibility of triumphing over death by merging with them. This illusory fusion is costly, however, because, as Rank pointed out, the individual feels too guilty to individuate and live his or her own life. Society strongly supports parents' assumption that they have proprietary rights over their children. Despite all facts about children's misery and teenage troubles, most courts of law hold sacred and inviolable parents' rights over their children's lives and destinies, except in cases of blatant child abuse or neglect.

INSTITUTIONALIZED DEFENSES

Nationalism, Totalitarianism, and the "Ultimate Rescuer"

The fear of death drives people to embrace various causes, groups, and totalitarian regimes in an unending search for immortality and security. Indeed, it has been my experience that behaviors such as desperate dependence on a group, idolization of a leader, and mindless allegiance to a cause are all defenses against death fears. Individuals tend to transfer the primitive feelings that initially characterized the bond with their parents onto new figures and ideologies. In discussing transference, Rank (1936/1972) described the dynamics of forming a bond with persons and groups for the purpose of preserving one's life:

With human beings this whole biological problem of individuation depends psychically on another person, whom we then value and perceive psychologically as parent, child, beloved friend. These several persons represent then for the individual the great biological forces of nature, to which the ego binds itself emotionally and which then form the essence of the human and his fate. (p. 82)

Transference of emotions from early interactions with parents to a leader or a group is responsible for the submissive behavior observed in members of a group. According to Kaiser (Fierman, 1965), people's compelling need to surrender or completely submit their will to another person or group through a "delusion of fusion" represents the universal neurosis. In this form of denial, the leader of the group becomes the "ultimate rescuer" and the cause a bid for immortality. The illusion of fusion and connection provided by being part of a patriotic or nationalistic movement is addictive and exhilarating because of the false sense of power it gives the individual.

The fear of leaving the security of the family for a world of decision and responsibility (the fear of individuation) can be avoided by conforming to the standards and values of the "kinship circle," "group," "nation," or "father-land." Allegiance and identification with the group and simultaneous devaluation of others ("outsiders," "aliens," those who do not belong), feeds narcissistic, omnipotent feelings and inflates a sense of self-importance. On the other hand, as Fromm (1964) pointed out, submission and conformity keep the individual "in the prison of the motherly racial-national-religious fixation" (p. 107).

Fromm extended Freud's (1921/1955) formulations about group behavior to include couple relationships that have elements of a symbiotic, dependent tie. My own analysis of marital relationships has shown that most people act out dominant/submissive (parent/child) modes in their coupling. In these cases, the partner becomes the ultimate rescuer, responsible for the individual's decisions, happiness, and life. Both partners participate in this damaging collusion and find it difficult to disengage from, because the polarization provides an illusion of safety, protection, and permanence (Firestone, 1985, 1988).

Religious Doctrine

> In both recent and ancient times certain Christian milieus have been so obsessed with sinfulness, particularly of a sexual nature, that one is led to posit an analogy between this exacerbated sense of sin and obsessional neurosis. (Vergote, 1978/ 1988, p. 72)

Traditional religious ideologies of both Western and Eastern cultures have contributed to a collective neurosis by unwittingly reinforcing people's tenden-cies to deny the body or obliterate the self (destroy the ego). Misinterpretations of teachings originally meant to enhance spiritual and humane qualities have led to self-denying, self-sacrificing, passive orientation to life in many individuals. For example, St. Augustine's misreading in the fifth century of the story of creation led to his adopting a view of nature that was

> utterly antithetical to scientific naturalism. It was human choice—Adam's sin—that brought mortality and sexual desire upon the human race and, in the process, de-prived Adam's progeny of the freedom to choose not to sin. (Pagels, 1988, p. 130)

Ever since, theologians have postulated that the punishment for Adam's act of disobedience was death and have held out the promise that if individuals deny sexual desire and bodily pleasures, their soul will triumph over the body and survive death.

In a similar manner, many people have misunderstood the teachings of Taoism and Buddhism, assuming that all desire, striving, and will (the ego) must be given up in order to attain enlightenment. Suzuki, Fromm, and DeMartino (1960) and Watts (1961) have attempted to overcome this misinterpretation of Eastern philosophers in their discourses on Zen Buddhism.

The question arises as to why millions of people blindly follow religious dogma based on serious distortions or misinterpretations of the original teaching. Dostoyevsky (1880/1958) partly answered this question in *The Brothers Kara-mazov*, listing, among other reasons, transcendence over the body (which must die), a guarantee of perpetual care from the institutionalized church, and the union with a powerful being.

> But we [the church] shall keep the secret and for their own happiness will entice them with the reward of heaven and eternity. (pp. 304–305)

> The most tormenting secret of their conscience—everything, everything they will bring to us, and we shall give them our decision for it all, and they will be glad to believe in our decision, because it will relieve them of their great anxiety. (p. 304)

As is true of relationships and sexuality, to use a spiritual teaching (whether of a god or a Buddha) to procure an absolute, unqualified security in the face of a realistically uncertain future often destroys the inherent value and meaning of that teaching. Moreover, religious ideologies based on distortions of these basic teachings tend to support a collective self-destructive process. Philosophies of self-sacrifice and self-denial of the personality or body that equate thought with action are in essence a form of thought control. Traditional religion's dogma of selflessness represents an externalization of the individual's destructive voices that underlie feelings of shame about basic wants and needs. These judgmental values have a devastating effect on people's lives because they support the internal voices' negative injunctions.

An Antisexuality, Antifeeling Existence

Secular attitudes toward sex and the human body derived from traditional religious beliefs could be construed to be institutionalized sexual abuse because they cause so much damage to people in their sexual lives. In my clinical experience, I have found that virtually every patient has developed a negative point of view about his or her body, especially the sexual region. In socializing their children, parents are under tremendous pressure from society to teach restrictive values and narrow, distorted views of sexuality. For example, parents typically perceive sex as dirty or a function that should be hidden or compartmentalized (Berke, 1988; Calderone, 1974/1977). Children internalize this distorted view of sex as a negative thought process, and their adult sexuality and closest relationships are profoundly influenced by it. Many men and women find themselves distracted during lovemaking by critical thoughts about their bodies and their performance or by cynical ''voices'' about their partner's body or performance. In this manner, the voice protects people from potential loss by causing them to withhold or inhibit their loving and sexual responses, so that relationships do not become too deep or meaningful.

Perhaps because feelings arise in the body, society has also created strong prohibitions against feelings, especially anger and sadness. People are taught to feel only in a socially prescribed manner. Children are socialized to suppress their genuine feelings, particularly those that would indicate that they are in pain. Parents who protect themselves against feelings of sadness and vulnerability related to death cannot help but stifle these same emotional responses in their children. Admonitions such as ''Don't wear your emotions on your sleeve!'', ''Why get so upset?'', and ''You're too thin-skinned, too sensitive'' effectively suppress the child's expression of feelings of weakness or helplessness. Efforts to restrict or suppress people's natural expressions (of both sexuality and ''unacceptable'' emotions) lead to an increase in human aggression and immoral, acting-out behavior.

Progressive Self-Denial

> The common denominator of all negative ways of dealing with anxiety is a shrinking of the area of awareness and of activity. . . . We are afraid to die, and therefore we are afraid to live, or, as Tillich puts it, we avoid nonbeing by avoiding being. The avoidance of anxiety then means a kind of death in life. (Rheingold, 1967, pp. 204–205)

A particularly insidious defense against death anxiety and one that has been largely neglected in the literature is the commission of small suicides on a daily basis to achieve mastery over death. The universal tendency toward microsuicide and self-destruction is *not* due to a death instinct; rather, it represents a powerful defense against the fear of death. People do *not* have innate death wishes toward the self, yet they do try to protect themselves when faced with the specter of death.

The circumstance faced by all human beings is analogous to the situation faced by the prisoner on death row. Like the convict, people are aware, on an intellectual level at least, that they face an inescapable sentence of death, as a function of life itself. Just as prisoners faced with the knowledge of the exact hour of their execution often attempt suicide to escape the unbearable anticipatory anxiety, ''normal'' individuals commit emotional or subclinical suicide in an attempt to accommodate death anxiety. In both cases, the suicide is a desperate attempt to avoid the dread and anxiety surrounding the awareness of death

(Firestone & Seiden, 1987). By withdrawing feeling and energy from personal pursuits and goal-directed activity, individuals reduce their vulnerability to the anticipated loss of self through death. Ironically, in deadening themselves in advance, people barely notice the transition from "living" to dying.

It is noteworthy that the indications or signs of suicidal intention listed by suicidologists Shaffer and Shneidman (MacNeil-Lehrer Productions, 1987) parallel the basic defenses against death anxiety. Indeed, the symptoms and behaviors in patients that alert therapists to the possibility of suicide are similar to those that "normal" people use to keep themselves dulled to an awareness of death. These symptoms include isolation, substance abuse, an unconcern with physical surroundings, misery and guilt reactions, and a progressive withdrawal from relationships and favored activities.

Psychosis and depersonalization are exaggerated forms of defensive accommodation to the fact of death. The "less serious" version in "normal" people includes feelings of estrangement from loved ones and from the world, an impairment of the feeling of being alive, a sense of not being connected to one's body (disembodiment), and the sense of no longer being touched by events i.e., isolation from affect; (Meyer, 1975). These symptoms can be found, albeit on a subclinical level, in a large majority of individuals in our society.

A negative thought pattern, or voice, saps motivation for purposeful goal-directed behavior. It administers suicidal tendencies and mediates a systematic decathexis process. People withdraw investment and interest from their most meaningful associations and increasingly trivialize their experiences. Most individuals are unaware that they are acting against their own best interests and fail to question their loss of vitality and enthusiasm. The voice rationalizes their diminished investment in life with familiar clichés: "This vacation is too expensive, too much trouble to arrange. Why not stay home?", or "Why begin this project at this stage in your life? You probably won't be around to see it finished", or "You're too old for sex."

This destructive voice can be elicited directly in voice therapy. In fact, nowhere is the evidence supporting the hypotheses stated in this chapter more clear-cut than in voice therapy sessions, in which people bring to the surface the alien, defended aspect of their personality and identify their negative thoughts and destructive attitudes. In these sessions, one can observe that this subliminal thought process promotes each self-protective defense and discourages the seeking of gratification in the real world.

For example, one of my clients approaching his 50th birthday decided to give up his avocation of flying and sell his private plane. He told himself that flying was too dangerous for someone his age. He reported thoughts such as "You're not as alert as you once were. You should just stay on the ground." Subsequently he became deeply depressed. His friends, concerned about his loss of vitality, urged him to take up flying again. In general, as people move into middle age, many become fearful and apprehensive, and the defense of withdrawing libido from favored activities and relationships is accelerated. The voice becomes more dominant, exerting increasing influence by dictating and rationalizing self-denying behavior.

Society reinforces the defense of self-denial by maintaining certain standards regarding "age-appropriate" behavior for people who have reached "maturity." Consensually validated attitudes on the part of most members of our society support disengagement from life in every area of human endeavor: early retirement, segregated retirement communities, a premature giving up of participation in athletics and other physical activities, a diminished interest in sex, a reduction in sexual activity, and a decline in social life. Indeed, remaining involved and energetic often elicits disparaging remarks from one's friends, relatives, and children, comments that reinforce the voice: "Still playing baseball at your age? You must be crazy!" Similarly, signs of romance in the elderly bring on ridicule: "There's no fool like an old fool!"

Thus, conventional attitudes about so-called mature behavior disguise a process of self-denial that appears to be almost universal, and people are able to gradually ease themselves out of the mainstream of life. They become emotionally deadened to life, yet maintain their physical life. In a recent book (Firestone, 1990b), I summarized my overall view of the destructive impact that society has on its members in reinforcing their gradual accommodation to death:

> Over the millennia, people have unknowingly created increasingly complex institutions, conventions, belief systems, and sanctions in their attempt to adapt to death anxiety by limiting life and dulling feeling and awareness. Each generation has been raised by people whose ancestors were themselves reared by parents who knew and feared death as a reality and defensively retreated from investing in their lives. Each succeeding generation has added its own incremental building blocks to the system of denial and accommodation, contributing to the increased rigidity and power of the defensive process. (pp. 323–324)

DISCUSSION

As noted earlier, a number of theorists subscribe to the view that death anxiety masks unfulfillment and dissatisfaction with one's life. However, my clinical experience supports the converse proposition: Death anxiety is related to degree of individuation and self-actualization. As I have shown, most people, beginning in early childhood, try to deny death on an immediate, personal level and gradually adapt to the fear of death by giving up, or at least seriously restricting, their lives. Most individuals never reach an optimal level of differentiation or individuation because they stubbornly refuse to step outside their customary defenses (Kerr & Bowen, 1988). They fear that they will experience a recurrence of the full intensity of terror and dread that tormented them as children when they first learned about death. However, humans who live defended, constricted, and unfulfilled lives in an attempt to minimize death anxiety are often tortured by ontological guilt about a life not fully lived.

My clinical data support the hypothesis that death anxiety increases as people relinquish defenses, refuse to conform to familial and societal standards, reach new levels of differentiation of the self, or expand their lives. For example, many of my clients have reported having death dreams immediately after a particularly happy or fulfilling experience. In addition, serious, long-term regression often follows an atypical success or achievement in high-functioning adults. This phenomenon was originally noted by Freud (1916/1957a) in his essay "Those Wrecked by Success." In a recent article (Firestone, 1990a), I documented cases of regression precipitated by positive circumstances and showed that this seemingly paradoxical reaction is understandable when death anxiety is taken into account.

> Any experience that reminds an invididual that he possesses strength, independence, personal power, or acknowledged value as a person will make him acutely conscious of his life and its eventual loss. (p. 127)

Finally, a negative therapeutic reaction or intensified resistance to the therapy process often indicates that clients have reached a certain stage in their therapy in which death anxiety is intensified. In becoming aware of the damage they sustained in their early development, they often react with anger and outrage. Experiencing this murderous rage in sessions is symbolically equivalent to expressing death wishes toward the parents. Intense guilt and separation anxiety arise during the symbolic destruction of parental figures. However, at the same time, the client is moving away from, or completely severing, the bond with the family and the sense of "belonging" that previously functioned as a powerful defense. The problem of expressing anger over childhood abuses, combined with the anxiety involved in breaking with the family bond, may well be the key factor underlying therapeutic failure.

Viewing death anxiety as natural, that is, taking the "morbid" view of death, and as proportionally related to degree of individuation facilitates an understanding of the full range of clients' resistance: their fear of change, the stubbornness with which they cling to a negative concept learned in the family, episodic regressions related to significant improvement or progress, and the anxiety involved in termination. It clarifies why patients persist in holding onto feelings of vanity and omnipotence and explains their fear of nonconformity and personal power, their overriding need for illusions of fusion, and the impact of destructive bonds on interpersonal relationships.

In contrast, the "life satisfaction/healthy" view of death may itself be a defense against death anxiety, because it denies the reality that people can conceptualize their own death. This view confuses death anxiety with the existential guilt inherent in withholding from life's satisfactions.

In this chapter, I have attempted to elucidate the manner in which people defend themselves against the fear of death. My approach has not been philosophical in the sense of expressing either optimism or pessimism about the dilemma humans face. My interest has been in the impact that defenses against death anxiety have on individuals and on society. I have outlined a theoretical framework that integrates psychoanalytic and existential thought concerning defense formation and its effect on the developing personality.

The data supporting this approach to death anxiety are primarily observational and longitudinal; thus there is a compelling need for experimental studies. Two types of research that might be fruitful are (a) clinical and empirical studies in which children's thoughts, feelings, and attitudes toward death are elicited and assessed at various stages in their development, and (b) research studies in which increased reliance on defense mechanisms known to be associated with the arousal of death anxiety is measured in experimental and control groups. Recent studies (Greenberg et al., 1990; Rosenblatt, Greenberg, Solomon, Pyszczynski, & Lyon, 1989; Solomon, Greenberg, & Pyszczynski, 1991) have demonstrated the feasibility of such empirical investigations.

The formulations set forth in this chapter have crucial implications for psychotherapy. First, the state of vulnerability to death anxiety brought about by the process of dismantling major defenses needs to be taken into account by clinicians. McCarthy (1980) has addressed this concern:

> If the goal of the psychoanalytic work is the patient's freedom and autonomy, and the patient retains the unconscious fears that autonomy equals death or the loss of the self, then the positive outcome of the analysis may be as anxiety-provoking as the original inner conflicts. (p. 193)

Indeed, the intensity of death anxiety appears to be in proportion to clients' freedom from neurotic propensities. I have found that many clients concerned with the trivialities of life and obsessed with worries about personal conflicts and pseudoissues have viewed death with a kind of friendly acceptance. Unless therapists recognize the implications of therapeutic progress related to the arousal of death anxiety, they run the risk of misinterpreting many of their clients' reactions, symptoms, and communications.

Second, it is more pragmatic to conceptualize mental illness as a form of suicide (related to the attempt to achieve control over death) than to consider suicide and microsuicide as a subclass of mental illness. This formulation provides a clearer perspective on the underlying meaning of clients' symptoms and distress.

Finally, therapists need to recognize more fully the essential dilemma of psychotherapy:

The alternatives are clear: without challenging destructive aspects of ourselves . . . we will gradually submit to an alien, inimical point of view and shut down on our authentic self and unique outlook; on the other hand, disrupting powerful, self-protective defenses intensifies our awareness of life's tragic aspects and threatens at times to overwhelm us with feelings of helplessness and dread. (Firestone, 1988, p. 271)

Thus, therapeutic progress may be disappointing to the client, because it does not lead to a state of prolonged happiness. In fact, by opening us up to genuine feeling about our lives, improvement gives us a sense of personal freedom that makes us more aware of potential losses. Appropriate affect, as contrasted with melodramatic reactions, deepens our sadness about the poignancy of life, death, illness, and aging as well as permitting us to enjoy the excitement and thrill of genuine positive experiences. The inevitability of future loss is a real problem for human beings, yet when they face this issue without defending themselves, their lives become rich, powerful, and sweet, and they are capable of true intimacy, friendship, and love. Indeed, the choice to invest in a life we must certainly lose leads to tenderness and compassion for ourself and others.

REFERENCES

Alexander, I. E., & Adlerstein, A. M. (1965). Affective responses to the concept of death in a population of children and early adolescents. In R. Fulton (Ed.), *Death and identity* (pp. 111–123). New York: Wiley. (Original work published 1958)

Anthony, S. (1971). *The discovery of death in childhood and after*. Harmondworth, England: Penguin Education.

Becker, E. (1973). *The denial of death*. New York: Free Press.

Berke, J. H. (1988). *The tyranny of malice: Exploring the dark side of character and culture*. New York: Summit Books.

Calderone, M. S. (1977). Eroticism as a norm. In E. S. Morrison & V. Borosage (Eds.), *Human sexuality: Contemporary perspectives* (2nd ed., pp. 39–48). Palo Alto, CA: Mayfield. (Original work published 1974)

Choron, J. (1964). *Modern man and mortality*. New York: Macmillan.

Dostoyevsky, F. (1958). *The brothers Karamazov* (D. Magarshack, Trans.). London: Penguin Books. (Original work published 1880)

Fierman, L. B. (Ed.). (1965). *Effective psychotherapy: The contribution of Hellmuth Kaiser*. New York: Free Press.

Firestone, R. W. (1985). *The fantasy bond: Structure of psychological defenses*. New York: Human Sciences Press.

Firestone, R. W. (1988). *Voice therapy: A psychotherapeutic approach to self-destructive behavior*. New York: Human Sciences Press.

Firestone, R. W. (1990a). The bipolar causality of regression. *American Journal of Psychoanalysis, 50*, 121–135.

Firestone, R. W. (1990b). *Compassionate child-rearing: An in-depth approach to optimal parenting*. New York: Plenum Press.

Firestone, R. W., & Seiden, R. H. (1987). Microsuicide and suicidal threats of everyday life. *Psychotherapy, 24,* 31–39.

Frankl, V. E. (1959). *Man's search for meaning.* New York: Washington Square Press. (Original work published 1946)

Freud, S. (1955). Group psychology and the analysis of the ego. In J. Strachey (Ed. and Trans)., *The standard edition of the complete psychological works of Sigmund Freud* (Vol. 18, pp. 67–143). London: Hogarth Press. (Original work published 1921)

Freud, S. (1957a). Some character-types met with in psychoanalytic work. In J. Strachey (Ed. and Trans.), *The standard edition of the complete psychological works of Sigmund Freud* (Vol. 14, pp. 311–333). London: Hogarth Press. (Original work published 1916)

Freud, S. (1957b). Thoughts for the times on war and death. In J. Strachey (Ed. and Trans.), *The standard edition of the complete psychological works of Sigmund Freud* (Vol. 14, pp. 273–302). London: Hogarth Press. (Original work published 1915)

Fromm, E. (1941). *Escape from freedom.* New York: Avon Books.

Fromm, E. (1964). *The heart of man: Its genius for good and evil.* New York: Harper & Row.

Greenberg, J., Pyszsczynski, T., Solomon, S., Rosenblatt, A., Veeder, M., Kirkland, S., & Lyon, D. (1990). Evidence for terror management theory: II. The effects of mortality salience on reactions to those who threaten or bolster the cultural worldview. *Journal of Personality and Social Psychology, 58,* 308–318.

Hall, G. S. (1915). Thanatophobia and immortality. *American Journal of Psychology, 26,* 550–613.

Hinton, J. (1975). The influence of previous personality on reactions to having terminal cancer. *Omega, 6,* 95–111.

Kastenbaum, R. (1974, Summer). Childhood: The kingdom where creatures die. *Journal of Clinical Child Psychology,* 11–14.

Kernberg, O. F. (1980). *Internal world and external reality: Object relations theory applied.* Northvale, NJ: Jason Aronson.

Kerr, M. E., & Bowen, M. (1988). *Family evaluation: An approach based on Bowen theory.* New York: Norton.

Lester, D. (1970). Relation of fear of death in subjects to fear of death in their parents. *Psychological Record, 20,* 541–543.

Levin, A. J. (1951). The fiction of the death instinct. *Psychiatric Quarterly, 25,* 257–281.

MacNeil-Lehrer Productions, WNET, WETA. (1987). Open door policy?/Teen suicide: Fall from grace (Transcript 2989 of the MacNeil/Lehrer NewsHour, March 12). New York: Author.

Maslow, A. H. (1976). *The farther reaches of human nature.* New York: Penguin. (Original work published 1967)

McCarthy, J. B. (1980). *Death anxiety: The loss of the self.* New York: Gardner Press.

McIntire, M. S., Angle, C. R., & Struempler, L. J. (1972). The concept of death in Midwestern children and youth. *American Journal of Diseases of Children, 123,* 527–532.

Meyer, J. E. (1975). *Death and neurosis* (M. Nunberg, Trans.). New York: International Universities Press.

Nagy, M. H. (1959). The child's view of death. In H. Feifel (Ed.), *The meaning of death* (pp. 79–98). New York: McGraw-Hill. (Original work published 1948)

Pagels, E. (1988). *Adam, Eve, and the serpent*. New York: Random House.

Rado, S. (1933). The psychoanalysis of pharmacothymia (drug addiction) (B. D. Lewin, Trans.). *Psychoanalytic Quarterly, 2*, 1–23.

Rado, S. (1958). Narcotic bondage: A general theory of the dependence on narcotic drugs. In P. H. Hoch & J. Zubin (Eds.), *Problems of addiction and habituation* (pp. 27–36). New York: Grune & Stratton.

Rank, O. (1958). *Beyond psychology*. New York: Dover. (Original work published 1941)

Rank, O. (1972). *Will therapy and truth and reality* (J. Taft, Trans.). New York: Alfred A. Knopf. (Original work published 1936)

Rheingold, J. C. (1967). *The mother, anxiety, and death: The catastrophic death complex*. Boston: Little, Brown.

Rochlin, G. (1967). How younger children view death and themselves. In E. A. Grollman (Ed.), *Explaining death to children* (pp. 51–85). Boston: Beacon Press.

Rosenblatt, A., Greenberg, J., Solomon, S., Pyszczynski, T., & Lyon, D. (1989). Evidence for terror management theory: I. The effects of mortality salience on reactions to those who violate or uphold cultural values. *Journal of Personality and Social Psychology, 57*, 681–690.

Searles, H. F. (1961). Schizophrenia and the inevitability of death. *Psychiatric Quarterly, 35*, 631–665.

Shneidman, E. S. (1973). *Deaths of man*. New York: Quadrangle/New York Times.

Solomon, S., Greenberg, J., & Pyszczynski, T. (1991). A terror management theory of self-esteem. In C. R. Snyder & D. R. Forsyth (Eds.), *Handbook of social and clinical pyschology: The health perspective* (pp. 21–40). Elmsford, NY: Pergamon Press.

Stern, M. M. (1972). Trauma, death anxiety and fear of death. *Psyche, 26*, 901–928.

Suzuki, D. T., Fromm, E., & DeMartino, R. (1960). *Zen Buddhism and psychoanalysis*. New York: Harper & Row.

Vergote, A. (1988). *Guilt and desire: Religious attitudes and their pathological derivatives* (M. H. Wood, Trans.). New Haven, CT: Yale University Press. (Original work published 1978)

von Gebsattel, V. E. (1951). Anthropology of anxiety. *Hochland, 43*, 352–364.

Wass, H., Dinklage, R. Gordon, S., Russo, G., Sparks, C., & Tatum, J. (1983). Young children's death concepts revisited. *Death Education, 7*, 385–394.

Watts, A. (1961). *Psychotherapy East and West*. New York: Vintage Books.

Wolfe, T. (1983). *The right stuff*. New York: Farrar, Straus, & Giroux.

Yalom, I. D. (1980). *Existential psychotherapy*. New York: Basic Books.

Zilboorg, G. (1943). Fear of death. *Psychoanalytic Quarterly, 12*, 465–475.

Chapter 13

Changing Death Attitudes Through Death Education

Joseph A. Durlak

Whereas several contributions to this volume have concentrated on the measurement of death attitudes, this chapter has an applied focus: the modification of death attitudes through death education. There are four major sections. A brief overview of death education is provided first, followed by a discussion of the impact of death education programs on various death attitudes. In the third section, I discuss basic theory and research on attitude change, and in the final section I show how these theories and techniques relate to death education.

OVERVIEW OF DEATH EDUCATION

Rationale for Death Education

There are two general reasons for offering death education programs. The first is scholarly or pedagogic in nature and is based on the development of thanatology as a legitimate scientific enterprise. Theory, concepts, and information related to death have been developed in many disciplines, including medicine, psychology, sociology, philosophy, and religion, and death education programs often survey these disciplines in an attempt to convey what is currently known about death-related phenomena.

There is also an individualized or personal objective in many death education programs that rests on the premise that American society does not currently handle death very well. For instance, there are many death-denying or death-avoiding aspects in American culture (Charmaz, 1980; Kastenbaum & Aisenberg, 1972; Wass, Berardo, & Neimeyer, 1988). Many salient cultural values, such as youth, achievement, health, individualism, and personal control, do not assist people in dealing with death. As a result, death is rarely treated as a natural event, and instead its occurrence and eventuality are sensationalized or distorted.

Therefore, it is generally believed that many individuals possess inaccurate or misleading information about death-related issues that might give rise to various insecurities. Also, many individuals do not have sufficient opportunity to examine their feelings about death in such a way that would permit them to come to terms with any discomfort or concerns they might have. Furthermore, on a professional level, it is believed that treatment of the terminally ill and bereaved is not as humane or comforting as it can be. For various reasons, many caregivers are not adequately prepared to deal with death-related issues (Kirchberg & Neimeyer, 1991; Kübler-Ross, 1969; Quint, 1967). Thus, in addition to scholarly objectives, death education programs are also offered to help participants deal with death more effectively on a personal or professional level.

A Brief History of Death Education

The first formal death education programs occurred in the 1950s; influenced by the work of several noted thanatologists (Richard Kalish, Robert Kastenbaum, Elizabeth Kübler-Ross, Herman Feifel, Earl Grollman, and Edwin Shneidman), death education practices proliferated in the 1960s and probably peaked in popularity during the 1970s. Pine (1977) has provided a helpful historical perspective on death education. At one point, there were more than 1,000 death education programs of some sort being offered each year in the United States. By 1978, at least 938 colleges and universities were offering death education courses (Crummins, cited by Crase, 1989).

The popularity of death education has diminished over the past few years on college campuses, but not necessarily in other settings. It has been estimated that approximately 11% of all elementary and secondary public schools offer a course or some instructional units on death education in general, 17% offer a grief intervention or support program, and 25% conduct suicide prevention and educational programs (Wass, Miller, & Thornton, 1990). Among schools of medicine, nursing, pharmacy, dentistry, and social work, 13–40% offer a full course on death education and 43–83% integrate such instruction into other courses (Dickinson, Sumner, & Frederick, 1992).

The field of death education has grown in other ways as well. There is an international, multidisciplinary organization (the Association for Death Education and Counseling [ADEC]) devoted to improving the quality of death education and death-related counseling and caregiving (Stillion, 1989). ADEC sponsors an annual conference and operates a certification program for death educators and grief counselors (Zinner, 1992). In addition, the International Work Group on Death, Dying and Bereavement (1992), whose work is compatible with ADEC's, has developed a statement of assumptions and principles for death education.

Diversity of Death Education Efforts

Death education efforts vary in terms of specific goals, formats, duration, characteristics of participants and instructors, and procedures used to evaluate program impact (Durlak & Reisenberg, 1991; Leviton, 1977). To illustrate some of these differences, death education programs may take the form of intensive semester-long courses (Bell, 1975; Leviton & Fretz, 1978), educational units (mini-courses) offered as part of semester course offerings (Glass & Knott, 1984), or brief (2–20 hr) specialized workshops or presentations (Combs, 1981; Durlak, 1978). Participants may include elementary (Mueller, 1975), junior high or high school (Glass & Knott, 1984), or undergraduate and graduate students (Bell, 1975; Hoelter & Epley, 1979); health care personnel (Miles, 1980; Yeaworth, Kapp, & Winget, 1978); funeral directors; clergy; and adult volunteers from the community (Trent, Glass, & McGee, 1981). Most death education occurs in schools or professional training programs, but some hospitals, clinics, and community agencies such as hospice organizations also sponsor and conduct death education programs.

To the extent that time permits, the topics typically covered in death education include social and community perspectives on death, the dying process, individual attitudes toward death, religious and cultural views about death, grief and bereavement, funerals, suicide, euthanasia, medical ethics, legal issues, and children's understanding of death. Some specialized topics might be acquired immune deficiency syndrome, war, abortion, capital punishment, and life-style choices (e.g., nutrition, risk taking, health care, and smoking).

Didactic Versus Experiential Programs

An important distinction in death education is whether a program is didactic or experiential. Didactic programs emphasize knowledge and information about thanatology. The focus is on enhancing participants' cognitive awareness and understanding of death-related issues. Readings, lectures, and large-group discussions are frequently used for this purpose. Experiential programs might use some of the same instructional techniques, but they devote considerable time toward encouraging participants to examine and discuss their personal feelings and concerns about death. The ultimate goal is to help participants become more comfortable with and accepting of any negative feelings engendered by the topic of death. In experiential programs, exploration and sharing of personal feelings and experiences are encouraged through the use of personal exercises, role playing, fantasy, media presentations, and simulations. Technically speaking, because there is overlap in the process and content of didactic and experiential programs, the important distinction is between programs that emphasize experiential elements and those that do not. For convenience's sake, however, the terms *didactic* and *experiential* are customarily used to make this distinction.

Programs reported by Bell (1975) and Irwin and Melbin-Helberg (1992) illustrate the primary differences between didactic and experiential death education. Bell described a university-based, semester-long didactic death education course. The course consisted primarily of lectures and selected guest speakers from the medical, legal, and religious professions. Students did extensive research and writing on a death-related topic and presented their work in class. In contrast, Irwin and Melbin-Helberg described a semester-long university course on dying and bereavement that contained several experiential elements. The course was 13 weeks long and consisted of 2 hr of lecture and discussion and 2 hr of small-group workshops each week. The lectures covered topics related to dying and bereavement and attitudes about death. The workshops built on the lecture material but featured sequenced exercises designed to help participants in their personal understanding and acceptance of death and expression of death-related feelings. Students also kept a personal journal in which they recorded their reactions and feelings about course topics.

The next section presents the results of a recent review of death education programs. The findings from this review reveal the magnitude and dimension of attitude change that occurs as a result of death education and begins the discussion of what factors may be important in achieving such changes.

The Impact of Death Education

The results of studies on the outcome of death education have not been consistent. Some reports indicate positive benefits from death education (Leviton & Fretz, 1978; Miles, 1980; Trent, Glass, & McGee, 1981); others suggest that death education has no impact (Glass & Knott, 1984; Hoelter & Epley, 1979); and a few studies describe apparently iatrogenic effects, that is, that participants leave death education with heightened death concerns (Combs, 1981; Mueller, 1975; Wittmaier, 1979). There are several possible explanations for these inconsistent findings, such as differences in the scope, duration, and goals of programs; differences in the methodologies of the evaluation studies; and differences in the implementation various instructional techniques across programs.

In an attempt to synthesize research on death education, Reisenberg and I conducted a meta-analytic review of controlled outcome studies (Durlak & Reisenberg, 1991). Meta-analysis is increasingly being used in the behavioral and social sciences to assess the magnitude of impact from interventions and evaluate the relationship between conceptual and methodological features of studies and outcome. For the details on our procedures, see our review (Durlak & Reisenberg, 1991); for information on meta-analysis in general, see Durlak and Lipsey (1991) and Light and Pillemer (1980).

Briefly, we examined the outcomes from 47 published reports of death education that had appeared through May 1987. These reports represented the range of programs that characterize death education. For example, the most common type of program was a semester-long college course, but the second most frequent type of program was a mini-course or workshop for health care workers that lasted less than 10 hr. To be included in the review, a study had to include a control group of some sort, but most studies used a nonequivalent control group design in which comparison data were collected from a convenience sample. In fact, the overall experimental quality of the 47 reviewed programs was not very high. The quality of the design of each study was evaluated along a 5-point scale. Each study received a point for each of the following: (a) random assignment of subjects to experimental and control groups; (b) use of placebo or waiting-list controls (the latter would control for motivation and interest in death); (c) use of reliable outcome measures; (d) use of multiple, reliable outcome measures; and (e) inclusion of a follow-up study of program effects. The experimental quality of the 47 programs averaged only 1.40 on this 5-point scale, indicating that many improvements need to be made in the basic methodological features of program evaluation studies.

In meta-analyses such as ours in which an experimental group is compared with a control group of some sort, the variable of interest for each study is the effect size (ES), which is calculated as follows:

$$ES = \frac{m_1 - m_2}{s_2},$$

where m_1 is the posttreatment mean of the death education group, m_2 is the posttreatment mean of the control group, and s_2 is the posttreatment standard deviation of the control group. In other words, in each study the performances of the two groups are compared at posttreatment. A positive ES indicates the death education group demonstrated more positive change than the control group; a negative ES has the reverse meaning. In studies in which detectable between-groups differences existed at pretreatment, adjusted ESs were calculated (Durlak & Reisenberg, 1991).

Separate ESs were calculated within each study for outcome measures assessing cognitive, affective, or behavioral components of death attitudes, although not all studies collected information on all of these dimensions. The cognitions assessed typically involved general beliefs about the study of thanatology (e.g., it is valuable to study death and dying and people should be able

Table 13-1 Mean Effect Sizes and Standard Deviations for Different Outcome Domains and Different Types of Death Education Programs

	Effect Size	
Outcome Domain	**M**	**SD**
Cognitions (N = 12)	0.67	0.60
Behaviors (N = 3)	0.69	0.23
Affective (N = 44)	0.18	0.43
Didactic program (N = 14)	−0.04	0.44
Experiential program (N = 26)	0.33	0.41

Note. Ns are numbers of studies. Findings for didactic and experiential programs differed significantly at the .01 level. The data for this table have been drawn from "The Impact of Death Education" by J. A. Durlak and L. A. Reisenberg, 1991, *Death Studies, 15*, pp. 47–48. Copyright © 1991 by Hemisphere Publishing Corporation.

to talk about their reactions to death) or opinions about specific death-related topics, such as euthanasia or suicide (e.g., people who attempt or complete suicide are crazy and the terminally ill should have a right to express their choices about their own medical care). In terms of affect, programs assessed a variety of negative feelings about personal death, such as anxiety, fear, threat, and discomfort. Many of the measures discussed elsewhere in this volume, such as the Threat Index (Chapter 4) and the Collett–Lester Fear of Death and Dying Scale (Chapter 3), were used. The behavioral outcome dimension included either data drawn from role-playing exercises that tapped the ability to talk effectively with the terminally ill or self-reports about changes in life-style that were prompted by the death education program (e.g., giving up smoking or making out a will or organ donation card).

Table 13-1 summarizes the major findings. The upper section indicates that the 12 studies of changes in death-relation cognitions achieved a mean *ES* of 0.67, and the 3 studies of changes in death-related behaviors achieved a similar average effect (0.69).

There is no absolute standard for evaluating the magnitude of *ES*s. Generally, a mean *ES* in the 0.67–0.69 range is considered to be moderately large and is similar to that achieved in many interventions in the behavioral and social sciences. For instance, the data reflect that the average participant in a death education program displayed more positive death-related cognitions or demonstrated more positive behavioral changes than did two thirds of the members of the control groups. Therefore, it can be concluded that death education programs have been moderately successful in changing death-related cognitions and behaviors. Unfortunately, the number of studies of these two dimensions, particularly behavioral changes, is not very high.

Findings for the 44 programs that assessed affective outcomes are also presented in the upper half of Table 7-1. The average *ES* achieved by these studies was only 0.18, a low overall effect. Hypothesizing that program format was an important moderator of impact, we separated the 44 studies into two groups, those in which the death education program was didactic and those in which education was experiential. We could not categorize 4 of the 44 programs in this fashion because of limited information. (Because of the small number of studies collecting data on cognitions and behaviors, didactic and experiential programs could not be effectively compared on these other outcome dimensions.)

As shown in the bottom half of Table 7-1, the 14 didactic programs achieved a mean *ES* of less than zero (-0.04), whereas the 26 experiential programs achieved a mean *ES* of 0.33 (*SD* = 0.41). This difference was significant. In other words, the type of death education program conducted was an important determinant in changing participants' feelings about death. Overall, experiential programs produced a modest decrease in death fears and anxieties, whereas didactic programs appeared to have no appreciable effect. Data from additional outcome studies that appeared after our review was completed (e.g., Hutchinson & Scherman, 1992; Irwin & Melbin-Helberg, 1992; Johansson & Lally, 1990–1991) are consistent with this conclusion.

Supplementary analyses were conducted to determine whether *ES* was significantly related to program length, setting (university vs. medical school), the number and characteristics of participants, or the quality of study design (according to the criteria listed earlier). None of these variables were significantly related to *ES*.

To summarize, our review (Durlak & Reisenberg, 1991) indicated that both the type of outcomes assessed and the type of program conducted were important determinants of the impact of death education. In general, programs are fairly successful in modifying participants' death-related cognitions and behaviors, but the type of program conducted makes a crucial difference in terms of influencing feelings about personal death. Experiential programs seem to produce modestly positive results, whereas didactic programs have no overall effect on feelings.

Before discussing the possible reasons for the preceding findings, it is necessary to switch topics temporarily, and discuss basic theory and research regarding attitude change. The following discussion draws heavily upon the work of McGuire (1985), Katz (1960), and Oskamp (1991).

ATTITUDES AND CHANGES IN THEM

Attitude research is perhaps the most complex topic studied by social and behavioral scientists. Approximately 1,000 new attitude studies appear each year (McGuire, 1985). Fishbein and Ajzen (1972) identified more than 500 different operational definitions of attitude and noted that findings often differ depending on the definition. Moreover, there are at least 38 different attitude theories (Shaw & Costanzo, 1982), each with its adherents and its limitations. Many variables have been studied in relation to attitude change; Oskamp (1991) listed 65 that have been frequently examined. Finally, McGuire (1985) suggested there are at least 12 successive steps (i.e., mediating processes) that individuals must complete before they will change their attitude toward something.

It is impossible to do justice to all attitude theory and research except to emphasize that the phenomenon of attitude change is complex, and there is no consensus about how attitudes are formed or modified. Nevertheless, it is helpful to describe several basic features of attitudes.

The Functions of Attitudes

Attitudes can serve four social–psychological functions: understanding, need satisfaction, ego defense, and value expression. Some attitudes may serve more than one function at a time. In terms of understanding, attitudes help individuals understand their world and their relationship to it; this so-called knowledge function of attitudes creates a sense of order and predictability to life. Attitudes may also serve to satisfy personal needs and be useful for reaching personal goals. Other attitudes serve ego-defensive functions by defending people against perceived threats or conflicts. Finally, value-expressive attitudes are those that help establish or solidify an individual's personal identity.

What implications do these attitude functions have for death education? Usually, attitudes must be aroused or stimulated before they can be changed, and different conditions are needed to change attitudes with different functions. For example, understanding-oriented attitudes are most likely to change when individuals are in new or ambiguous situations and are given information that reduces the ambiguity. This might occur for individuals who enter death education programs with minimal or inaccurate information about death-related phenomena. For these individuals the knowledge offered in lectures and readings could lead to change in attitudes toward death that serve a knowledge function. Need-oriented attitudes are more likely to change if the person's current attitudes no longer serve his or her needs (perhaps because the needs have changed) or if it is clear that adopting a new attitude will help the person achieve a goal. Regarding death education, individuals who have a need for personal control over their lives might be affected by information about the importance of completing Living Wills and communicating with significant others about their last wishes. In the case of ego-defensive attitudes, factors that alleviate the presumed threat or discomfort are important. Perhaps individuals who are threatened by the potential pain or social isolation of dying can be made to feel more comfortable by being informed about the hospice movement, the management of physical and psychological pain in the terminally ill, and case studies suggesting that the final days of life can be characterized by peace and acceptance (Kübler-Ross, 1969).

Value-expressive attitudes may be the most difficult of all to change, because they relate to individuals' basic core beliefs and sense of self. An individual's sense of self might have to change before he or she can adopt a particular new attitude. A less extreme possibility is for individuals to become aware that a particular attitude that they currently hold really is not consistent with their values and thus should be changed. Individuals who perceive no value in death because it destroys the sense of self might experience a change in attitude as they learn that the dying process can draw loved ones closer together and enhance personal meaning and life satisfaction.

For the preceding formulations to be helpful to efforts to change people's attitudes toward death, it is important to specify the possible functions served by different death attitudes. With few exceptions (see Chapters 1 and 4), this has not occurred.

The Components of Attitudes

As if the different functions of attitudes did not make the study of attitudes complex enough, there are other aspects of attitudes to consider. As noted by McGuire (1985), early theorists viewed attitudes as possessing three related components: cognitions, affect, and behavior. That is, attitudes were thought to consist of ideas and beliefs (cognitions) that were related to certain emotions (affect), and both components were believed to be related to the action taken concerning the object of the attitude (behavioral component). More recent theoretical and empirical work maintains that these three components may or may not be related, depending on many factors. Thus an individual can feel positively about something but not necessarily act in line with these feelings. The fact that the three components of attitudes are not always related has implications regarding attitude measurement. For instance, had Reisenberg and I not evaluated the impact of death education programs separately for all three outcome dimensions (cognitions, behavior, and affect) in our meta-analysis (Durlak & Reisenberg, 1991), the differential findings achieved for these dimensions would have been obscured. Furthermore, in evaluating a death education program, researchers must choose an outcome measure that directly relates to the program's objectives; for example, using a measure that assesses death-related feelings when the program is primarily directed at changing death-related cognitions will not provide a fair test of the program's impact.

Target, Integration, and Complexity of Attitudes

Attitudes are held in regard to a specific target or object, and it is important to be precise in identifying these targets. Although it is generally assumed that individuals strive for some type of coherence, connection, and consistency in their beliefs, it is unknown exactly how individuals integrate their attitudes toward similar or different topics. Thus, attitudes about the dying process, euthanasia, the deaths of others, and personal death may or may not be related and should be measured with this in mind. Unfortunately, several death education studies have assessed attitudes in a global manner, making it difficult to pinpoint the specific death-related attitudes that were examined.

Finally, attitudes toward the same target can be multidimensional or complex. That is, it is theoretically possible (Durlak, Horn, & Kass, 1990; Lonetto & Templer, 1986) for individuals to hold multiple and perhaps contradictory attitudes on the same topic. For example, a person can have both positive and negative feelings about personal death at the same time. Thus it cannot be assumed that individuals who are highly anxious about their own death have no positive feelings about it whatsoever or that those who feel positively about personal death have absolutely no anxiety or concern about it. Although this point seems elemental, it is not reflected in current measures of death attitude. Most research to date has focused almost exclusively on assessing negative feelings about personal death.

In addition, some data (Feifel & Nagy, 1980, 1981) suggest that individuals' attitudes toward death can differ at conscious, preconscious, and unconscious levels. The validity of measures of unconscious death attitudes has yet to be established (Neimeyer, 1988). Nevertheless, simple self-report measures might not be sufficient to assess the true depth and complexity of individual reactions to death.

In summary, the phenomenon of attitude change is complex and involves at the very least considerations of attitude functions, components, targets, integration, and multidimensionality. Because these issues have not been completely clarified in basic (much less applied) research, the outcome data from death education programs must be interpreted cautiously.

CHANGE IN ATTITUDE TOWARD DEATH AS A RESULT OF DEATH EDUCATION

What factors or mechanisms cause attitudes toward death to change as a result of death education? Unfortunately, in the controlled outcome research that Reisenberg and I examined (Durlak & Reisenberg, 1991) and in most other reports of death education, crucial information has been lacking that would permit a clear answer to this question. Three primary factors contribute to the confusion. First, the educators' specific goals are not always described in reports and in many cases must be inferred from the types of outcome measures that were used. If an assessment of personal feelings about death was used, then it must be assumed that changing participants on this dimension was one of the primary goals of the program. Second, researchers have seldom operationalized all their teaching techniques or intervention practices. Usually, it is possible to identify only the most prominent program features, and much potentially valuable information on exactly what occurred in the program is unavailable. Third, death education is a complex phenomenon in its own right, with numerous factors potentially in operation. For example, characteristics of the source of information can influence attitude change, but in death education there are frequently many interacting sources of information. These include not only the educator, but also the authors of the reading material offered to participants, guest speakers, the characters depicted in any media presented, and any participants who offer information and share their experiences.

In this section, I describe some mechanisms that possibly underlie the attitude changes that have occurred in various programs. Future investigators could make a substantial contribution to death education research by putting some of the following suppositions to experimental test.

The Central Importance of Affect

This section discusses efforts to change negative feelings about death, rather than death-related cognitions or behaviors, because of the fundamental importance attached to the former dimension by many thanatologists. The assumptions are that personal feelings can interfere with individuals' ability to help others or themselves deal with death and, furthermore, that the resolution of death-related concerns occurs best on a personal and emotional level rather than an abstract or intellectual level (Grollman, 1967; Kübler-Ross, 1969; Quint, 1967). Irwin and Melbin-Helberg (1992) described the possible dangers for caregivers of not coming to terms with death: "Counselors' own unresolved issues can so contaminate their interactions with clients that the capacity to assist clients is seriously impaired, and in fact the behavior of counselors might even be so self-protective as to be counterproductive for clients' welfare" (p. 73). Therefore, coming to a personal understanding and acceptance of death is a central theme in many death education efforts.

Although there is much clinical evidence and some correlational data (Bugen, 1979; Cullinan, 1990) to support the central hypothesis that emotional issues influence death-related behaviors, direct experimental evidence is lacking. Nevertheless, the reduction of negative affect about personal death has been a primary goal of most death education programs.

The general process of attitude change in death education appears to be consistent with basic attitude theory and research, which maintains that the first goal is to arouse an attitude and the second is to use various techniques to change the beliefs. Each of these dimensions is now discussed.

Arousal of Death-Related Attitudes

Research indicates that direct positive experience with the target of an attitude can induce change. Although death education cannot, of course, provide direct experience with death, many other methods can be used to stimulate death-related attitudes, thereby making them open to change. These include readings, films, videos, role playing, field trips, interviews with terminally ill persons or bereaved persons, and experiential exercises (Durlak, 1978; Glass & Knott, 1984; Miles, 1980; Yeaworth et al., 1974).

Experiential exercises appear to be particularly effective in stimulating personal feelings about death. Two examples include the Do-It-Yourself Death Certificate (Simpson, 1975) and the 24-hours-to-live scenario (Hammer, 1971). In the former, participants are given an official death certificate form and asked to complete it in detail regarding their own eventual death; a group discussion follows. In the latter 24-hours-to-live scenario, students are typically instructed to "Imagine you have just learned you have 24 hours left to live. You are mobile and can go or do what you want. Please spend a few moments thinking about how you would spend your last day on earth." After a few minutes of introspection, participants are asked to pair off and share their plans for their last day, including an explanation of why they would do certain things. A large-group discussion follows. Many other experiential exercises are available (for descriptions, see Knott, Ribar, Duson, & King, 1989).

It is essential to proceed carefully in this regard, however. Instructors must recognize the motivations and abilities of participants to deal with personal feelings about death. If time permits, a gradual approach is advisable to ensure that cohesiveness and trust are present in the group and to reduce the likelihood of negative effects (Corr, 1978). It is possible that didactic programs have failed to change feelings about death because although the readings, lectures, and other activities in these programs arouse death-related attitudes, there is insufficient opportunity for personal discussions through which participants could process these attitudes. In contrast, experiential programs regularly provide opportunities for individuals to discuss their personal feelings and learn how others deal with their death-related concerns.

In summary, various elements of death education can arouse relevant death attitudes and create need states in participants. That is, they arouse anxiety and other negative feelings about death that individuals are motivated or feel the need to reduce. Anxiety is often a strong motivator for change, but a natural reaction is for individuals to avoid the source of their anxiety, rather than to work through their discomfort. Therefore, it is important in death education to create a climate of acceptance and support that encourages participants to share and work through their negative death-related feelings. This climate is usually achieved through group discussions and the resulting interactions among students, a topic that is considered further in the next section.

Mechanisms of Attitude Change

The group discussions that are invariably used as a supplement to other features of death education appear to be a crucial ingredient of effective death education programs. This is so for two main reasons. Group discussions (a) contain many factors that contribute to attitude change and (b) foster a climate of openness and acceptance that helps participants remain willing to deal with their death-related feelings.

For example, group situations offer the possibility for empathy, modeling, mutual support and encouragement, and reinforcement for positive change. The instructor also has the opportunity to tailor material to suit the motivations, needs, capacities, interests, and experiences of different group members. Instructors can use repeated suggestions to change attitudes, provide critical information, and detail specific arguments and persuasions for various attitude positions. Instructors can also selectively enhance the salience of certain aspects of a reading or videotape, present new information as needed, clarify ambiguous situations, and respond specifically to participants' needs. For instance, participants who value "death with dignity" and personal control can be directed to the arguments for Living Wills, durable powers of attorney, and the importance of communicating their wishes to significant others. Information and discussion about each of these issues can induce positive attitude change in participants who value personal choice in health care decisions.

Some death educators use the Socratic method during group discussions. The Socratic method can change attitudes by requiring participants to clarify certain attitudes, which might reveal inconsistencies in their beliefs. As noted earlier, revealing inconsistencies in thinking can induce attitude change in individuals who value coherency and order. The Socratic technique might also be particularly effective in changing death attitudes related to core values of the self and one's philosophy of life, which ordinarily are difficult to modify. Furthermore, many persons find the Socratic process a comfortable way to examine feelings and cognitions and thus remain involved in and motivated during the dialogue.

Group discussions in death education parallel the process of group therapy in the sense that a climate of trust and acceptance is fostered and participants feel encouraged to take risks and share personally meaningful material. Personal disclosure followed by acceptance and support reduces discomfort for the discloser and leads others to share. Even if all the feelings disclosed are initially negative, the eventual result can be positive as group members experience relief at learning their concerns are shared by others. Over time, some participants express lower death concern, and they function as positive role models for others. Positive changes occurring in some group members thus serve to establish peer norms, encouraging improvement in others. In other words, a positive social milieu is created that influences attitude development and change. These processes are entirely consistent with basic findings regarding attitude change.

In summary, the major goals of experiential death education programs have been (a) to increase awareness of personal death attitudes and then (b) to develop a group atmosphere that fosters sharing and acceptance of these attitudes, followed by (c) use of attitude change techniques to modify participants' beliefs.

Unfortunately, it is not possible at present to specify exactly which techniques have been responsible for the positive results achieved in different programs.

To conclude this chapter I shall briefly discuss three additional issues that are relevant to changing death attitudes: the durability of attitude change, individualized assessment of attitudes, and the skills or qualifications needed by death educators.

Durability of Attitude Change

Attitude research offers no clear prediction regarding whether induced change in attitude will remain at the same intensity or strength or diminish quickly or slowly over time. There does not seem to be much empirical support for delayed-action or sleeper effects, however (McGuire, 1985). Therefore, unless attitudes have been positively affected immediately after death education, no change is likely to be present later, unless intervening events are responsible. In our review (Durlak & Reisenberg, 1991), we found that participants from experiential programs displayed exactly the same level of positive change at a mean follow-up of 4 months (range—2 weeks to 1 year) as they did at the end of the death education experience. These encouraging data indicate that the effects of death education are not transitory; however, the mean follow-up period was short, and follow-up data were collected for only seven programs.

Individual Level of Analysis

It is important to stress that participants enter death education with different motivations and needs. Not everyone is afraid of or uncomfortable about death, and thus not every participant should be expected to show reduced negative feelings about death after a death education program. Even if all participants are highly anxious about death, one particular program might work more effectively for some than for others. Rainey and Epting (1977) reported that although no significant mean change was found in death attitudes of participants in a death education program, the variance of these attitudes increased over time, suggesting that the program had affected individuals differently. Analyses that focus exclusively on group-level change can provide a misleading assessment of the impact of death education, failing to determine differential effects among participants. A more informative evaluative strategy would be to conduct both group and individual levels of analysis, such as were recently conducted by Knight and Elfenbein (1993).

Knight and Elfenbein (1993) reported that after a death education program the total group of participants reported *more* negative death-related feelings than those in a control group. However, they also found that, depending on which one of three outcome measures was examined, 31–41% of participants showed reduced death anxiety after the program, 7–17% showed no change over time, and 48–52% demonstrated heightened death concern. Overall, Knight and El-fenbein reported, that more religious individuals displayed more positive changes across measures. Studying individuals in relation to their preprogram status and their change over time can provide an understanding of how death education specifically affects different individuals. Ultimately, such studies can determine which methods of death education are useful for which individuals.

Characteristics of Effective Death Educators

Several authors have written about the experience and training necessary to be an effective death educator (e.g., Corr, 1978; International Work Group on Death, Dying and Bereavement, 1992). In addition to the qualities needed by any good teacher, death educators should be comfortable with the topic of death and have no hidden agendas or needs with respect to teaching thanatology, such as working through their own unresolved grief or death attitudes.

However, if the earlier comments about the mechanisms of attitude change in death education are correct, one important implication for death educators is that they must be quite skilled in leading group discussions and in the basic features of group dynamics. Among other things, they should be attentive and good listeners; skilled in asking appropriate questions; empathic and supportive when emotions are expressed; able to model effective expression of feelings; able to engage quieter individuals and manage the contributions of more active group members; aware of how bonds and attachments form among different members in groups; and able to deal with any conflicts or differences of opinion that might arise.

To date, there has been no research on how well different instructors have implemented their death education programs or components of these programs. Before examining whether participants' death attitudes have changed, it is important to confirm that instructors are effectively using the various teaching strategies and attitude change techniques that are necessary for a program to achieve its specific educational objectives.

SUMMARY

A review of controlled outcome studies (Durlak & Reisenberg, 1991) suggests that both the type of program conducted and the type of outcome measures used moderate the impact of death education. Programs have been moderately suc-cessful in changing death-related cognitions; a few programs have also achieved success in modifying death-related behaviors. Experiential programs have had some success in reducing participants' negative feelings about death, whereas didactic programs as a whole have had no significant impact in this area.

Death education programs are complex interventions that incorporate several principles of attitude change theory. These include modeling, support, provision of information, and various persuasion techniques that are effective in engaging participants and responding to their needs and motivations. Theory building is now needed that would lead to testable hypotheses of how specific attitudes change or fail to change in death education. Such studies may well represent the next wave of research in the field. There are several indications that educational efforts can affect participants positively; now we need a greater understanding of the mechanisms of change in different programs.

The previous chapters in this volume serve as an important context for the current discussion. The importance of adequate measurement of relevant constructs cannot be underestimated. Any attempt to understand to what extent and how death attitudes are influenced by death education is highly dependent on reliable and valid measurement of the death attitudes in question. Although the chapters in Part II indicate a growing sophistication in the measurement of death attitudes, current measures are still far from perfect. In other words, there is still much to learn about how various death attitudes can be measured most effectively under different circumstances. Therefore, the conclusions and interpretations presented here must be offered tentatively until greater precision is gained in the measurement of various death attitudes.

REFERENCES

Bell, B. (1975). The experimental manipulation of death attitudes: A preliminary investigation. *Omega, 6*, 199–205.

Bugen, L. (1979). State anxiety effects on counselor perceptions of dying stages. *Journal of Counseling Psychology, 26*, 89–91.

Charmaz, K. (1980). *The social reality of death*. Reading, MA: Addison-Wesley.

Combs, D. (1981). The effects of selected death education curriculum models on death anxiety and death acceptance. *Death Education, 5*, 75–81.

Corr, C. A. (1978). A model syllabus for death and dying course. *Death Education, 1*, 433–457.

Crase, D. (1989). Death education: Its diversity and multidisciplinary focus. *Death Studies, 13*, 25–29.

Cullinan, A. L. (1990). Teachers' death anxiety, ability to cope with death, and perceived ability to aid bereaved students. *Death Education, 14*, 147–160.

Dickinson, G. E., Sumner, E. D., & Frederick, L. M. (1992). Death education in selected health professions. *Death Education, 16*, 281–289.

Durlak, J. (1978). Comparison between experiential and didactic methods of death education. *Omega, 9*, 57–66.

Durlak, J. A., Horn, W., & Kass, R. A. (1990). A self-administering assessment of personal meanings of death: Report on the revised Twenty Statements Test. *Omega, 21*, 301–309.

Durlak, J. A., & Lipsey, M. W. (1991). A practitioner's guide to meta-analysis. *American Journal of Community Psychology, 19*, 291–332.

Durlak, J. A., & Reisenberg, L. A. (1991). The impact of death education. *Death Studies, 15*, 39–58.

Feifel, H. (Ed.). (1977). *New meanings of death* (2nd ed.). New York: McGraw-Hill.

Feifel, H., & Nagy, V. T. (1980). Death orientation and life-threatening behavior. *Journal of Abnormal Psychology, 89*, 38–45.

Feifel, H, & Nagy, V. T. (1981). Another look at fear of death. *Journal of Consulting and Clinical Psychology, 49*, 278–286.

Fishbein, M., & Ajzen, I. (1972). Attitudes and opinions. *Annual Review of Psychology, 23*, 487–544.

Glass, J., & Knott, E. (1984). Effectiveness of a lesson series on death and dying in changing adolescents' death anxiety and attitudes toward older adults. *Death Education, 8*, 299–313.

Grollman, E. (1967). *Explaining death to children*. Boston: Beacon Press.

Hammer, M. (1971). Reflections on one's own death as a peak experience. *Mental Hygiene, 55*, 264–265.

Hoelter, J., & Epley, R. (1979). Death education and death-related attitudes. *Death Education, 3*, 67–75.

Hutchison, T. D., & Scherman, A. (1992). Didactic and experiential death and dying training: Impact upon death anxiety. *Death Studies, 16*, 317–330.

Johansson, N., & Lally, T. (1990–91). Effectiveness of a death-education program in reducing death anxiety of nursing students. *Omega, 22*, 25–33.

International Work Group on Death, Dying and Bereavement. (1992). A statement of assumptions and principles concerning education about death, dying, and bereavement. *Death Studies, 16*, 59–65.

Irwin, H. J., & Melbin-Helberg, E. B. (1992). Enhancement of death acceptance by a grief counseling course. *Omega, 25*, 73–86.

Kastenbaum, R., & Aisenberg, R. (1972). *The psychology of death*. New York: Springer.

Katz, D. (1960). The functional approach to the study of attitudes. *Pubic Opinion Quarterly, 6*, 248–268.

Kirchberg, T. M., & Neimeyer, R. A. (1991). Reactions of beginning counselors to situations involving death and dying. *Death Education, 15*, 603–610.

Knight, K. H., & Elfenbein, M. H. (1993). Relationship of death education to the anxiety, fear, and meaning associated with death. *Death Studies, 17*, 115–130.

Knott, J. E., Ribar, M. C., Duson, B. M., & King, M. R. (1989). *Thanatopics: Activities and exercises for confronting death*. Lexington, MA: Lexington Books.

Kübler-Ross, E. (1969). *On death and dying*. New York: Macmillan.

Leviton, D. (1977). Death education. In H. Feifel (Ed.), *New meanings of death* (2nd ed., pp. 254–272). New York: McGraw-Hill.

Leviton, D., & Fretz, B. (1978). Effects of death education on fear of death and attitudes towards death and life. *Omega, 9*, 267–277.

Light, R. J, & Pillemer, D. B. (1984). *Summing up: The science of reviewing research*. Cambridge, MA: Harvard University Press.

Lonetto, R., & Templer, D. I. (1986). *Death anxiety*. Washington, DC: Hemisphere.

McGuire, W. J. (1985). Attitudes and attitude change. In G. Lindzey & E. Aronson (Eds.), *The handbook of social psychology: Vol. II. Special fields and applications* (3rd ed., pp. 233–346). Hillsdale, NJ: L. Erlbaum Assoc.

Miles, M. (1980). The effects of a course on death and grief on nurses' attitudes toward dying patients and death. *Death Education, 4*, 245–260.

Mueller, M. L. (1975). Fear of death and death education. *Notre Dame Journal of Education, 6*, 84–91.

Neimeyer, R. A. (1988). Death anxiety. In H. Wass, F. Berardo, & R. A. Neimeyer (Eds.), *Dying: Facing the facts* (2nd ed., pp. 97–136). Washington, DC: Hemisphere.

Oskamp, S. (1991). *Attitudes and opinions* (2nd ed.). Englewood Cliffs, NJ: Prentice-Hall.

Pine, V. R. (1977). A socio-historical portrait of death education. *Death Education, 1*, 57–84.

Quint, J. (1967). *The nurse and the dying patient.* New York: Macmillan.

Rainey, L. C., & Epting, F. R. (1977). Death threat constructions in the student and the prudent. *Omega, 8*, 19–28.

Shaw, M. E., & Costanzo, P. R. (1982). *Theories of social psychology* (2nd ed.). New York: McGraw-Hill.

Simpson, M. A. (1975). The do-it-yourself death certificate in evoking and estimating student attitudes toward death. *Journal of Medical Education, 50*, 475–478.

Stillion, J. M. (1989). Association for Death Education and Counseling: An organization for our times and for our future. *Death Studies, 13*, 191–201.

Wass, H., Berardo, F. M., & Neimeyer, R. A. (Eds.). (1988). *Dying: Facing the facts* (2nd ed.). Washington, DC: Hemisphere.

Wass, H., Miller, M. D., & Thornton, G. (1990). Death education and grief/suicide intervention in the public schools. *Death Education, 14*, 253–268.

Wittmaier, B. (1979). Some unexpected attitudinal consequences of a short course on death. *Omega, 10*, 271–275.

Yeaworth, R. C., Kapp, F. T., & Winget, C. (1974). Attitudes of nursing students toward the dying patient. *Nursing Research, 23*, 20–24.

Zinner, E. S. (1992). Setting standards: Certification efforts and considerations in the field of death and dying. *Death Studies, 16*, 67–77.

Part IV

Conclusion

Chapter 14

Death Attitudes in Adult Life: A Closing Coda

Robert A. Neimeyer

An implicit theme in many of the chapters in this book could be stated as a question: How can we conduct more meaningful research on the role of death attitudes in adult life? In their own ways, each of the authors provides one possible answer to this question, whether by arguing for better articulation of research with theory, promoting the use of promising scales or instruments, or exemplifying the application of these concepts or methods to particular populations or contexts concerned with death and dying. In this closing coda, I share a few of my own responses to this question, offering leads for others engaged in the development of thanatological theory, research, and practice. For the sake of impact, these reflections are presented as prescriptions for future work; however, I realize that creative contributions can (and indeed should) go beyond simple adherence to the guidelines I offer.

PRESCRIPTION 1: CONDUCT THEORETICALLY GROUNDED RESEARCH

As Tomer points out in Chapter 1, much of the research on death attitudes is atheoretical, with many researchers at most making a casual reference to a larger conceptual framework in which their findings can be placed. Nonetheless, investigators often design their studies with an implicit theory in mind, without explicating for themselves or their readers the assumptions on which their studies are based. Thus, they may hypothesize that a particular death education program should reduce students' fear of death, without explaining why such an outcome might be expected. Similarly, authors may use disembedded concepts (e.g., denial of death anxiety) without situating them in a larger theory (e.g., psychoanalysis) that gives them meaning, suggesting conditions under which they operate, and so on. Even when theories are systematically invoked (e.g., in the frequent references to existential or search-for-meaning theories), they are typically used retrospectively as heuristic devices for interpreting findings on a post hoc basis, rather than prospectively to formulate incisive hypotheses that can support or disconfirm key tenets of the theories. If the field of death studies is to move beyond its tendency toward chaotic fragmentalism, stricter derivation of empirical research from overarching theories is essential.

This respect for theory, however, does not imply that existing theories have cornered the market in defining suitable frameworks for organizing future research. In particular, imaginative application of psychosocial theories from other domains could yield novel hypotheses that could be evaluated empirically, resulting in useful links between well-developed research areas and thanatological research. For example, what might theories of social cognition predict about the role of self-schemas in mediating an individual's awareness of mortality (Marcus, 1977)? How might fear of the death of others vary as a function of an individual's attachment style (secure, anxious, or avoidant) in close relationships (Hazan & Shaver, 1987)? Does rendering a satisfying "interpersonal account" of a loss subtly influence one's own acceptance of death (Harvey, Weber, & Orbuch, 1990)? Much of the impoverishment of the field of death attitudes owes to the intellectual isolationism that characterizes the majority of research efforts, a limitation that could be redressed by suitable bridge-building with the work of productive scholars in related disciplines.

PRESCRIPTION 2: BUILD INTEGRATIVE THEORIES

Theories themselves could benefit from integration or selective synthesis with one another, much as the field of psychotherapy is now making concerted efforts to surmount the limitations of commitment to existing schools (Norcross & Goldfried, 1993). At least two benefits might be expected to ensue from such integration. First, needless duplication in conceptualization might be avoided, or, alternatively, communication among the adherents to different theories might be increased. For example, in Chapter 1, Tomer suggests that several theories (e.g., self-actualization and certain existential and self-concept discrepancy models) converge on the hypothesis that death anxiety varies with the degree of compatibility between the self and ideal self. A systematic attempt at bridging such theories might reveal important but subtle distinctions among them, or might suggest still other points of agreement that could allow for the development of a more parsimonious model that encompasses the key predictions of each theory. This sharpened (and perhaps simplified) theory might then be a clearer guide to subsequent research than its parent theories, although it may lack some of their interpretive resources.

A second and perhaps more important contribution of theoretical integration could be the development of more comprehensive theories that articulate or reconcile the sometimes competing predictions of their predecessors. For example, in self-realization models death anxiety is usually viewed as a sign of psychological disturbance, whereas Heideggerian theory views this same fear of death as an inevitable concomitant of humans' existential predicament, engendered by their contemplation of eventual nonbeing. (For an explication of these contrasting perspectives, see Chapter 1 in this volume and Warren, 1989). But these predictions might be reconciled from the standpoint of an expanded constructivist model, which assumes with Kelly (1961) that "the very essence of life is the use of the present to bridge the past with the future" (p. 260). If life is viewed as an ongoing process of identity construction, both reflection on the past and anticipation of the future would be components of this process. Glancing back over their lives, individuals confront the challenge of reconciling the self that has been with their core values and ideals. Glancing forward toward their eventual death, individuals face the threat to their sense of identity and continuity posed by the cessation or transformation of their being. Thus, death anxiety could be considered a function of both the discrepancy people sense between themselves and their ideals (as in the self-realization position) and their incapacity to anticipate the reality of death within the structure of their present life (as in Heideggerian position).[1]

This constructivist view could also accommodate certain aspects of the psychoanalytic position, with its emphasis on denial and defense (see Chapter 12, by Firestone). For construct theorists, the meaningful anticipation of events is fundamental to individuals' psychological processes (R. A. Neimeyer, 1987). When people encounter events that threaten to overwhelm their anticipatory systems, they sometimes constrict their perceptual field, narrowing their aware-

---

[1]Strictly speaking, *anxiety* is defined from a personal construct view as "the recognition that the events with which one is confronted lie outside the range of convenience of one's construct system" (Kelly, 1955, p. 495). In other words, individuals experience anxiety when they are confronted with something that is fundamentally unknown, that cannot be interpreted within the confines of their present meaning system. Similarly, *threat* also represents a "transitional" emotion, referring to "the awareness of imminent comprehensive change in one's core [identity] structures" (Kelly, p. 489). It is this latter concept that has been operationalized by the development of the Threat Index and related personal construct methods (see Chapter 4). In contrast to both of these anticipatory emotions, construct theorists define *guilt* as the "perception of one's apparent dislodgment from his core role structures" (Kelly, p. 502). Thus, the self–ideal self discrepancy recognized in retrospective contemplation of one's life might be more properly considered a kind of existential guilt over having lived at variance with one's most central values, rather than a state of anxiety per se. For the present purposes, however, the key point is that both contemplation of one's life and anticipation of one's death can contribute to one's level of apprehension or unease about personal mortality.

ness of events to minimize apparent incompatibilities (Kelly, 1955). Viewed in this light, denial of death may not be so much pathological as it is understandable; it can represent an individual's healthy if temporary refuge against a chaotic reality that cannot be accommodated within the individual's present meaning system. Eventually, however, it is more fruitful for a person to elaborate or extend his or her meaning system to render such events interpretable. If successful, this "effort after meaning" permits a person once again to dilate his or her focus to include the prospect of personal death, thereby making more comprehensive sense of his or her life.

This constructivist theory does not assume that death has any single, real meaning that should hold for all people all of the time. Thus, striving for symbolic immortality through one's works, one's offspring, or the survival of one's soul is not seen as a variant of self-deluding denial of the reality of eventual nonbeing, as in the analytic view. Instead, these and the myriad of other meanings people attribute to death can be seen as equally valid attempts on the part of individuals and cultures to infuse death with significance and to develop a construction of death that supports and extends people's construction of their lives. The validity of these constructions can be judged only in terms of their viability, that is, in terms of the constructive or destructive implications they carry for the individuals or groups that espouse them. This constructivist analysis is compatible with a positive illusions perspective (R. A. Neimeyer, 1993; Tomer, Chapter 1 of this volume).

In summary, existing research on death attitudes has placed too much emphasis on the accumulation of supposedly neutral facts at the expense of the development of comprehensive theories capable of subsuming the facts and giving them order and significance. This imbalance needs to be redressed if the field is to make substantial conceptual advances.

PRESCRIPTION 3: EXPLORE THE DIMENSIONALITY OF DEATH ATTITUDES

If a single trend is evident in the 25-year history of intensive research on death attitudes, it is the shift from unidimensional measures of death attitudes to multidimensional forms of assessment (R. A. Neimeyer, 1988). Thus, instruments originally designed to measure a single global construct such as Templer's (1970) Death Anxiety Scale and Krieger, Epting, and Leitner's (1974) Threat Index have undergone improvement and refinement, yielding useful measures whose component subscales discriminate various aspects of death anxiety or threat (see Chapters 2 and 4). Moreover, other reliable and valid multifactorial scales have been devised that assess a range of specific death fears (Hoelter, 1979; R. A. Neimeyer & Moore, Chapter 5 in this volume) and other attitudes, including varieties of death acceptance (Wong, Reker, & Gesser, Chapter 6 in this volume). Finally, initial attempts have been made to assess a broader range of positive death attitudes, such as coping and self-efficacy (Robbins, 1992, Chapter 7 in this volume).

In general, the accelerating differentiation of measures is a positive development, permitting the more precise identification of nuances of death attitudes in future studies. Substitution of multidimensional for unidimensional scales could reveal in what respects women experience greater death anxiety than men (e.g., fear of bodily disfigurement or fear of the deaths of others) and what aspects of death attitudes change as a function of death education. For example, DePaola and his colleagues (Chapter 11) assessed a large group of nursing home staff and a comparison group of workers in other settings using the Multidimensional Fear of Death Scale and discovered that the nursing home group showed less fear of the dead and concern about the impact of the deaths of significant others than did the control group. In contrast, these same nurses and aides reported greater apprehension about the unknown aspects of the state of death than did the comparison sample. Specific results such as these, which may clarify the impact of working in terminal care settings, could not have been obtained using a single, global measure of death anxiety.

But the utility of multidimensional assessments should not blind us to their hidden limitations. One of these is their possible redundancy. As new measures proliferate, it is important to guard against the assumption that they necessarily tap distinctive constructs. For example, Durlak and Kass (1981) factor-analyzed 12 measures of death attitudes and reported that they loaded on only five empirically distinguishable dimensions, identified as negative evaluation of personal death, reluctance to interact with the dying, negative reaction to pain, reactions to reminders of death, and preoccupation with thoughts of death. It is not even safe to assume that measures designed to assess different attitudinal domains necessarily do so in a given population. An illustration of this point is provided by Hintze, Templer, Cappelletty, and Frederick in Chapter 10. Although they had hoped to study the relationship between symptomatology related to acquired immune deficiency syndrome and death depression and death anxiety in gay men who tested positive for the human immunodeficiency virus (HIV), the .91 correlation between the depression and anxiety measures in this sample indicated that these two affective states were functionally identical, at least as measured. Thus, no separate conclusions about the respective elevations in death-related depression and anxiety were warranted. A similar point can be made about purportedly independent subscales of an inventory. As an example, consider Lester's research using the Collett–Lester Fear of Death Scale (Chapter 3). Although it was rationally constructed to measure distinguishable fears clustering around the death of self, dying of self, death of others, and dying of others, empirical studies of its factor structure departed dramatically from this model. Findings such as these imply that future researchers need to go beyond the titles of published scales or subscales to select a measure appropriate to their needs.

A more basic and subtle error in using multidemensional instruments involves the interpretation of their component factors. As Gould (1981) has pointed out with reference to studies of intelligence using factor-analytic methods, a factor or "principal component is a mathematical abstraction that can be calculated from any matrix of correlation coefficients; it is not a 'thing' with physical reality" (p. 250). Simply identifying a statistical pattern accounting for the variation in a set of items does not explain them in any causal or ontological sense—it is only a convenient way of summarizing a more complex and unruly set of relationships. In the case of intelligence tests, for example, this cautions against interpreting a factor on which several quantitative tasks load as a reflection of the "underlying" nature of (mathematical) intelligence. Yet the apparent human need to carve the world up into essential structures is so strong that factor analysts have repeatedly been drawn into just this kind of error, viewing the factors they distill out of a pattern of data as indicating a reality that somehow transcends the individual items themselves. As Gould has observed "the history of factor analysis is strewn with the wreckage of misguided attempts at reification" (1981, p. 269).

These cautions apply with equal force to the history of factorially derived measures for the multidimensional assessment of death attitudes. Although there are important respects in which such instruments may represent an improvement on their unidimensional predecessors (greater precision, utility, etc.), they are not intrinsically more valid than are omnibus measures. Even more pointedly, a stable factor structure—even one established by state-of-the-art confirmatory factor-analytic methods (e.g., Moore & Neimeyer, 1991)—does not indicate the true nature of death anxiety. This is so because (a) the same pattern of interrelationships in any particular data set can be accounted for by more than one factor structure (depending on the decision rules for extraction, rotation, and factor specification one selects), and (b) quite different patterns could emerge from a different pool of initial items. Thus, we would do well to remember that the multidimensional measures of death attitudes we use are themselves human constructions; they do not offer a means of direct access to the irreducible nature of death anxiety itself.

This cautionary statement is not meant to detract from the obvious usefulness of existing measures of death attitudes, but it should make us humble in their application. At a pragmatic level, two approaches are suggested for the further sophistication of research in this area. First, in view of the documented complexity of human responses to death, investigators would do well to rely less on single, global measures of death concern and more on multifaceted measures that tap a broader range of death attitudes. Moreover, because no single inventory is (or can be) comprehensive, researchers are advised to construct batteries of multiple instruments, whose selection should be tailored to the objectives of a particular investigation. Second, the existence of several good scales (reviewed in Part II) should not discourage the judicious development of new measures, as long as these are constructed to measure clearly distinguishable constructs. Theory-based measures are particularly needed, if the field is to achieve the greater coherence and direction that theory-guided research can provide. For example, existential thinkers maintain that confrontation with one's own mortality, although anxiety producing, is essential if one is to be dislodged from one's everyday world and live more fully and genuinely. Unfortunately, this prediction cannot be adequately tested using death anxiety measures alone, because a high score on such measures could result from factors other than confrontation with eventual nonbeing (e.g., general maladjustment). What seems required in such a case is a new, theory-driven measure, with items such as "I have often reflected on my death as a way of determining what is of ultimate importance in my life" and "Life is too short to become preoccupied with trivial concerns." Use of such a scale in conjunction with valid measures of death fear or threat could permit the documentation of a hypothesized process of self-actualization, whereby individuals might move from shunning awareness of death as a way of buffering themselves from death anxiety, through confronting death in all of its fearfulness, to eventual acceptance of mortality, accompanied by reduced anxiety or dread. Grounding instrument development in provocative and comprehensive theories pays dividends for both the theorist and empiricist, on the one hand providing guidance in scale construction and research design and on the other yielding data with greater capability for confirming or disconfirming hypotheses derived from the theory.

PRESCRIPTION 4: DEVELOP INNOVATIVE METHODS

Although increased use of psychometrically adequate measures and construction of new theory-based questionnaires should improve the quality and coherence of the literature on death attitudes, bolder experimentation with alternative methods is also desirable. Researchers working in the various areas of death attitudes have been reluctant to complement direct self-report scales with indirect measures, particularly since projective testing fell out of favor in the 1970s because of its unreliability (R. A. Neimeyer, 1988). Much of this early work was based on a psychodynamic perspective that posited conscious, fantasy, and below-the-level-of-awareness death fears, assessed by a purportedly distinctive set of tasks (e.g., self-report, imagery, and color-word interference tasks; Feifel & Nagy, 1980, 1981). It was assumed that these less direct tasks, in circumventing conscious ego-defensive mechanisms, yielded a more valid assessment of real death anxiety. Unfortunately, evidence for the validity of many of these procedures is lacking, and empirical efforts to substantiate the existence of three distinctive and internally consistent levels of death fear have not been encouraging (Epting, Rainey, & Weiss, 1979; Rigdon, 1983).

What seems called for is a reconsideration of measurement strategies, which might be facilitated by relaxation of the field's traditional commitment to a psychodynamic model.[2] Researchers could select from among a range of sophisticated conceptual models, derived from fields as diverse as sociology, life-span development, and social psychology (see Chapter 1 for examples). For example, computer-administered lexical decision tasks or perceptual identification procedures adapted from cognitive psychology (Graesser & Clark, 1985) might tell us something about the cognitive schemas that people develop to assimilate and react to information concerning death. Narrative or constructivist assessment techniques (G. J. Neimeyer, 1993) might be used to illuminate the idiosyncratic meanings that people attribute to their own mortality. Ethnographic or behavioral measures (Samarel, 1991) might be used to disclose the way people cope with death on a day-to-day basis in the workplace. Although experimentation with such novel methods may require the development of competencies not found in the average investigator of death attitudes, the broadening of our knowledge base may make such methodological extension worth the effort.

Indeed, there are signs that a movement toward technical diversification may already be under way. A number of researchers within personal construct theory have explored the use of repertory grids to elucidate the knowledge structures people develop to understand death and its relation to life (Meshot & Leitner, Chapter 9 in this volume; R. A. Neimeyer, Bagley, & Moore, 1986). Others have used reliable content analysis procedures to code respondents' narratives about death obtained in interviews (Viney, 1984), sentence completion tasks (Durlak, Horn, & Kass, 1990), and written "personal philosophies" (Holcomb, Neimeyer, & Moore, 1993). Finally, preliminary attempts have been made to assess the behavior change that should accompany attitude change in response to death education (see Chapter 13). The integration of these and other, yet-to-be-devised methods into the repertoire of techniques used by death attitude researchers should not only lead to better answers to old questions, but enable the framing of fresh questions as well.

PRESCRIPTION 5: CONSIDER THE TEMPORAL DIMENSION

Human attitudes toward mortality are inherently temporal, in the sense that they are essentially about living in time. For this reason, it is ironic that so little effort in the field has been directed toward this temporal dimension. Instead, study after study treats death anxiety as a stable trait or individual-difference variable,

---

[2]Of course, as I have argued earlier, this commitment has often been implicit, rather than explicit, as is revealed in the prevalent concern with defensive processes, denial, unconscious death anxiety and the like. In the absence of explicit ties to theory, research using such free-floating concepts obfuscates more than it reveals. In contrast, I applaud the occasional study or analysis (see Chapter 12 by Firestone) that is thoroughly grounded in an analytic perspective, particularly if it suggests some disciplined means by which its viability can be evaluated.

as if it were unchanging across the course of a person's life. As a result, research on death attitudes is characterized by at least three lacunae.

First, little empirical attention has been given to the development of death attitudes throughout childhood, although these attitudes are the logical predecessors of such attitudes in adult life.[3] This is not to say that children's concerns about death have been ignored; indeed, there is a rich clinical literature on how best to understand and assuage children's fear of death. The difficulty is that in the absence of research on the incidence, causes, and consequences of death anxiety in normal children, clinical opinions can vary widely, sometimes to the point of contradiction. For example, Firestone's experience as a psychotherapist has led him to posit an anxiety-arousing encounter with the death of others and, by implication, of the self, as a universal developmental marker in the life of every child (see Chapter 12). In response, he believes that children begin building character defenses that provide protection against such narcissistic injury, but also set in motion patterns of denial that cripple mature recognition of life's poignancy and distort future adult relationships. In contrast, reflecting on his work as a family therapist, Bowen (1991) concluded, ''I have never seen a child hurt by exposure to death. They are hurt only by the anxiety of survivors'' (p. 90). Because these two assessments carry quite different implications for intervention in the lives of children who are touched by death, research on the inevitability and effects of fear of death in childhood is all the more important.

Curiously, the dearth of research on death attitudes in healthy children is at variance with the considerable empirical attention given to such topics as youth suicide, the exposure of children to death and violence in the media, and the reactions of terminally ill children (Wass & Stillion, 1988). Moreover, a large research literature has focused on the acquisition of a mature understanding of death across the course of the childhood, as children gradually develop conceptions of death as universal, irreversible, and entailing nonfunctionality (Speece & Brent, 1984, 1992). What seems lacking is a parallel investigation of the way in which normal children's *emotional* responses develop in tandem with these benchmarks in cognitive sophistication. Do certain aspects of death anxiety (e.g., fear of nonbeing) require the acquisition of a more abstract conception of death, whereas others (e.g., fear of disfigurement) represent ontogenetically less mature fears? Although conjectures such as this may receive occasional anectodal support, systematic research on such questions has yet to be designed.

A second lacuna in the temporal dimension of death attitudes is the lack of significant longitudinal data on adults, whose own postformal cognitive devel-

[3]I am using the word *attitude* as it is typically used in the death anxiety literature, namely, to describe predominantly affective reactions to death. In the social-psychological literature, a broader definition of attitude is often used, including not only emotional but also cognitive and behavioral components (Berscheid, 1985). This discussion is important, because a surprisingly large number of studies have focused on the development of children's cognitive understanding of death, leaving its emotional components relatively unexplored.

opment (see Chapter 1), ongoing experiences with loss, and increasing proximity to death might be expected to continue to shape their views of death across the life span. Of course, a substantial literature suggests that elderly persons display less anxiety about death than those in midlife (see Chapter 6), but this could be attributable to cohort differences in socialization, religious belief, normative stage in the family life cycle, or a host of other variables rather than to developmental maturation per se. Although it is inherently difficult to conduct, genuinely longitudinal research that tracks evolving death attitudes alongside other major events such as cognitive shifts, life transitions, and changing health status is needed to answer fundamental questions of this kind.

Finally, a third temporal lacuna is the rarity of longitudinal experimental studies of even very short duration. To establish a confident causal inference, scientists typically conduct well-controlled studies in which they predict changes in one or more dependent variables as a function of manipulation of an independent variable. Of course, our limited control over the variables that influence individuals' attitudes toward death makes such experiments more difficult to conduct in death studies in other domains of social science. The single exception in the field of death studies is the use of experimental or quasiexperimental designs (Cook & Campbell, 1979) to study the impact of death education, which has yielded a sizeable and informative literature (see Chapter 13). However, studying phenomena over time in response to planned or unplanned events is possible in other areas of death attitudes. One ingenious example is the work of Kuzendorf (1985), who was interested in the role of repression in suppressing death fears. Kuzendorf first asked subjects to write answers to a series of quesitons assessing fear of death, and then induced a mild hypnotic trance state, in which they were instructed to allow their "subconscious minds" to "automatically" give their true answers to the same questions. As predicted by the repression hypothesis, one dimension of death fear (fear of inexistence) was greater under hypnosis. This effect was especially strong for subjects who had expressed a conscious belief in an afterlife. Although a single study of this kind should be interpreted cautiously in light of the substantial literature suggesting that religious belief ameliorates death anxiety (R. A. Neimeyer, 1988), the imaginative use of more experimental designs could represent a step forward in sophistication for the largely correlational study of death attitudes.

PRESCRIPTION 6: STUDY PROBLEMS WITH CLINICAL SIGNIFICANCE

I was recently asked the earnest question, "Why study death anxiety? Why is it so important?" What made the question unique was that it was not asked by a curious layperson or inquisitive student, but by the author of one of the best-selling textbooks on death and dying! Indeed, the book contained substantial and intelligent coverage of a host of topics, including suicide, children and death, bereavement, cultural practices, care for the dying, and more—but discussion of the several hundred studies of attitudes toward death was omitted almost entirely.

Ultimately, part of the responsibility for this ironic state of affairs must be borne by death attitude researchers themselves. For the clinician, counselor, nurse, or physician dealing with real people whose lives are disrupted by the loss of a loved one or imminent death, academic research on such topics as the relationship between death anxiety and attitude toward fertility must seem like a luxury at best and irrelevant at worst. Even more theoretically incisive questions such as those concerning the role of self-actualization in reducing the fear of death are rarely asked in a way that indicates their significance to those working in clinical contexts.

Several of the chapters in this book (as well as an increasing number of contributions to the literature) reflect an effort to narrow the gap between research and practice. Greyson's study of near-death experiences (Chapter 8) and Hintze, Templer, Cappelletty, and Frederick's research on HIV-positive men (Chapter 10) contribute to a clearer understanding of the emotional reactions of these individuals for the caregivers working with them. Research of this kind would be especially valuable if it laid the groundwork for more sensitive dialogue between these two patient groups and those who care for them, in view of the psychological isolation from the normal population that each may feel. But research like that of DePaola and his colleagues (Chapter 11) illustrates that it is not only the death attitudes of patients that must be taken into account, but also those of personnel in health care settings. In particular, it was found that compared with control subjects working in other occupations, nursing staff were inured to the deaths of others and to contact with the dead. But elevated fear of death went hand in hand with greater anxieties about aging, especially for the nursing home sample. This research contributes to a growing literature suggesting that different work settings can subtly or unsubtly shape an employee's attitudes toward death.

Although preliminary, Robbins's study (Chapter 7) hints at the opposite effect as well—that individuals' death attitudes can shape their choice of work. Investigating death competencies as well as death anxieties in hospice volunteers, she discovered that both experienced staff and new trainees were higher in "death self-efficacy" (the belief that they could respond to the challenges posed by death and dying) than were nonhospice controls. Interestingly, coping with death (operationalized as Bugen's Coping with Death Scale) showed a somewhat different pattern of results, discriminating only between more experienced volunteers and other groups. Thus, a scale of one type of death competency may hold promise as an outcome measure to evaluate the efficacy of training, whereas a measure of another type of death competency may prove useful as a screening device in volunteer selection. The scales that Robbins used require further validation in terms of predicting job performance or reflecting training effects, but her findings indicate that such additional studies are worth undertaking.

The one area in which measures of death attitudes have been extensively applied is death education (see Chapter 13). In general, these measures have been useful in documenting the greater impact of experiential over didactic death education in ameliorating individuals' death concern, so that such scales might justifiably be used as indices of "affective learning" in future evaluation efforts. But studies such as those by Rainey and Epting (1977) and Knight and Elfenbein (1993) indicate that these normative reductions in death anxiety may mask huge variability among students, with some showing markedly greater and some markedly less death fear as a result of a death education course. This fuels the concerns of critics like Warren (1989), who question whether anxiety reduction is a legitimate goal of death education. Instead, what seems called for is a closer consideration of the idiographic meanings students attribute to death and the way these are challenged and elaborated by education.

Perhaps the largest applied literature in the field of thanatology concerns bereavement and grieving. This makes it all the more unfortunate that there has been so little contact between researchers studying grief and those studying death attitudes (Tokunuga, 1985), despite clinical evidence that suggests the fruitfulness of studying the relationship between grief and attitudes toward death. For example, in my own psychotherapeutic practice, I am currently working with three men who are grappling with issues of death and loss, each in his own way. The first, Terry, is a 30-year-old stockbroker who consulted with me specifically about his acute (but medically unfounded) anxiety about dying after the death of an older mentor in his firm. The sudden and accidental death of his friend and colleague undercut Terry's own sense of invulnerability and aroused a fear of the death of his (apparently healthy) parents as well. The second client, Richard, sought help with his depression after the dissolution of his second marriage at age 70. In the course of our contacts, he was called away to minister to his dying mother, whom he strongly resembled. Looking at her sleeping and emaciated features, he felt himself "come face up to death" as a wave of despondency and fear washed over him. He was imbued with a keen sense of the meaninglessness and ultimate futility of his own life, despite an illustrious career spent as a diplomat and administrator at the highest levels of government service. John, the third client, was referred by his girlfriend, who had become concerned about his propensity toward suicide since the death of his mother a few months before. As his relationship with his girlfriend became more and more angry and combative, John's yearnings for death as a form of release intensified. Although he had dropped out of high school 3 years before, he began to write powerful and poetic odes to death, conjuring it as a beckoning friend reaching out to him with cold and lifeless, but comforting arms. Tragically, it was at this very point in our brief therapy when John's younger brother was murdered in an episode of gang-related violence.

What these and other psychotherapy clients teach us is something about the complex interplay between loss or imminent loss and attitudes toward death on an individual level. There may not be a simple cause-and-effect relationship to be discovered—each of the preceding patients' attitudes toward death (as feared, inevitable, or beckoning) both influenced their response to loss and was shaped by it. What is important is recognizing the delicate interweaving of personal meanings, fears, and responses to death, which play themselves out not only within the private experience of the individual client, but also interpersonally within his or her most intimate relationships.[4] Although close observation of such struggles in the context of therapy reveals them all ultimately to be unique, there nonetheless is much to be gained by serious study of the subtle connections among death attitudes, grief responses, and subsequent enactment of close relationships. The work of Meshot and Leitner (Chapter 9) represents one step in this direction.

CONCLUSION

Psychological research on attitudes toward death has made considerable strides in the last few decades, emerging from the general obscurity with which death and dying have been shrouded in contemporary society. But researchers' enthusiasm for the study of death anxiety has not always been matched by careful attention to building conceptually satisfying theories, using the best available measures, or conducting applied research that offers something of value to practitioners. I hope that this volume makes a modest contribution to the sophistication of this literature, so that psychology might make its own distinctive contribution to our understanding of the role of death in human life.

REFERENCES

Berscheid, E. (1985). Interpersonal attraction. In G. Lindzey & E. Aronson (Eds.), *Handbook of social psychology* (pp. 413–484). New York: Random House.

Bowen, M. (1991). Family reaction to death. In F. Walsh & M. McGoldrick (Eds.), *Living beyond loss* (pp. 79–92). New York: Norton.

Cook, T. D., & Campbell, D. T. (1979). *Quasi-experimentation.* Chicago: Rand-McNally.

[4]Readers interested in the psychotherapeutic exploration of death attitudes, intimate relationships, and response to loss might like to obtain the home-study videotape entitled *Death in the Family*, available through PsychoEducational Resources, P. O. Box 141231, Gainesville, FL 32614.

Durlak, J. A., Horn, W., & Kass, R. A. (1990). A self-administering assessment of personal meanings of death: Report on the revised Twenty Statement Test. *Omega, 21*, 301–309.

Durlak, J. A., & Kass, R. A. (1981). Clarifying the measurement of death attitudes: A factor analytic evaluation of fifteen self-report scales. *Omega, 12*, 129–141.

Epting, R. R., Rainey, L. C., & Weiss, M. J. (1979). Constructions of death and levels of death fear. *Death Education, 3*, 21–30.

Feifel, H., & Nagy, V. T. (1980). Death orientation and life-threatening behavior. *Journal of Abnormal Psychology, 89*, 38–45.

Feifel, H., & Nagy, V. T. (1981). Another look at fear of death. *Journal of Consulting and Clinical Psychology, 49*, 278–286.

Gould, S. J. (1981). *The mismeasure of man*. New York: Norton.

Graesser, A. C., & Clark, L. F. (1985). *Structures and procedures of implicit knowledge*. Norwood, NJ: Ablex.

Harvey, J. H., Weber, A. L., & Orbuch, T. L. (1990). *Interpersonal accounts*. Cambridge, MA: Blackwell.

Hazan, C., & Shaver, P. (1987). Romantic love conceptualized as an attachment process. *Journal of Personality and Social Psychology, 52*, 511–524.

Hoelter, J. W. (1979). Multidimensional treatment of fear of death. *Journal of Consulting and Clinical Psychology, 47*, 996–999.

Holcomb, L. E., Neimeyer, R. A., & Moore, M. K. (1993). Personal meanings of death: A content analysis of free-response narratives. *Death Studies, 17*, 299–318.

Kelly, G. A. (1955). *The psychology of personal constructs*. New York: Norton.

Kelly, G. A. (1961). Suicide: The personal construct point of view. In N. L. Farberow & E. S. Shneidman (Eds.), *The cry for help* (pp. 255–280). New York: McGraw-Hill.

Knight, K. H., & Elfenbein, M. H. (1993). Relationship of death education to the anxiety, fear, and meaning associated with death. *Death Studies, 17*, 115–130.

Krieger, S. R., Epting, F. R., & Leitner, L. M. (1974). Personal constructs, threat, and attitudes toward death. *Omega, 5*, 299–310.

Kuzendorf, R. G. (1985). Repressed fear of inexistence and its hypnotic recovery in religious students. *Omega, 16*, 23–33.

Marcus, H. (1977). Self-schemata and processing of information about the self. *Journal of Personality and Social Psychology, 35*, 63–78.

Moore, M. K., & Neimeyer, R. A. (1991). A confirmatory factor analysis of the Threat Index. *Journal of Personality and Social Psychology, 60*, 122–129.

Neimeyer, G. J. (1993). *Constructivist assessment: A casebook*. Newbury Park, CA: Sage.

Neimeyer, R. A. (1987). An orientation to personal construct therapy. In R. A. Neimeyer & G. J. Neimeyer (Eds.), *Personal construct therapy casebook* (pp. 3–19). New York: Springer.

Neimeyer, R. A. (1988). Death anxiety. In H. Wass, F. Berardo, & R. A. Neimeyer (Eds.), *Dying: Facing the facts* (2nd ed., pp. 97–136). Washington, DC: Hemisphere.

Neimeyer, R. A. (1993). An appraisal of constructivist psychotherapies. *Journal of Consulting and Clinical Psychology, 61*, 221–234.

Neimeyer, R. A., Bagley, K. J., & Moore, M. K. (1986). Cognitive structure and death anxiety. *Death Studies, 10*, 273–288.

Norcross, J. C., & Goldfried, M. R. (Eds.). (1993). *Handbook of psychotherapy integration*. New York: Basic Books.

Rainey, L. C., & Epting, F. R. (1977). Death threat constructions in the student and the prudent. *Omega, 8*, 19–28.

Rigdon, M. A. (1983). Levels of death fear: A factor analysis. *Death Education, 6*, 365–373.

Robbins, R. A. (1992). Death competency: A study of hospice volunteers. *Death Studies, 16*, 557–570.

Samarel, N. (1991). *Caring for life and death*. Washington, DC: Hemisphere.

Speece, M. W., & Brent, S. B. (1984). Children's understanding of death: A review of three components of a death concept. *Child Development, 55*, 1671–1686.

Speece, M. W., & Brent, S. B. (1992). The acquisition of a mature understanding of three components of the concept of death. *Death Studies, 16*, 211–230.

Templer, D. I. (1970). The construction and validation of a fear of death scale. *Journal of General Psychology, 82*, 165–177.

Tokunuga, H. T. (1985). The effect of bereavement upon death-related attitudes and fears. *Omega, 16*, 267–380.

Viney, L. (1984). Concerns about death among severely ill people. In F. R. Epting & R. A. Neimeyer (Eds.), *Personal meanings of death* (pp. 143–158). Washington, DC: Hemisphere.

Warren, W. G. (1989). *Death education and research: Critical perspectives*. New York: Haworth.

Wass, H., & Stillion, J. M. (1988). Death in the lives of children and adolescents. In H. Wass, F. Berardo, & R. A. Neimeyer (Eds.), *Dying: Facing the facts* (2nd ed., pp. 201–228). Washington, DC: Hemisphere.

Index